PRAISE FOR *INTRODUCTION TO HOSPITALITY AND TOURISM MANAGEMENT*

"A truly enriching read—this comprehensive account of hospitality management offers not only pedagogical precision but also a profound and timely exploration of the industry as a fundamental human necessity. It beautifully captures the essence of global interaction and the human quest to embrace diversity.

Structured, clear, and caring, the narrative engages all the senses, presenting hospitality management as both a professional discipline and a deeply human, enduring adventure. This work is bound to become an international classic for future generations of hospitality management students—a sustainable, touching journey that will be remembered."
Dr Sini Bask, Senior Lecturer in Professional Teacher Education, Haaga-Helia UAS, Finland

"This dynamic introduction textbook offers an excellent foundation for students entering the hospitality and tourism field. Covering a broad range of essential topics from the foundation of hospitality, different sectors, cultural diversity and core business functions, wellness, managed services, and career exploration. More importantly, the textbook provides a comprehensive, contemporary approach. Its flexible structure allows instructors to tailor content to their course needs, while its clear, engaging writing makes complex ideas accessible. A valuable resource for both learners and educators in the discipline."
Carl A. Boger Jr., Clinton L. Rappole Distinguished Chair, Conrad N. Hilton College of Global Hospitality Leadership at the University of Houston, USA

"*Introduction to Hospitality and Tourism Management* stands out for its leadership and recruitment-focused perspective. It moves beyond traditional industry overviews to provide students with a clear map of diverse career pathways, essential market trends, and concrete advancement opportunities.

I particularly commend the author's thoughtful inclusion of cultural competence, recognizing the global nature of tourism from both customer and employee standpoints. The text successfully highlights the exciting overlap with related sectors like managed services, healthcare, and real estate, demonstrating the true breadth of professional possibilities. This is essential reading for any aspiring student ready to explore the dynamic future of the hospitality and tourism industry."
Vanja Bogicevic, Clinical Associate Professor, New York University, USA

"*Introduction to Hospitality and Tourism Management* offers a refreshing and well-balanced integration of theory, management practice, and service excellence. Particularly commendable is how the book contextualizes core hospitality and tourism management concepts through vivid, up-to-date industry examples and global case insights. The accessible writing style and reflective activities make it especially effective for engaging today's students, while its academic rigor ensures strong alignment with course learning outcomes. This is a book that truly bridges the classroom and the industry."
Professor Faizan Ali, Established Professor of Marketing, J.E. Cairnes School of Business and Economics, University of Galway, Ireland

"Turpin's *Introduction to Hospitality and Tourism Management* is an insightful and timely exploration of the industry through a human-centered and culturally conscious lens. Her focus on cultural diversity, global interconnectedness, and intersectionality offers readers a deeper understanding of how hospitality extends beyond service; it's about fostering meaningful human connection across borders. A must-read for anyone passionate about inclusive and globally aware leadership in the hospitality field and organizational development as well."
Jad-Évangelo Nasser, Associate Faculty Instructor, Communications, Post University, USA

"*Introduction to Hospitality and Tourism Management* is a comprehensive and forward-thinking guide that equips future hospitality leaders with both practical expertise and cultural intelligence. By emphasizing the human dimension of service and the significance of cultural awareness, Turpin offers readers a deeper understanding of what drives excellence in hospitality. The book skillfully integrates sector insights, career pathways, and the critical importance of resilience amid emerging global trends—making it an essential resource for students, educators, and professionals alike."
Wlla E. Obeidat Assistant Professor, Mutah University, Jordan

"Turpin skillfully integrates her extensive industry experience with her passion for education in *Introduction to Hospitality and Tourism Management*. The book captures the dynamic and culturally rich nature of the hospitality and tourism industry, offering practical and globally relevant insights that prepare students to lead with understanding and empathy. It's an engaging and valuable resource for the next generation of hospitality and tourism professionals."
Dr Stephanie Liu, Associate Professor and Chair of Hospitality Management Undergraduate and Graduate Studies, The Ohio State University, USA

"*Introduction to Hospitality and Tourism Management* is a transformative generational wealth of investment in learning, understanding, and the awareness of the hospitality and tourism industry powered by Turpin. It ties the connectivity and intersectionality of foundations and global significance by interconnecting the human intelligence, excellence, technology, and service at the core of the hospitality industry. This book will equip anyone with the transformative skills to empower people and communities on risk, compliance, procurement, revenue, reputation, safety, operations, crafting, management, strategy, career pathways, transferrable skills, and cross-sector opportunities. It is the ultimate workforce development guide for the hospitality and tourism industry."
Professor Felix Quayson, Assistant Professor, Texas State University, USA

"*Introduction to Hospitality and Tourism Management* provides a comprehensive and engaging overview of the dynamic hospitality and tourism industry. The textbook effectively bridges theory and practice, offering real-world examples that prepare students for leadership roles in a global service environment. It is an essential resource for anyone seeking to understand the foundations and future directions of hospitality and tourism."
Dr Tingting Zhang, Associate Professor, School of Hospitality and Sport Management, Muma College of Business, University of South Florida, USA

"*Introduction to Hospitality and Tourism* is a forward-thinking, comprehensive resource for current and future professionals in this dynamic field. It provides detailed insights into the latest trends and clear descriptions of the different career sectors. What sets this book apart is its thoughtful inclusion of cultural and societal issues, offering a well-rounded perspective on the complexities and opportunities in hospitality and tourism management."
Amanda Cecil, Professor, Indiana University-Indianapolis, USA

"Turpin's experience and connection with her students inspired her to author this comprehensive and forward-thinking textbook, which expands students' understanding of tourism and combines it with hospitality's economics to highlight exciting career opportunities. Details include historical importance, current issues, and trends for the future. The textbook is designed to engage the reader while encouraging further study and is a great introduction to hospitality and tourism in our current times."
Gretchen Friend, Professor, School of Hospitality Management and Culinary Arts, Columbus State Community College, USA

"This book offers a refreshing and inclusive vision of hospitality, that truly reflects the evolution of our industry."
Maïté Berrier Cybal, Head of user experience, Sodexo

"I especially appreciate the 'Think Like a Manager' sections in *Introduction to Hospitality and Tourism Management*. These connect classroom learning with real-world leadership—like procurement efficiency, food waste reduction, and cost control — which I deal with every day in my current role. Guest experience will always be the heart of hospitality, but understanding the business side is just as important. This book helps build the confidence and mindset every future new manager needs to be successful."
Claudia DelFavero, Director of Catering Operations and 2019 The Ohio State University alumni, Hospitality Management Program

"This book is a timely and insightful contribution to hospitality and tourism education. Turpin skillfully weaves contemporary industry perspectives with an essential inclusive and forward-thinking approach that challenges and empowers readers to lead with empathy, awareness, and authenticity. Her passion for teaching and her deep respect for what educators and students learn from one another give this work both heart and scholarly depth. She inspires readers to see hospitality not just as a profession, but as a practice of understanding and connection."
Melissa Johnson, VP and Operating Partner, Cameron Mitchell Premier Events and CMR Community Relations

Introduction to Hospitality and Tourism Management

A Contemporary Approach

Annemarie M. Turpin

Publisher's note
Every possible effort has been made to ensure that the information contained in this book is accurate at the time of going to press, and the publishers and author cannot accept responsibility for any errors or omissions, however caused. No responsibility for loss or damage occasioned to any person acting, or refraining from action, as a result of the material in this publication can be accepted by the editor, the publisher or the author.

First published in Great Britain and the United States in 2026 by Kogan Page Limited

All rights reserved. No part of this publication may be reproduced, stored in a retrieval system or transmitted in any form or by any means – including electronic, mechanical, photocopying, recording or by any artificial intelligence (AI) or machine learning system – without the prior written permission of the publisher. Unauthorized use, including the use of text or images to train AI models, is strictly prohibited and may result in legal action.

Kogan Page
Kogan Page Ltd, 2nd Floor, 45 Gee Street, London EC1V 3RS, United Kingdom
Kogan Page Inc, 8 W 38th Street, Suite 902, New York, NY 10018, USA
www.koganpage.com

EU Representative (GPSR)
Authorised Rep Compliance Ltd, Ground Floor, 71 Baggot Street Lower, Dublin D02 P593, Ireland
www.arccompliance.com

Kogan Page books are printed on paper from sustainable forests.

© Kogan Page, 2026

The moral rights of the author have been asserted in accordance with the Copyright, Designs and Patents Act 1988.

ISBNs
Hardback   978 1 3986 2227 2
Paperback   978 1 3986 2225 8
Ebook   978 1 3986 2226 5

British Library Cataloguing-in-Publication Data
A CIP record for this book is available from the British Library.

Library of Congress Control Number
A CIP record for this book is available from the Library of Congress.

Typeset by Integra Software Services, Pondicherry
Printed and bound by CPI Group (UK) Ltd, Croydon CR0 4YY

CONTENTS

Walkthrough of textbook features and online resources xii
About the author xv
Acknowledgments xvi

1 **Foundations of hospitality and tourism** 1
Introduction to hospitality and tourism: The interwoven nature of service and exploration 1
The evolution of hospitality and tourism: A historical journey 2
Hospitality and tourism: A unified force of service and exploration 10
Key segments of a global industry 12
Global significance of hospitality and tourism 13
Hospitality education: Shaping the next generation of leaders 17
Interconnectedness with other industries 19
Foundations of hospitality and tourism 23
Looking ahead 25
References 25

2 **The core of hospitality: Human interaction, connectivity, and service** 27
Introduction 27
Human connectivity at the heart of hospitality 29
Empathy and emotional intelligence in service excellence 32
Applying industry service models 39
Technology as a tool for human interaction 49
Conclusion: The core of hospitality—human interaction, connectivity, and service 52
Looking ahead 53
References 54

3 **Cultural diversity and intersectionality in hospitality and tourism** 56
Introduction 57
Defining cultural diversity and cultural competence in hospitality and tourism 57
Theoretical frameworks that guide us 59
A shift in focus 64

Understanding cultural identity in a globalized hospitality context 65
The role of intersectionality in hospitality 69
Digital accessibility in hospitality 73
Experiences of historically marginalized groups 74
Challenges to identity affirmation in diverse settings 75
Frameworks for cultural responsiveness 77
Looking ahead 83
References 84

4 Core business functions: Service, sales, and people 86

Introduction: The backbone of hospitality excellence 86
Theoretical framework: Service-profit chain 87
Understanding guest experience management in hospitality and tourism 88
Operations management: The engine of seamless hospitality 93
Marketing and sales: Crafting demand and driving revenue 96
Reputation management in the age of online reviews 101
Human resources management: Empowering people, elevating service 102
Looking ahead 108
References 109

5 Core business functions: Finance, risk, and infrastructure 112

Introduction 112
Theoretical framework: Resource-based view theory 113
Financial management in hospitality 113
Revenue and yield management: Turning strategy into profit 117
Risk management and compliance: Safeguarding hospitality's reputation and operations 121
Supply chain and procurement management: The backbone of hospitality operations 124
Sustainability and environmental management: Building a greener future 129
Facilities and asset management: Preserving the foundations of hospitality 134
Looking ahead 138
References 138

6 Career exploration in hospitality and tourism 140

Introduction: Envisioning your future in hospitality 140
Building bridges: Transferable skills and cross-sector opportunities 142
Exploring the segments: Where will your career take you? 147

Gaining real-world experience: Internships, employment, and practical learning 159
Networking and industry engagement 163
Mentorship: Accelerating your career growth 167
Looking forward: Turning connections into career opportunities 169
Conclusion: Shaping your unique hospitality journey 169
Looking ahead 170
References 170

7 Managed services in hospitality 173

Introduction 173
Understanding managed services: Serving two audiences 174
Historical evolution of managed services 174
Managed services across key sectors 175
Applying core business functions in managed services 183
Operational considerations: A more conversational approach 184
Technology and innovation: Directly engaging guests 186
Global impact and scope: A more storytelling tone 190
Career pathways in managed services: Property, above-property, and corporate levels 194
Looking ahead 197
References 198

8 Events 201

Introduction: What is event management? 201
Historical overview and evolution of events 202
Events across key sectors 204
Inclusive event planning framework 212
Emerging trends in events 220
Event management structures: Models, partnerships, and integrated approaches 224
Career pathways within event management structures 225
Getting started in your career exploration 229
Looking ahead 232
References 232

9 The tourism industry 235

Introduction: Tourism as a global industry 235
Historical development and evolution of tourism 236
Economic, community, and global impact 237

Key tourism segments 242
Customer behavior and traveler influences 247
Sustainable tourism and ecotourism 250
UNESCO world heritage and tourism 253
Emerging trends in tourism 257
Careers in tourism: Pathways and opportunities 261
Looking ahead 266
References 267

10 Lodging 271
Introduction: Lodging—where hospitality meets home 271
Historical evolution of lodging 272
Lodging segments 274
Hotel management, ownership, and branding: Understanding the structures 279
Emerging trends and innovations in lodging 284
Hotel organizational structure: Understanding executive leadership and operations 289
Core business and operational functions in lodging: The backbone of hospitality excellence 290
Career pathways in lodging 295
Connecting career pathways to foundational hospitality concepts 299
Looking ahead 301
References 301

11 The food and beverage industry 303
Introduction: The universal language of food and beverage 303
Historical evolution of food and beverage 305
Key food and beverage segments 307
Key beverage segments 314
Ownership, management, and branding in food and beverages 319
Key trends in the food and beverage industry 321
Core business functions in food and beverage 323
Inclusive practices in food and beverage 325
Food and beverage careers and professional development 328
Career development and professional associations 331
Looking ahead 333
References 334

12 Entertainment and recreation 337

Introduction 337
Historical evolution of entertainment and recreation 338
Key segments in entertainment and recreation 339
Specialized and niche recreation segments 354
Key trends in entertainment and recreation 356
Core business functions in entertainment and recreation 357
Careers in entertainment and recreation 357
Looking ahead 361
References 361

13 Intersection of the wellness and health industry with healthcare 365

Introduction 365
Historical evolution of health and wellness hospitality and tourism 366
Segment overview: Spas, health clubs, and wellness retreats 367
Hospitality in senior living communities 372
Hospitality in hospitals and clinics 375
Integrating wellness across hospitality and tourism 381
Emerging trends and future directions 383
Nuanced considerations in wellness and healthcare hospitality 386
Core business functions in wellness hospitality 387
Career pathways and industry associations 387
Looking ahead 388
References 389

14 Resilience in hospitality and tourism 391

Introduction 391
Historical timeline of economic challenges and industry responses 392
Crisis management and recovery 396
Sustainable tourism and resilience 403
Building resilient businesses 404
Career mobility: The hospitality and tourism subway map 406
Inclusive strategies for workplace resilience 410
Emerging trends in hospitality and tourism: Personalization, values, and flexibility 413
Emerging trends in wellness, immersive experiences, and resilience 414
References 417

Index 420

WALKTHROUGH OF TEXTBOOK FEATURES AND ONLINE RESOURCES

Learning Objectives

A bulleted list at the beginning of each chapter summarizes what you can expect to learn, to help you to track your progress.

LEARNING OBJECTIVES

- Describe the scope and importance of the hospitality and tourism industry, including its key sectors and global significance.
- Explain how hospitality services are interconnected with other industries, such as healthcare, education, and entertainment, and their shared focus on human-centered service.
- Explore the evolution of hospitality by exploring historical milestones and connecting them to modern trends such as sustainability, diversity, and technological innovation.

Real-world Examples

A range of global examples illustrates how key ideas and theories are operating in practice to help you to place the concepts discussed in a real-life industry context.

REAL-WORLD EXAMPLE:
INDUSTRY SPOTLIGHT   Edinburgh Fringe Festival

The Edinburgh Fringe Festival is the largest arts festival globally, annually hosting over 3,000 performances across more than 300 venues.

Career Spotlights

Insights from professionals working in hospitality and tourism highlight the opportunities and career paths available in this industry.

> **CAREER SPOTLIGHT**
> Zach Clapper, General Manager & Regional Safety Lead, Red Rocks Amphitheatre and Denver Coliseum, Aramark Facilities Management

Think Like a Manager

Questions and scenarios to help you start to think like a manager in your future career.

> **THINK LIKE A MANAGER**
> Addressing Overtourism Challenges
>
> You manage a popular but overcrowded UNESCO site (e.g. Cinque Terre). Identify one immediate solution you could implement to reduce overcrowding sustainably while preserving revenue. Briefly explain how you'd effectively communicate this solution to visitors.

Interactive Exercises

Questions and activities throughout to encourage you to reflect on what you have learned and to apply your knowledge and skills in practice.

> **INTERACTIVE EXERCISE**
> Tourism trends pitch
>
> **Objective:** Apply current tourism trends to rejuvenate a destination's visitor appeal.
>
> **Instructions:** Identify a tourism destination currently experiencing declining visitation or needing revitalization (examples: Atlantic City, Marseille).

Key Takeaways

A bulleted list at the end of each chapter summarizes the main themes and key points, to help you synthesize your learning.

Key Takeaways

- **Global Economic and Cultural Influence:** Tourism significantly boosts economies, enriches cultural exchange, and strengthens global connections, shaping communities worldwide.
- **Historical Foundations:** Understanding tourism's evolution—from ancient pilgrimages and explorations to today's mass travel and digital nomadism—highlights its dynamic adaptability and growth.
- **Diverse Tourism Segments and Traveler Behavior:** Clearly differentiating segments (leisure, business, cultural, ecotourism, niche markets) and analyzing traveler motivations helps professionals strategically manage and market destinations.

References

Detailed references provide quick and easy access to the research and underpinning sources behind the chapter.

Online Resources:

This book includes online resources for lecturers and students comprising:

- Lecturer slides for each chapter
- Real-world examples
- Practitioner videos

These resources can be accessed through the Kogan Page website: www.koganpage.com/ITHM

ABOUT THE AUTHOR

Annemarie M. Turpin is Clinical Assistant Professor of Hospitality Management in the Department of Human Sciences at The Ohio State University, USA, where she also serves as Director of the Hospitality Management Advisory Board. With over three decades of combined experience in the hospitality industry and higher education, she has held leadership roles at Marriott and Starwood Hotels & Resorts across general management, operations, and training and development. She was honored as General Manager of the Year by both the Ohio Hotel & Lodging Association and Fairfield Inn by Marriott, recognizing her excellence in leadership, operations, and service.

ACKNOWLEDGMENTS

Empowering the next generation of hospitality leaders through cultural insight and industry innovation

First and foremost, I thank God for placing this calling in my heart and guiding me along a more beautiful journey than I could have imagined. Every step, challenge, and person along the way has been part of a greater plan—one I'm humbled and grateful to be living.

This book would not have been possible without the many individuals who poured into both this project and my professional journey spanning hospitality and higher education—offering encouragement, insight, and belief, and providing opportunities that shaped who I am as an educator and now as an author. Some of you are featured in these pages; all of you are carried in my gratitude.

To my students: Your passion, curiosity, and willingness to grow have shaped this book as much as any chapter I've written. Thank you for bringing energy, ideas, and authenticity into each classroom and conversation. You are the reason this work matters.

To Susan Furber, my editor at Kogan Page: Thank you for your guidance, collaboration, and unwavering support. Your thoughtful feedback, enthusiasm, and care brought clarity and confidence to this project. You also reflect many of the values at the heart of this book—genuine hospitality, thoughtful empathy, and a commitment to creating spaces where others feel seen and supported.

To my daughters—Allie, Annalise, and Alexis: You are my greatest joy, and I hope this book reminds you that your voice, ideas, and the purpose God places in your hearts are there for a reason. Stay true to that calling. Thank you for your patience and support—and for inspiring me to be more present, more hopeful, and more whole.

To Dr. Erik Porfeli: Thank you for your leadership, mentorship, and belief in my work and potential. I'm grateful for your support and the example you've set as a thoughtful educator and collaborator.

And finally, to the future leaders of hospitality and tourism: May you lead with curiosity, courage, empathy, and care—and never underestimate the power of service to create belonging, impact, and innovation.

Foundations of hospitality and tourism

1

LEARNING OBJECTIVES

- Describe the scope and importance of the hospitality and tourism industry, including its key sectors and global significance.
- Explain how hospitality services are interconnected with other industries, such as healthcare, education, and entertainment, and their shared focus on human-centered service.
- Explore the evolution of hospitality by looking at historical milestones and connecting them to modern trends such as sustainability, diversity, and technological innovation.
- Identify and explain examples of how hospitality and tourism create economic value and cultural exchange in communities around the world.
- Analyze real-world scenarios to evaluate the ripple effects and multiplier impact of hospitality on job creation, tourism spending, and related industries.

Introduction to hospitality and tourism: The interwoven nature of service and exploration

In 2023, 1.3 billion international travelers crossed borders, reconnecting families, fueling economies, and creating memories that span generations (UNWTO, 2024). Behind each of these journeys is an intricate web of hospitality, quietly working to transform ordinary moments into extraordinary experiences.

Consider a traveler arriving late at night in a distant city after hours of delays. At the hotel front desk, she's met not only by her reservation but also by thoughtful gestures—a warm towel, a soothing cup of tea, and a list of personalized recommendations for her stay. This small act of care doesn't just alleviate fatigue; it redefines her entire journey.

Such experiences illustrate the profound impact hospitality and tourism have on our lives—far beyond mere vacations or business trips. These interconnected industries are critical drivers of global prosperity, cultural exchange, and personal growth. In this chapter, we'll explore how hospitality and tourism have become integral to our human experience, underpinning not just economic vitality but also the meaningful connections that shape our world.

Hospitality and tourism segment overview

To ensure clarity as you explore this and subsequent chapters, the following is a concise summary of the key industry segments introduced here and referenced throughout the book:

- **Lodging**: Hotels, resorts, inns, and alternative accommodations providing comfort, rest, and spaces for guests to recharge and connect.
- **Food and beverage**: Restaurants, cafés, bars, and catering services that offer culinary experiences, fostering cultural connections and community interactions.
- **Tourism**: Guided tours, museums, cultural and historical attractions, and immersive experiences that encourage exploration and meaningful connections to destinations.
- **Entertainment and recreation**: Theaters, theme parks, sports venues, concerts, and recreational activities enriching travel experiences through joy, excitement, and inspiration.
- **Events and conferences**: Coordinated gatherings including weddings, festivals, conventions, and community celebrations, emphasizing meticulous planning and creative execution to bring people together.

Understanding these segments will enhance your ability to connect the foundational concepts explored in this and following chapters—such as guest experience management, operations, marketing, sales, and human resources—to real-world applications across diverse hospitality and tourism contexts.

The evolution of hospitality and tourism: A historical journey

Hospitality and tourism are among the world's oldest industries, rooted in humanity's enduring desire to connect, explore, and share experiences. From ancient inns offering shelter to weary travelers to cutting-edge digital innovations shaping modern guest experiences, the history of these industries reflects their resilience, adaptability, and global impact.

Ancient beginnings: The foundations of hospitality

Hospitality has been a cornerstone of human culture for millennia. In Ancient Greece and Rome, the concept of *hospitia* represented the duty of hosts to care for travelers, often providing food, shelter, and protection. Similarly, along the Silk Road, merchants relied on roadside lodges for rest and trade, fostering the exchange of goods, ideas, and cultures. Meanwhile, Middle Eastern caravanserais offered rest and safety to travelers crossing deserts, emphasizing hospitality as a universal cultural value. In Japan, ryokans (traditional inns) embodied meticulous attention to detail, offering travelers lodging, dining, and cultural immersion. These early establishments were not only practical but also deeply symbolic, reflecting the values of generosity and community care that continue to define hospitality today.

Medieval innovations: Pilgrimages and taverns

During the medieval era, hospitality evolved to meet the needs of religious pilgrims. Monasteries across Europe provided free lodging and meals, embodying the spirit of service and care. As travel expanded, coaching inns and taverns emerged as vital hubs for social and economic activity, offering basic accommodations and food to visitors traveling on horseback or by carriage.

In the Islamic world, institutions such as caravanserais and funduqs played a pivotal role, providing travelers with safe havens that fostered trade, cultural exchange, and intellectual discourse (Touati, 2010). These establishments became gathering places not only for merchants and politicians but also for scholars and adventurers, significantly contributing to the vibrant exchange of ideas, goods, and cultures. Collectively, these medieval innovations laid the foundational structure for modern hotels, restaurants, and hospitality practices.

The Industrial Revolution: Transforming travel and lodging

The Industrial Revolution dramatically reshaped hospitality and tourism, introducing exciting new technologies such as steamships and railroads. Suddenly, journeys to distant cities became faster, more affordable, and accessible—not just for the elite, but for the growing middle class eager to explore the world (Walton, 2005).

During this transformative period, hotels began offering guests experiences they had not dreamed possible. A standout example is Boston's Tremont House, which opened its doors in 1829 (Figure 1.1). Imagine travelers stepping into a hotel with private rooms, bell service, indoor plumbing, and gas lighting—all revolutionary at the time. These innovations didn't just set new standards for comfort; they transformed hotels from simple places to rest into desirable destinations in their own right.

Figure 1.1 Tremont House, Boston (1829–1894), wood engraving

SOURCE (Boston Public Library)

Across the Atlantic, London's Savoy Hotel further revolutionized luxury when it opened in 1889 (Figure 1.2). According to Olivia Williams (2021), the Savoy was more than just opulent—it was a technological marvel, showcasing electric lighting in every room, futuristic elevators that whisked guests effortlessly between floors, and private bathrooms with hot and cold running water. Visitors enjoyed a remarkable blend of cutting-edge convenience and refined service, establishing the Savoy's international reputation as synonymous with elegance and innovation.

The Industrial Revolution also transformed hospitality management. As cities expanded rapidly and commerce flourished, there was an increasing demand for structured lodging and dining facilities. Hotels transitioned from modest, family-run operations to larger, professionally managed enterprises, significantly raising service standards and guest expectations (Sandoval-Strausz, 2007). This era established the foundational structures of today's global hospitality industry, in which quality, comfort, and innovative guest experiences remain central.

The 20th century: Globalization and modern tourism

The 20th century ushered in significant transformations in hospitality and tourism, fueled by advances in air travel, increased globalization, and technological innovation. In the period after World War II, particularly the 1950s and 1960s, airlines

Figure 1.2 Grand Foyer of the Savoy Hotel restaurant, London, c. 1900; illustration by Max Cowper

SOURCE (Gallica Digital Library via Wikimedia Commons)

partnered strategically with hotels and tour operators to offer all-inclusive packages, significantly broadening international tourism's reach to the growing middle class. This era saw rapid enhancements in travel infrastructure, enabling exploration of destinations that were previously inaccessible (Gyr, 2010).

Renowned hospitality chains such as Hilton and Marriott expanded globally during this time. The first hotel bearing the Hilton name opened in 1925, quickly becoming a symbol of consistent quality and service worldwide (Sandoval-Strausz, 2007). Similarly, Marriott, initially a modest root-beer stand set up in 1927, entered the hotel industry officially in 1957 and soon became synonymous with reliability and standardized guest experiences across diverse locations.

Iconic destinations significantly defined this transformative era. Las Vegas emerged prominently in the 1940s and 1950s, particularly with the opening of the Flamingo Hotel in 1946, which catalyzed the famed Las Vegas Strip's evolution into a premier global resort destination renowned for gambling, entertainment, and luxury hospitality (Schwartz, 2013). Similarly, Disney introduced groundbreaking themed entertainment experiences, reshaping the tourism landscape profoundly. Disneyland's launch in Anaheim, California, in 1955 created a new category of immersive family vacation, combining attractions, lodging, and dining experiences. Building upon

Disneyland's success, Walt Disney World Resort opened in Orlando, Florida, in 1971, offering a vastly expanded and integrated resort experience that set new standards in destination tourism (Bryman, 2004).

The late 20th century marked a crucial turning point, with the advent of digital technology fundamentally altering how travelers planned and booked their journeys. By the mid-1990s, online platforms such as Expedia and Travelocity had revolutionized trip planning by providing unprecedented convenience, customization, and control to travelers. These innovative digital tools enabled consumers to effortlessly compare prices, tailor itineraries, and access a wide array of options, shifting travel planning power directly into their hands (Xiang et al., 2015). Together, these developments significantly shaped modern tourism, laying the foundations for contemporary global hospitality standards and consumer expectations.

The digital age: Hospitality in the 21st century

The internet and mobile technology have transformed hospitality, providing travelers with exciting new ways to connect with places and cultures. Platforms such as Airbnb and Vrbo have disrupted traditional lodging, offering unique, localized experiences in which travelers can stay in accommodations ranging from cozy urban lofts to secluded mountain retreats. Artificial intelligence (AI) has further revolutionized hospitality, enabling highly personalized guest experiences through tailored recommendations, automated check-ins, and predictive analytics.

Sustainability and inclusivity have become central to hospitality's evolution. Eco-friendly practices such as renewable energy use, waste reduction, and responsible sourcing are increasingly common as companies align with environmentally conscious travelers.

These advances reflect the industry's ability to adapt to a more connected, environmentally conscious, and diverse world, reinforcing hospitality's role as a dynamic force shaping modern travel experiences.

Post-pandemic trends: Resilience and innovation

The Covid-19 pandemic tested the hospitality industry profoundly, challenging its resilience and forcing rapid adaptation. The crisis prompted many students and professionals to question their chosen paths, yet industry leaders emphasized hospitality's extraordinary resilience and its essential role in human connection (Baum et al., 2020). History has consistently demonstrated that hospitality emerges stronger and more adaptable after each challenge.

One of the most notable transformations during Covid was the rise of contactless technology. Mobile check-ins, digital menus, and AI-driven customer service became essential rather than optional. Post-pandemic, the shift toward these solutions has continued, with mobile check-ins, touchless payments, and digital menus becoming standard industry practices (Sharma et al., 2021).

Another significant shift was the growing emphasis on sustainability. Sodexo, for example, integrated eco-friendly practices into its operations, focusing on waste reduction, renewable energy, and responsible sourcing. Marriott's initiative Work Anywhere with Marriott Bonvoy illustrated the industry's flexibility, catering to professionals seeking safe, inspiring spaces during lockdowns.

Hospitality professionals demonstrated transferable skills, transitioning successfully into sectors like healthcare, logistics, technology, and the public sector. Their expertise in communication, service delivery, and problem-solving reinforced the versatility and adaptability of hospitality's workforce.

The pandemic highlighted hospitality's enduring importance, affirming that the industry is more than a career—it's a calling to bring people together and foster meaningful connections.

Modern trends: Shaping the future of hospitality and tourism

As the industry evolves, it continues to reflect societal values and technological advances, reshaping service delivery and guest engagement.

Sustainability and ecotourism

Environmental conservation and considerations are now a defining focus as consumers increasingly seek eco-friendly leisure options. Companies are adopting renewable energy, reducing waste, and emphasizing responsible sourcing. Sodexo has embedded sustainability into its operations, utilizing advanced food-waste tracking systems and partnering with local farmers. Marriott launched its Serve360 initiative, aiming to reduce landfill waste by 45 percent and achieve net-zero greenhouse gas emissions by 2050 (Marriott International, 2024).

Ecotourism destinations such as Costa Rica continue to lead the way, combining conservation efforts with cultural engagement. Visitors can explore rainforest tours, eco-lodges, and wildlife preservation programs while supporting local communities. New Zealand has also become a benchmark for sustainable tourism, promoting environmental conservation through initiatives such as the Tiaki Promise—which encourages visitors to care for land, sea, and culture—and extensive eco-friendly practices integrated throughout its hospitality industry (Tourism New Zealand, n.d.).

Certifications like LEED (Leadership in Energy and Environmental Design) and Green Globe are worldwide benchmarks for sustainable operations. Iconic properties such as the Plaza Hotel in New York demonstrate how sustainability and luxury coexist, highlighting hospitality's potential as a leader in environmental stewardship.

Diversity and inclusion

Hospitality thrives by welcoming wide ranges of audiences, making diversity and inclusion essential to its success. Companies are investing in workforce diversity, equitable opportunities, and inclusive practices to better serve visitors from varied cultural, gender, and socioeconomic backgrounds.

Guest services continually evolve to reflect inclusivity demands. From halal and kosher dining options to accessibility features such as braille menus and adaptive technologies, the best hospitality actively creates inclusive spaces. Research consistently demonstrates that companies which embrace diversity enhance guest satisfaction, foster innovation, and strengthen workplace collaboration (Kalargyrou and Volis, 2014). As industries and populations diversify, commitment to inclusivity remains vital.

Technological innovation

Technology continues to revolutionize hospitality, enhancing operational efficiency and delivering personalized guest experiences. AI provides tailored recommendations and seamless interactions, while virtual reality (VR) and augmented reality (AR) improve trip planning and on-site engagement. Smart hospitality, powered by the Internet of Things (IoT), includes "smart rooms," allowing guests to control amenities through digital devices, elevating guest satisfaction and promoting energy efficiency (Buhalis and Leung, 2018).

The Covid pandemic accelerated touchless technology adoption, revolutionizing check-ins, payments, and service delivery. Emerging technologies such as blockchain streamline processes including reservations and loyalty programs, improving security and integrating travel experiences. Alongside these evolving tools and trends, technology consistently fosters efficiency, sustainability, and personalized service, meeting the demands of a dynamic global audience.

Honoring the past, embracing the future

The evolution of hospitality and tourism illustrates a compelling story of adaptation and innovation. From ancient inns to modern eco-lodges, the industry continually meets travelers' needs while embracing technological advances, sustainability, and inclusivity.

As hospitality develops, its foundational principles—welcoming, serving, and connecting—remain vital. Understanding its historical trajectory and modern trends equips students and professionals to contribute meaningfully, ensuring hospitality remains a dynamic, impactful force for generations.

The symbolism of the pineapple: A universal icon of hospitality

The pineapple has long been a cherished symbol of hospitality, embodying warmth, welcome, and generosity. This association originates from the colonial era when sea captains returning from long voyages would place a pineapple at their door to signify their safe return and invite friends and neighbors to gather. Over time, the pineapple gained prominence across Europe and the Americas, symbolizing luxury, cordiality, and the spirit of gracious hosting. Today, it continues to serve as a universal emblem of hospitality, seen in hotel logos, restaurant decor, and welcome signs worldwide (Figure 1.3).

A marker of generosity and affluence

The fruit's distinctive appearance and rarity further reinforced its status as a symbol of affluence and generosity, especially in colonial societies. Hosts often placed pineapples at the center of their gatherings, showcasing their commitment to creating an inviting and inclusive atmosphere. This enduring legacy of hospitality reminds us of the timeless value of making others feel at home.

Figure 1.3 Pineapple: Symbol of hospitality

SOURCE (Taylor Friel on Unsplash)

The complex legacy of the pineapple

While the pineapple symbolizes positivity and welcome, its history carries a more complicated narrative. During the colonial era, the cultivation and trade of pineapples were intertwined with exploitative economic systems, including the transatlantic slave trade. Enslaved individuals labored to produce this luxury good for European and American markets: injustices that underpin the pineapple's rise as a marker of wealth and hospitality. Recognizing this history encourages us to reflect on the systems of exploitation behind symbols of abundance and generosity.

Lessons for future hospitality professionals

For those entering the global hospitality industry, understanding the full history of the pineapple adds depth to its symbolism. It reminds us to embrace the true spirit of hospitality—not just creating spaces that are welcoming, but also fostering equity and inclusion for all. By celebrating the pineapple's positive legacy while acknowledging its complex past, we uphold the values of care, respect, and connection that define hospitality.

Future hospitality professionals can draw inspiration from the pineapple's continued influence in modern applications:

- **Design and branding:** The pineapple is a popular motif in luxury hotel decor, symbolizing excellence and service.
- **Cultural resonance:** Exploring similar cultural symbols, such as the olive branch in the Mediterranean or tea in Asia, can help brands create experiences that resonate globally.

The pineapple's story, both inspiring and complex, serves as a powerful symbol for the hospitality industry. It urges us to reflect on its dual legacy: one of warmth and inclusion, and another shaped by historical inequalities. As we celebrate the values of connection and care, let us also strive to honor the principles of equity and diversity that make hospitality truly meaningful.

Hospitality and tourism: A unified force of service and exploration

Hospitality and tourism are intrinsically linked; crafting seamless experiences for travelers through complementary roles. Hospitality provides essential infrastructure—hotels, restaurants, and transportation hubs—while tourism facilitates adventure, exploration, and discovery. Whether returning to a cool hotel after an African safari or experiencing a bustling resort as the gateway to Orlando's famed theme parks, these industries share a unified goal: to create unforgettable moments for guests.

Together, hospitality and tourism significantly impact the global economy, contributing approximately $9.5 trillion to global GDP—over 10 percent of global economic activity—and employing around 334 million people worldwide (WTTC, 2024). Their expansive reach underscores their critical role in fostering cultural exchange, global understanding, and connection. For instance, a family visiting New York City not only enjoys local attractions but simultaneously supports numerous businesses, from taxi services to neighborhood cafés, illustrating the deep interdependence within this vibrant ecosystem.

The power of human-centered experiences

At the heart of these industries is a commitment to service excellence and human connection. The Merriam-Webster dictionary defines hospitality as the "friendly and generous reception and entertainment of guests, visitors, or strangers." Tourism complements this by inspiring exploration, encouraging people to venture beyond their usual environments to seek leisure, business, or cultural engagement. Together, they form a dynamic global network that invites people to connect, grow, and create memories that last a lifetime.

Hospitality is characterized by care, connectivity, and innovation—centered on creating memorable experiences. At its essence, hospitality ensures guests feel valued and welcomed, through seamless operations, thoughtful service, and inspiring environments. Many successful organizations embrace a "people first" philosophy, prioritizing employee well-being to foster exceptional service delivery. When employees feel supported and empowered, they consistently enhance guest satisfaction and contribute to sustained business success (Baum et al., 2020).

Tourism reflects humanity's intrinsic desire for exploration and discovery. Derived from the Latin word *tornare*, meaning "to turn or travel in a circle," tourism encapsulates the excitement of experiencing diverse cultures, landscapes, and histories. According to the United Nations World Tourism Organization (UNWTO, n.d.), tourism comprises "the activities of persons traveling to and staying in places outside their usual environment for leisure, business, or other purposes," driving economic growth and global connectivity.

Shared goals, distinct contributions

Though distinct, hospitality and tourism align in their goals to create transformative experiences. Hospitality offers physical comfort and emotional warmth—through welcoming accommodations, exceptional dining, and attentive service—that enrich the traveler's experience. Tourism motivates individuals to explore and meaningfully engage with the world around them.

Looking forward, the industries' full potential continues to evolve, with emerging technologies, greater accessibility, and an increasing emphasis on sustainable travel. Collectively, hospitality and tourism remain powerful drivers of economic prosperity, cultural exchange, and human connection, reinforcing that every journey begins and ends with genuine care and endless exploration.

Key segments of a global industry

The hospitality and tourism industry can be visualized like a bustling subway system, where each segment functions as a distinct yet interconnected line, all working together to create seamless experiences. Just as different subway lines cross and converge at various stations, these segments often intersect, supporting each other to transport travelers smoothly from one memorable experience to another.

- The **Lodging** Line provides foundational comfort and rest. It includes everything from luxurious five-star resorts to cozy bed-and-breakfast inns, offering spaces where guests relax, recharge, and find meaningful connections.
- Intersecting closely is the **Food and Beverage** Line, nourishing guests and fueling their adventures. Restaurants, cafés, bars, and catering services create cultural connections through cuisine, making dining experiences as much about community as about sustenance.
- Extending outward is the adventurous **Tourism** Line, encouraging exploration and discovery. Guided tours, museums, cultural attractions, and immersive experiences invite travelers to engage deeply with new destinations, creating purposeful journeys and lasting memories.
- Crossing paths frequently is the vibrant **Entertainment and Recreation** Line. Theaters, theme parks, sports venues, concert halls, and outdoor activities add joy and excitement, enriching the travel experience by engaging guests in ways that delight and inspire.
- Running alongside these is the dynamic **Events and Conferences** Line, coordinating and orchestrating gatherings both large and small. Weddings, festivals, conventions, and community celebrations represent stations along this route, bringing people together through meticulous planning and creative execution.

Putting it all together: An example

Compare attending a major music festival with using the subway. There's a central "station" where all lines converge seamlessly:

- The Lodging Line provides accommodations for attendees.

- The Food and Beverage Line ensures diverse dining options, energizing festival-goers.
- The Tourism Line allows visitors to explore the local attractions and culture around the festival.
- The Entertainment and Recreation Line delivers thrilling live performances and engaging recreational activities.
- The Events and Conferences Line ensures smooth event logistics and unforgettable experiences.

Each hospitality and tourism segment—like a well-coordinated subway system—plays a crucial role, intersecting strategically to ensure guests navigate effortlessly through enriching experiences.

Why the subway analogy?

This metaphor clearly illustrates how the distinct hospitality and tourism segments are interconnected and interdependent. Later chapters will further explore each "line" and intersection in detail, illustrating how their collaborations shape operational strategies, business functions, and innovations.

As one hospitality student insightfully observed, "Hospitality is often right underneath our noses," much like subway lines quietly running beneath a bustling city—connecting everyday moments, from the barista preparing your morning coffee to the event planner orchestrating a global sporting event. Together, these interconnected segments form a vibrant global network that drives economic growth, cultural exchange, and meaningful human connections, making hospitality and tourism a dynamic, continuously evolving industry.

Global significance of hospitality and tourism

Imagine your ideal getaway—perhaps a vibrant city break bursting with culture, a tranquil beach escape, or a breathtaking mountain adventure. Hospitality and tourism make these moments a reality, yet their impact reaches far beyond memorable vacations. These industries fuel global economies, generate millions of jobs, and foster cross-cultural empathy and understanding. Let's explore the transformative influence hospitality and tourism have worldwide.

Economic contributions

Hospitality and tourism significantly influence the global economy. In 2024 alone, they contributed an impressive $10.9 trillion to global GDP, accounting for over

10 percent of global economic activity (WTTC, 2024). To put this into perspective, this economic contribution rivals some of the world's largest national economies.

Multiplier effects

The economic impact of hospitality and tourism extends far beyond direct spending, sending a powerful ripple effect across diverse sectors. For every dollar spent by tourists, an additional $1.50 to $2.00 flows into related industries such as agriculture, technology, and construction (UNWTO, 2024). This multiplier effect highlights tourism's transformative capacity to stimulate broader economic growth, enriching entire communities.

Major destinations vividly illustrate this phenomenon. Las Vegas, once a humble desert town, is now a global entertainment capital, contributing a remarkable $55.1 billion in visitor spending in 2024, with a total economic impact of $87.7 billion. The city welcomed over 41 million visitors, fueling local businesses and directly supporting approximately 385,000 jobs (Las Vegas Convention and Visitors Authority, 2024). Beyond the casinos and entertainment venues, tourism spending supports countless small businesses—from restaurants and retail shops to event planning and transportation services—amplifying its economic reach.

Dubai similarly epitomizes tourism's powerful economic multiplier effect. In 2024, the city attracted 18.72 million international overnight visitors, a 9 percent increase over the previous year (Dubai DET, 2024). Iconic attractions such as the Burj Khalifa and Palm Jumeirah not only define Dubai's skyline; they also stimulate significant employment in sectors including construction, retail, hospitality, and aviation. This interconnected economic landscape underscores tourism's critical role in driving sustained economic growth and urban development.

The benefits extend beyond major cities to smaller communities worldwide. Caribbean cruise tourism significantly boosts local economies by sourcing fresh seafood, produce, and artisanal products from regional farmers and suppliers, fostering sustainable agriculture and supporting small-scale businesses. Likewise, large-scale global events such as the Paris 2024 Olympics can leave lasting legacies beyond tourism revenue, rejuvenating infrastructure, revitalizing neighborhoods, and enhancing public transportation systems to benefit both visitors and residents.

The Maldives offers a compelling example of integrating economic prosperity with environmental stewardship. Tourism contributes approximately 21 percent of the nation's GDP, making it a cornerstone of its economic structure (World Bank, 2024). Recognizing its environmental fragility, the Maldives proactively balances economic growth with sustainability through initiatives such as the Maldives Coral Institute, which spearheads coral restoration and marine conservation efforts. This sustainable tourism model helps to preserve the Maldives' spectacular marine ecosystems and supports resilient communities, exemplifying responsible and inclusive economic development.

These diverse examples underscore hospitality and tourism's expansive economic reach, demonstrating how thoughtful investment in tourism can foster comprehensive economic and social benefits.

Job creation: The industries as a workforce engine

Hospitality and tourism rank among the largest global employers, offering diverse and exciting career opportunities at every skill and leadership level. Direct employment spans a wide range of roles, from essential front-line positions such as receptionists, tour guides, and chefs, to prestigious executive-level careers including hotel general managers, event directors, senior marketing executives, and chief sustainability officers. These leadership roles offer significant career advancement and personal growth and allow professionals to influence and shape industry trends.

Beyond the direct roles, hospitality and tourism have an extraordinary impact on broader economic ecosystems. Remarkably, for every job directly created in tourism, an additional six to eight jobs are indirectly supported, powering sectors such as agriculture, construction, technology, finance, and logistics (WTTC, 2024). This impressive multiplier effect underscores the vast economic influence of hospitality and tourism, highlighting their crucial role as a driver of comprehensive economic development worldwide.

The dual impact of direct and indirect job roles positions the industry as a cornerstone of employment, particularly in developing economies where tourism drives both income generation and skills development.

Direct employment

Direct employment in hospitality is about creating memorable experiences. Professionals in roles such as housekeeping supervisors, event coordinators, transportation specialists, spa therapists, and culinary experts are vital in crafting quality guest experiences. Luxury resorts, such as those in Bali, employ a diverse range of talented individuals—from skilled front-desk agents welcoming guests to dedicated activity coordinators ensuring unforgettable adventures—thus significantly supporting regional economies and enriching local communities.

Indirect employment

Indirect employment reveals the expansive impact of hospitality and tourism, where the industry's demands stimulate substantial job growth across various complementary sectors. Local farmers benefit from supplying fresh produce to hotels, construction firms thrive building state-of-the-art accommodations, airlines depend on advanced logistics, and tech companies innovate booking platforms and guest services applications. This interconnected network amplifies economic growth and showcases the industry's pivotal role in supporting millions of livelihoods globally (WTTC, 2024).

Role of SMEs in tourism economies

Small and medium-sized enterprises (SMEs) are crucial drivers of tourism economies, fostering growth, innovation, and local economic resilience. These businesses—including boutique hotels, local tour operators, restaurants, and artisan shops—play a central role in job creation, especially in rural and underserved regions. Leveraging their unique cultural and geographic assets, SMEs often lead innovation in specialized markets such as ecotourism, adventure travel, and culinary experiences.

In Bali, for instance, small guesthouses and family-operated eateries known as warungs dominate the tourism landscape. These businesses offer visitors authentic cultural interactions, channeling tourism revenue back into the local economy, thereby enhancing overall community prosperity. SMEs in settings like these underscore the potential for smaller-scale enterprises to cultivate meaningful exchanges between travelers and local communities.

Beyond economic impact, SMEs empower communities by providing platforms for entrepreneurs to showcase their heritage, crafts, and cuisine. This empowerment creates deeper community pride and ownership, further enriching tourist experiences. Rwanda provides an exemplary model of integrating SMEs within its tourism economy through gorilla trekking. Local guides, small-scale lodgings, and community-run initiatives form the core of this niche tourism segment, ensuring revenues directly benefit local populations. Rwanda's approach demonstrates that SMEs can effectively balance economic prosperity with cultural preservation, fostering sustainable tourism ecosystems. When thoughtfully structured, SME-led models can support local livelihoods and reduce environmental harm, including disturbance to wildlife.

Cultural exchange and global connections

At their core, hospitality and tourism are about creating connections between people. Whether sharing a meal, exploring a new city, or engaging in conversations with local hosts, these industries facilitate cultural exchanges and promote global understanding.

Programs such as Airbnb Experiences enhance these connections by offering personalized interactions. Imagine learning to prepare matcha tea in a traditional Japanese ceremony or cooking a Kenyan meal alongside a local family. These experiences transcend typical sightseeing, fostering genuine connections and lasting memories. Similarly, culinary tourism enriches travel experiences, allowing visitors to engage deeply with local traditions through activities like French wine tastings or exploring Moroccan spice markets.

Tourism can also play an essential role in preserving cultural heritage. Iconic landmarks such as Machu Picchu in Peru and the Taj Mahal in India attract millions of tourists whose entrance fees contribute directly to preservation and maintenance. Tourist visits, when carefully managed, thus support the protection of historical sites while fostering pride among local communities. Detailed exploration of tourism's cultural impacts will be made in subsequent chapters.

Hospitality education: Shaping the next generation of leaders

Hospitality management programs are more than academic pathways—they are launchpads for future leaders who will shape one of the most dynamic and impactful global industries. These programs impart foundational knowledge, inspire creativity, cultivate leadership skills, and foster innovation within a fast-paced, people-centered profession.

In the classroom, students begin to understand the principles underlying successful hospitality management. From exploring the factors influencing guest satisfaction and learning the fundamentals of revenue management to building cultural competence, theoretical knowledge lays the groundwork for future success. Structured learning significantly reduces the learning curve, preparing students to confidently navigate professional settings and make informed decisions.

The importance of industry experience

> My internships brought classroom lessons to life—from creating and coordinating social media campaigns to assisting guests at a hotel front desk and planning events—internships taught me essential leadership, communication, and problem-solving skills. More importantly, they showed me how genuine connection and kindness can make a meaningful impact on successful hospitality operations; giving me a well-rounded understanding of the industry and preparing me to confidently enter a career after graduation.
>
> —*Sophia Troutman, hospitality management student*

Hospitality is inherently practical, making hands-on experience crucial to fully grasping its dynamic nature. Internships, co-op programs, on-campus roles, and paid industry positions offer invaluable insights beyond classroom instruction.

Internships and co-ops

Internships and co-op schemes immerse students in real-world hospitality operations, building their adaptability, problem-solving skills, and resilience. These situations serve as bridges between academic theory and industry practice, providing live-learning environments where students can apply and expand their classroom knowledge.

- *Example*: A rotational internship at a resort might involve guest services, event planning, and food and beverage operations, offering a comprehensive view of departmental collaboration.
- *Skills gained*: Service excellence, operational planning, and leadership.

Paid positions

Paid industry roles offer students invaluable opportunities to gain hands-on experience while earning an income. Whether working as a front desk associate at a boutique hotel or assisting with banquet setups, these positions help develop professionalism, teamwork, problem-solving, and customer service excellence. Like internships and co-ops, they allow students to apply classroom lessons in real settings, bridging the gap between theory and practice.

It's also worth noting that, in some cases, students can combine an internship with a paid position. If this option interests you, be sure to inquire about paid internships! While there is not a universal standard for paid internships, I can confidently share that many of my students have secured them. Additionally, some have found paid roles customized to fulfill the learning objectives of their internships, offering a best-of-both-worlds experience.

REAL-WORLD EXAMPLE:
INDUSTRY SPOTLIGHT Taylor Penn: Designing experiences that inspire

Taylor Penn, an event designer at Together & Company, exemplifies the importance of gaining diverse industry experience to succeed in hospitality. Together & Company is a leading catering and event design firm known for creating thoughtfully curated experiences and exceptional hospitality at events ranging from intimate gatherings to large corporate celebrations.

Penn began her career serving and bartending, roles that honed her interpersonal and customer service skills. Building on these foundational experiences, she advanced into catering sales before becoming an event designer, crafting memorable events and meaningful guest experiences. Now, leveraging her comprehensive expertise, she is launching her own event business, reflecting the entrepreneurial opportunities available through dedicated industry engagement.

Reflect

- Identify one professional skill you'd like to develop through industry experiences. Why is this skill particularly important to you?
- Think about a hospitality professional you admire. What experiences do you believe contributed significantly to their success?

Success happens when preparation meets opportunity

A guiding principle in hospitality is that success happens when preparation meets opportunity. Every class, internship, job, and leadership experience serves as a stepping stone toward future success. As you explore careers in hospitality, consider how experiences like internships, campus roles, or community events can prepare you for leadership.

Hospitality education is more than just learning about the industry—it's a transformative journey that blends theoretical knowledge with hands-on experience, shaping the leaders of tomorrow. It fosters transferable skills, instills a commitment to excellence, and cultivates a mindset of lifelong learning that transcends the hospitality field.

Reflect

Think about a time when your preparation helped you successfully navigate an unexpected opportunity—whether in school, work, extracurricular activities, or your personal life:

- Briefly describe the situation and the opportunity you encountered.
- What specific preparation (skills, knowledge, experiences, or mindset) enabled you to seize this opportunity effectively?
- Reflect on how this experience can help you recognize and leverage future opportunities in your education or career, including those within hospitality and tourism.

Interconnectedness with other industries

Hospitality is not confined to hotels, restaurants, or resorts. Its integration into industries such as senior living, healthcare, and education highlights hospitality's expansive scope and transformative impact. Its foundational principles of comfort, care, and meaningful connections extend into diverse sectors, enhancing community support and fostering innovation. This interconnected ecosystem creates a dynamic network of collaboration and advancement across various fields.

Professionals experienced in hospitality frequently observe how its core tenets of service excellence, operational efficiency, and human-centered care open new opportunities, drive innovation, and raise standards across multiple industries.

Senior living: Where hospitality meets home

Senior living facilities exemplify how hospitality values can transform everyday experiences into moments of care and connection. These establishments often operate with the same level of precision and attention to detail as boutique hotels, blending personalized care with operational excellence. An example of this connection can be seen in senior living communities managed by global hospitality leaders like Sodexo, which bring industry expertise to enhance residents' experiences. By integrating hospitality principles into their operations, senior living facilities demonstrate the far-reaching influence of the industry, extending its impact into new and meaningful territories.

Senior living communities are thoughtfully designed to prioritize quality of life for residents, offering tailored services such as concierge-style assistance, curated meal plans, wellness programs, and personal care services. These settings go beyond functionality to create warm, welcoming environments that foster comfort and connection. Recreation and social opportunities are also a vital part of senior living. Communities often organize excursions, fitness classes, cultural events, and lifelong learning programs, fostering connection and enriching the lives of residents. These offerings mirror the recreation-focused aspects of the hospitality industry, where experiences are designed to engage and delight guests.

Food and beverage services in senior living are another area where hospitality principles shine. Trends such as farm-to-table dining, cooked-to-order meals, and community gardens emphasize fresh, high-quality ingredients and create opportunities for residents to be part of the food preparation process. This supports health and wellness and cultivates a sense of purpose and community.

A seamless combination of care and service in senior living underscores its alignment with hospitality principles. For professionals, this sector offers many and varied career pathways in areas such as operations, human resources, sales, marketing, and events. Moreover, the transferable skills gained in hospitality education—such as empathy, problem-solving, and teamwork—prepare individuals to thrive in this growing and deeply rewarding industry.

Healthcare: Where healing meets hospitality

Hospitals and healthcare facilities increasingly draw upon the operational best practices and guest service standards of the hospitality industry to improve patient care and overall experience. For example, professionals with hospitality backgrounds have successfully applied their lodging expertise to healthcare settings, highlighting the versatile nature of hospitality skills.

Hospitality professionals often transition into healthcare roles, leveraging their expertise in guest relations, housekeeping, and foodservice. For instance:

- A former hotel veteran becoming a director of patient experience to enhance service culture and responsiveness.
- A director of food and nutrition at a multi-site hospital system bringing restaurant-quality dining to patients and staff.
- A director of environmental services using housekeeping management experience to improve hygiene and operational efficiency in healthcare settings.

These transitions reflect the close parallels between the two industries, offering hospitality professionals boundless opportunities to grow while applying their skills in meaningful new ways.

Key areas of hospitality's influence in healthcare include, but is not limited to:

- **Patient services:** Some hospitals now employ concierge-style services to improve patient navigation and satisfaction, ensuring a seamless experience. As an example, the Mayo Clinic, a globally renowned healthcare institution, incorporates hospitality-trained staff to prioritize empathy and responsiveness, enhancing patient care and outcomes.
- **Food operations:** Hospital dining can be transformed to offer restaurant-quality meals, focusing on nutrition and presentation to elevate patient satisfaction. Providers like Sodexo and Compass Group integrate culinary excellence into healthcare settings, mirroring the high standards of hotel dining.
- **Facility management:** Hygiene, safety, and ambiance in healthcare facilities now reflect the rigorous standards seen in luxury hotels.

REAL-WORLD EXAMPLE:
INDUSTRY SPOTLIGHT   Pioneering culinary excellence in healthcare

Sodexo, a global leader in food and facilities management, exemplifies how hospitality principles elevate patient care in healthcare environments. Known for bringing restaurant-quality dining experiences to hospitals, Sodexo combines culinary excellence, nutritional expertise, and innovative hospitality-driven services. Through meticulous menu planning and attentive service, Sodexo transforms hospital dining, significantly enhancing patients' satisfaction and supporting their recovery.

Education: Hospitality as a catalyst for growth

Service excellence, operational efficiency, and creating meaningful connections—some of hospitality's core principles—extend into educational settings in diverse and impactful ways. Whether a university boasts iconic event venues like Ohio Stadium or operates smaller-scale facilities, hospitality principles enhance the campus experience, create a sense of community, and provide students with unique opportunities to learn and grow.

Imagine a university with dining halls that offer the convenience and ambiance of a high-end restaurant, a conference center that hosts global events, or even a stadium that welcomes over 100,000 fans for game days and concerts. These spaces showcase the breadth of hospitality and tourism segments that can be integrated into a campus environment. While not all universities have such facilities, many offer opportunities for students to engage with hospitality-driven practices on some level—whether through a bustling student union, campus events, or residence hall operations.

For example, The Ohio State University's campus features multiple segments of hospitality and tourism, including event venues, dining services, and a full-service hotel. Iconic spaces such as Ohio Stadium bring together elements of entertainment, food and beverage, and event planning, creating a vibrant hub of activity. At the same time, smaller satellite campuses or fully remote programs may focus on other aspects of hospitality, such as virtual event coordination or remote community engagement. No matter the setting, the underlying hospitality principles—creating meaningful connections, delivering excellent service, and fostering operational efficiency—remain the same.

In dining facilities, hospitality practices elevate the experience beyond simple meals. For instance, adopting a restaurant-style approach to customer service transforms a routine activity into a chance to build community. Similarly, campuses that host large-scale events, such as academic conferences or cultural festivals, apply hospitality-driven logistics to ensure seamless operations and memorable guest experiences. These activities mirror professional hospitality environments. Other segments seen on campus may include club management, lodging, transportation, and more.

Campuses that include iconic venues like Ohio Stadium also demonstrate how diverse hospitality segments coexist within a single environment. From managing crowd logistics to offering VIP experiences, these venues provide a microcosm of the hospitality industry. Students might find opportunities in event planning, food and beverage operations, marketing, and guest services—all within their university.

Additionally, for hospitality students, campuses can serve as their own living laboratories. Whether managing events, working in dining services, or assisting with conference center operations, students can gain practical experience that aligns with career pathways in hospitality and tourism. These roles offer a chance to develop skills in guest relations, logistics, and operational planning, for example, preparing students for dynamic roles in the industry.

Ultimately, the integration of hospitality into education goes beyond operations—it creates environments that foster connection, inclusion, and growth. Whether on a large campus with iconic venues or in a smaller setting with focused opportunities, hospitality principles empower universities to deliver meaningful experiences. For students, these settings not only enhance their education; they also prepare them to lead in an industry defined by care, innovation, and human connection.

Reflect

Consider how hospitality principles enhance settings beyond traditional hotels and restaurants, such as hospitals and university campuses.

- In your opinion, what specific hospitality practice would significantly improve patient experiences in healthcare settings, and why?
- Reflect on a personal experience (perhaps visiting a hospital or attending a campus event). Identify one hospitality-related interaction that notably improved your experience. How did it change your perception of that environment?

Foundations of hospitality and tourism

Hospitality and tourism are far more than services—they are dynamic forces that weave together cultures, economies, and experiences to create transformative value for individuals and societies. By understanding the historical trajectory, economic contributions, and modern trends of these industries, students can see hospitality not just as a career but as a powerful lens for global interconnectedness and human connection.

INTERACTIVE EXERCISE
Bridging hospitality to new industries

A large, metropolitan hospital wants to significantly improve patient and visitor satisfaction. You have been hired—as a hospitality management consultant—to propose practical strategies adapted from the hospitality industry.

1. Identify three core hospitality principles from this chapter that you believe will significantly enhance patient experience (for instance, service excellence, personalized attention, operational efficiency).
2. Propose at least two specific hospitality-driven actions for each principle you identified (offering concierge services for patient navigation, enhancing dining experiences with customized menus, improving waiting-area ambiance, and so on).
3. Explain briefly how each action aligns with the task of improving patient satisfaction and operational efficiency.
4. Share and discuss your solutions with a small group or class. Select one best practice from your discussion to share with the larger class, explaining why your group considers it particularly impactful.

Having explored how hospitality principles can be creatively applied across diverse settings, you've gained deeper insights into hospitality's expansive influence. As we conclude this foundational exploration, let's reflect on key points that summarize hospitality's global significance, interconnectivity, and continuous evolution.

Key takeaways

- Hospitality creates meaningful, guest-centered experiences, reflected in the symbolism of the pineapple.
- Hospitality serves as a global economic powerhouse, driving innovation and resilience.
- It fosters cultural exchange, strengthening mutual respect and understanding.
- The industry's impact extends beyond core sectors, influencing diverse industries including healthcare and education.
- Its legacy of evolution—from ancient inns to AI-driven innovations—demonstrates adaptability and forward-thinking.

Looking ahead

As we conclude this foundational exploration, you are encouraged to view hospitality and tourism as more than an industry—they are transformative agents that shape how people connect with the world and one another. The opportunities within this field are vast, offering pathways to impact economies, uplift communities, and foster global understanding.

In the next chapter we will dive deeper into the human-centered nature of the industry. This journey will explore the vital roles of empathy, emotional intelligence, and service excellence in creating guest experiences that leave lasting impressions.

References

Baum, T., Mooney, S.K.K., Robinson, R.N.S., & Solnet, D. (2020) COVID-19's impact on the hospitality workforce: New crisis or amplification of the norm?, *International Journal of Contemporary Hospitality Management*, 32 (9), 2813–2829. doi.org/10.1108/IJCHM-04-2020-0314 (archived at https://perma.cc/T7HD-9DXD)

Bryman, A. (2004) *The Disneyization of Society*. London: Sage Publications.

Buhalis, D. & Leung, R. (2018) Smart hospitality: Interconnectivity and interoperability towards an ecosystem, *International Journal of Hospitality Management*, 71, 41–50. doi.org/10.1016/j.ijhm.2017.11.011 (archived at https://perma.cc/647Y-YMA4)

Dubai DET (Department of Economy and Tourism) (2024) *Dubai Tourism Performance Report 2024*. dubaitourism.gov.ae (archived at https://perma.cc/H89N-NH9P)

Gyr, U. (2010) *The History of Tourism: Structures on the Path to Modernity*, European History. ieg-ego.eu/en/threads/europe-on-the-road/the-history-of-tourism (archived at https://perma.cc/7LCD-TZV6)

Kalargyrou, V. & Volis, A.A. (2014) Disability inclusion initiatives in the hospitality industry: An exploratory study of industry leaders, *Journal of Human Resources in Hospitality & Tourism*, 13 (4), 430–454. doi.org/10.1080/15332845.2014.903152 (archived at https://perma.cc/SV6U-F278)

Las Vegas Convention and Visitors Authority (2024) *Las Vegas Tourism Statistics: 2024 Overview*. lvcva.com/research/visitor-statistics (archived at https://perma.cc/2LTG-RLQV)

Marriott International (2024) *Environmental, Social & Governance: Global Progress*. serve360.marriott.com/wp-content/uploads/2024/07/2024ESGProgress.pdf (archived at https://perma.cc/Z9YF-XW7K)

Merriam-Webster (n.d.) Hospitality. merriam-webster.com/dictionary/hospitality (archived at https://perma.cc/F9M3-VLPK)

Sandoval-Strausz, A.K. (2007) *Hotel: An American History*. New Haven, CT: Yale University Press.

Schwartz, D.G. (2013) *Grandissimo: The First Emperor of Las Vegas: How Jay Sarno Won a Casino Empire, Lost It, and Inspired Modern Las Vegas*. Las Vegas, NV: Winchester Books.

Sharma, A., Shin, H., Santa-María, M.J., & Nicolau, J.L. (2021) Hotels' COVID-19 innovation and performance', *Annals of Tourism Research*, 88, 103180. doi.org/10.1016/j.annals.2021.103180 (archived at https://perma.cc/6JPP-Z8XK)

Touati, H. (2010) *Islam and Travel in the Middle Ages*, trans. L.G. Cochrane. Chicago: University of Chicago Press.

Tourism New Zealand (n.d.) Tiaki: Care for New Zealand. tourismnewzealand.com/partner-with-us/tiaki (archived at https://perma.cc/7DQQ-PQE6)

UNWTO (United Nations World Tourism Organization) (2024) *International Tourism Highlights, 2024 Edition*. Madrid: UN Tourism. doi.org/10.18111/9789284425808 (archived at https://perma.cc/6JPP-Z8XK)

UNWTO (n.d.) *Glossary of Tourism Terms*. unwto.org/glossary-tourism-terms (archived at https://perma.cc/V4WZ-7RXG)

Walton, J.K. (2005) *Histories of Tourism: Representation, Identity and Conflict*. Bristol: Channel View Publications.

Williams, O. (2021) *The Secret Life of the Savoy: Glamour and Intrigue at the World's Most Famous Hotel*. New York: Pegasus Books.

World Bank (2024) Maldives development update: Seeking stability in turbulent times. worldbank.org/en/country/maldives/publication/maldives-development-update-2024 (archived at https://perma.cc/4YK9-5TPF)

WTTC (World Travel & Tourism Council) (2024) *Economic Impact Research*. wttc.org/research/economic-impact (archived at https://perma.cc/S9AD-XTW3)

Xiang, Z., Magnini, V.P., & Fesenmaier, D.R. (2015) Information technology and consumer behavior in travel and tourism: Insights from travel planning using the internet, *Journal of Retailing and Consumer Services*, 22, 244–249. doi.org/10.1016/j.jretconser.2014.08.005 (archived at https://perma.cc/37BH-2JVB)

The core of hospitality: Human interaction, connectivity, and service

2

LEARNING OBJECTIVES

- Explain the importance of human connection and service excellence in creating memorable hospitality experiences.
- Apply established industry service models (Ritz-Carlton, Hilton, Disney) and original instructional frameworks (CARES and REACT) to effectively address diverse guest and traveler scenarios.
- Illustrate how empathy and emotional intelligence directly enhance guest satisfaction and loyalty in hospitality and tourism settings.
- Evaluate the interplay between technology and human interaction, assessing its impact on guest experiences in hospitality.
- Analyze diverse practical examples of empathy-driven service excellence, identifying best practices applicable across hospitality contexts.

Introduction

Picture this: After a long, exhausting day spent exploring bustling city streets, fascinating museums, and vibrant local markets, you finally return to your hotel. As you step into the lobby, a front-desk associate greets you warmly with a genuine smile, addresses you by name, and anticipates your needs by suggesting a nearby restaurant that aligns perfectly with your tastes and today's adventures. In that moment, you're no longer just another traveler; you feel recognized, appreciated, and genuinely cared for—a powerful reminder of the transformative impact of meaningful human connections. Can you recall a similar moment when someone's personal attention transformed your travel experience?

At their core, hospitality and tourism revolve around people—serving them, connecting authentically, and enriching their experiences. Research underscores that memorable travel and guest experiences are largely defined by human interaction, warmth, and personalization, extending far beyond standard service elements (Kandampully et al., 2014). Whether it's a tour guide thoughtfully tailoring the pace of sightseeing to your family's interests, the housekeeper ensuring every detail in your room feels just right, or the concierge going the extra mile to craft a personalized itinerary, these thoughtful interactions profoundly shape the traveler's journey.

> Hospitality is fundamentally about human connection. Outstanding guest service is achieved when businesses genuinely prioritize emotional engagement and build lasting relationships, creating meaningful experiences that guests carry with them long after their visit.
>
> *—Dr. Jay Kandampully, professor of service management and hospitality*

Yet delivering exceptional service in today's fast-paced, global environment requires more than good intentions. It demands a deep understanding of diverse guest and traveler needs, emotional intelligence to navigate complex interactions, and structured frameworks to maintain consistency without sacrificing the personal touch. Emotional intelligence, as described by Goleman (2005), includes essential skills such as self-awareness, empathy, and relationship management—all vital for excelling across hospitality and tourism contexts. Leading brands such as Hilton, Ritz-Carlton, and Disney have operationalized these concepts, creating structured service models that empower teams to consistently exceed expectations while remaining flexible enough to handle unique situations. These models are more than theoretical—they are practical, actionable tools actively used by industry professionals every day to enhance guest loyalty and satisfaction, ultimately driving business success.

As a (future) hospitality and tourism professional, your ability to meaningfully connect with others will distinctly set you apart. According to Bain & Company (n.d.), businesses that prioritize authentic human connection achieve substantially higher levels of guest loyalty, translating directly into greater profitability and sustained competitive advantage. In this chapter, we'll delve into practical strategies for fostering genuine human connection, explore renowned industry service frameworks, and examine how empathy and emotional intelligence serve as essential tools for service excellence in hospitality and tourism.

Let's embark on this journey together to uncover the heart of hospitality and tourism—where every interaction holds the potential to make a profound difference, and the simple act of connecting transforms ordinary service into something extraordinary.

Human connectivity at the heart of hospitality

Hospitality is built on human connection. At its core, the industry thrives by meeting emotional and social needs, transforming routine interactions into unforgettable experiences. Even in today's technology-driven world, the personal touch remains the hallmark of exceptional service. This section explores why human connection matters, how it drives guest satisfaction and loyalty, and the vital role cultural awareness plays in creating meaningful interactions.

The psychology of connection

Why does a warm greeting or thoughtful gesture resonate so deeply? Connection is a fundamental human need, deeply rooted in evolutionary biology. As social beings, humans thrive on interaction, cooperation, and the sense of being seen and valued.

Daniel Goleman (2005), an expert on emotional intelligence, highlights how empathy, self-awareness, and strong social skills build authentic relationships—an essential skill set in hospitality. Imagine a hotel guest returning from a long day of meetings to find their favorite snack and a handwritten note waiting in their room. This simple gesture not only addresses a practical need; it also creates an emotional bond, reinforcing the sense of value and care. Such thoughtful moments, while small, significantly enhance guest satisfaction and loyalty, emphasizing the emotional depth of hospitality.

How human connection drives satisfaction and loyalty

Guests choose hospitality experiences for reasons beyond comfort or convenience. Clean rooms, delicious meals, and convenient locations matter—but it's the personal touch that truly inspires loyalty.

- **Satisfaction:** Emotional connection greatly enhances guest satisfaction. When a server remembers a repeat guest's dietary preferences, it transforms an ordinary meal into a personal, memorable experience, leaving the guest feeling deeply valued.
- **Loyalty:** Genuine connections turn satisfied guests into loyal advocates. Increasing customer retention by just 5 percent can boost profits by as much as 95 percent (Reichheld and Markey, 2011). Exceptional hospitality inspires guests not just to return but to enthusiastically recommend their experiences to others.

The Ritz-Carlton's renowned "Gold Standards" exemplify this principle, training staff to anticipate needs and create special moments that delight guests, underscoring the transformative power of structured yet personalized care.

The role of cultural awareness in hospitality

In an increasingly global industry, cultural awareness has become essential. Understanding and respecting diverse cultural norms, values, and expectations isn't just thoughtful—it's essential business practice. For instance, in Japanese culture, quiet and respectful interactions signify professionalism, while Italian guests often value warmth and expressive attentiveness. Hospitality teams who understand these cultural nuances can offer more personalized, meaningful interactions. However, effective cultural awareness emphasizes understanding broad cultural expectations while recognizing individual differences to avoid stereotypes and ensure genuine guest engagement. Hospitality professionals must always remember that guests are individuals first, whose preferences and behaviors might differ from broader cultural trends.

Training teams to recognize and adapt to cultural differences enriches guest experiences and strengthens internal cohesion, reflecting hospitality's global nature. Leaders fostering inclusive environments empower teams to deliver exceptional, culturally sensitive service.

> **THINK LIKE A MANAGER**
>
> You are the front office manager at a busy downtown hotel. A front-desk associate unintentionally offends an international guest by misunderstanding a cultural norm. As a manager, how would you:
>
> - Immediately address the situation with both the guest and your employee?
> - Coach your team to prevent future cultural misunderstandings?
> - Foster an inclusive environment that values ongoing cultural education?

Bridging cultural differences

Cultural awareness is essential for hospitality success. Recognizing and respecting diverse cultural norms, values, and expectations allows hospitality organizations to connect authentically with guests from around the globe. Understanding these subtle nuances enhances guest experiences, increases satisfaction, and builds loyalty by fostering environments of genuine inclusion and respect.

REAL-WORLD EXAMPLE:
INDUSTRY SPOTLIGHT Disneyland Paris

Disneyland Paris offers a compelling story of lessons learned from cultural adaptation. When the park opened in 1992, Disney unintentionally overlooked key cultural norms, leading to guest frustration and financial setbacks. Predominantly American food offerings, strict dress codes, and heavy reliance on English-language signage alienated many European visitors.

Recognizing these missteps, Disney thoughtfully introduced authentic French cuisine, adjusted operational norms to align with European expectations, and provided multilingual communication. These culturally aligned operational improvements significantly boosted guest satisfaction and financial performance, turning initial setbacks into lasting successes. These adjustments dramatically improved guest experiences and highlighted the transformative power of genuine cultural sensitivity and "glocalization"—the adaptation of global strategies to meet local cultural expectations (Matusitz, 2011).

Reflect

Consider your current comfort level with cultural awareness.

- What cultures are you familiar with, and which cultures would you like to learn more about?
- How will you actively seek opportunities to broaden your cultural competency to become a more inclusive hospitality leader?

Anticipating needs: The cornerstone of connection

Anticipating guest needs defines exceptional hospitality. It involves insightful observation and thoughtful actions, transforming ordinary moments into lasting memories. As mentioned, increasing customer retention rates by just 5 percent can boost profits by 25–95 percent, underscoring the tangible value of proactive service (Reichheld and Markey, 2011).

In tourism, consider a tour guide noticing guests' keen interest in local culinary traditions. By spontaneously arranging a visit to a renowned local market, the guide enriches their cultural experience, creating an unexpected and memorable highlight. Similarly, in air travel, personnel trained to recognize passenger cues can significantly enhance comfort. For example, a flight attendant observing a passenger's anxiety can proactively offer reassurance and friendly conversation, turning a stressful situation into a comforting interaction.

These thoughtful actions demonstrate genuine empathy and attentiveness—qualities consistently recognized in industry research as foundational to outstanding hospitality (Goleman, 2005). Such proactive service highlights the importance of training teams to recognize subtle cues, allowing for personalized experiences that resonate deeply with guests.

Reflect

Recall a time when personalized service significantly enhanced your experience as a guest.

- What made this interaction memorable?
- How can you incorporate similar thoughtful actions into your professional hospitality career?

Building meaningful connections

Human connectivity is deeply woven into the fabric of hospitality. Beyond transactional exchanges, meaningful interactions enrich guest experiences, leaving lasting emotional impressions. Understanding the psychology behind human connections, embracing diverse cultural insights, and anticipating guest needs are necessary tools to craft impactful, memorable experiences. As the industry continues to evolve, the emphasis on authentic, meaningful relationships will remain central, sustaining hospitality's enduring strength and appeal.

Empathy and emotional intelligence in service excellence

In hospitality and tourism, exceptional professionals understand that their roles extend beyond delivering services—they curate meaningful emotional experiences that make lasting memories. Empathy and emotional intelligence serve as cornerstones for these transformative moments, empowering hospitality leaders and employees to forge genuine connections with guests and colleagues. This section explores empathy's pivotal role in leadership, examines the critical relationship between emotional labor and staff well-being, and highlights actionable strategies for using emotional intelligence to elevate service excellence.

Empathy as a leadership strength

Often underestimated as merely a soft skill, empathy is a powerful leadership advantage in hospitality. It enables leaders to approach challenges with genuine understanding, cultivating trust and stronger connections with both guests and staff. Defined as the ability to recognize, understand, and share the feelings of others, empathy equips leaders to address immediate issues and anticipate unspoken needs.

Empathetic leaders build trust, foster collaboration, and nurture a sense of belonging within their teams (Baumeister and Leary, 1995). Consider, for example, a hotel general manager who listens attentively to an employee who is struggling to balance family and work responsibilities. By offering flexible scheduling solutions, the leader significantly enhances employee morale and productivity. Such thoughtful gestures create a positive ripple effect: employees who feel genuinely supported are more inclined to deliver outstanding guest experiences (Reichheld and Markey, 2011).

Empathy also equips leaders to navigate the complexities of culturally diverse teams. In today's global hospitality landscape, teams frequently include members from varied cultural, linguistic, and personal backgrounds. Leaders who engage with these differences with curiosity and respect cultivate inclusive environments where every team member feels valued and empowered. This inclusive approach directly enhances service quality, as employees naturally mirror the care they receive from their leaders in their guest interactions.

REAL-WORLD EXAMPLE:
INDUSTRY SPOTLIGHT   Emirates Airline: Elevating service through empathy and cultural intelligence

Emirates Airline, consistently recognized as a global leader in aviation hospitality, attributes much of its success to the empathetic and culturally intelligent approach of its cabin crew (Emirates, 2023). With a cabin crew workforce representing over 130 nationalities and serving passengers from every corner of the globe, Emirates emphasizes rigorous emotional intelligence training to ensure outstanding guest experiences on every flight.

Crew members undergo comprehensive training not only in technical and safety procedures but also in cross-cultural communication, empathy, and interpersonal sensitivity. For instance, flight attendants are trained to recognize subtle emotional cues from passengers who might feel anxious, stressed, or unfamiliar with flying. They proactively engage guests through personalized gestures of comfort and reassurance—such as gently checking in with nervous passengers, offering calming conversations, or subtly providing culturally familiar amenities.

By embedding empathy and cultural understanding into their training programs, Emirates empowers its staff to deliver personalized and memorable interactions, fostering passenger loyalty and creating an exceptional onboard experience (Earley and Mosakowski, 2004; Goleman, 2005). This holistic approach demonstrates how emotional intelligence can transform standard service interactions into emotionally resonant experiences cherished by a global audience.

Reflect

Think of a challenging situation you have faced (or witnessed) in a guest-service setting.

- How was empathy demonstrated or overlooked?
- What would you personally do differently as a hospitality professional to ensure empathy consistently guides your interactions?

Balancing emotional labor with supportive practices

Hospitality professionals do more than execute tasks—they engage in emotional labor, a concept introduced by sociologist Arlie Hochschild (1983) to describe managing emotions and maintaining a positive demeanor consistent with expectations. While emotional labor significantly enhances guest satisfaction, it can also lead to burnout if employees are not adequately supported.

Emotional labor often involves two actions: *surface acting*—modifying outward expressions—and *deep acting*—genuinely aligning internal emotions with expected displays (Hochschild, 1983). For example, a concierge empathizing with a stressed traveler, or a server anticipating a diner's preferences engages in emotional labor to improve guest experiences. Without proper support, such continuous emotional regulation can leave professionals feeling isolated, undervalued, or emotionally exhausted (Grandey, 2000).

Leaders play a crucial role in proactively identifying signs of emotional burnout, such as reduced engagement, fatigue, and increased absenteeism. They can provide immediate support through counseling resources, flexible scheduling, and by actively promoting work–life balance.

Strategies for supporting emotional well-being

Hospitality leaders play a crucial role in addressing the demands of emotional labor. By implementing supportive practices, organizations can foster resilience and reduce burnout. Effective strategies include:

- **Emotional resilience training:** Equip employees with skills to manage stress and emotional balance through mindfulness practices, stress management workshops, and scenario-based training (Grandey, 2000).
- **Employee empowerment:** Allow employees autonomy to resolve guest issues, reducing frustration, building confidence, and increasing job satisfaction (Karatepe, 2013).
- **Open communication:** Establish safe channels where employees can express concerns, seek support, and share feedback without judgment. Regular check-ins and team debriefings help normalize conversations about emotional challenges (Grandey, 2000).

Connecting theory to practice

Hochschild (1983) emphasizes that emotional labor is not only an individual effort; it is shaped by organizational expectations. Leaders who validate emotional demands and foster a culture prioritizing employee well-being can significantly reduce workplace stress. For example, Ritz-Carlton empowers employees to take their own immediate actions to resolve guest concerns, providing resources to reduce emotional strain (Goleman, 2005).

Thoughtful attention to emotional labor enables hospitality leaders to support teams in delivering exceptional guest experiences while preserving their own emotional health. Ultimately, fostering a supportive environment benefits employees and enhances service quality, creating a positive ripple effect of care and connection.

THINK LIKE A MANAGER

As the general manager of a popular luxury resort, you notice rising fatigue and lower engagement levels among your frontline staff during peak season. As a manager, how would you:

- Identify the early warning signs of emotional burnout?
- Implement proactive strategies to support your team emotionally and physically?
- Balance immediate operational needs with your employees' long-term well-being?

Emotional intelligence as a framework for excellence

Emotional intelligence involves recognizing, understanding, and managing emotions while effectively navigating interpersonal relationships (Goleman, 2005). For hospitality professionals, emotional intelligence is fundamental to exceptional service:

- **Self-awareness:** Recognizing personal emotions and their impact on interactions. For example, a front-desk associate managing a long line of check-ins should be able to pause to acknowledge their frustration, take a deep breath, and refocus on creating positive guest experiences.
- **Self-regulation:** Maintaining composure and adapting to changing circumstances. A banquet manager who remains calm during a last-minute schedule change models grace under pressure and sets the tone for their team.
- **Motivation:** Using intrinsic drive to maintain energy and enthusiasm. Hospitality professionals who find meaning in their work are better equipped to deliver consistent service, even during demanding shifts.
- **Empathy:** Understanding and validating others' feelings. Explicitly acknowledging a guest's emotions by stating, for instance, "I understand why this situation is frustrating, and I would likely feel the same way," fosters deeper emotional connections.
- **Social skills:** Building rapport and resolving conflicts effectively. Strong social skills, whether addressing guest concerns or mediating team interactions, ensure smoother operations and enhance guest satisfaction.

REAL-WORLD EXAMPLE:
INDUSTRY SPOTLIGHT Chick-fil-A: Embedding emotional intelligence in quick-service dining

Chick-fil-A, a leader in the quick-service restaurant industry, is renowned for its exceptional customer service, which is deeply rooted in emotional intelligence and empathy. The company's training programs emphasize the development of emotional intelligence competencies among employees to enhance customer interactions.

One notable initiative is the Emotional Intelligence course offered by Chick-fil-A Baytown, which focuses on self-awareness, self-regulation, motivation, empathy, and social skills. The course is designed to help team members understand and manage their emotions, recognize the emotions of others, and handle interpersonal relationships judiciously and empathetically.

Additionally, Chick-fil-A's Leadership Development Program incorporates emotional intelligence principles to cultivate effective leaders. Participants engage in hands-on experiences that challenge them to apply emotional intelligence skills in real-world scenarios, fostering personal and professional growth (Chick-fil-A Baytown, n.d.).

These structured programs demonstrate the company's commitment to integrating emotional intelligence into its organizational culture, resulting in meaningful customer experiences and a supportive work environment.

Empathy in action: Memorable moments

Empathy transforms ordinary service into unforgettable experiences. Consider the following real-world scenarios showcasing how hospitality professionals apply empathy effectively.

Transforming challenges with empathy

When a guest at a boutique hotel was frustrated by an unexpected room cancellation, the front-desk manager immediately stepped in with understanding. The manager listened attentively to the guest's concerns, offered a complimentary upgrade, and included a thoughtful handwritten note stating, "I understand how disruptive this must have been, and we're committed to making it right." This genuine, empathetic response not only resolved the issue but also transformed a disappointed guest into a loyal advocate.

Personalized experiences that create lifelong memories

During a family vacation, resort staff noticed a young guest's excitement about soccer from the jersey they were wearing. Seizing the opportunity to create a special moment, the concierge arranged tickets to a local match, presenting them with heartfelt words: "I saw how much you love soccer and wanted to make your evening extra special." This thoughtful gesture turned a simple observation into a memorable, cherished experience for the entire family.

Strengthening team bonds through empathy

In a busy hotel kitchen, a sous chef observed a junior cook struggling with a task. Instead of criticizing, the chef offered hands-on assistance coupled with encouraging words: "I see how hard you're working. Let's tackle this together." This empathetic leadership boosted the junior cook's confidence, reinforced a supportive workplace culture, and fostered mutual respect among the team.

Interactive exercise
Practicing empathy in real-time

Imagine you are the guest experience manager on a popular luxury cruise line. A family approaches you, visibly distressed. Their scheduled shore excursion—one they had planned months in advance as the highlight of their trip—was unexpectedly canceled due to weather conditions.

Step 1: Reflect and empathize

Take a moment to genuinely imagine the family's perspective. Beyond the inconvenience, what deeper emotions might they be experiencing (disappointment, frustration, sadness)?

Step 2: Craft an empathetic response

Write down exactly how you would respond to the family—what you would say and how you would say it. Focus not only on acknowledging the situation but also on explicitly recognizing their feelings. Avoid simply apologizing; instead, demonstrate sincere understanding and emotional validation.

Example response

"I can imagine how disappointed you must be—especially since you planned this excursion months ago as a special highlight for your trip. I would feel just as frustrated. Let's explore some options together to make sure your day is still memorable."

Step 3: Suggest solutions with empathy

List at least two actionable solutions you could offer, clearly connecting these solutions to the family's emotional needs and expectations.

Step 4: Analyze and share

Briefly reflect on how your empathetic approach would likely affect the family's feelings, satisfaction, and overall perception of the cruise line. How does this practice help you understand the difference between empathizing and merely apologizing?

Conclusion: Empathy as the differentiator

Empathy and emotional intelligence are critical to hospitality success, setting exceptional organizations apart from mere good ones. Leaders who embody empathy inspire their teams to deliver service that resonates deeply with guests. Consistently integrating empathy into interactions not only transforms routine service into extraordinary experiences, it also builds lasting loyalty and elevates a brand's reputation.

Emotional intelligence equips hospitality professionals with the tools to navigate diverse interactions and deliver thoughtful, personalized service. The next section looks at how service models such as Ritz-Carlton's Gold Standards and Hilton's HEART build on these principles, providing structured frameworks that show how empathy and EI can be scaled to create consistent, exceptional guest experiences across diverse settings.

Applying industry service models

The hospitality and tourism industries thrive on service excellence, which requires structured, actionable frameworks to guide interactions, empower teams, and ensure consistency without losing the personal touch. Leading brands have developed unique service models that cater to specific contexts, offering valuable insights into creating exceptional guest and traveler experiences.

Ritz-Carlton: The gold standards of service

> Exceptional hospitality goes beyond providing service—it's about creating lasting impressions through sincere care, attention to detail, and the ability to anticipate the unspoken needs of each guest.

—Tony Herasme, director of rooms, Ritz-Carlton South Beach, reflecting on his personal experience

Ritz-Carlton's Gold Standards epitomize luxury, personalization, and anticipatory service, forming a robust foundation for consistently delivering exceptional guest experiences. Central to this renowned service philosophy are the company's Three Steps of Service:

1 **A warm and sincere greeting**: Engage guests warmly, always using their names to personalize interactions.

2 Anticipation and fulfillment: Proactively recognize and fulfill each guest's expressed—and unexpressed—needs.

3 A fond farewell: Give a genuine goodbye, reaffirming the personal connection by again using the guest's name.

Complementing these foundational steps, Ritz-Carlton's 12 Service Values reinforce the brand's dedication to excellence, personalized care, and employee empowerment:

1. **Relationship building:** Cultivate authentic relationships to build lifelong Ritz-Carlton guests.
2. **Responsiveness:** Be attentive and proactive in meeting both stated and unstated guest desires.
3. **Empowered decisions:** Grant employees ("Ladies and Gentlemen") autonomy, including the ability to spend up to $2,000 per guest, to swiftly resolve issues or craft memorable experiences.
4. **Brand commitment:** Actively contribute to the brand's Key Success Factors, Community Footprints initiatives, and the distinctive Ritz-Carlton Mystique.
5. **Continuous improvement:** Consistently seek ways to innovate and elevate guest experiences.
6. **Problem ownership:** Immediately and personally resolve guest issues to their satisfaction.
7. **Teamwork:** Encourage lateral support and collaboration across teams to surpass guest expectations.
8. **Growth opportunities:** Support continuous learning and development opportunities for all staff.
9. **Involvement:** Empower employees by involving them in planning and decision-making processes.
10. **Professionalism:** Uphold high standards of professional appearance, language, and conduct.
11. **Privacy and security:** Maintain stringent protection of guest privacy, confidential information, and company resources.
12. **Cleanliness and safety:** Adhere strictly to uncompromising cleanliness and safety standards, ensuring a safe and welcoming environment.

Leadership takeaway: Empowering teams

Ritz-Carlton's emphasis on empowerment instills confidence and fosters innovation among its employees. By enabling staff to make impactful decisions independently, the organization ensures every interaction authentically reflects its commitment to luxury and excellence.

By operationalizing the Three Steps of Service and the 12 Service Values, Ritz-Carlton establishes a benchmark within the hospitality industry. This structured yet personalized approach demonstrates how deliberate empowerment, meticulous attention to detail, and genuine empathy transform everyday interactions into extraordinary experiences (Ritz-Carlton Leadership Center, 2024).

> **CAREER SPOTLIGHT**
> Tony Herasme, director of rooms, Ritz-Carlton South Beach
>
> Tony Herasme's hospitality journey exemplifies perseverance, resilience, and leadership excellence. As a college student studying hospitality management, Herasme began his career as a rooms operations intern at the Hilton/Polaris in Columbus, Ohio. Shortly after his Hilton internship, Herasme also interned at the Oakbrook Hills Marriott Resort in Oak Brook, Illinois. From those early experiences, he embraced every opportunity to learn, advance, and grow professionally, demonstrating exceptional dedication along the way.
>
> Herasme's career advanced steadily through key operational roles at iconic Marriott properties, including the New York Marriott Marquis, Orlando World Center Marriott, and Marriott Stanton South Beach. Each role allowed him to develop deeper expertise in guest service, operational efficiency, and team leadership.
>
> Currently, he serves as the director of rooms at the Ritz-Carlton, South Beach, leading the division with a passion for excellence and guest satisfaction. His journey from intern to executive leader embodies the impact of hard work, determination, and resilience, inspiring others who follow in his footsteps.
>
> Herasme's personal advice for future hospitality leaders is that *every role matters*. "Treat each position as an essential building block toward your future. Leadership grows from daily dedication, attention to detail, and the relationships you build along your journey."

Hilton: The HEART model

Hilton's HEART model is a highly effective framework for service recovery, guiding employees through challenging situations with empathy and accountability (Hilton/SweetRush, n.d.):

Hear: Actively listen to the guest's concerns without interruption.

Empathize: Acknowledge and validate the guest's emotions, demonstrating understanding and care.

Apologize: Offer a sincere and thoughtful apology for the issue at hand.

React: Take immediate action to resolve the concern effectively.

Thank: Show gratitude to the guest for their patience and for bringing the issue to your attention.

The HEART model in action

A guest at a Hilton hotel misses a scheduled airport shuttle due to a staff error. Applying the HEART model, the front-desk colleague listens carefully to the guest's frustration (Hear), acknowledges their inconvenience by saying, "I can imagine how stressful this must be for you" (Empathize), offers a heartfelt apology (Apologize), arranges immediate transportation with a private taxi (React), and follows up with a handwritten note thanking the guest for their understanding and a voucher for a future stay (Thank).

Leaders who encourage employees to own and resolve service failures create a culture of trust and empowerment. By training staff to take responsibility and act decisively, Hilton fosters confidence among its teams and ensures that guests feel valued, even during service recovery scenarios.

Introducing CARES and REACT models

To support professionals in mastering both guest engagement and service recovery, this book introduces two original instructional frameworks: *CARES* (for proactive guest engagement) and *REACT* (for service recovery). These models reflect widely adopted industry principles and provide a clear, actionable foundation for delivering exceptional service, while also supporting practices that promote a sense of belonging and inclusive guest experiences.

The CARES model: Proactive guest engagement

Connect warmly: Begin with eye contact, a sincere greeting, and welcoming body language that sets the tone for inclusion and belonging.

Acknowledge the guest: Use names when possible; demonstrate that their presence is seen, valued, and respected as part of the community.

Recognize needs: Listen attentively to understand guest preferences or concerns.

Engage meaningfully: Demonstrate empathy, offer support that respects diverse backgrounds, and foster interactions that affirm identity and promote belonging.

Show appreciation: Thank the guest for their time, feedback, or loyalty.

The REACT model: Structured service recovery

Respectfully listen: Give the guest your full attention without interruption, creating space for them to feel genuinely heard and valued.

Empathize sincerely: Try to understand the situation from the guest's perspective, validating their emotions and demonstrating genuine care for their experience.

Apologize meaningfully: Offer a specific, heartfelt apology, taking responsibility without excuses.

Correct the issue swiftly: Promptly and respectfully take clear actions to restore the guest's sense of comfort, dignity, and satisfaction.

Thank and follow through: Express sincere appreciation for the guest's patience and trust, and confirm the resolution to ensure the guest feels valued.

Guest engagement in action

Imagine a traveler participating in a guided cultural heritage tour who appears uncertain and hesitant, perhaps due to unfamiliar surroundings or language differences. The tour guide warmly greets the traveler with friendly eye contact and an inviting smile, immediately fostering a welcoming atmosphere (*Connect warmly*). The guide quickly learns and frequently uses the traveler's name, clearly signaling respect and appreciation for their presence (*Acknowledge the guest*). Throughout the tour, the guide attentively observes and listens to identify the traveler's particular interests or concerns, noticing their curiosity about local traditions and cuisine (*Recognize needs*). Noticing these preferences, the guide thoughtfully tailors the tour by providing clear explanations and relatable examples, ensuring the traveler feels included and connected to the cultural experience (*Engage meaningfully*). At the end of the excursion, the guide personally thanks the traveler for joining, emphasizing genuine appreciation for their participation and highlighting how their involvement enriched the tour experience for everyone (*Show appreciation*).

Choosing the right model

Hospitality professionals are encouraged to select service models based on the guest's position in their journey and the nature of each interaction:

- **Proactive engagement models** (such as CARES) are most effective during initial touchpoints, routine interactions, and opportunities where guest needs can be anticipated and exceeded. These models foster comfort, trust, and loyalty by creating thoughtful connections and a genuine sense of belonging.
- **Service recovery models** (such as REACT) are essential when guests experience a problem or disappointment. These frameworks provide structured guidance for

active listening, responding with empathy, and restoring trust through decisive, compassionate actions.

- **Comprehensive service cultures** integrate both proactive engagement and responsive recovery—starting with warm, intentional connections and seamlessly transitioning to resolution when challenges arise. This holistic approach ensures teams are empowered to interact with authenticity, empathy, and consistency throughout the guest journey, continuously reinforcing a sense of belonging and value.

By understanding the strengths and appropriate applications of each model, hospitality professionals can dynamically tailor their approach to ensure exceptional experiences—whether they're creating welcoming first impressions or thoughtfully addressing unexpected issues. Models such as Ritz-Carlton's Gold Standards, Hilton's HEART, and Disney's Five Keys (discussed shortly) provide prominent industry examples of operationalized service excellence. CARES and REACT build upon these principles, offering accessible, adaptable frameworks for students and emerging professionals to deliver thoughtful guest engagement and responsive care in any hospitality environment.

Integrated example of models in action

Imagine a guest arrives for check-in visibly frustrated. A front-desk associate begins by applying the CARES model: greeting the guest warmly, offering eye contact and a genuine smile to establish a welcoming and inclusive atmosphere (*Connect warmly*). The associate uses the guest's name while confirming reservation details, clearly conveying respect and appreciation (*Acknowledge the guest*). They then actively listen and inquire if everything leading up to the stay has met the guest's expectations, creating space to uncover underlying concerns (*Recognize needs*). The guest reveals they were transferred multiple times during a pre-arrival call, felt dismissed, and began their trip feeling unheard. The associate expresses genuine empathy, validating the guest's frustration and reassuring them that their experience matters (*Engage meaningfully*). They thank the guest for openly sharing their concerns, reinforcing a sincere appreciation for the opportunity to improve their experience (*Show appreciation*).

Recognizing the need for additional resolution, the associate seamlessly transitions to the REACT model. They Respectfully listen, maintaining calm, reassuring body language as the guest elaborates further. They then Empathize sincerely: "I'm genuinely sorry you felt dismissed—that's not the welcoming experience we strive for, and your frustration is completely understandable." They follow this with a Meaningful apology and Correct the issue swiftly by offering an upgraded room and arranging a personalized welcome amenity. Finally, to Thank and follow through, the manager personally sends a handwritten note to the guest's room, inviting further feedback and reaffirming the team's commitment to the guest's comfort and satisfaction throughout their stay.

This intentional combination of CARES and REACT transforms a challenging start into a meaningful opportunity to strengthen guest relationships, demonstrating the team's dedication to empathetic, inclusive service excellence.

Disney: The five keys to guest experience

Disney's legendary reputation for exceptional guest experiences is built upon its Five Keys—Safety, Courtesy, Show, Efficiency, and Inclusion. These guiding principles underpin every interaction, blending practical operations with immersive storytelling to deliver consistent, memorable experiences.

The Five Keys in action

Consider guests waiting for a popular attraction or parade. Disney's Cast Members (employees) skillfully manage crowd flow to prioritize guest Safety, maintaining order while never sacrificing Courtesy and warmth. Simultaneously, Cast Members elevate the Show aspect by spontaneously arranging interactive character meet-and-greets or engaging activities, transforming wait times into delightful experiences. This approach masterfully balances Efficiency and Inclusion with Disney's renowned magical atmosphere.

Leadership insight: Embedding brand values through storytelling

Disney's emphasis on "Show" highlights the power of embedding cohesive storytelling into service interactions. Leaders across the hospitality and tourism sectors can leverage this model, ensuring teams consistently reflect brand values through their actions. By integrating narrative-driven service, organizations foster authenticity, strengthen guest connections, and create compelling experiences that guests will remember and share with enthusiasm (Kober, n.d.).

Adapting service models across industries

Although initially designed with specific hospitality contexts in mind, these service models offer versatile principles that extend well beyond traditional boundaries. Organizations in sectors such as retail, healthcare, and education have successfully adapted these hospitality frameworks to enhance their customer or client interactions. For example:

- **Hilton's HEART model** has inspired empathy-driven care frameworks in healthcare, emphasizing the critical role of emotional support in patient experiences.

- **Disney's Five Keys,** centered around immersive storytelling and operational consistency, have influenced the creation of engaging educational settings, transforming classrooms into environments that encourage active participation and memorable learning experiences.
- **Frameworks grounded in personalization and structured responsiveness,** like CARES and REACT, have also been adapted to foster inclusive communication and swift resolution.

Choosing the right model

Selecting an appropriate service model goes beyond simply enhancing guest experiences—it involves strategically aligning these models with organizational goals, core values, and operational realities:

- For luxury and highly personalized interactions, Ritz-Carlton's Gold Standards set a global benchmark.
- To compassionately address service failures and facilitate guest recovery, Hilton's HEART model is particularly effective.
- For building rapport and fostering inclusivity, proactive engagement frameworks like CARES offer structured guidance.
- When aiming for immersive and cohesive customer interactions, Disney's Five Keys provide a robust, narrative-driven framework.

In practice, hospitality leaders can thoughtfully combine elements from multiple models or tailor these frameworks to fit their organization's unique cultural and operational needs, ensuring consistent and exceptional service across varied contexts and situations (see Table 2.1).

Table 2.1 Service models and potential uses

Model	Focus	Key strengths	Ideal application
Ritz-Carlton Gold Standards	Anticipatory personalized luxury	Empowerment, attention to detail	Luxury hospitality
Hilton's HEART	Service recovery	Empathy, structured accountability	Handling guest complaints/issues
CARES engagement framework	Warm engagement	Personalization, inclusivity	Day-to-day guest interactions
REACT recovery framework	Structured recovery	Clear communication, swift action	Resolving service breakdowns
Disney's Five Keys	Immersive experiences	Storytelling, guest engagement	Entertainment and themed venues

REAL-WORLD EXAMPLE:
INDUSTRY SPOTLIGHT Cross-industry application: Cleveland Clinic

These hospitality-inspired frameworks transcend their original contexts, influencing fields such as healthcare to improve client experiences. For instance, the Cleveland Clinic, an internationally acclaimed nonprofit academic medical center recognized for outstanding patient care, research, and education, adopted an empathy-based H.E.A.R.T. model (similar in approach and structure to Hilton's HEART service recovery model) to significantly enhance patient engagement and satisfaction (Cleveland Clinic, n.d.). By incorporating elements from hospitality service models, the Clinic demonstrates how empathy and structured responsiveness can dramatically improve patient outcomes and satisfaction.

Integrating technology with human connection

By adopting and creatively adapting these proven service frameworks, hospitality leaders strike an essential balance between operational consistency and the human touch that defines affective and memorable experiences. While technology provides powerful tools for efficiency, convenience, and personalization, it is ultimately the depth of emotional connection—rooted in empathy and genuine human interaction—that distinguishes good hospitality from exceptional experiences. In this section, we explore how technological innovation complements rather than replaces the critical human element at the heart of outstanding hospitality.

INTERACTIVE EXERCISE
Putting principles into practice

This exercise is designed to help students explore, understand, and apply industry-leading service models to real-world scenarios. Through reflection, role-playing, brainstorming, and actionable planning, students will discover how structured frameworks such as Ritz-Carlton's Gold Standards, Hilton's HEART model, Disney's Five Keys, and the original models CARES and REACT can enhance guest experiences, empower teams, and foster meaningful connections.

1. Review service models

Explore the key principles of each model:

- **Ritz-Carlton**: Personalization, anticipation, and empowerment.
- **Hilton**: Empathy-driven service recovery (HEART).

- **Disney**: Safety, courtesy, show, efficiency, and inclusion.
- **CARES**: Connect warmly, Acknowledge the guest, Recognize needs, Engage meaningfully, Show appreciation.
- **REACT**: Respectfully listen, Empathize sincerely, Apologize meaningfully, Correct swiftly, Thank and follow through.

2. Reflect on experiences

Think of a time you experienced or delivered a hospitality service:

- What made it successful or challenging?
- How could a service model improve the interaction?
- Which model most aligns with your personal approach to service?

3. Practice scenarios

Choose and act out a real-world situation using a service model:

Ritz-Carlton

Scenario: A guest arrives to celebrate their anniversary, but the room is not decorated as requested during booking.

Use Ritz Carlton's Gold Standards: Greet warmly, anticipate needs, and, later, give a personalized farewell.

Hilton

Scenario: A guest misses an airport shuttle due to a scheduling error on the hotel's part.

Use HEART to address the guest's concern empathetically.

CARES and REACT

Scenario: A guest from another country is struggling with the language barrier and is unsure how to navigate the hotel's amenities.

Use CARES to establish trust and clarity, then transition into REACT to resolve concerns with care and accountability.

Disney

Scenario: A child loses their favorite stuffed animal during a busy parade at a theme park.
Balance operational needs with magical moments.

4. Brainstorm solutions

In groups, discuss challenges from the scenarios and propose solutions guided by the models:

- How can personalization, empowerment, or empathy address guest needs?
- In REACT, how do empathy and apology play distinct but complementary roles?
- What actions ensure consistency while maintaining a human touch?

5. Action plan

Develop a personal plan to apply these principles in your work:

- Which model(s) fit your goals?
- What steps will you take to integrate them into daily interactions?

While service models offer structured approaches to elevating guest experiences, technology provides innovative tools to enhance efficiency and personalization. However, it is critical to ensure that these advances complement the human touch rather than detract from it, preserving the emotional connections at the heart of hospitality.

Technology as a tool for human interaction

Technology in hospitality and tourism should always enhance—never replace—the human connections that define meaningful guest and traveler experiences. In hospitality, technology has become an indispensable tool for enhancing guest experiences and streamlining operations. Yet, at its core, hospitality remains a profoundly human endeavor. Technology complements the emotional intelligence, empathy, and personal connection that define exceptional service. While digital tools are valuable, travelers still highly value human interaction in their experiences (Deloitte, 2024).

High-tech meets high-touch: The role of technology in hospitality

As guests' expectations evolve, hospitality organizations increasingly turn to technology to deliver convenience and personalization. From mobile check-ins to AI-powered chatbots, these innovations offer speed and efficiency, addressing guests' needs in real time. Examples of high-tech solutions are:

- **AI-powered concierge services**: Hotel chains including Hilton and Marriott use AI in virtual concierges for routine queries, enabling staff to focus on more complex interactions.
- **Internet of Things (IoT)**: Smart room technologies, such as voice-activated lighting and temperature control, allow guests personalized comfort through intuitive mobile apps.

Balancing efficiency with connection

These innovations enhance convenience and streamline operations, but their true value lies in how they work alongside the human touch that defines memorable hospitality. Imagine a scenario where a guest requires emotional support following a travel delay. A chatbot is unlikely to suffice in alleviating their frustration or stress, underscoring the importance of retaining human engagement in certain contexts.

Hospitality professionals must strategically integrate technology to complement—not replace—human interaction. By doing so, they can meet operational needs while preserving the personal touch guests value most.

Humanizing technology: Strategies for retaining personal connection

Hospitality professionals must strategically integrate technology to preserve genuine connection. According to PwC (2023), travelers increasingly prioritize personalized experiences. Hospitality providers effectively meet this expectation through advanced customer relationship management (CRM) systems, enabling tailored experiences based on guest data and preferences. Key strategies include:

- **Pair technology with human support**: Chatbots can answer FAQs, but complex queries should be managed by staff trained in personalized guest interactions.
- **Use data to personalize interactions**: Brands such as Ritz-Carlton leverage guest data to anticipate preferences, ensuring returning guests find tailored experiences awaiting them upon arrival.
- **Ensure accessibility**: Marriott has developed apps compatible with screen readers for visually impaired guests, demonstrating technology's role in promoting inclusivity.

Real-world application

A prominent luxury hotel brand recently introduced smart rooms equipped with IoT technology. Guests could adjust lighting, curtains, and entertainment systems through a user-friendly mobile app or voice-activated commands. To further enhance the experience, AI-powered digital assistants provided tailored recommendations, such as local attractions or spa services, based on guest preferences.

Challenges and solutions

While guests appreciated the convenience, some expressed frustration with technology glitches or a perceived lack of warmth. To address this, the hotel complemented the system with a 24/7 support line staffed by knowledgeable team members trained to troubleshoot issues and provide a personal touch.

Outcome

By blending cutting-edge technology with accessible human support, the hotel successfully enhanced the guest experience without sacrificing connection. This approach also reinforced brand loyalty, as guests felt their concerns were acknowledged and addressed.

Emerging technologies and their impact on service excellence

Several emerging technologies have the potential to reshape how the hospitality industry interacts with guests:

- **Augmented reality (AR) and virtual reality (VR)**: Guests can virtually explore hotels and destinations, creating immersive pre-arrival experiences and fostering trust. Trainees can learn, practice, and gain confidence in service situations.
- **Facial recognition**: While facial recognition streamlines check-ins, it raises privacy considerations that must be addressed to maintain guest trust. Hospitality organizations must transparently communicate data use policies and maintain stringent data protection standards. Clear communication, robust security measures, and explicit guest consent are critical to addressing privacy concerns associated with this technology.
- **Robotics**: Robots assist increasingly with room service deliveries and back-of-house operations such as inventory management. According to Markets and Markets (2024), the hospitality robotics market is projected to reach $7.3 billion by 2028, highlighting the rapidly increasing role of robotic assistance in enhancing service efficiency and consistency. Robots excel in repetitive tasks, but they lack the emotional intelligence required for nuanced guest interactions, emphasizing the need to maintain a careful balance between technological innovation and a personal human touch.

> **INTERACTIVE EXERCISE**
> Balancing technology and human connection
>
> The discussion questions in this exercise will enhance your critical thinking and problem-solving skills, preparing you to handle real-world challenges involving technology and human interaction.
>
> Imagine you're integrating a new AI chatbot into hotel operations. While it efficiently handles routine queries, guests occasionally express dissatisfaction when seeking personalized assistance.
>
> 1. How would you coach your staff to manage guest frustrations stemming from chatbot interactions, rebuild trust, and enhance future experiences?
> 2. What steps could ensure the chatbot conveys your brand's warmth and welcoming tone?
> 3. How would you evaluate whether technology enhances or detracts from your guests' overall experiences?

Technology is reshaping the hospitality industry, offering tools to improve efficiency, personalization, and accessibility. However, its greatest potential lies in complementing—not replacing—the human connection that defines the guest experience. By strategically integrating innovations like AI, IoT, and AR/VR with empathetic, culturally responsive interactions, hospitality professionals can create seamless, memorable moments for their guests.

As the next generation of leaders, it is essential to view technology as an enabler rather than a substitute for the emotional intelligence and personal touch that guests cherish.

Conclusion: The core of hospitality—human interaction, connectivity, and service

The hospitality industry thrives on human connection, empathy, and genuine engagement, making guests and team members feel valued and cared for. Renowned restaurateur Danny Meyer (2008) emphasizes this core principle: "Hospitality is present when something happens *for* you. It is absent when something happens *to* you."

Empathy and adaptability remain central, with service models like Ritz-Carlton's Gold Standards and Hilton's HEART model illustrating how care and thoughtful action elevate guest experiences. Empathy is more than a skill—it's a mindset, strengthening guest relationships and fostering supportive workplace cultures.

Hospitality and tourism are more than industries—they represent missions driven by authentic connection. Each interaction holds the potential to profoundly impact guests, travelers, and staff. By operationalizing empathy, leveraging effective service models, and using technology to complement human interactions, hospitality professionals consistently deliver excellence.

Key takeaways

- Human connection lies at the heart of hospitality and tourism, forming the foundation of guest and traveler loyalty, satisfaction, and competitive advantage.
- Empathy and emotional intelligence are indispensable tools, empowering hospitality and tourism professionals to create personalized, meaningful experiences that directly enhance guest and traveler loyalty and organizational success.
- Established service models—such as Ritz-Carlton's Gold Standards, Hilton's HEART model, Disney's Five Keys—and the original CARES and REACT frameworks offer actionable frameworks for service excellence, applicable across hospitality and related sectors.
- Cultural awareness drives inclusive environments, enhances internal team cohesion, and ensures service delivery effectively meets the diverse and unique needs of global guests.
- Technology, such as advanced CRM systems and IoT solutions, enhances human connections by complementing—rather than replacing—the personalized, emotional interactions valued by guests and travelers.
- Practical examples and interactive exercises in cultural responsiveness and inclusiveness equip hospitality professionals with the tools to foster environments in which all individuals can thrive.

Looking ahead

This chapter explored the foundational role of empathy and service models in hospitality. In the next chapter, on cultural diversity and intersectionality, we will expand on these principles by examining how identity, belonging, and inclusivity shape the experiences of guests and employees. Together, these insights will provide a deeper understanding of how hospitality professionals can foster environments that celebrate diversity and create meaningful connections across cultures.

References

Bain & Company (n.d.) Retaining customers is the real challenge. Available at: bain.com/insights/retaining-customers-is-the-real-challenge (archived at https://perma.cc/AH2L-N8KJ)

Baumeister, R.F. & Leary, M.R. (1995) The need to belong: Desire for interpersonal attachments as a fundamental human motivation, *Psychological Bulletin*, 117 (3), 497–529. researchgate.net/publication/15420847_The_Need_to_Belong_Desire_for_Interpersonal_Attachments_as_a_Fundamental_Human_Motivation (archived at https://perma.cc/8E6N-N2NE)

Chick-fil-A Baytown (n.d.) *Emotional Intelligence*, https://www.cfaleadership.org/courses/emotional-intelligence-?utm; Leadership Development Program, chick-fil-a.ca/en/leadership-development-program (archived at https://perma.cc/E3UR-RLEKK)

Cleveland Clinic (n.d.) *Communicate with H.E.A.R.T.* my.clevelandclinic.org/departments/patient-experience/depts/experience-partners/licensed-programs/communicate-with-heart (archived at https://perma.cc/7ALD-RFUX)

Deloitte (2024) *2025 Travel Industry Outlook*. deloitte.com/us/en/Industries/consumer/articles/travel-hospitality-industry-outlook.html (archived at https://perma.cc/5MJL-F4BJ)

Earley, P.C. & Mosakowski, E. (2004) Cultural intelligence, *Harvard Business Review*, 82 (10), 139–146. hbr.org/2004/10/cultural-intelligence (archived at https://perma.cc/AMJ3-UPRU)

Emirates (2023) *Celebrating International Cabin Crew Day the Emirates way*, emirates.com/media-centre/celebrating-international-cabin-crew-day-the-emirates-way (archived at https://perma.cc/XG89-2RZ8); *Learning and Talent Development*: Course offering, learning.emirates.com/knowledge_centre_courses/courses/emerge/standalone_files/ltp/res/Learning-and-Talent-2022-Offering.pdf (archived at https://perma.cc/L4GJ-LVCQ)

Goleman, D. (2005) *Emotional Intelligence: Why It Can Matter More Than IQ*. New York: Bantam Books.

Grandey, A.A. (2000) Emotional regulation in the workplace: A new way to conceptualize emotional labor, *Journal of Occupational Health Psychology*, 5 (1), 95–110. doi.org/10.1037/1076-8998.5.1.95 (archived at https://perma.cc/MA2P-SM47)

Hilton/SweetRush (n.d.) Hilton and SweetRush have teamed up to support leaders and team members in living the Make it Right Promise. xrhilton.com (archived at https://perma.cc/9JW3-YFJY)

Hochschild, A.R. (1983) *The Managed Heart: Commercialization of Human Feeling*. Berkeley: University of California Press.

Kandampully, J., Keating, B.W., Kim, B.(P.), Mattila, A.S., & Solnet, D. (2014) Service research in the hospitality literature: Insights from a systematic review, *Cornell Hospitality Quarterly*, 55 (3), 287–299. doi.org/10.1177/1938965514536778 (archived at https://perma.cc/3NF4-PJK2)

Karatepe, O.M. (2013) High-performance work practices and hotel employee performance: The mediation of work engagement, *International Journal of Hospitality Management*, 32, 132–140. doi.org/10.1016/j.ijhm.2012.05.003 (archived at https://perma.cc/F8WR-57HX)

Kober, J.J. (n.d.) Disney's Four Keys to a great guest experience, Disney Insights. disneyinsights.com/disneys-four-keys-to-a-great-guest-experience (archived at https://perma.cc/DYX9-UEER)

MarketsandMarkets (2024) Hospitality robots market by type: Global forecast to 2028. marketsandmarkets.com/Market-Reports/hospitality-robots-market-76205823.html (archived at https://perma.cc/Z7K7-QD2F)

Matusitz, J. (2011) Disney's successful adaptation in Hong Kong: A glocalization perspective, *Asia Pacific Journal of Management*, 28 (4), 667–681. doi.org/10.1007/s10490-009-9179-7 (archived at https://perma.cc/DD3T-UQBW)

Meyer, D. (2008) *Setting the Table: The Transforming Power of Hospitality in Business*. New York: HarperCollins.

PwC (2023) *June 2023 Global Consumer Insights Pulse Survey*. pwc.com/gx/en/industries/consumer-markets/consumer-insights-survey.html (archived at https://perma.cc/FK8S-9ECD)

Reichheld, F.F. & Markey, R.G. (2011) *The Ultimate Question 2.0: How Net Promoter Companies Thrive in a Customer-Driven World*. Boston: Harvard Business Review Press.

Ritz-Carlton Leadership Center (2024) Foundations of our brand: Gold Standards. ritzcarltonleadershipcenter.com/about-us/about-us-foundations-of-our-brand (archived at https://perma.cc/T8U3-FX5M)

Cultural diversity and intersectionality in hospitality and tourism

3

LEARNING OBJECTIVES

- Define cultural competence, cultural diversity, cultural responsiveness, and intersectionality, and explain why these concepts matter in hospitality and tourism.
- Identify the five components of cultural competence—awareness, knowledge, sensitivity, skills, desire—and describe how they can be applied to enhance guest and employee experiences.
- Describe the social identity wheel and discuss how intersecting identities affect personal experiences, interactions, and workplace dynamics in hospitality.
- Explain how theoretical frameworks including social identity theory, Maslow's hierarchy of needs, and belongingness theory can help hospitality professionals create inclusive environments.
- Evaluate practical strategies and industry examples for improving inclusivity and addressing common challenges in hospitality workplaces.
- Reflect on your own attitudes and practices related to empathy, allyship, and cultural responsiveness, and identify ways you can apply these insights in your hospitality career.

Introduction

Think of a time when you entered a new workplace or classroom and felt immediately comfortable—fully able to be yourself, without worry about fitting in or being misunderstood. Maybe someone warmly introduced you to others, recognized your individual strengths, or took the time to learn something meaningful about your background or interests. In these moments, inclusion isn't just a buzzword; it's a powerful experience that shapes how connected, engaged, and motivated you feel.

Have you ever considered how deeply cultural responsiveness and genuine inclusivity influence the guest experience and workplace dynamics?

Research highlights that cultural competence and thoughtful recognition of intersectionality—the unique blend of identities each person holds—directly impact both employee engagement and guest satisfaction in hospitality environments (Baumeister and Leary, 1995; Crenshaw, 2016). Leading hospitality organizations, such as Disney, Hyatt, and Sodexo, understand this and have embedded intentional cultural responsiveness into their operations, creating environments where diverse identities are authentically valued, celebrated, and leveraged for success.

In this chapter, you'll gain insights into foundational concepts such as cultural competence, intersectionality, and cultural responsiveness. More importantly, you'll explore practical strategies that empower you, as future hospitality professionals, to build inclusive experiences for guests and meaningful workplaces for employees—because exceptional hospitality thrives where everyone feels they truly belong.

Defining cultural diversity and cultural competence in hospitality and tourism

One element that makes hospitality and tourism truly unique is its inherent cultural diversity across all aspects. With a geographic footprint spanning every continent, the industry naturally thrives on a rich variety of cultural influences. Cultural diversity is defined as the existence of a variety of cultural groups within a setting. In hospitality and tourism, both guests and employees bring diverse cultural backgrounds to the forefront, creating opportunities to unite people and deliver memorable experiences that celebrate diversity.

The foundation of diversity: Culture

At the core of cultural diversity is culture—the accumulation of beliefs, values, attitudes, habits, behaviors, customs, and traditions shared by a group of people. These shared elements serve as a lens through which groups view and respond to the world (Ford, 2022).

However, culture is not static—it is dynamic, encompassing *universal*, *cultural*, and *individual* aspects that shape how people navigate and interpret their lives:

- At the *universal* level, culture reflects the fundamental components shared by all humans, such as the needs for connection, communication, and safety. These universal traits remind us of our shared humanity, transcending specific cultural differences.
- At the *cultural* level, shared practices, values, and norms define specific groups. These traits shape traditions, languages, and social roles, influencing how communities interact, celebrate, and find meaning in their experiences.
- At the *individual* level, culture becomes deeply personal. Each person experiences and interprets cultural norms uniquely, shaped by their own preferences, identities, and lived experiences. This individuality means that, even within the same cultural group, beliefs and behaviors can vary significantly.

Moving beyond awareness: What is cultural competence?

Cultural competence builds on an understanding of cultural diversity and culture. It is the ability to recognize, respect, and effectively engage with cultural differences. In the context of hospitality and tourism, cultural competence means creating and maintaining environments where diverse perspectives are not only acknowledged but actively embraced to enrich guest and employee experiences.

Think about the last time you felt truly welcomed in a new environment. Was it because someone anticipated your needs, honored your traditions, or tried to understand your perspective? Cultural competence involves recreating that feeling for others. It's the ability to anticipate needs, respect cultural practices, and provide personalized service. This is more than a skill—it's a mindset.

As the hospitality industry evolves and embraces global diversity, cultural competence has become essential for thriving in today's competitive landscape. It is no longer a "nice-to-have" but a foundational aspect of both operational excellence and human connection.

From competence to action: Cultural responsiveness

While cultural diversity reflects the variety of cultural identities within a group, cultural responsiveness—a key component of cultural competence—focuses on taking thoughtful and meaningful action to embrace and support diverse individuals. Cultural responsiveness ensures that diversity is not just acknowledged but celebrated and supported through intentional actions.

We will discuss cultural responsiveness in greater detail later in this chapter; in the meantime, an example is a culturally diverse team that includes employees who have different first languages. A culturally competent workplace recognizes this diversity and provides inclusive resources, such as language-appropriate materials or opportunities for cultural exchange. A culturally responsive workplace takes this further by offering training materials in multiple languages and providing cultural sensitivity training to ensure every employee feels valued and supported.

> Cultural responsiveness goes beyond awareness. It's about actively integrating diverse perspectives and experiences into everyday practices, policies, and interactions—creating environments where everyone genuinely feels respected, understood, and valued.
>
> *—Dr. Donna Y. Ford, distinguished professor and expert in cultural competence and educational equity*

Why cultural competence matters

Cultural competence doesn't just benefit guests—it transforms workplaces by fostering belonging and purpose among employees. A workplace that embraces diversity is inclusive and powerful. Employees who feel valued and seen perform better, stay longer, and serve guests with genuine enthusiasm. By prioritizing cultural responsiveness, organizations improve satisfaction while building loyalty and trust, both internally and externally.

To fully understand cultural competence, it's important to revisit cultural diversity. Cultural diversity extends beyond race or ethnicity to include language, religion, gender, age, and socioeconomic background. It includes the unique experiences and perspectives that individuals bring into a shared space, creating a dynamic environment with plentiful opportunities for collaboration and growth.

Tourism—with its constant movement of people—and hotels—which welcome travelers from around the globe—are perfect examples of cultural diversity in action. Guests and employees alike bring unique traditions, preferences, and cultural backgrounds, making the hospitality environment diverse, enriching, and complex.

Theoretical frameworks that guide us

Cultural diversity and competence are essential for creating inclusive and meaningful hospitality experiences, but how can we better understand the underlying principles that drive belonging and connection? To deepen our understanding, we turn to theoretical frameworks that explain how human needs and social dynamics shape interactions in hospitality. These frameworks provide valuable insights into how employees and guests experience belonging, identity, and fulfillment, guiding hospitality professionals to foster environments that are both inclusive and impactful.

Understanding and implementing cultural competence in hospitality requires more than surface-level awareness—it calls for a deeper exploration of the principles that shape human interactions and experiences. Theoretical frameworks provide this foundation, offering insights into the universal need for belonging, the motivations that drive behavior, and the ways social identities influence relationships. By applying these frameworks, hospitality professionals can design inclusive environments that foster meaningful connections, empowering both guests and employees to thrive.

Belongingness theory

Authentic and inclusive hospitality includes making people feel they belong. Have you ever noticed how a small act of kindness, like remembering someone's name or cultural preferences, can turn a routine interaction into a meaningful connection? Belongingness theory, proposed by Baumeister and Leary (1995), is a psychological framework emphasizing the universal human need to form meaningful and lasting relationships. In the hospitality world, this need manifests in two critical areas: the employee experience and the guest experience.

For employees, a sense of belonging means a workplace where, for example, a manager warmly introduces new hires to their colleagues, highlights each person's unique strengths, and quickly involves them in team decisions, transforming initial uncertainty into lasting loyalty. Imagine a new hire joining a hotel's front desk team. Instead of feeling like an outsider, they are warmly welcomed, their unique skills recognized, and they quickly become part of a cohesive group. This sense of belonging fosters loyalty, boosts morale, and leads to better collaboration.

Guests experience belonging when their interactions feel meaningful and personal. Consider a family staying at a resort for the first time. As soon as they arrive, staff members greet them by name, anticipate their needs, and ensure their cultural preferences are acknowledged. Perhaps the resort even offers amenities or dining options that align with the family's values or dietary restrictions, showing that their individuality is not only recognized but embraced. When guests feel they belong, they are more likely to return and share their positive experiences with others.

Hospitality professionals have the unique ability to create these transformative moments of connection. By weaving belonging into every interaction, we fulfill a universal human need, leaving a lasting impact on both employees and guests.

Maslow's hierarchy of needs

A well-known framework that categorizes human needs, ranging from basic physiological requirements (like food and safety) to self-actualization (achieving one's potential), is Maslow's hierarchy of needs (Figure 3.1). Positioned between physiological and safety needs at the base and self-actualization at the top, belonging is the vital bridge that connects basic human requirements to higher aspirations.

Figure 3.1 Maslow's hierarchy of needs

SOURCE Adapted from Maslow, 1987; McLeod, 2025

In the workplace, Maslow's hierarchy reveals why meeting basic needs is critical for fostering growth and innovation. Take the example of an employee working in a high-pressure kitchen environment. If their basic needs—like fair pay, reasonable working hours, and physical safety—are unmet, it's impossible for them to focus on belonging, let alone achieving excellence. However, when these foundational needs are satisfied, and the employee feels part of a team that values their contributions, they are empowered to reach their full potential. This might be collaborating on creative menu ideas or taking the lead in training new staff, showing how a sense of belonging fuels growth.

Hospitality guests provide another lens for applying Maslow's hierarchy, which emphasizes experiences that exceed basic expectations. A traveler staying at a hotel expects cleanliness, safety, and comfort—these are the foundations of a positive stay. But what elevates the experience to one that creates lasting memories? Let's suppose they arrive after a delayed, exhausting flight. Recognizing their basic need for comfort, the hotel proactively provides complimentary refreshments, a personalized note, and clear instructions for relaxing onsite amenities, which turns an ordinary arrival into an extraordinary welcome. Later, when they mention an interest in local art, the front desk colleague provides a curated list of galleries nearby, along with a map and recommendations for lunch. On their return, a handwritten note welcomes them back and asks if they enjoyed their outing. These personalized touches of anticipating needs and demonstrating care build a sense of connection and belonging, transforming a routine hotel stay into an exceptional one.

By understanding Maslow's hierarchy, hospitality professionals can align their strategies with human needs, creating environments where both employees and guests can thrive. But meeting individual needs is just one part of the equation—understanding how people identify within groups adds another dimension to fostering truly inclusive spaces. Social identity theory (which we explore later) provides a framework for exploring how group affiliations shape behaviors and perceptions, offering further insights into creating hospitality environments where everyone feels they belong.

Reflect

- What thoughtful gestures have made you feel especially valued and welcomed, either as a guest or as an employee?
- How can you proactively anticipate and meet guests' needs to foster a sense of belonging?

Social identity theory

As we've explored with the social identity wheel, reflecting on our own identities is a vital step toward self-awareness. However, understanding ourselves is just one part of the equation. Social identity theory, developed by Henri Tajfel and John Turner (1979), explains how people categorize themselves and others into social groups to make sense of the world and establish a sense of belonging. These categorizations help individuals define their identities through group memberships, influencing their self-esteem and shaping their attitudes toward both in-group (groups they belong to) and out-group (groups they do not belong to) members (Hogg, 2018; Tajfel and Turner, 1979). Research highlights that this self-categorization process affects behaviors such as stereotyping, group conformity, and intergroup dynamics (Abrams and Hogg, 2004).

In hospitality, social identity theory reveals both opportunities and challenges for creating genuinely inclusive environments. Shared identities foster camaraderie, connection, and teamwork. However, they can also unintentionally exclude individuals who don't "fit the mold," reinforcing separation between in-groups (those similar to us) and out-groups (those perceived as different) (Hornsey, 2008).

Consider a hospitality team member who identifies as neurodiverse, such as someone with autism. Differences in communication styles, sensory sensitivities, or work approaches can unintentionally create social distance between this individual and colleagues, placing them in an out-group. Without intentional efforts toward inclusion, their unique strengths may be overlooked and they may feel isolated or misunderstood. However, when inclusivity is prioritized—through accommodations like quiet workspaces, adjusted communication styles, or team education—it transforms the team dynamic. By recognizing and valuing diverse ways of thinking, inclusivity bridges these gaps, enabling the entire team to thrive (Austin and Pisano, 2017).

An illustrative example occurred during a professional event involving a conversation with an attendee who has cerebral palsy. After engaging in meaningful dialogue about the attendee's interests and motivations for joining the event, the individual expressed sincere gratitude, noting that others frequently avoided interactions due to discomfort or uncertainty. Moments like these underscore the critical importance of intentional inclusivity and highlight how thoughtful interactions can counteract unintentional exclusion and isolation (Sue and Spanierman, 2020).

Consider another scenario of a new culinary team member who has recently joined a bustling kitchen from another country, with English as a second language. Although they possess exceptional cooking skills and creativity, the team often communicates quickly using industry jargon, colloquial expressions, or humor specific to native English speakers. While not deliberately exclusive, these interactions unintentionally create social distance, making the new team member feel isolated and undervalued. By intentionally fostering inclusion—such as clearly explaining culinary terms, encouraging participation in menu development and conversations, and thoughtfully translating or clarifying unfamiliar expressions—the kitchen team can bridge these divides, leveraging diversity to enhance overall collaboration and innovation (Cox and Blake, 1991).

Social identity theory can guide inclusive action in hospitality by:

- **Reducing in-group biases.** Be intentional about engaging diverse team members and guests. For example, encourage collaboration across departments or proactively inquire about guests' cultural preferences.
- **Fostering inclusion.** Adopt inclusive practices, such as multilingual services, accessible accommodations, and employee resource groups. Thoughtful interactions affirm that diverse identities are valued.
- **Creating exceptional experiences.** Inclusive environments elevate guest satisfaction and employee performance. Guests who feel personally welcomed and employees who feel valued experience deeper belonging and satisfaction (Kandampully et al., 2015).

Social identity theory reminds us that, although categorization is natural, it doesn't need to divide us. By recognizing biases and intentionally bridging gaps, hospitality professionals foster spaces where everyone—employees and guests—feels they belong. In hospitality, where connection is central, these intentional actions have a profound impact.

Imagine the transformative power of proactively engaging someone who typically feels overlooked. Whether recognizing a team member's overlooked strengths or ensuring guests feel authentically welcomed, seeing and celebrating diversity leaves lasting impressions. By embracing these principles, hospitality professionals create environments where everyone is genuinely valued.

Reflect

- Consider a time when you strongly identified with an "in-group." How did this sense of belonging influence your behavior, attitudes, or interactions with those who were not part of this group?
- Reflect on a hospitality experience—either as a guest or employee—where you observed or experienced in-group favoritism or out-group exclusion. How could use of social identity theory have improved the inclusivity and outcomes of that situation?
- As a future hospitality professional, what intentional steps will you take to recognize and reduce in-group biases, ensuring inclusive interactions for all?

A shift in focus

Historically, the hospitality industry has built its success on efficiency. Standardized protocols and uniformity have been essential for ensuring smooth operations and delivering consistent service across global brands. Efficiency remains a cornerstone of any successful business, playing a vital role in streamlining processes and achieving operational excellence. However, as the industry has evolved, so too have the expectations of guests and employees.

Today's guests increasingly seek experiences tailored to their preferences and needs. Customization has become a defining trend, with personalized touches and thoughtful gestures standing out as drivers of memorable stays. Similarly, employees increasingly value workplaces that offer more than just a paycheck. Many are seeking opportunities to grow, contribute meaningfully, and a sense of connection and purpose in their work.

This doesn't mean abandoning efficiency, but rather balancing it with empathy and personalization. Cultural competence bridges this gap by enabling businesses to meet operational goals while delivering human, customized service. It's about moving beyond a one-size-fits-all approach and embracing the richness of diversity that is inherently woven throughout the fabric of hospitality and tourism. It's about ensuring that guests and employees feel valued and connected.

As we consider these principles of cultural competence and responsiveness, remember: hospitality is fundamentally about human connection—making everyone feel they belong. By embracing these ideas, we foster a more inclusive, empathetic industry. With these theoretical frameworks in mind, let's explore how identity shapes the real-world experiences of hospitality employees and guests.

Understanding cultural identity in a globalized hospitality context

Developing critical consciousness—the ability to recognize systems of inequality (awareness), reflect on their impact (reflection), and take meaningful steps to challenge them (action)—is essential to creating transformation in the world. As we deepen our understanding of our own social identities and develop critical consciousness, we cultivate empathy and insight, empowering hospitality professionals to create, inclusive, accessible, and meaningful experiences that honor the dignity of every individual.

—*Dr. Ashley A. Hicks, clinical associate professor and expert in family science, cultural identity, and inclusive practices*

In today's interconnected world, the hospitality industry operates on a global stage. Hotels host guests from every corner of the world; restaurants serve dishes with flavors spanning continents; events celebrate traditions that transcend borders. Amid this diversity, awareness of cultural identities becomes a critical aspect of hospitality.

Cultural identity is deeply personal—it shapes how people view themselves and how they interact with the world. For hospitality professionals, understanding and respecting these identities are key to creating environments where every guest and employee feels welcome. In a globalized industry, cultural awareness isn't just about avoiding faux pas—it's about building trust and creating experiences that resonate on a human level.

While cultural identity provides a lens for understanding global diversity, the social identity wheel offers a framework to explore the individual facets of identity that shape our experiences and interactions in more personal and tangible ways.

The social identity wheel

The social identity wheel is a tool designed to help individuals explore and reflect on their personal identities. It breaks down identity into categories, including race, ethnicity, gender, age, ability, socioeconomic status, sexual orientation, and others. Each category provides an opportunity to consider how this aspect influences your interactions, decisions, and perceptions of the world around you.

The wheel also encourages reflection on how these identities interact with each other. The concept of intersections of identity, known as intersectionality, will be explored later in this chapter; for now, understanding the individual categories sets the stage for a deeper discussion of how these identities overlap and influence experiences.

Categories of the social identity wheel

To gain a foundational understanding of the social identity wheel (Figure 3.2), let's break down some of its key categories and explore their significance:

1 Race
- Race refers to physical characteristics, such as skin color or facial features, that societies use to categorize people.
- *Example*: Someone identifying as Black, White, or Asian based on physical attributes.

Figure 3.2   Social identity wheel

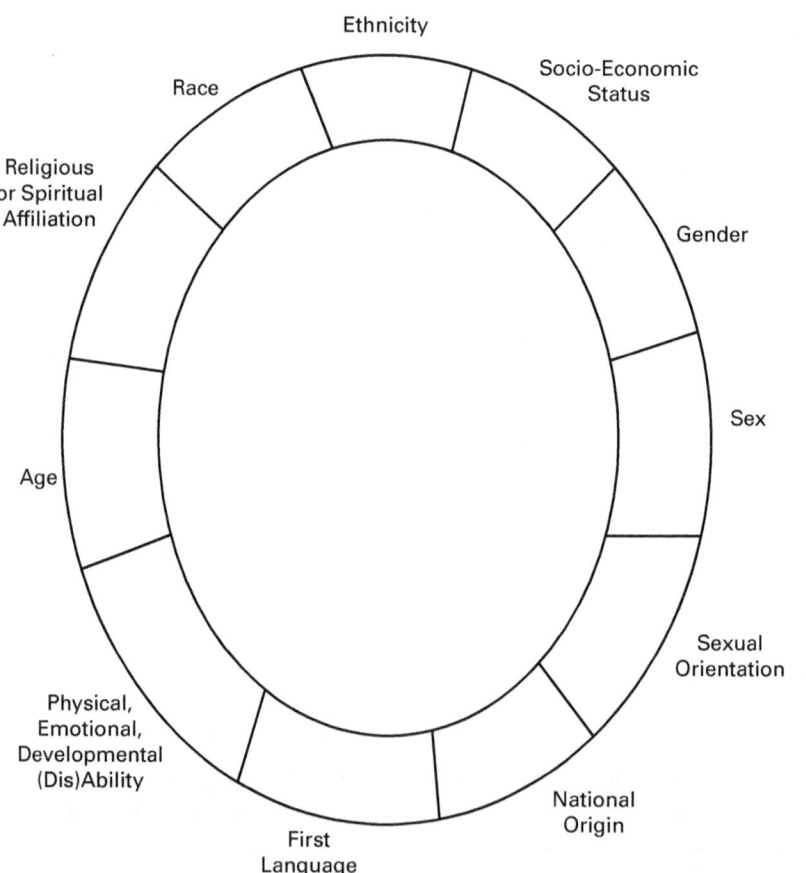

SOURCE Adapted from the University of Michigan, 2017

2 Ethnicity
- Ethnicity focuses on cultural aspects, such as nationality, language, and traditions.
- *Example*: A person identifying as Mexican or Ethiopian based on cultural heritage.

3 Gender
- Gender refers to societal roles and expectations associated with being male, female, or nonbinary, distinct from biological sex.
- *Example*: Someone identifying as a woman, a man, or gender nonbinary.

4 Age
- Age refers to the stage of life a person is in, from childhood to older adulthood.
- *Example*: A person in their 20s being described as a young adult.

5 (Dis)ability
- Ability encompasses physical, emotional, and developmental capacities, as well as disabilities.
- *Example*: A person who uses a wheelchair due to limited mobility.

6 Socioeconomic status (SES)
- SES considers factors such as income, education, and occupation.
- *Example*: A schoolteacher with a steady income may represent a middle SES, while someone working multiple part-time jobs to meet basic needs could represent a lower SES. Conversely, a successful business executive with significant assets might exemplify a higher SES.

7 Sexual orientation
- Sexual orientation refers to an individual's romantic or sexual attraction to others.
- *Example*: Someone identifying as heterosexual, gay, or bisexual.

8 First language
- First language refers to the primary language a person learned and used during early childhood.
- *Example*: A person who grew up speaking Spanish as their first language.

9 National origin
- National origin refers to a person's country of origin or citizenship.
- *Example*: A person born in Canada and holding Canadian citizenship.

How identities shape experiences

Our identities serve as lenses through which we interpret and navigate life. They influence how we interact with others, access opportunities, and experience the world. Some identities, such as physical characteristics, are apparent to others, while others, such as socioeconomic status or neurodiverse abilities, may remain invisible unless shared. The following examples highlight these dynamics:

- **First language:** Growing up speaking a language different from the dominant language in a region can lead to communication challenges. For instance, a guest at a hotel might feel more comfortable and included if the staff speaks their first language or provides translated materials.
- **Socioeconomic status:** Access to education, leisure, and career opportunities can vary greatly based on SES. For example, a student from a low-income background may face financial challenges that shape their approach to pursuing internships or overseas study opportunities, compared to a peer with greater resources.
- **Ability:** Physical, emotional, or developmental abilities can shape experiences in significant ways. For example, a traveler using a wheelchair might select destinations based on accessibility features such as ramps and elevators. Similarly, an employee with a disability might prioritize workplaces with inclusive policies and accommodations that enable them to thrive.

> **Reflect**
>
> - Which of your personal identities from the social identity wheel most significantly shapes your interactions with others?
> - Have you considered how your identities may influence your perspectives or biases toward guests or colleagues in hospitality settings?

The value of the social identity wheel

The social identity wheel is more than a tool for personal reflection—it's a bridge to understanding and empathy. By exploring your own identities, you gain a deeper awareness of how you interact with the world and how others experience it differently. This awareness is vital in hospitality and tourism, where the ability to build authentic interactions with diverse guests, colleagues, and team members is at the heart of the industry.

Using the social identity wheel helps uncover assumptions and biases that might otherwise go unnoticed. It also prompts consideration of aspects of identity that we might simply not be aware of or have thought about, broadening our understanding of both ourselves and others. It provides an opportunity to reflect on our own perspectives while considering the varied experiences of others. This process fosters self-awareness and creates space for growth as a culturally responsive professional. With an open mind and an appreciation for diversity, you'll be better equipped to create inclusive environments that honor the unique identities of all individuals.

For students entering the hospitality and tourism industry, understanding the complexities of identity offers a strong foundation for empathy and cultural competence. These skills are critical in a field where every interaction—with a guest, coworker, or community member—can leave a lasting impression. The social identity wheel helps future professionals recognize their own identities while cultivating an awareness of how identity shapes experiences for others.

By engaging in this reflective exercise, you not only enhance your ability to create welcoming environments but also contribute to shaping an industry that values and celebrates the richness of human identity. Through intentional learning and self-reflection, you will be better prepared to lead with understanding, serve with care, and foster connections that define excellence in hospitality and tourism.

The role of intersectionality in hospitality

> Intersectionality helps us recognize that identities are interconnected and multilayered. In hospitality, embracing intersectionality deepens our understanding of belonging, enabling organizations to create truly inclusive experiences for both employees and guests.
>
> —*Tony Tenicela, global / North America head of culture and belonging, Sodexo*

Identity shapes everyone's experiences, but the interplay of multiple identities—intersectionality—creates unique challenges and opportunities. Coined by Kimberlé Crenshaw (1989), intersectionality highlights how overlapping aspects of identity, such as race, gender, ability, and socioeconomic status, can amplify both marginalization and privilege.

For a deeper understanding of intersectionality and its relevance across various contexts, consider watching Crenshaw's TED Talk, "The Urgency of Intersectionality" (2016). It offers insightful examples and underscores the importance of recognizing and addressing intersecting identities in creating equitable and inclusive environments.

In hospitality, these dynamics influence daily interactions. Imagine a young woman working as a lead engineer in a high-end resort. Her intersecting identities of gender and profession—fields typically dominated by men—may lead some colleagues or guests to question her technical expertise or authority. While confidently applying her skills is an important part of breaking down these biases, the solution also requires awareness from others that they might hold these biases. By fostering open dialogue and creating opportunities for shared understanding, she and her team can work together to capitalize on their diversity and recognize her unique identity and strengths.

Now consider the guest scenario of a father traveling with his two young daughters who is also navigating a physical disability. He may face challenges accessing family-friendly spaces that accommodate both his needs as a parent and as a person with a disability, such as play areas that are wheelchair accessible. Addressing these intersecting considerations requires a hospitality professional who not only anticipates practical solutions but also fosters an environment where he feels fully welcome and supported in both roles.

For team dynamics, think about a young female manager leading a boutique hotel. Her intersecting identities of gender and age may lead some guests or team members to perceive her as inexperienced, even though she is fully qualified. She may feel added pressure to demonstrate her authority while fostering a collaborative environment. A supportive team that recognizes her leadership skills and values her contributions can help create a workplace culture where her abilities shine, inspiring confidence and trust.

Now consider a new employee from a low-income background starting their first job in private aviation, where they are working with high-net-worth clients. Their intersecting identities of economic status and inexperience might make them feel intimidated by the luxury environment or hesitant to ask for guidance in navigating the high expectations of this exclusive industry. A thoughtful leader who offers mentorship, provides clear and thorough training, and acknowledges their unique potential can help them build confidence, develop their skills, and foster a sense of belonging, ensuring they thrive in their new role.

THINK LIKE A MANAGER
Improving accessibility

A family checks into your hotel, and you notice one parent uses a wheelchair. They express concern about accessing family-friendly amenities like the pool and dining areas.

How could you proactively address their needs to ensure every family member feels genuinely welcomed and comfortable? Consider the roles that thoughtful preparation, empathy, and clear communication play in creating a seamlessly inclusive experience.

INTERACTIVE EXERCISE
Understanding intersectionality in hospitality

This exercise is designed to help students reflect on personal experiences, develop empathy through role-playing, and collaboratively create solutions for fostering inclusion in hospitality environments. Intersectionality isn't just about recognizing identity—it's about applying that understanding to create meaningful change. Hospitality leaders and employees can design inclusive policies, enhance team cohesion, and elevate guest experiences by considering the complexities of identity. By doing so, we not only improve service but also foster a hospitality industry that values every individual's uniqueness and contribution.

1. Reflect on your own experiences

- Start by reflecting on a time when you felt "different" or "out of place" in a professional or social setting.
    - What factors contributed to that feeling?
    - Did it relate to your identity or how others perceived you?
    - How did this experience shape your interactions or your sense of belonging?

This step sets the foundation for empathy, helping you connect with others who may face similar challenges.

2. Empathize through role play

- Building on your reflection, step into someone else's shoes by selecting one of the following scenarios:
    - You are a solo traveler practicing a religious tradition requiring prayer at specific times of the day, but the hotel lacks designated prayer spaces.
    - You are an employee who speaks English as a second language, working in a team where English is the dominant language.
    - You are a guest with a dietary restriction (such as, gluten-free) at a resort where the menu is not clearly labeled for allergens.
- From the perspective of the individual in the scenario, consider:
    - How do their intersecting identities influence their experience in this hospitality environment?
    - What unique challenges might they face?

By empathizing, you can deepen your understanding of how identity shapes experiences in hospitality.

3. Brainstorm inclusive solutions

- Next, work in a pair or small group to brainstorm practical, inclusive solutions for the challenges identified in the scenarios. Build on the empathy developed in the previous steps to consider actions that could improve these experiences, such as:
    - Creating designated, multipurpose spaces for prayer or reflection to accommodate religious needs.
    - Providing multilingual training materials or translation support for employees.
    - Offering flexible dining options and clearly labeled allergen menus for guests with dietary restrictions.
- Discuss how these solutions can address the specific challenges posed by intersecting identities while promoting inclusion and belonging.

This process is an opportunity to design meaningful changes that enhance team cohesion, improve guest experiences, and demonstrate the hospitality industry's commitment to valuing every individual's uniqueness and contribution.

4. Commit to taking action

- Finally, bring everything together by identifying one actionable step you can take as a hospitality professional to foster inclusion in your workplace. Consider:
    - How your own reflections and empathy-building influence your proposed action.
    - How the solutions discussed can be implemented effectively in real-world hospitality settings.
- Share your commitment with the class, explaining why it's important and how it can make a difference for both individuals and the industry as a whole.

By taking thoughtful action, you help create a hospitality environment that recognizes and values the complexity of identity, ensuring that everyone feels respected and included.

Digital accessibility in hospitality

In today's increasingly digital hospitality landscape, accessibility extends beyond physical spaces. Digital accessibility—ensuring websites, applications, and online content are usable and inclusive for individuals of all abilities—is essential for delivering comprehensive hospitality and tourism experiences. Inclusive digital platforms enable all guests, including those with visual, auditory, cognitive, or motor disabilities, to independently research, book, and customize their travel and hospitality experiences.

Industry standards and practices

The Web Content Accessibility Guidelines (WCAG), developed by the World Wide Web Consortium (W3C), provide a globally recognized framework for inclusive digital design. WCAG outlines principles and criteria ensuring websites and applications are perceivable, operable, understandable, and robust for diverse users (W3C, 2025).

Major hospitality and tourism organizations across various sectors incorporate WCAG to enhance guest experiences. Examples include Marriott and Hyatt in lodging, Delta Airlines in aviation, Royal Caribbean in cruising, and Disney in theme parks. Common practices include accessible reservation and booking systems, compatibility with screen-reader technology, multilingual and captioned multimedia, and optimized platforms for assistive technologies. These efforts aim to improve guest satisfaction and ensure compliance with accessibility regulations such as the Americans with Disabilities Act, the European Accessibility Act, and similar international standards.

Significance of digital accessibility in hospitality and tourism

Digital accessibility directly enhances guest experiences, aligning closely with the hospitality and tourism industry's core values of inclusion and personalized service. Accessible digital design expands market reach, mitigates legal and reputational risks, and positions organizations as leaders in inclusive hospitality. As international regulatory bodies increasingly emphasize digital accessibility, hospitality and tourism businesses are advised to proactively embed these standards into their digital strategies.

Reflect

- How accessible are the digital platforms (websites, apps, booking systems) you commonly use for travel and hospitality experiences? Have you noticed any strengths or gaps in their accessibility?
- As a future hospitality professional, what practical steps could you take to improve digital accessibility in your workplace or role?
- In what ways could initiatives to enhance digital accessibility positively influence guest experiences and support organizational goals?

Experiences of historically marginalized groups

Hospitality is uniquely positioned to serve as a beacon of inclusion, ensuring people from diverse backgrounds feel genuinely welcomed and valued. Challenges persist, but they can offer meaningful opportunities for industry leaders to demonstrate their commitment to equity and belonging. Recognizing and understanding the lived experiences of historically marginalized groups empowers hospitality professionals to transform potential barriers into genuine connections.

Meanwhile, a microaggression is a subtle or indirect remark or action that reinforces stereotypes or unintentionally excludes or harms someone based on their identity (Sue and Spanierman, 2020). Remarks that may seem harmless can communicate underlying assumptions or biases. Awareness of microaggressions highlights the importance of equipping team members with training and resources to interact respectfully, cultivating an environment in which diverse identities are consistently celebrated and valued.

THINK LIKE A MANAGER
Addressing microaggressions

Imagine a scenario where a server overhears a guest remarking to a colleague, "Your English is surprisingly good!", causing visible discomfort. As the manager, how would you proactively prepare your team to handle such a situation sensitively, ensuring a respectful and inclusive environment for both guests and staff?

Consider another scenario in which a guest with a visual impairment visits a luxury resort. While physical accommodations like ramps may be in place, the guest might still encounter communication or navigational challenges. This scenario

> presents hospitality staff with the opportunity to go beyond physical solutions by actively listening to the guest's needs, offering thoughtful assistance, and creating a comfortable, welcoming experience. Such intentional efforts can leave a lasting positive impression, reinforcing the industry's commitment to inclusivity.

These scenarios are not unique to hospitality—they occur across many industries. However, what sets hospitality apart is its intrinsic focus on people and its ability to make a profound difference through intentional action. Equipped with the right tools and mindset, hospitality professionals can champion inclusivity, setting new standards for welcoming and belonging.

To address these challenges and leverage opportunities effectively, current and emerging industry leaders can:

- **Lead with empathy**: Foster genuine engagement with both employees and guests, prioritizing understanding and mutual respect.
- **Train for inclusivity**: Provide comprehensive training that builds awareness, equips teams with practical skills to address diverse needs, and prevents harmful behaviors such as microaggressions.
- **Create pathways for growth**: Invest in professional development opportunities for employees from all backgrounds, ensuring everyone feels supported, valued, and empowered to succeed.

Hospitality excels when it authentically reflects the diversity and vibrancy of the communities it serves. By addressing the experiences of historically marginalized groups with empathy, intentionality, and purpose, the industry fosters environments that not only warmly welcome all but also inspire lasting loyalty.

Challenges to identity affirmation in diverse settings

The hospitality industry often celebrates diversity, but true inclusion requires more than acknowledgment—it demands affirmation. Affirming identity means creating spaces where individuals can express their authentic selves without fear of judgment, exclusion, or barriers. This is especially vital in an industry built on personal connection and care.

However, affirming identity in diverse settings is not without challenges. Cultural misunderstandings, unconscious biases, or rigid corporate policies can unintentionally suppress individual expression. Imagine a hotel's dress code that prohibits head coverings, thereby marginalizing employees or guests who wear them for religious reasons. Or consider a training program designed for "typical" guest scenarios that fails to address cultural nuances or accessibility needs. These oversights risk alienating the very people the industry seeks to serve.

Addressing these challenges requires intentionality and foresight. Organizations must prioritize policies that accommodate and celebrate diverse identities. This could mean creating uniforms that align with religious practices, offering multilingual training resources, or even establishing a floating holiday policy that allows employees to celebrate their cultural traditions. These actions send a clear message: every identity matters, and everyone belongs.

Building on this foundation, it's crucial to examine identity affirmation from two key perspectives—those of internal and external guests. By understanding the experiences of employees and customers alike, hospitality professionals can better address challenges and create a culture of inclusion that resonates on every level.

Perspectives on identity: Internal and external guests

Hospitality thrives on human connection, and understanding identity is essential for fostering meaningful relationships. Both employees and guests bring their unique identities into every interaction, shaping their experiences and the culture of the organizations they engage with. By exploring the distinct perspectives of internal guests (employees) and external guests (customers), we can better understand how inclusion and identity affirmation intersect to create positive environments for all. This dual perspective not only highlights the challenges faced; it also uncovers opportunities to build a more inclusive and thriving industry.

Internal guests: Employees

Employees are the heartbeat of hospitality, and their sense of belonging directly shapes the guest experience. When employees feel valued and affirmed, they bring their full selves to work, creating an environment of genuine care and enthusiasm.

However, identity can introduce complexities into workplace dynamics. Consider a young female manager in a male-dominated team. Her gender and age might intersect to create additional pressures, such as needing to prove her competence repeatedly. Or an employee navigating the challenges of a multilingual workplace and diverse cultural norms might struggle to feel fully integrated into team camaraderie.

These examples highlight the importance of creating workplaces where all identities are embraced. When leaders actively support their employees through mentorship, clear communication, and inclusive policies, they foster a sense of belonging that empowers staff to excel and enhances the overall workplace culture.

External guests: Customers

Visitors bring their identities into every interaction, whether it's checking into a hotel or attending a conference. For some, travel represents a joyful escape; for others, it's fraught with anxiety about how they'll be perceived or treated.

The key is to approach every guest interaction with cultural competence and a mindset of authentic empathy. Asking thoughtful questions, using inclusive language, and anticipating needs are simple yet powerful ways to make guests feel at ease. For instance, a restaurant that offers diverse dietary options signals to guests from different cultural backgrounds that their requirements are understood and respected.

Understanding the role of identity in hospitality is not just theoretical—it's practical. It enables professionals to shape environments that automatically welcome and celebrate diversity.

Frameworks for cultural responsiveness

To create inclusive and welcoming environments, hospitality professionals must move beyond just recognizing identity to actively cultivating the skills and mindset needed for cultural responsiveness. Building on earlier discussions of culture, cultural diversity, and cultural responsiveness, as well as tools like the social identity wheel and frameworks such as social identity theory, achieving meaningful change requires practical application. This is where cultural competence becomes essential. By integrating awareness, knowledge, sensitivity, skills, and a genuine desire for inclusivity, leaders and teams can transform insights into action, ensuring that every interaction reflects a commitment to celebrating diversity and fostering belonging.

Components of cultural competence in hospitality

Cultural competence is a cornerstone of effective hospitality. It equips professionals across the industry, from event managers to sales directors, to navigate and celebrate diversity while creating environments where guests and employees feel respected, valued, and included. Achieving cultural competence involves five interrelated components, each requiring practical application to create meaningful impact: awareness, knowledge, sensitivity, skills, and desire. These interconnected elements form the foundation for creating meaningful and inclusive experiences in hospitality.

Cultural awareness

Cultural awareness begins with self-awareness. Hospitality professionals must recognize how their own biases, assumptions, and cultural influences shape their decisions and interactions. For instance, an event manager planning a corporate conference might reflect on how their personal preferences could unintentionally overlook the diverse needs of attendees, such as incorporating multi-faith prayer rooms or scheduling meal breaks that accommodate fasting times.

Recognizing these influences fosters better decision-making and helps create environments where all individuals feel acknowledged and valued. While awareness lays the groundwork for understanding, it's knowledge that enables us to navigate cultural nuances effectively.

Reflect

- Can you recall a situation where your cultural assumptions or biases unintentionally influenced a decision or interaction?
- What steps can you take to become more mindful of your biases in future hospitality interactions?

Cultural knowledge

Knowledge about different cultures, traditions, and communication styles is essential in the globalized hospitality industry. For sales and marketing directors, this could mean tailoring promotional campaigns to resonate with specific audiences. A campaign targeting international tourists might highlight local experiences that connect with their cultural values, such as showcasing sustainable tourism practices for environmentally conscious travelers.

Cultural knowledge enables professionals to anticipate and meet unique needs, transforming interactions into personalized interactions and demonstrating respect for diverse perspectives. However, knowledge alone isn't enough—it must be paired with cultural sensitivity to ensure empathy and adaptability in real-world interactions.

Cultural sensitivity

Cultural sensitivity goes beyond knowing—it's about feeling. It requires empathy and an acute awareness of how words, actions, and decisions impact others. A director of food and beverage services, for example, might notice a team member hesitating to participate in wine tasting due to religious or cultural reasons. A culturally sensitive leader would respect this, ensuring the team member can still contribute without feeling excluded or diminished.

Sensitivity fosters trust, breaking down barriers that might otherwise prevent collaboration or connection, creating a sense of inclusion for everyone involved.

Cultural diversity and intersectionality

> **THINK LIKE A MANAGER**
> Cultural sensitivity in action
>
> You notice a team member declining a wine tasting event for cultural and religious reasons. As a manager, how do you accommodate this team member's needs while ensuring their continued engagement and inclusion in team-building activities?

REAL-WORLD EXAMPLE:
INDUSTRY SPOTLIGHT   Disney's "Inclusion Key"

Disney's commitment to inclusion is exemplified through its Inclusion Key, one of the company's five foundational service keys (Safety, Courtesy, Show, Efficiency, and Inclusion). This framework guides "Cast Members" in delivering personalized experiences that thoughtfully address diverse guest needs. Disney parks, for instance, offer sensory-friendly resources and quiet zones for neurodivergent guests, adaptive services such as the disability access service, comprehensive dietary accommodations, and accessibility tools, including audio descriptions, Braille materials, assistive listening devices, and sensory-friendly film screenings. These practices clearly demonstrate cultural sensitivity, accessibility, and responsiveness (Matusitz, 2011; Walt Disney Company, n.d.).

In early 2025, Disney strategically restructured aspects of its corporate diversity, equity, and inclusion (DEI) strategy, removing specific DEI performance metrics from executive pay evaluations and integrating diversity efforts into a broader "Talent Strategy" framework (Financial Times, 2025). This shift coincides with the evolving nature of DEI practices and stresses the importance for hospitality professionals to remain adaptable and responsive to changing industry approaches.

Corporate inclusion in action

Disney's corporate inclusion efforts extend beyond guest-facing practices, with initiatives such as barrier-free recruitment, voluntary employee-led resource groups supporting diverse populations (including Veterans, Asian American and Pacific Islanders, Historically Black Colleges and Universities alumni, and Latinx communities), and robust creative inclusion programs. Additionally, Disney invests in measurable outcomes, including increased supplier diversity spending and representation of women and other underrepresented groups in leadership positions. Collectively, these corporate practices highlight a systemic and enduring commitment to inclusion across all levels of the organization (Walt Disney Company, n.d.).

> **Reflect**
>
> - How does Disney's Inclusion Key illustrate cultural sensitivity in action, especially within the context of evolving corporate DEI strategies?
> - What lessons from Disney's inclusive service approach and organizational DEI initiatives could you apply in your future hospitality roles?

Cultural skills

Cultural skills translate awareness, knowledge, and sensitivity into actionable tools. Whether it's a concierge who learns key phrases in multiple languages to greet international guests or an event manager who adapts seating arrangements to reflect cultural norms, these skills demonstrate inclusivity in action.

For instance, a sales director planning a trade show might create materials in multiple languages and ensure interpreters are available. By doing so, they not only accommodate diverse participants but also strengthen relationships that transcend language barriers.

These actionable efforts create memorable experiences and drive success. All these components hinge on cultural desire—a genuine commitment to foster inclusion and continually learn from diverse perspectives.

Cultural desire

At the heart of cultural competence lies the genuine willingness to embrace diversity and continually learn. Cultural desire isn't about checking a box—it's about fostering an enduring commitment to inclusion. For example, a regional director overseeing multiple venues might launch an initiative to celebrate underrepresented voices in hospitality, inviting employees to share stories about their heritage or background as part of a larger cultural appreciation program.

Leaders who embody cultural desire inspire others to do the same, cultivating environments where inclusivity thrives. But understanding these components isn't enough—what truly matters is how they're applied in practice to create inclusive and thriving hospitality environments.

REAL-WORLD EXAMPLE:
INDUSTRY SPOTLIGHT   Hyatt's "World of Care"

Hyatt's World of Care initiative highlights its strategic commitment to DEI, deeply embedding these values across global operations. The initiative includes robust supplier diversity programs, employee-led diversity business resource groups, and intentional efforts to enhance representation and retention of employees from underrepresented communities. Hyatt's proactive outreach and strategic partnerships illustrate how actionable DEI steps can foster genuine inclusion, cultural responsiveness, and belonging while driving innovation, enhancing guest experiences, and strengthening overall business performance (Hyatt Hotels, n.d.).

Reflect

- How can you demonstrate a genuine desire to learn from others with diverse cultural backgrounds and identities?
- What specific steps can you take now, as a student, to foster openness and continuous learning within your future hospitality career?

Putting cultural competence into practice

Understanding the components of cultural competence is only the first step—it's the application that makes the difference. Hospitality professionals must translate these principles into everyday actions that foster belonging, inclusivity, and connection across all interactions.

Imagine a marketing team tasked with organizing a global hospitality summit. Their cultural competence shines as they anticipate diverse dietary preferences, offering vegan, kosher, halal, and allergen-free options. They design schedules mindful of global attendees' time zones and holidays, ensuring maximum participation. Promotional materials highlight inclusivity by showcasing diverse cultures and languages, making every attendee feel represented. These thoughtful actions elevate the event from functional to memorable.

Now imagine an event manager overseeing a multicultural wedding. Understanding the importance of cultural rituals, they meet with the couple to learn about traditions such as the tea ceremony or Mehendi. They collaborate to ensure these customs are seamlessly integrated into the event, coordinating with vendors to honor the cultural dress code and dietary restrictions. By prioritizing inclusivity, the manager delivers a successful event and creates a deeply meaningful celebration for the couple and their families.

Consider a hotel manager onboarding a diverse team of employees. By incorporating cultural competence into training, they ensure materials are available in multiple languages and include examples reflecting employees' cultural experiences. Regular check-ins address concerns related to cultural dynamics, helping team members feel supported and respected, fostering a stronger, more inclusive workplace culture.

REAL-WORLD EXAMPLE:
INDUSTRY SPOTLIGHT Sodexo's "Spirit of Inclusion"

Sodexo's Spirit of Inclusion program demonstrates the company's commitment to fostering an inclusive workplace culture. It features mandatory inclusive training focused on unconscious bias, respectful communication, and inclusive behaviors. Sodexo supports targeted mentoring circles such as SheLeads for women's leadership and employee-led networks such as SoTogether to promote gender inclusion. These efforts are supported through ongoing campaigns, regular gender pay-gap audits, and family-friendly workplace policies to integrate inclusion into daily operations (Sodexo, n.d.).

Reflect

- Identify a practical action you can take today to improve your awareness of unconscious bias.
- How will stronger inclusion awareness enhance your effectiveness as a future hospitality leader?

Why cultural competence matters

Cultural competence isn't about memorizing a checklist—it's about embodying an ethos of empathy, adaptability, and inclusivity. Cultural competence transcends checklists. It involves adopting a mindset of empathy, adaptability, and inclusivity in every interaction. Whether you're greeting guests at the front desk, leading a kitchen team, or managing a global brand, these principles empower you to deliver exceptional experiences. They are the foundation for building trust, inspiring loyalty, and driving innovation in an increasingly diverse world.

By integrating self-awareness, knowledge, sensitivity, skills, and desire into your professional journey, you don't just meet the standards of hospitality—you redefine them. As you move forward in your hospitality journey, consider how you can embody cultural competence in your daily interactions. What steps can you take to create spaces where every individual—guest or team member—feels valued and included? By committing to these principles, you become a catalyst for change, shaping a future where hospitality reflects the beauty of human diversity. As you reflect on the examples and strategies discussed, keep these key insights in mind to guide your own journey toward becoming a culturally competent hospitality professional.

Key takeaways

- **Cultural competence** involves awareness, knowledge, sensitivity, skills, and a genuine desire to create inclusive environments—essential for success in hospitality and tourism.
- **Intersectionality** recognizes that individuals hold multiple, overlapping identities, influencing how they experience hospitality settings as both guests and employees.
- Concepts such as **belongingness theory, Maslow's hierarchy of needs**, and **social identity theory** help hospitality professionals understand how to foster inclusive and welcoming environments.
- **Empathy and cultural responsiveness** are core skills in hospitality, shaping authentic, meaningful interactions with guests and colleagues.
- **Intentional reflection and allyship** strengthen your ability to support diverse individuals, positively influencing guest satisfaction and workplace dynamics.
- **Practical application of cultural competence** involves proactively addressing potential barriers, affirming diverse identities, and continuously learning from real-world scenarios and industry best practices.

Looking ahead

As we conclude our exploration of cultural diversity and intersectionality, remember that cultural competence is an ongoing journey, not a final destination. Hospitality professionals are uniquely positioned to lead with empathy, inclusivity, and a commitment to belonging, profoundly impacting both guest experiences and workplace dynamics.

In the next chapter, on service, sales, and people, we shift attention to the operational essentials that underpin hospitality excellence. We'll explore how managing guest experiences, leveraging personalization, and implementing proactive crisis management strategies enhance brand reputation and guest loyalty. Additionally, we'll examine the critical roles of operations management, strategic marketing and sales, effective human resource practices, and how employee engagement directly shapes guest satisfaction and organizational success. Understanding these interconnected core functions will equip sustainable, service-driven hospitality organizations poised for lasting success.

References

Abrams, D. & Hogg, M.A. (2004) Collective identity: Group membership and self-conception, in M.B. Brewer & M. Hewstone (eds.), *Self and Social Identity*. Malden, MA: Blackwell Publishing, pp. 147–181.

Austin, R.D. & Pisano, G.P. (2017) Neurodiversity as a competitive advantage, *Harvard Business Review*. hbr.org/2017/05/neurodiversity-as-a-competitive-advantage (archived at https://perma.cc/HHZ7-LXH8)

Baumeister, R.F. & Leary, M.R. (1995) The need to belong: Desire for interpersonal attachments as a fundamental human motivation, *Psychological Bulletin*, 117 (3), 497–529. doi.org/10.1037/0033-2909.117.3.497 (archived at https://perma.cc/4YV9-NLPZ)

Cox, T.H. & Blake, S. (1991) Managing cultural diversity: Implications for organizational competitiveness, *Academy of Management Executive*, 5 (3), 45–56. doi.org/10.5465/ame.1991.4274465 (archived at https://perma.cc/63PY-6J99)

Crenshaw, K. (1989) Demarginalizing the intersection of race and sex: A Black feminist critique of antidiscrimination doctrine, feminist theory and antiracist politics, *University of Chicago Legal Forum*, 1989 (1), 139–167. chicagounbound.uchicago.edu/uclf/vol1989/iss1/8 (archived at https://perma.cc/HN4N-FNSA)

Crenshaw, K. (2016) The urgency of intersectionality (TED Talk). ted.com/talks/kimberle_crenshaw_the_urgency_of_intersectionality?subtitle=en (archived at https://perma.cc/ENZ8-N4WX)

Financial Times (2025) Walt Disney cuts diversity category from executive pay scheme, February 11. ft.com/content/158edbd0-cada-4af2-b1ed-94fb7bb32ebe (archived at https://perma.cc/2WH7-T9EE)

Ford, D.Y. (2022) in class.

Hogg, M.A. (2018) Social identity theory, *Stanford Encyclopedia of Philosophy*. psycnet.apa.org/record/2018-19142-005 (archived at https://perma.cc/45T7-ZGSF)

Hornsey, M.J. (2008) Social identity theory and self-categorization theory: A historical review. *Social and Personality Psychology Compass*, 2 (1), 204–222. doi.org/10.1111/j.1751-9004.2007.00066.x (archived at https://perma.cc/YQ9Z-Z3QM)

Hyatt Hotels (n.d.) World of Care: Caring for People. hyatt.com/world-of-care/en-US/caring-for-people (archived at https://perma.cc/BLB8-5HZG)

Kandampully, J., Zhang, T., & Bilgihan, A. (2015) Customer loyalty: A review and future directions with a special focus on the hospitality industry, *International Journal of Contemporary Hospitality Management*, 27 (3), 379–414. doi.org/10.1108/IJCHM-03-2014-0151 (archived at https://perma.cc/4D7B-P23P)

Maslow, A.H. (1987) *Motivation and Personality* (3rd edn). New York: Harper & Row.

Matusitz, J. (2011) Disney's successful adaptation in Hong Kong: A glocalization perspective, *Asia Pacific Journal of Management*, 28 (4), 667–681. doi.org/10.1007/s10490-009-9179-7 (archived at https://perma.cc/GT86-D89X)

McLeod, S. (2025) *Maslow's Hierarchy of Needs*, Simply Psychology. simplypsychology.org/wp-content/uploads/simplypsychology.org-Maslows-Hierarchy-of-Needs.pdf (archived at https://perma.cc/K3QW-2JGV)

Sodexo (n.d.) *Belonging and inclusion*. sodexo.com/working-at-sodexo/belonging-and-inclusion (archived at https://perma.cc/FCB5-VQZT)

Sue, D.W. & Spanierman, L. (2020) *Microaggressions in Everyday Life: Race, Gender, and Sexual Orientation* (2nd edn). Hoboken, NJ: John Wiley & Sons.

Tajfel, H. & Turner, J.C. (1979) An integrative theory of intergroup conflict, in W.G. Austin & S. Worchel (eds.), *The Social Psychology of Intergroup Relations*. Monterey, CA: Brooks/Cole, pp. 33–47.

Walt Disney Company (n.d.) At Disney, we want everyone to belong and thrive, inclusion. twdc.com (archived at https://perma.cc/F38Y-3DER) Guests with disabilities overview, disneyworld.disney.go.com/guest-services/guests-with-disabilities (archived at https://perma.cc/UCB7-BRNM)

University of Michigan (2017) Social identity wheel. LSA Inclusive Teaching Initiative. sites.lsa.umich.edu/equitable-teaching/social-identity-wheel (archived at https://perma.cc/FWH7-CAMY)

W3C (World Wide Web Consortium) (2025) *Web Content Accessibility Guidelines*. w3.org/TR/WCAG21 (archived at https://perma.cc/PP3S-GDYA)

Core business functions: Service, sales, and people

4

> **LEARNING OBJECTIVES**
>
> - Describe the key front-facing business functions in hospitality and tourism, including guest experience management, operations, marketing, sales, and human resources.
> - Analyze how these functions, guided by theoretical frameworks such as the service-profit chain, lean management, and social exchange theory, work together to deliver cohesive, memorable guest experiences.
> - Evaluate strategies that drive service excellence, brand loyalty, and team performance.
> - Discuss the impact of digital tools and technologies on guest engagement and operational efficiency.
> - Apply insights from real-world industry examples and interactive exercises to hospitality and tourism management scenarios across lodging, food and beverage, entertainment, events, wellness, tourism, and managed services.

Introduction: The backbone of hospitality excellence

Recall a moment when hospitality made you feel special—perhaps it was the warm greeting at a luxury hotel, a personalized dining experience at a fine restaurant, the excitement of a theme park visit, or the effortless check-in for your cruise vacation. These moments don't happen by chance—they are the result of strategic, interconnected business functions working in perfect harmony (Pizam and Tasci, 2019). These experiences result from interconnected hospitality functions, including guest experience management, sales, marketing, operations, and human resources, that collectively foster lasting impressions and brand loyalty (Lovelock and Wirtz, 2020).

Hospitality and tourism segment overview

To ensure clarity as you explore this and subsequent chapters, the following quick reference guide summarizes the key industry segments introduced in this book:

- **Managed services**: Providers delivering contracted food and support services within institutional or organizational settings (universities, hospitals, corporations, airports), balancing the needs of direct clients and their guests.
- **Events**: Carefully planned gatherings such as weddings, festivals, conventions, corporate meetings, and cultural celebrations, emphasizing detailed planning, coordination, and guest experience.
- **Tourism**: Experiences involving exploration, cultural exchange, and travel to diverse attractions and destinations, enriching personal growth and cultural understanding.
- **Lodging**: Hotels, resorts, inns, and alternative accommodations providing personalized guest services, comfort, and memorable stays.
- **Food and beverage industry**: Restaurants, cafés, bars, catering services, food trucks, and institutional dining, creating culinary experiences that foster community connections and cultural interactions.
- **Entertainment and recreation**: Theme parks, casinos, cruise entertainment, water parks, museums, theaters, sports events, and recreational activities, providing engaging, exciting, and immersive guest experiences.
- **Wellness and health industry and healthcare intersection**: Spas, wellness retreats, senior living communities, fitness centers, and healthcare institutions that integrate hospitality principles to enhance physical, mental, and emotional well-being.

Understanding these segments will help you connect foundational hospitality concepts explored throughout the book (such as guest experience management, operations, marketing, sales, and human resources) to real-world applications across diverse hospitality and tourism contexts.

Theoretical framework: Service-profit chain

The service-profit chain (Heskett et al., 1994) provides a foundational framework for understanding how internal service quality impacts employee satisfaction, which in turn drives guest satisfaction and loyalty—ultimately leading to revenue growth and profitability. This theory emphasizes that organizations investing in employee training, empowerment, and engagement create a cycle of success: engaged employees deliver exceptional service, satisfied guests become repeat customers, and businesses achieve sustainable financial success (Rust et al., 1995).

In hospitality, this framework underscores why service excellence, guest experience management, and strong sales and marketing strategies are critical (Solnet et al., 2018). The service-profit chain serves as a guide for designing customer-focused operations that align team performance, brand loyalty, and financial success across hospitality sectors (Bowen and Ford, 2004).

Understanding guest experience management in hospitality and tourism

Guest experience management is more than just providing good service—it is the strategic design and execution of interactions that create emotional connections, build loyalty, and enhance brand reputation across hospitality and tourism sectors. Every guest touchpoint, from initial research to post-experience reflection, shapes overall perceptions and influences guests' likelihood of returning or recommending the service.

Professionals in hospitality and tourism utilize guest journey mapping to intentionally design and enhance these interactions. Every experience—booking a hotel, dining at a restaurant, attending a festival, exploring a wellness retreat, touring a new destination, or enjoying a scenic rail journey—is defined by critical touchpoints. By strategically managing these touchpoints, hospitality and tourism businesses create cohesive, memorable experiences that foster emotional connections and enduring brand loyalty.

Pre-experience

The guest journey begins with research, booking, and anticipation. Hotels personalize booking confirmations; restaurants provide interactive online menus; event venues optimize ticketing platforms; tourism organizations inspire anticipation by showcasing compelling travel content, interactive itineraries, and personalized recommendations. Brands like Starbucks enhance anticipation through mobile apps for personalized ordering and loyalty rewards. Similarly, the My Disney Experience app, with what was formerly known as the Genie+ skip-the-line service and is now offered through Lightening Lane Multi Pass and Lightening Lane Single Pass, exemplifies personalized itinerary creation for guests.

Arrival and first impressions

First impressions significantly impact guest satisfaction. Hotels prioritize welcoming check-in experiences, including mobile check-ins for convenience. Restaurants emphasize ambiance and attentive greetings; events streamline registrations. In tourism, destinations and attractions welcome visitors through clearly marked signage, convenient access points, engaging visitor centers, and welcoming local interactions. Resorts like Marriott ensure ease of arrival through digital keys and personalized greetings, while festivals such as Coachella optimize entry points with technology-driven efficiency and engaging welcome experiences.

Core experience and service delivery

Central to guest satisfaction in hospitality and tourism are personalized services and quality interactions. Hotels ensure room comfort, efficient housekeeping, and responsive concierge services. Restaurants emphasize meal quality and attentive table service. Entertainment venues like Broadway theaters or performances by Cirque du Soleil present immersive storytelling alongside exceptional guest care. Tourism providers such as guided tour companies or Eurail integrate knowledgeable guides, engaging commentary, and smooth service delivery to enrich visitor experiences. Wellness resorts like Canyon Ranch integrate personalized health and mindfulness programs, with the aim of elevating the hospitality and tourism experience.

Departure and post-experience

Final impressions shape guest loyalty. Hotels refine checkout processes and solicit feedback; restaurants deliver personalized farewells and smooth settlements. Events follow up through emails or surveys. Tourism providers encourage guest feedback through post-visit surveys, follow-up communications, or personalized recommendations for future trips. Transportation services such as Eurail maintain engagement through inspiring post-trip communications. Hospitality and tourism brands consistently utilize feedback to improve future guest experiences and nurture ongoing relationships.

INTERACTIVE EXERCISE
Turning frustration into loyalty

Imagine you're the assistant manager of a popular restaurant inside a luxury hotel. A couple arrives for their 7:30 anniversary dinner, only to find their reservation is missing. The restaurant is fully booked, and the next available table requires a 45-minute wait. Frustrated, the couple tweets about their disappointment, tagging both the restaurant and hotel. Their post gains traction, catching the attention of your general manager, who asks you to handle it.

When using guest journey mapping, consider how theoretical frameworks such as the service-profit chain (employee satisfaction driving guest loyalty) and social exchange theory (reciprocal positive interactions between guests and employees) can guide your strategic response:

1 **Pre-experience**: How could the reservation system or confirmation process have prevented this issue?
2 **Arrival and first impressions**: What can you do immediately to ease frustration? A complimentary drink or priority seating?
3 **Core experience**: Once seated, how can you restore trust? How can you use the information you have to create a special and memorable experience?
4 **Post-experience**: How could you respond to the social media complaint to turn a negative moment into a loyalty-building opportunity?

Reflect

Consider a memorable hospitality or tourism experience you've had.

- How was your journey intentionally managed?
- Identify specific touchpoints that stood out positively or areas for improvement.

Personalization at scale: Balancing high-touch and high-tech

In today's hospitality landscape, brands must strike the right balance between high-tech (automation, AI, digital personalization) and high-touch (warm, personalized human interactions) (Sigala, 2018). Some luxury hotels, for example, use AI-driven concierge services to recognize repeat guests and customize recommendations (Cobanoglu et al., 2011). Cruise lines might offer wearable technology, such as radio-frequency identification (RFID) wristbands, to streamline guest interactions while maintaining personalized service (Kwortnik, 2008).

Today's hospitality industry faces an important challenge: how do businesses provide personalization at scale? Guests expect tailored experiences, but companies must deliver these on a large scale without losing the warmth of human service. The key lies in blending high-tech solutions with high-touch, thoughtful, human-driven interactions. Different sectors within hospitality implement personalization in unique ways. Luxury hotels use AI-driven concierge services to recognize repeat guests, offering customized recommendations based on past stays. Restaurants store digital menu preferences for frequent diners, making it easy to suggest past favorites or accommodate dietary needs without requiring guests to repeat their requests. Cruise lines employ wearable technology, pre-loading guest preferences such as drink selections or room temperature settings for onboard convenience. Airlines leverage predictive analytics to anticipate traveler needs, adjusting seating options, meal selections, or loyalty perks based on past travel behavior. Theme parks use smart ride reservation systems to optimize guest flow while offering tailored park experiences, ensuring a balance between personalization and operational efficiency.

An excellent example of this balance is the Four Seasons Chat app, which allows guests to request services, room changes, or amenities directly from their phones. While the technology streamlines communication, the human touch remains central—hotel staff personally fulfill requests, ensuring interactions feel warm and thoughtful rather than purely automated.

> **THINK LIKE A MANAGER**
>
> A hotel guest has stayed five times in the past year but never dines at the hotel restaurant. What personalized strategies could you implement to enhance their experience and drive revenue?

Multisensory branding: Designing emotional connections

Guest experience management extends beyond service interactions—it involves crafting a multisensory brand identity that influences guest emotions through sight, sound, scent, taste, and touch. Inclusive multisensory branding also ensures experiences accommodate guests with sensory sensitivities or disabilities, such as offering fragrance-free spaces, sensory-friendly hours, or alternative ways to experience auditory and visual elements. By intentionally designing experiences that engage all five senses as appropriate, hospitality brands across various sectors create stronger emotional connections, deepen brand recognition, and enhance guest satisfaction.

Sight is often the first impression of a brand, setting the tone for the experience. Airlines use mood lighting in cabins to create a relaxing atmosphere, while stadiums and event venues employ dynamic LED displays to build excitement. Cruise lines carefully design interior aesthetics and themed decor and enable panoramic views to elevate guest perception and reinforce brand identity.

Sound plays a critical role in shaping mood and engagement. Fine dining restaurants curate custom playlists to match their culinary themes, while casinos use strategic background noise to enhance energy and encourage longer stays. Theme parks create immersive soundscapes, where each attraction has a unique soundscape that transports guests into different worlds.

Scent is a powerful stimulus and a memory trigger that enhances brand recall and emotional connection. Resorts and spas often diffuse signature scents throughout their properties to promote relaxation, while entertainment venues may use themed scents to complement experiences, such as the smell of fresh popcorn at a movie theater or an outdoor festival. Singapore Airlines, for example, use light floral scents in cabins to contribute to a calming environment and reinforce their luxury brand identity.

Taste reinforces a brand's authenticity and uniqueness, often tied to local culture or exclusivity. Cruise lines feature destination-inspired menus that highlight regional flavors, while stadiums and arenas offer signature food items that become part of the fan experience. High-end airlines curate premium, chef-designed meals based on passenger preferences, elevating their in-flight service beyond basic catering.

Touch influences perceptions of quality and comfort through physical interactions. Hotels focus on high-thread-count linens, plush carpets, soft robes, and ergonomic furniture to enhance relaxation, while spas use silk-like massage oils and warm towels to deepen the sensory experience. Even transportation sectors integrate tactile branding, such as the smooth leather seating in luxury train cabins or soft-touch materials in first-class airline suites to reinforce exclusivity and comfort.

An excellent example of multisensory branding in action is Disney Parks, where every sense is engaged—from the iconic visuals and themed music to the scent of waffle cones, and tactile experiences within interactive attractions. Similarly, Westin Hotels' white tea scent has become synonymous with relaxation, while Delta Airlines' cabin lighting shifts to promote rest and comfort. British Airways strategically uses curated in-flight music playlists featuring prominent British artists, such as Adele and Coldplay, to evoke a sense of place and cultural connection before passengers even arrive.

THINK LIKE A MANAGER

Your hotel is experiencing high employee turnover, and guest satisfaction scores are declining.

- What initiatives would you implement to enhance employee engagement and service quality? Would you focus on better training, recognition programs, or career growth opportunities?
- How could improving workplace culture and employee satisfaction lead to better guest experiences and, ultimately, stronger business performance?

The link between employee satisfaction, service quality, and guest loyalty

A truly exceptional guest experience begins with the people who serve them. In the hospitality industry, satisfied and engaged employees are the foundation of outstanding service. They directly influence guest satisfaction, brand reputation, and long-term business success. A disengaged workforce can result in lackluster service, negative guest experiences, and declining loyalty, while a well-supported team creates an environment where exceptional service thrives.

The service-profit chain (Heskett et al., 1994), mentioned earlier, is a widely recognized framework that illustrates the direct link between employee experience and guest loyalty. The model explains that strong hiring, training, and workplace culture create a motivated workforce (internal service quality), which leads to higher employee satisfaction and engagement. When employees feel valued, supported, and empowered, they are more likely to go above and beyond in delivering exceptional service. This, in turn, enhances guest satisfaction, increasing the likelihood of repeat business, positive reviews, and brand advocacy. Ultimately, loyal guests drive revenue growth and long-term profitability, proving that investing in employees is an investment in business success (Heskett et al., 2003).

REAL-WORLD EXAMPLE:
INDUSTRY SPOTLIGHT Ritz-Carlton's Gold Standards

As we saw in Chapter 2, Ritz-Carlton embodies exceptional hospitality through their Gold Standards, empowering employees to proactively manage the guest experience. Team members are authorized and encouraged to immediately resolve guest issues, such as offering personalized room upgrades or unexpected amenities to delight guests. This culture of trust and empowerment leads directly to higher employee engagement and superior guest satisfaction, solidifying Ritz-Carlton's industry-leading reputation.

Operations management: The engine of seamless hospitality

Guest experience design is only as good as its execution. Even the most well-planned service strategy can fail without thoughtful behind-the-scenes coordination. This is where operations management plays a crucial role, in ensuring that every process, from check-ins to foodservice, runs smoothly to create consistent, high-quality guest experiences. Let's explore how hospitality businesses optimize their operations to deliver excellence at every touchpoint.

Imagine arriving at a bustling hotel after a long flight. You're exhausted, but, within moments, the front desk agent warmly welcomes you, hands over your key, and offers a complimentary beverage. As you step into your room, it's immaculately clean, and a note on your pillow welcomes you by name. The next morning, breakfast arrives exactly as you requested—fresh coffee, croissants, and fruit. These experiences don't happen by chance—they are the result of effective operations management, the backbone of the hospitality industry.

Operations management in hospitality is the art and science of coordinating people, processes, and technology to ensure guests receive exceptional service efficiently and consistently. It involves anticipating guest needs, optimizing workflows, and integrating technology to enhance the overall experience. Successful operations managers balance guest satisfaction, cost control, and efficiency while ensuring that safety, compliance, and innovation remain at the forefront.

At its core, operations management focuses on five key objectives:

- Delivering exceptional service, ensuring that guest experiences are smooth and memorable
- Optimizing efficiency, reducing wait times and streamlining workflows
- Managing costs, balancing high-quality service with profitability
- Ensuring safety and compliance, adhering to industry regulations and best practices
- Embracing innovation, leveraging technology to improve efficiency and personalize guest interactions

> **THINK LIKE A MANAGER**
>
> You're an operations director at a large convention center. A major conference with 5,000 attendees is happening next weekend, and you must ensure smooth check-ins, catering, and security. What key areas would you prioritize to prevent operational breakdowns?

Front office management: The first and the last impression

The front office is the heartbeat of hospitality operations, shaping a guest's first and last impressions. From a warm welcome at check-in to an easy departure, this department plays a pivotal role in ensuring guest satisfaction. A well-run front office handles reservations and check-ins efficiently, ensuring a smooth arrival process, while also managing guest services such as special requests, transportation, and concierge assistance. The front office is typically the hub of communication with various other departments in the business. Additionally, the team oversees billing and payment processing, ensuring flawless transactions at check-out.

Luxury hotels like the Ritz-Carlton empower their front desk staff to create "wow" moments by providing them with a discretionary budget to surprise guests with personalized room upgrades or special amenities. These small but meaningful gestures elevate the guest experience and foster brand loyalty.

> **THINK LIKE A MANAGER**
>
> Your hotel's check-in process is causing long wait times during peak hours, leading to negative guest reviews.
>
> - What solutions would you implement, for instance mobile check-ins, self-service kiosks, or additional staffing?
> - How would you balance efficiency with personalized service?

Theoretical framework: Lean management

Developed by Taiichi Ohno for Toyota, lean management aims to maximize value while minimizing waste. In hospitality, this means optimizing operations by reducing inefficiencies, improving service speed, and enhancing guest satisfaction (Ohno, 1988):

- **Reducing wait times**: Streamlining check-ins, room turnovers, and restaurant service.
- **Eliminating waste**: Preventing food waste and unnecessary inventory stockpiling.
- **Enhancing efficiency**: Using automation and staff cross-training to improve service quality.

By integrating lean principles, hospitality organizations can optimize operations, reduce costs, and enhance the overall guest experience.

Exceptional operations lay the foundation for outstanding guest satisfaction. However, even the most efficiently managed hospitality businesses may struggle to attract and retain guests without equally effective marketing and sales strategies. Marketing and sales bridge the gap between a great service offering and a steady stream of guests, ensuring that strong operations translate into sustained profitability.

Let's explore how branding, digital engagement, and strategic promotions shape demand and drive long-term business success. How do leading hospitality brands craft compelling stories that drive bookings and revenue? Let's find out.

Marketing and sales: Crafting demand and driving revenue

> Effective hospitality marketing means connecting emotionally with guests. We're not just promoting rooms or events—we're sharing compelling stories and unique experiences that inspire guests to choose us, stay with us, and share their experiences with others.
>
> —*Cassandra Seaman, senior sales manager, Signia by Hilton*

Hospitality marketing involves more than selling rooms, event tickets, or cruise packages—it sells experiences, emotions, and lasting memories. A compelling marketing strategy captures attention, builds trust, and transforms interest into bookings across various hospitality segments. Imagine launching a boutique hotel in a crowded market. Will you differentiate through luxury personalization, sustainability, or local culture? Effective hospitality marketing clearly communicates these unique value propositions, converting guest interest into bookings. Leading brands excel by clearly defining their unique strengths and crafting compelling marketing strategies accordingly. Successful hospitality marketing focuses on three key goals:

1. **Attracting guests:** Sparking interest through engaging content, promotions, and advertising.
2. **Driving revenue:** Encouraging bookings, reservations, or ticket purchases through strategic pricing and promotions.
3. **Building loyalty:** Creating long-term relationships through personalized experiences, loyalty programs, and exceptional service.

Marketing in hospitality bridges emotion and logic—it entices guests with the promise of a memorable experience while ensuring they perceive value in their purchase.

THINK LIKE A MANAGER

You are the marketing director of a new luxury resort opening in Bali. With several established competitors, how would you differentiate your resort to attract bookings? Would you focus on pricing, unique experiences, sustainability, or a combination of strategies?

The hospitality brand: More than a logo; it's a promise

In hospitality, a brand is more than a logo, name, or tagline—it represents a company's identity and the promise it delivers to guests. A strong brand does more than attract customers; it can create an emotional connection that transforms first-time visitors into lifelong advocates.

Successful hospitality brands are built on key elements that shape guest perceptions. Brand identity defines what the company represents—whether it embodies luxury, adventure, relaxation, exclusivity, or affordability. Consistency ensures that every interaction, from a hotel's website to the in-person guest experience, aligns with the brand's promise. The most successful brands also make an emotional connection, evoking feelings of trust, excitement, nostalgia, or exclusivity that keep guests returning. Ultimately, the guest experience must reflect the brand's core message. If a luxury resort markets itself as an oasis of relaxation, every touchpoint, from the spa to customer service, must deliver on that promise.

A powerful example of branding excellence is Disney. Built on a foundation of magical experiences, immersive storytelling, and world-class service, Disney integrates its brand promise across multiple segments, from theme parks and hotels to cruise lines and entertainment ventures. Every interaction aims to reinforce the brand's identity, ensuring that guests associate Disney with wonder, nostalgia, and exceptional hospitality—a formula that keeps millions returning year after year.

REAL-WORLD EXAMPLE:
INDUSTRY SPOTLIGHT Disney Parks: Mastering anticipation and emotional engagement

Disney Parks have mastered the art of anticipation, emotional engagement, and strategic guest journey mapping. From the moment a guest considers visiting, Disney intentionally builds excitement and emotional connection through carefully crafted marketing and personalized interactions at every touchpoint.

A classic illustration is Disney's renowned advertising campaign from 1997, in which two children famously declare, "I'm too excited to sleep!" before their Disney trip (Disney Parks, 1997). This iconic commercial effectively captured the anticipation and emotional build-up guests feel prior to their experience—a hallmark of Disney's guest journey approach. Disney has continued to build upon this legacy with more recent and equally impactful campaigns, including "The Magic is Calling," which marked Walt Disney World's 50th anniversary, evoking nostalgia and excitement through powerful storytelling (Disney Parks, 2021). In 2023, the global campaign "Disney100 – The Magic is Calling" celebrated the company's 100th anniversary, inviting guests worldwide to join in commemorating a century of storytelling and memorable experiences (Disney Parks, 2023).

Internationally, Disney consistently applies this formula of anticipation-building and emotional engagement. The campaign for the Disneyland Paris 30th anniversary vividly captured the joy and energy of celebrating three decades of magic in Europe (Disneyland Paris, 2022). Similarly, Disneyland Resort's announcement of its 70th anniversary showcases how Disney continues to evolve, maintaining excitement across generations (Disney Parks, 2025). Shanghai Disney Resort further expanded the global storytelling with a promotional video highlighting cultural resonance and emotional connection for guests in Asia (Shanghai Disney Resort, 2023). Disney Cruise Line followed suit, offering emotive, adventure-filled advertisements that inspire guests to anticipate unique family experiences at sea (Disney Cruise Line, 2023).

Collectively, these milestone campaigns and strategic guest journey experiences demonstrate Disney's enduring ability to create genuine anticipation, emotional resonance, and lasting loyalty—qualities that exemplify best practices in hospitality and tourism marketing and guest engagement strategies.

Digital marketing: The new front door to hospitality

In today's digital-first world, a guest's first impression of a hotel, restaurant, or event venue often happens long before they step through the door—it begins online. From scrolling through Instagram reels and TikTok videos to reading TripAdvisor reviews and searching for "best beach resorts" on Google, digital marketing plays a critical role in shaping consumer decisions. Hospitality businesses that master digital marketing can attract new guests, build brand loyalty, and drive direct bookings, often before a potential guest even lands on their website.

Successful hospitality brands leverage multiple digital marketing channels to engage and convert audiences. Social media marketing allows brands to showcase experiences visually, bringing destinations to life. For instance, Ritz-Carlton's Instagram doesn't just highlight luxury suites—it tells compelling behind-the-scenes stories of employees, reinforcing the brand's personal touch. Search engine optimization helps businesses rank higher in Google searches, making them more discoverable. Mountain Top Resort, for example, leveraged targeted search and Google's Performance Max—with high-intent keywords including "Vermont wedding destinations"—and saw a 30 percent increase in wedding inquiries and a 31 percent rise in paid-search leads (O'Rourke Hospitality, 2025).

Email marketing is another powerful tool, allowing brands to build relationships with past and potential guests through personalized offers and updates. Marriott Bonvoy utilizes this strategy effectively, sending targeted email campaigns with discounts tailored to a guest's past travel behavior. Meanwhile, influencer marketing has reshaped how travelers discover destinations. A single TikTok influencer's video tour of a Maldives resort recently resulted in a 20 percent increase in direct bookings, underscoring the power of social media in informing decisions (TravelBoom Hotel Marketing, 2025).

For hospitality businesses—especially smaller boutique properties with limited budgets—choosing the right digital marketing strategy is crucial. Should a business invest in Instagram promotions, Google ads, influencer partnerships, or email campaigns? The answer depends on the target audience, budget, and brand positioning, but a strong digital presence is no longer optional—it's the new front door to hospitality.

> **THINK LIKE A MANAGER**
>
> Your boutique hotel has a limited marketing budget. Where would you focus your efforts—Instagram promotions, Google ads, influencer partnerships, or email campaigns? Why?

Sales in hospitality: Turning interest into revenue

Marketing may generate interest, but it's sales teams that turn that interest into bookings, reservations, and revenue. In hospitality, effective sales strategies go beyond simply filling rooms or selling event space—they involve building relationships, understanding guest needs, and creating tailored offerings that drive long-term business success.

There are several key types of hospitality sales. Direct sales involve personalized outreach, such as phone calls, emails, and loyalty programs, to convert individual guests into repeat customers. Group sales focus on securing large bookings, such as wedding packages, conferences, and corporate retreats, which can bring in significant revenue. Corporate sales involve partnerships with businesses to accommodate frequent business travelers, offering special rates and perks that encourage repeat stays. Finally, third-party sales leverage travel agents and online travel agencies like Expedia and Booking.com, which help hospitality businesses reach a broader audience but often come with commission fees. An example of strategic hospitality sales is a luxury resort that partners with corporate travel planners, offering discounted rates to executives who book frequent stays. Over time, these exclusive partnerships create a steady revenue stream and increase brand loyalty among business travelers.

Sales teams must continuously adapt to market trends and guest expectations. If an event venue sees a decline in wedding bookings, for instance, managers must explore solutions such as discounted packages, referral incentives, exclusive vendor partnerships, or enhanced services to make their venue more appealing. By combining relationship-building with data-driven sales strategies, hospitality businesses can maximize revenue and deliver exceptional guest experiences.

> In hospitality, successful sales are built on trust, empathy, and a deep understanding of guest needs. Planners, partners, and guests often come with different levels of event knowledge; It takes patience and a genuine connection to meet them where they are, with respect. Great salespeople don't just sell; they build lasting relationships that turn first-time visitors into lifelong advocates.
>
> —*Lesley G Cornathan, sales manager, Greater Columbus Convention Center / ASM Global*

The power of loyalty programs: Turning guests into lifelong customers

Loyalty programs in hospitality extend far beyond simple point systems—they are strategic relationship-builders that foster guest retention, encourage brand loyalty, and boost profitability. Research from Bain & Company (n.d.) reveals that even a modest 5 percent increase in customer retention can amplify profits by 25–95 percent, as returning guests typically spend more and actively refer friends and family, driving organic growth.

Recent industry insights further emphasize loyalty programs' critical role in hospitality. According to CBRE (2025b), hotel loyalty memberships across major global brands grew by more than 14 percent in 2024, surpassing 675 million members. Remarkably, these members accounted for almost 53 percent of occupied room nights, underscoring their importance in maintaining consistent occupancy and predictable revenue streams throughout the year.

KPMG's comprehensive report, *The Evolution of Loyalty Programs* (2024), highlights the significant influence on consumer behavior, noting that 88 percent of satisfied premium members remain brand loyal despite competing offers, while 83 percent affirm that joining loyalty programs motivates future purchases. Additionally, 70 percent actively recommend these programs to friends and family.

An effective hospitality loyalty program offers personalized rewards, such as room upgrades, early check-ins, or exclusive experiences, making repeat guests feel genuinely valued. Tiered benefits provide increasing incentives to encourage continued stays, rewarding frequent visitors with, for example, complimentary nights or priority reservations. Many hospitality brands also include experiential perks, offering VIP event access, complimentary spa treatments, or curated local experiences, making deeper emotional connections and lasting memories.

A prime example of loyalty program innovation is Marriott Bonvoy, enabling members to earn and redeem points not only for hotel stays but also for exceptional experiences like private concerts, culinary masterclasses, and adventure tours. By offering memorable moments rather than mere discounts, Marriott effectively develops guest loyalty and differentiates its brand beyond conventional accommodations.

In today's highly competitive landscape, hospitality businesses must continuously develop their loyalty strategies, ensuring programs remain engaging, rewarding, and aligned with evolving guest preferences. By doing so, hospitality providers transform one-time visitors into lifelong customers and brand advocates (CBRE, 2025a; KPMG, 2024).

Reputation management in the age of online reviews

In the hospitality industry, your reputation is your currency—and in the digital age, guest feedback can make or break a business. Most customers read online reviews before booking, meaning every rating, comment, and response directly impacts revenue and brand perception. A strong reputation builds trust, attracts new guests, and fosters long-term loyalty.

Effective reputation management starts with encouraging positive reviews, as satisfied guests are more likely to share their experiences when prompted by friendly staff. Addressing negative feedback professionally is equally critical. Responding to concerns with genuine apologies and actionable solutions can turn dissatisfied guests into returning customers. Monitoring multiple platforms, such as TripAdvisor, Yelp, Google Reviews, and social media, ensures businesses stay ahead of their online reputation and respond promptly to guest concerns. Additionally, successful brands use feedback to pinpoint operational weaknesses and improve their service.

As an illustrative example, imagine a hotel restaurant receives a negative TripAdvisor review about slow service. By effectively applying the REACT model introduced in Chapter 2, the manager would respectfully listen to the guest's feedback, sincerely empathize with their frustration, offer a meaningful apology, swiftly correct the issue by inviting the guest back for a complimentary meal, and follow through with a thoughtful, transparent response that publicly thanks the guest for their patience and trust. This structured approach addresses the immediate issue and demonstrates the organization's genuine commitment to guest satisfaction and continuous improvement, reinforcing a positive brand image.

Reputation management is not just about damage control—it's about proactive engagement and continuous improvement. By fostering positive interactions, addressing concerns transparently, and learning from guest feedback, hospitality businesses can strengthen their brand image and build lasting trust with guests.

Reflect

- Consider how online reviews influence your personal hospitality choices, whether selecting a hotel, restaurant, or vacation activity. Have you ever changed your plans based on a review?
- Reflect on a time you shared feedback online (positive or negative). What motivated you to do so, and how did the business's response—or lack of—impact your perception of their brand?

Human resources management: Empowering people, elevating service

Human resources plays a critical role in hospitality and tourism by developing talent, shaping culture, and driving employee engagement. By prioritizing the growth and well-being of our teams, we not only enhance guest satisfaction but also build sustainable, high-performing organizations that thrive in a dynamic industry.

—*Mie Young Reed, dual director of human resources, JW Marriott and Marriott*

Behind every memorable guest experience is a dedicated team, carefully recruited, trained, and motivated to deliver exceptional service. In hospitality, human resources (HR) goes beyond hiring and payroll. HR helps to cultivate a strong workplace culture, fostering leadership and ensuring continuous employee development. A well-managed HR strategy reduces employee turnover, increases job satisfaction, and improves service skills, directly impacting guest experiences and brand reputation.

Hospitality thrives on a global, multicultural workforce, with employees from diverse backgrounds, languages, and traditions. This diversity enriches the guest experience and helps businesses better understand and serve an international clientele. HR plays a key role in ensuring that employees are equipped with cross-cultural communication skills, have respect for different traditions, and can provide personalized service to guests from all walks of life.

Successful organizations focus on key HR functions to build high-performing teams. The right talent acquisition and recruitment policies ensure that new hires align with the company's service culture and have the necessary skills and mindset to thrive in a guest-centric industry. Training and development programs should hone essential service skills, empowering staff to anticipate guest needs, resolve issues effectively, and exceed expectations. Just as crucial is fostering a positive workplace culture, where employees feel valued, engaged, and motivated to contribute to the company's success.

A robust HR strategy prioritizes workplace collaboration, fairness, and professional growth, ensuring that all employees have opportunities to succeed. Organizations that emphasize clear career pathways, leadership development, and employee engagement build stronger, more resilient teams that reflect the diverse guests they serve. Additionally, HR ensures compliance with labor laws, safety regulations, and ethical employment standards, helping businesses avoid legal risks while fostering a safe and respectful work environment.

Ultimately, HR in hospitality is about people—hiring the right talent, nurturing their growth, and creating a culture that inspires excellence. When employees feel empowered and supported, they are more likely to deliver service that leaves a lasting impression on guests, turning everyday stays, meals, and experiences into unforgettable moments.

Theoretical framework: Social exchange theory

Social exchange theory (Blau, 1964) explains that relationships, such as those between employers and employees, are built on mutual exchange or reciprocity. When employers invest in their staff through fair compensation, professional growth opportunities, and genuine appreciation, employees typically reciprocate by becoming more engaged, committed, and loyal.

For instance, consider a guided tour company that invests significantly in their guides by providing competitive wages, continuous training, and recognition awards for exceptional guest service. The guides, in turn, feel valued and reciprocate by consistently delivering knowledgeable, enthusiastic, and memorable experiences to travelers. This positive exchange strengthens the company's reputation, resulting in repeat bookings, excellent reviews, and sustainable business success.

Recruitment and retention strategies in hospitality

Recruiting and retaining top talent is one of the biggest challenges in hospitality, where high turnover rates can disrupt service quality and increase operational costs. Successful recruitment strategies focus on attracting individuals who have not only the necessary skills but also a genuine passion for hospitality. Hiring for personality and service-oriented attitudes is key, as technical skills can often be developed through training. Employee referral programs can also be effective, in which existing staff recommend candidates who align with the company's culture and values. Additionally, career growth opportunities, such as internal promotions, training programs, and leadership development, can attract ambitious candidates looking for long-term careers rather than short-term jobs.

Retention strategies are equally crucial to reducing turnover and maintaining a motivated workforce. Competitive compensation and benefits, including fair wages, healthcare, and performance incentives, help businesses remain attractive in a competitive job market. Recognition programs that celebrate employee contributions, for example through employee-of-the-month awards, bonuses, or simple acknowledgments, boost morale and encourage engagement. Flexible scheduling and work–life balance initiatives can also improve retention, particularly in roles with demanding hours, by demonstrating a commitment to employee well-being.

> **THINK LIKE A MANAGER**
>
> You are hiring for a housekeeping team, a department with historically high turnover. What strategies would you implement to attract and retain employees in this critical role while ensuring service quality remains high?

Training and development: Building a service-oriented workforce

A well-trained team is the secret ingredient behind every five-star guest experience. In hospitality, training isn't just about learning the job—it's about mastering the art of service, problem-solving, and creating memorable moments that keep guests coming back. Service excellence training teaches employees how to anticipate guest needs, handle unexpected challenges, and deliver experiences that exceed expectations. Skills-based training ensures employees are proficient in essential tools, whether it's mastering front-desk software, perfecting culinary techniques, or co-ordinating flawless events.

And training doesn't stop at the basics. Leadership development programs help ambitious employees grow into management roles, ensuring career progression within the company. Cultural competency training is equally important, preparing employees to serve a diverse guest base with empathy and respect. In a global industry like hospitality, understanding different customs, preferences, and communication styles can make all the difference in creating welcoming and inclusive experiences. By investing in engaging, hands-on training, hospitality businesses do more than develop skilled employees—they build a confident, service-oriented workforce ready to handle anything that comes its way.

Service, sales, and people

> **THINK LIKE A MANAGER**
>
> You're launching a new boutique hotel with a team of employees from different backgrounds and experience levels. How would you structure training to ensure they work together to deliver outstanding service from day one?

Employee well-being, compliances, and ethical responsibilities

In hospitality, taking care of employees is just as important as taking care of guests. A well-supported workforce leads to high-quality service, high job satisfaction, and long-term business success. Ensuring fair compensation is the first step: competitive wages and benefits help attract and retain top talent in an industry known for high turnover. Financial stability alone isn't enough, however—employees also need a safe and secure workplace. Adhering, as a minimum, to OSHA (Occupational Safety and Health Administration) standards (in the US) and implementing proactive safety measures, whether in hotel kitchens, event venues, or housekeeping departments, minimizes injury risks and ensures operations run smoothly.

Beyond physical safety, fostering a respectful and inclusive work culture is essential. Anti-harassment policies, clear reporting procedures, and regular training reinforce a culture where all employees feel valued and supported. When hospitality businesses prioritize well-being, employees are more engaged, motivated, and empowered to deliver exceptional service. After all, a positive employee experience translates directly into a positive guest experience.

Measuring HR success: Key metrics

In hospitality and tourism, exceptional guest experiences begin with exceptional employees. Just as organizations carefully measure guest satisfaction, they must also closely monitor their HR practices. Effective HR metrics highlight industry challenges and reveal critical opportunities for leadership, innovation, and strategic workforce development. By approaching these metrics not just as challenges but as opportunities, leaders at every level can drive meaningful change, creating vibrant workplace environments and outstanding guest experiences.

Employee turnover rate

High turnover remains one of hospitality's greatest challenges—and opportunities. According to a report by the American Hotel & Lodging Association (AHLA, 2023), the cost to replace a hospitality employee averages about 30 percent of that employee's annual salary. This significant expense underscores why retention strategies are not just beneficial but crucial for organizational success. Leaders who prioritize employee retention through supportive workplace cultures, competitive wages, and clear career advancement paths can significantly enhance their organization's stability and reputation (Deloitte, 2023).

Employee satisfaction and engagement scores

Engaged employees don't just enjoy their jobs—they contribute directly to organizational success. Gallup's (2024) extensive global research demonstrates that companies with highly engaged workforces achieve:

- 23 percent higher profitability
- 41 percent lower absenteeism
- 17 percent greater productivity.

These powerful statistics underscore the direct link between investing in employee engagement and achieving superior operational results, including higher guest satisfaction and loyalty.

Training investment and return on investment

Investing in employee training goes beyond skill enhancement—it directly impacts financial performance. Research from the Association for Talent Development (ATD, 2019) found that organizations with comprehensive training programs consistently report:

- 218 percent higher income per employee
- 24 percent higher profit margins.

Furthermore, according to ATD's 2024 report, organizations continue to increase their investment in training, spending an average of $1,283 per employee in 2023. These figures highlight how strategic investments in employee development boost individual performance and significantly strengthen an organization's financial health.

Guest satisfaction correlation

The relationship between employee engagement and guest satisfaction is powerful. Research (Gallup, 2024; McKinsey, 2023) consistently shows that organizations with highly engaged employees experience:

- up to 21 percent higher profitability
- 17 percent increased productivity.

This data makes clear that investing in employee experience directly translates to improved guest satisfaction, loyalty, and overall organizational performance.

> **INTERACTIVE EXERCISE**
> Strengthening workplace culture
>
> Your resort has been experiencing high staff turnover and inconsistent service quality. Guest feedback consistently highlights issues around communication and varying attentiveness. Additionally, recent exit interviews indicate that employees feel undervalued and do not see clear pathways for career growth within the organization.
>
> As the newly appointed HR manager, you must propose initiatives to enhance employee engagement and improve training effectiveness, creating a motivated, service-driven team.
>
> 1 Identify and briefly describe two specific HR initiatives that address both employee satisfaction and service excellence. Your initiatives should consider:
>   - Recognition programs that boost morale and reward service excellence.
>   - Cross-cultural training to strengthen communication and guest interactions.
>   - Clear, structured career pathways to enhance retention and professional growth.
> 2 For each initiative, clearly explain:
>   - What the initiative involves.
>   - How it specifically addresses current employee concerns.
>   - How you will measure the initiative's success using relevant HR metrics (such as employee satisfaction scores, turnover rates, guest satisfaction ratings).
>
> As you reflect on these initiatives, remember that a hospitality organization's success fundamentally relies on well-integrated strategies across guest experiences, employee satisfaction, operations, marketing, and branding.

Now, let's summarize the key insights covered throughout this chapter to reinforce your understanding of how these core business functions collectively drive excellence in hospitality.

Key takeaways

- Guest experience management shapes success. Every guest interaction, from pre-arrival to post-experience, influences satisfaction and loyalty. Thoughtful experience design ensures cohesive, memorable stays across all hospitality sectors.

- Personalization balances high-tech and high-touch. Leveraging data and technology enables businesses to customize guest experiences while maintaining genuine, human-driven service.

- Crisis management protects brand trust. Proactive planning, clear communication, and rapid response strategies help mitigate service disruptions and maintain guest confidence.

- Employee satisfaction drives guest loyalty. The service-profit chain emphasizes that engaged employees lead to superior service, which directly impacts guest retention and revenue.

- Operations management is the backbone of hospitality. From front-office efficiency to housekeeping and food and beverage service, well-coordinated operations ensure smooth experiences for guests and financial stability for businesses.

- Hospitality branding creates emotional connections. A strong brand identity fosters guest loyalty by delivering consistent, memorable experiences aligned with brand values.

- Marketing and sales convert interest into revenue. Digital marketing, social media engagement, and targeted sales strategies attract guests and maximize profitability.

- HR management shapes workplace culture and performance. Recruiting, training, and retaining passionate hospitality professionals are essential for delivering high-quality service and sustaining a strong workforce.

Looking ahead

This chapter has explored the front-facing functions that define hospitality excellence: guest experience management, branding, marketing, operations, and human resources. These elements work together to shape service quality, employee engagement, and financial success.

While front-facing functions define the guest experience, the long-term success of hospitality businesses depends on financial strategy, risk management, and sustainable infrastructure. In the next chapter, we'll explore how businesses ensure financial health, mitigate risks, and create scalable operations that support long-term success in the hospitality industry.

References

AHLA (American Hotel & Lodging Association) (2023) *Turning Down Turnover: Key Insights and Recommendations to Improve Business Operations*. ahla.com/sites/default/files/Turning_Down_Turnover-10.16.23.pdf (archived at https://perma.cc/8BXZ-E6MG)

ATD (Association for Talent Development) (2019) *2019 State of the Industry Report*. td.org/product/state-of-the-industry--2019-state-of-the-industry/791911 (archived at https://perma.cc/TR7V-4KBN)

ATD (2024) *State of the Industry Report: Workplace learning spending in 2023*, HRTechEdge summary. hrtechedge.com/news/2024-state-of-the-industry-report-workplace-learning-spending-increases-and-key-insights (archived at https://perma.cc/CV5P-U62X)

Bain & Company (n.d.) Prescription for cutting costs: Loyal relationships. https://www.bain.com/insights/prescription-for-cutting-costs-bain-brief/?utm_source (archived at https://perma.cc/N9A5-JACN)

Blau, P.M. (1964) *Exchange and Power in Social Life*. New York: Wiley.

Bowen, J. & Ford, R.C. (2004) What experts say about managing hospitality service delivery systems, *International Journal of Contemporary Hospitality Management*, 16 (7), 394–401.

CBRE (2025a) Hotel loyalty programs continue to prove their value: Key findings from 675 million members. cbre.com/insights/articles/hotel-loyalty-programs-continue-to-prove-their-value-key-findings-from-675-million-members (archived at https://perma.cc/K5ED-6M3A)

CBRE (2025b) Hotel loyalty program membership surges 14.5% in 2024, Hotel News Resource. hotelnewsresource.com/article136035.html (archived at https://perma.cc/HDD5-W65J)

Cobanoglu, C., Berezina, K., Kasavana, M.L., & Erdem, M. (2011) The impact of technology amenities on hotel guest overall satisfaction, *Journal of Quality Assurance in Hospitality & Tourism*, 12 (4), 272–288. doi.org/10.1080/1528008X.2011.541842 (archived at https://perma.cc/F2HJ-BEDS)

Deloitte (2023) *The Future of the Frontline Workforce: A Roadmap for the Transportation and Hospitality Industries*. Deloitte Insights. deloitte.com/content/dam/Deloitte/us/Documents/consumer-business/us-the-future-of-the-frontline-workforce-2024.pdf (archived at https://perma.cc/P28B-CB7Q)

Disney Cruise Line (2023) *Adventure awaits with Disney cruise Line*. youtu.be/pGjDzfXoOg0 (archived at https://perma.cc/BE9F-ANHM)

Disneyland Paris (2022) *Disneyland Paris 30th anniversary launch*. youtube.com/ watch?v =ma7WoWRBLUQ (archived at https://perma.cc/D8UM-7H9D)

Disney Parks (1997) *"I'm too excited"*. https://www.youtube.com/watch?v=0eci1ZUbxaM (archived at https://perma.cc/8SKS-W887)

Disney Parks (2021) *The magic is calling: Walt Disney World's 50th anniversary*. youtube. com/ watch?v =SmWv-t5ogrg (archived at https://perma.cc/5RXC-F4TY)

Disney Parks (2023) *Disney100 – The magic is calling*. youtu.be/tSncj9IUEz0 (archived at https://perma.cc/YQN3-5SWU)

Disney Parks (2025) Disneyland resort to celebrate 70th anniversary. https://disneyparksblog.com/disney-experiences/bob-iger-josh-damaro-disneyland-70/ (archived at https://perma.cc/2EDB-CUUD)

Gallup (2024) *State of the Global Workplace: Understanding Employees, Informing Leaders 2024 Report*. gallup.com/workplace/349484/state-of-the-global-workplace.aspx (archived at https://perma.cc/E6FG-534L)

Heskett, J.L., Jones, T.O., Loveman, G.W., Sasser, W.E., & Schlesinger, L.A. (1994) Putting the service-profit chain to work, *Harvard Business Review*, 72 (2), 164–170.

Heskett, J.L., Sasser, W.E., & Schlesinger, L.A. (2003) *The Value Profit Chain: Treat Employees Like Customers and Customers Like Employees*. The Free Press.

KPMG (2024) *The Evolution of Loyalty Programs*. kpmg.com/us/en/articles/2024/evolution-loyalty-programs.html (archived at https://perma.cc/ND3K-WRWE)

Kwortnik, R.J. (2008) Shipscape influence on the leisure cruise experience, *International Journal of Culture, Tourism and Hospitality Research*, 2 (4), 289–311. doi.org/10.1108/17506180810908961 (archived at https://perma.cc/YFT9-9XDV)

Lovelock, C. & Wirtz, J. (2020) *Services Marketing: People, Technology, Strategy* (9th edn). New Jersey: World Scientific Publishing.

McKinsey & Company (2023) Some employees are destroying value. Others are building it. Do you know the difference? *McKinsey Quarterly*, September 11. mckinsey.com/capabilities/people-and-organizational-performance/our-insights/some-employees-are-destroying-value-others-are-building-it-do-you-know-the-difference (archived at https://perma.cc/J757-MZWU)

Ohno, T. (1988) *Toyota Production System: Beyond Large-Scale Production*. Portland, OR: Productivity Press.

O'Rourke Hospitality (2025) Paid marketing grows wedding inquiries by 30% at Vermont resort. orourkehospitality.com/results/paid-marketing-grows-wedding-inquiries-at-vermont-resort (archived at https://perma.cc/REU6-PZ66)

Pizam, A. & Tasci, A.D.A. (2019) Experienscape: Expanding the concept of servicescape with a multi-stakeholder and multi-disciplinary approach, *International Journal of Hospitality Management*, 76 (B), 25–37. doi.org/10.1016/j.ijhm.2018.06.010 (archived at https://perma.cc/93TX-955D)

Rust, R.T., Zahorik, A.J., & Keiningham, T.L. (1995) Return on quality (ROQ): Making service quality financially accountable, *Journal of Marketing*, 59 (2), 58–70. doi.org/10.1177/002224299505900205 (archived at https://perma.cc/94QM-TWV9)

Shanghai Disney Resort (2023) Shanghai Disney Resort promotional video. youtu.be/IcN7C3KBDW0 (archived at https://perma.cc/HW6B-QTW5)

Sigala, M. (2018) New technologies in tourism: From multi-disciplinary to anti-disciplinary advances and trajectories, *Tourism Management Perspectives*, 25, 151–155. doi.org/10.1016/j.tmp.2017.12.003 (archived at https://perma.cc/UL4V-UMCY)

Solnet, D., Ford, R., & McLennan, C.-L. (2018) What matters most in the service-profit chain? An empirical test in a restaurant company, *International Journal of Contemporary Hospitality Management*, 30 (1), 122–143.

TravelBoom Hotel Marketing (2025) *Empowering Independent Hotels: Maximizing Direct Bookings Through Strategic Influencer Partnerships*. admin.travelboommarketing.com/wp-content/uploads/2025/03/TravelBoom_Empowering_Independent_Hotels_Maximizing_Direct_Bookings_Through_Strategic_Influencer_Partnerships.pdf (archived at https://perma.cc/G8WX-VY3C)

Core business functions: Finance, risk, and infrastructure

5

LEARNING OBJECTIVES

- Identify the critical back-end business functions in hospitality, including financial management, revenue management, risk management, supply chain management, and facilities management.
- Explain how financial and revenue strategies drive profitability, sustainability, and guest experiences.
- Analyze the role of risk management and compliance in ensuring guest safety, legal adherence, and business continuity.
- Evaluate how efficient supply chain and asset management enhance operational performance and financial efficiency.
- Apply best practices from industry case studies to develop proactive strategies for managing business functions effectively.

Introduction

Imagine you're the general manager of a luxury resort hosting a high-profile wedding. Suddenly, a power outage plunges the entire venue into darkness, just as the couple prepares for their first dance. Within seconds, backup generators hum to life, the lights return, and the music resumes. Guests cheer, and the celebration continues without a hitch. Behind this seamless recovery are decisions and systems you helped put in place: smart budgeting that funded the generator, a reliable vendor who performed routine maintenance, and a well-trained team ready to respond.

These moments—the ones guests post about, rave about, and remember—are possible because of what happens behind the scenes. From financial planning to risk management, these core business functions are the invisible forces driving exceptional hospitality experiences.

Theoretical framework: Resource-based view theory

To understand why business functions are critical to success, we turn to the resource-based view theory (Barney, 1991). This highlights that competitive advantage comes from using internal resources, such as expertise, brand equity, and technology, effectively. In hospitality, this means leveraging what makes your business unique:

- A renowned culinary team can drive restaurant profits.
- A loyalty program can increase repeat bookings.
- Investing in green technology can attract eco-conscious travelers.

By managing resources wisely, hospitality businesses can drive both profitability and guest satisfaction—two pillars of long-term success.

Financial management in hospitality

Behind every seamless guest experience is a well-structured financial plan that ensures hospitality businesses run efficiently, sustainably, and profitably. Financial management—the strategic planning, organizing, controlling, and monitoring of financial resources (money, assets, and investments)—is essential for the long-term viability and success of hotels, restaurants, and tourism enterprises.

Effective financial management ensures revenues consistently exceed expenses, resources are allocated wisely, and cash flow remains stable. This allows businesses to invest in growth opportunities, adapt to changing market conditions, and maintain high-quality guest experiences even during challenging periods. From operating budgets and cost controls to financial reporting and forecasting, strong financial management is foundational to hospitality operations. By making informed financial decisions, hospitality managers drive profitability, enhance service quality, and secure sustainable growth.

Budgeting and cost control: Maintaining financial health

Budgeting is the process of creating a financial plan (budget) to allocate resources (money and assets) and set financial goals. In hospitality, budgets cover everything from labor costs to marketing expenses. Think of budgeting like managing your personal expenses for the semester. You have a set amount of money and need to decide how much goes toward essentials like rent and groceries, how much to save for future needs, and what's left for entertainment or extras. In hospitality, businesses do the same—allocating resources for payroll, utilities, marketing, and guest services to ensure smooth operations while staying financially stable.

Understanding hospitality budgets and cost control

Running a successful hospitality business requires careful financial planning, and budgeting plays a crucial role in ensuring long-term stability and profitability. Hospitality leaders must balance revenue and expenses while anticipating future needs, from daily operations to large-scale investments. While various budgeting approaches exist, three key types of budgets are fundamental to managing a hospitality business effectively: operating budgets, capital budgets, and cash flow budgets. As an example, let's look at a simplified breakdown of how revenue and expenses interact within a hospitality business budget (Table 5.1).

Revenue represents the money earned by selling hospitality services, while expenses are the costs of providing these services. Understanding this relationship clearly helps managers make informed financial decisions, optimize profitability, and maintain long-term financial health.

An *operating budget* covers the essential day-to-day expenses that keep a business running smoothly, including payroll, utilities, housekeeping supplies, food and beverage costs, and routine maintenance. Essentially, it serves as the financial roadmap for managing recurring expenses while maintaining high-quality service. In contrast, a *capital budget* focuses on long-term investments that improve or expand the business. These are typically high-cost expenditures, such as renovating a hotel lobby, upgrading kitchen equipment, or installing new guestroom technology. Since these projects require significant financial planning, businesses often allocate capital budgets separately from daily operating expenses. The third major budget, *cash flow*, tracks how money moves in and out of the business to ensure there is enough liquidity to cover expenses. Hospitality businesses experience fluctuations in revenue due

Table 5.1 Hospitality budget: Revenue and expenses

Revenue (money coming in)	**Expenses (money going out)**
Guest room sales ($10,000)	Staff salaries ($4,000)
Restaurant sales ($5,000)	Food and beverage ($2,000)
Spa treatments ($3,000)	Utilities ($1,000)
Event space rental ($2,000)	Marketing ($500)
Total revenue: $20,000	*Total expenses: $7,500*
Profit: $12,500	

to seasonality, special events, or economic shifts, making cash flow management essential for preventing financial strain during slower periods.

In addition to budgeting, cost control strategies help hospitality businesses maximize profitability while maintaining service quality. One of the most significant expenses in the industry is labor, which can be managed through cross-training staff, optimizing scheduling, and leveraging automation for repetitive tasks. Energy efficiency is another key area where cost savings can be achieved. Initiatives such as switching to LED lighting, using smart thermostats, and adopting energy-efficient appliances reduce utility expenses over time. Inventory management is equally important, particularly in food and beverage operations, where waste can be minimized using the "first in, first out" (FIFO) method to ensure older stock is used before new inventory. Lastly, vendor negotiations can have a significant impact on cost savings. Strong relationships with suppliers allow businesses to secure better rates, flexible payment terms, and bulk purchase discounts, ultimately lowering expenses without compromising quality. By understanding these budgeting principles and cost control strategies, hospitality leaders can make informed financial decisions that sustain operations, support strategic investments, and improve guest experiences.

Financial reporting: Tracking performance and informing decisions

In the fast-paced world of hospitality, financial reporting serves as a critical tool for understanding a business's financial health and making informed decisions. By analyzing financial data, hospitality leaders can assess performance, identify trends, and adjust strategies to optimize profitability. Whether managing a hotel, restaurant, or event venue, leaders must regularly review financial reports to ensure the business remains financially stable and competitive.

Several key financial statements provide a comprehensive view of a hospitality provider's financial position. The *income statement*, often referred to as the profit and loss statement, outlines revenues, expenses, and profits over a specific period, offering insight into whether the business is making money. The *balance sheet* provides a snapshot of assets, liabilities, and equity, helping leaders understand the company's financial standing at any given time. Meanwhile, the *cash flow statement* tracks how money moves in and out of the business, ensuring there is enough liquidity to cover expenses and plan for investments. Additionally, *variance reports* compare actual performance against budgeted figures, highlighting areas where spending is higher or lower than expected. These reports help managers make timely adjustments to financial plans and ensure the business stays on track toward its goals.

Through their financial reporting, hospitality professionals can make data-driven decisions that enhance operational efficiency and long-term sustainability. Whether identifying cost-saving opportunities, reallocating resources to high-performing areas, or determining when to reinvest in upgrades, these reports provide the insights needed to navigate financial challenges and seize growth opportunities.

> **THINK LIKE A MANAGER**
>
> You are the general manager of a restaurant, and your profit margins are falling. Which cost control areas would you address first—labor, inventory, or marketing—and why?

The impact of financial management on guest experience

Effective financial management is more than just balancing budgets—it directly shapes guest satisfaction and brand reputation. When hospitality businesses optimize financial strategies, they can reinvest in areas that enhance the guest experience, ensuring long-term success. Well-managed finances allow for critical improvements such as staff training to elevate service quality, property upgrades that modernize facilities and amenities, sustainability initiatives that attract eco-conscious travelers, and loyalty programs that encourage repeat business.

A prime example of strategic financial management in action is Marriott International's asset-light model—a business approach focused on franchising and managing properties rather than owning them outright. This model enables Marriott to minimize financial risk while expanding its global footprint. In 2023, Marriott reported a 15 percent increase in global revenue per available room (RevPAR), with net income rising by 26 percent compared to 2022 (Marriott International, 2024). These financial gains allowed Marriott to enhance its Bonvoy loyalty program, invest in property renovations, and expand brand offerings—initiatives that directly improve guest experiences. By using an asset-light model, Marriott successfully aligns financial efficiency with guest-centric innovation, reinforcing the critical role of financial management in hospitality success.

Financial management isn't just about numbers—it's about impact. Behind every budget is a guest experience, and behind every forecast is a future opportunity. As you lead hospitality businesses, let your financial strategies fuel both profitability and unforgettable experiences. In the next section, we'll explore revenue and yield management—where financial strategies come to life through efficient pricing models, demand forecasting, and innovative revenue optimization techniques that keep hospitality businesses competitive and profitable.

Revenue and yield management: Turning strategy into profit

Just like financial management, revenue and yield management are essential business functions that sustain hospitality operations and drive profitability. These strategies go beyond setting prices—they leverage data, technology, and forecasting to maximize revenue, optimize inventory, and enhance financial performance across all hospitality segments. From theme parks and spas to event venues and transportation services, businesses that master revenue management can stay competitive, adapt to market shifts, and reinvest in order to offer exceptional guest experiences.

Understanding revenue and yield management in hospitality

Revenue and yield management are essential for adjusting pricing, optimizing inventory, and enhancing profitability. They rely on analyzing customer demand, booking trends, and competitor positioning to *sell the right product, at the right price, to the right customer, at the right time.*

Revenue management focuses on increasing overall income (revenue – the money earned from sales and services) through strategic pricing, promotions, and distribution strategies. Yield management, a subset of revenue management, ensures that perishable inventory items, such as concert seats, spa appointments, and guided tour slots, are sold at the optimal price before they expire.

Perishability and its role in revenue optimization

One of the defining characteristics of hospitality services is perishability—the fact that, once a service goes unsold, the opportunity for revenue is permanently lost. An empty airline seat, an unsold hotel room, or an unused spa appointment cannot be resold the next day. This makes effective pricing and inventory management critical to ensure businesses capture revenue before their product expires.

For example, a theater cannot sell tickets for yesterday's performance, making it essential to fill seats in advance. This is why venues often use discounting strategies for last-minute tickets, allowing them to earn some revenue rather than letting seats remain empty. Perishability is the reason why revenue managers must balance demand forecasting, pricing adjustments, and overbooking strategies to optimize sales.

Strategic approaches to revenue management

> Effective revenue management in hospitality involves strategically balancing pricing, inventory, and distribution channels. By anticipating market trends and consumer behavior, we maximize revenue and profitability while delivering exceptional guest value.
>
> —Kurt Furlong, *chief revenue officer and partner, Genuine Hospitality*

One of the most impactful revenue management tools is *dynamic pricing*, where rates change based on demand, competitor pricing, and availability. The airline industry pioneered dynamic pricing in the 1980s, using computerized systems to adjust fares in real time. Today, event venues, cruise lines, and theme parks use similar strategies. For instance, a ski resort may increase lift ticket prices during peak weekends while offering discounts midweek to attract more visitors.

Market segmentation also plays a critical role, allowing businesses to tailor pricing and promotions to different customer groups. An amusement park may offer discounted weekday tickets for local residents while keeping peak pricing on weekends for tourists. Similarly, a cruise line might provide family packages while charging higher rates for luxury suites aimed at affluent travelers.

Inventory control is essential for managing capacity across multiple booking channels. Spas and wellness centers often reserve peak-time appointments for direct bookings while allocating off-peak slots to third-party platforms. Sports stadiums use this strategy by holding premium seating for season-ticket holders while offering flexible pricing for general admission.

Overbooking is a calculated risk used by various industries to account for expected cancellations and maximize revenue. A luxury train service may slightly overbook first-class seating, knowing that a percentage of travelers will cancel or reschedule. However, overbooking requires careful management to prevent guest dissatisfaction.

Think of the process like some concert ticket pricing: as demand surges, prices rise. Hospitality uses the same logic, whether for rooms, dining experiences, or spa services.

Revenue metrics in hospitality

To track financial performance, hospitality businesses rely on key revenue metrics that assess pricing effectiveness, demand patterns, and profitability. The *average daily rate* (ADR) calculates the average revenue per occupied unit, while the *occupancy rate* measures how much of the available inventory is sold. Together, these determine RevPAR, which helps hotels evaluate how effectively they are generating revenue from their available inventory (Table 5.2).

Table 5.2 Typical revenue metrics

Metric	Definition	Formula	Example
Average daily rate (ADR)	Average revenue earned per occupied unit	ADR = total revenue / units sold	$20,000 revenue ÷ 100 rooms = $200 ADR
Occupancy rate	Percentage of units sold	Occupancy rate = (units sold / units available) × 100	(80 rooms ÷ 100) × 100 = 80% occupancy
Revenue per available unit (RevPAR)	Revenue earned per available unit (room, table, etc.)	RevPAR = ADR × occupancy rate	$200 ADR × 80% occupancy = $160 RevPAR
Gross operating profit per available unit (GOPPAR)	Measures profitability per unit	GOPPAR = gross operating profit / units available	$16,000 profit ÷ 100 rooms = $160 GOPPAR

Theoretical foundations of revenue management

Revenue management is built on business and economic theories that help hospitality leaders optimize pricing, manage inventory, and stay competitive. Together, these theories guide revenue strategies across hospitality. Whether setting the ideal price for a sold-out concert, adjusting spa offerings based on seasonal demand, or optimizing VIP lounge pricing, these frameworks ensure businesses make data-driven decisions that balance guest satisfaction with profitability.

Yield management theory

First used in the airline industry by Kimes (1989), this focused on adjusting prices based on demand, time before departure, and seat availability. Today, this approach shapes pricing in theme parks, event venues, and resorts, where admission fluctuates based on season, special events, and last-minute demand. A theme park, for example, may raise prices for fast-track passes on high-traffic days while discounting off-peak tickets.

Resource-based view

Resource-based view (Barney, 1991) highlights how businesses can command premium pricing by leveraging exclusive assets. In hospitality, scarcity creates value, whether it's a luxury cruise offering private island access, a high-end spa providing one-on-one consultations with renowned wellness experts, or a stadium reserving VIP skyboxes with gourmet dining. These unique experiences drive revenue by offering something guests can't get elsewhere.

Game theory

Game theory (Von Neumann and Morgenstern, 1944/2021) helps businesses anticipate competitor pricing moves and adjust their own strategies accordingly. For instance, if a rival tour company discounts last-minute bookings, a competitor might counter with bundled deals, such as a free meal or behind-the-scenes access, to add value without cutting profits. From adventure parks to ticketed festivals, businesses use this approach to stay competitive with strategic promotions, dynamic pricing, and bundled experiences.

Revenue optimization as a competitive advantage

Effective revenue management blends analytics with strategic decision-making. Hospitality businesses that leverage key revenue metrics, pricing models, and market insights can optimize financial performance while enhancing guest experiences.

Revenue optimization ensures that businesses can adjust pricing based on demand, maintain financial stability, and reinvest in guest-focused improvements. However, with increased revenue comes the responsibility of protecting against financial risks, such as economic downturns, cybersecurity threats, and operational disruptions. In the next section, we will explore risk management, examining how businesses identify, assess, and mitigate financial and operational risks across various industry segments.

INTERACTIVE EXERCISE
Revenue management in action

You're the revenue manager at Sunset Bay Resort, a popular beachfront hotel with 300 rooms. It's spring break, and the hotel is busy—currently at 90 percent occupancy and an ADR of $180. A nearby competitor suddenly lowers their rate to $150, potentially drawing your guests away.

Using what you've learned about revenue management (setting the right price at the right time to maximize profit) and yield management theory (adjusting prices based on demand), decide your next steps:

1 **Understand your position**: With your hotel nearly full, how might lowering your price affect your revenue or brand?

2 **Evaluate your options**:
   a Lower your rate to $155 to match the competition.
   b Keep your rate at $180 but include a $25 dining credit.
   c Keep your current pricing and highlight your premium amenities and superior guest experience through marketing.

3. **Make your decision**: Choose one option and explain why this choice helps your resort remain profitable and appealing to guests.

4. **Measure success**: List two specific metrics (such as occupancy rate, guest satisfaction, ADR) you would track to know if your strategy is working.

Reflect

Think of a time you chose a hotel or service because of pricing or a special promotion.

- How did this impact your perception of quality and value?
- How can hospitality businesses balance competitive prices with maintaining a high-quality image?

Risk management and compliance: Safeguarding hospitality's reputation and operations

Again, imagine you're the operations manager of a luxury resort. A guest slips and falls near the pool. Within minutes, your team responds with care and professionalism. The guest is helped, an incident report is filed, and the area is secured with extra signage, all without disrupting other guests' experiences. The quick response is the result of meticulous planning in emergency protocols, employee training, and regular safety audits. This is risk management in action: quietly protecting guests, employees, and your business's reputation.

In hospitality, where every experience involves human interaction, technology, food service, and facilities, risk management and compliance are not just policies—they're promises; promises to ensure safety, protect against legal issues, and maintain trust while supporting profitability.

What is risk management in hospitality?

Risk management in hospitality and tourism is the proactive process of identifying, assessing, and mitigating risks that could harm guests, employees, or overall business operations. Think of it as packing an emergency kit before a road trip—you hope you'll never need it, but you're prepared just in case.

Risks in hospitality and tourism can vary widely, from slip-and-fall incidents in hotels and food-borne illnesses in restaurants, to cybersecurity breaches and natural disasters impacting tourist destinations. Without proactive risk management, businesses risk legal actions, financial losses, operational disruptions, and severe damage to their reputation.

Effective risk management does more than simply prevent incidents—it actively builds trust, enhances guest experiences, and strengthens brand reputation. For instance, according to the International Association of Amusement Parks and Attractions (IAAPA, n.d.), the odds of experiencing a serious injury on a permanent amusement park ride in the US are approximately 1 in 15.5 million rides. This exceptional safety record results directly from rigorous safety protocols, routine inspections, thorough staff training, and clear emergency response plans. By maintaining these high standards, hospitality and tourism businesses reduce incidents, boost guest confidence, minimize liability costs, and support uninterrupted operations—forming the foundation for long-term success and resilience.

Theoretical framework: Enterprise risk management

Enterprise risk management (ERM) is a strategic approach that integrates risk assessment into business decision-making. It helps organizations identify, analyze, and mitigate risks across all operational areas, ensuring long-term sustainability. As an example, a large convention center implements ERM by analyzing risks in event safety, cyber threats, and food handling. By proactively addressing these concerns, it enhances visitor trust and avoids financial losses from potential lawsuits.

Risks and mitigation strategies

Hospitality businesses face a range of risks, including guest safety incidents, cybersecurity threats, operational disruptions, and reputational damage. A proactive risk management strategy ensures businesses prevent legal liabilities and financial losses.

Effective risk management in hospitality requires a proactive approach to guest safety, food hygiene, cybersecurity, and labor compliance. By implementing preventive measures and training staff, businesses can minimize risks and create a secure and trustworthy environment for guests and employees alike.

Guest safety and security

These measures are essential for protecting guests and ensuring a safe environment. Hospitality businesses can reduce security risks by installing surveillance systems, using secure access controls, and maintaining a visible on-site security presence 24/7. Conducting regular emergency drills, such as fire, natural disaster, and medical incidents, helps staff respond swiftly to crises. Hilton Hotels, for example, improved guest security by implementing encrypted room keys, CCTV monitoring, and mobile security alerts, leading to a reduction in security incidents (Hilton Hotels & Resorts, 2024). Similarly, amusement parks and large event venues invest in crowd control strategies, ensuring guest safety through well-placed security checkpoints, emergency exits, and surveillance monitoring.

Food safety and hygiene

Food hygiene protocols play a critical role in preventing food-borne illnesses and maintaining health standards. Following Hazard Analysis and Critical Control Points protocols ensures that food safety risks are identified and managed effectively. Regular staff training in proper food handling and sanitation practices, along with frequent kitchen and equipment inspections, further strengthens food safety efforts. Marriott International has implemented a digital food safety system that monitors kitchen temperatures and ensures hygiene compliance across its restaurants. Similarly, cruise lines with large-scale dining operations use automated tracking systems to monitor food storage temperatures and prevent cross-contamination.

Cybersecurity and data protection

Cybersecurity has become increasingly important as hospitality businesses increasingly handle sensitive guest information. Encrypted payment systems protect financial transactions, while staff training on phishing awareness reduces the risk of cyberattacks targeting employee credentials. Implementing multifactor authentication strengthens internal system security, minimizing vulnerabilities. In late 2015, Hyatt identified and dealt with malware on its payment processing systems, affecting customer payment card data at multiple properties (Hyatt Hotels, 2015). Casinos and theme parks, which process thousands of guest transactions daily, have also increased security by incorporating biometric authentication and fraud detection systems to prevent identity theft and data breaches.

Employee safety and labor compliance

These are key to maintaining a fair and safe work environment. Adhering to OSHA standards helps prevent workplace injuries, while mandatory harassment prevention training fosters a culture of respect. Fair scheduling practices, including compliance with overtime and break regulations, contribute to employee well-being and retention. Accor Hotels introduced a comprehensive anti-harassment policy with extensive staff training, which has led to improved employee satisfaction and compliance scores (Accor, 2020). Similarly, convention centers and stadiums with large event staff implement ergonomic assessments to reduce workplace injuries and provide structured scheduling policies to prevent employee burnout. By implementing such risk mitigation strategies, hospitality businesses across all sectors, including hotels, restaurants, event venues, cruise lines, and casinos, can protect their guests, employees, and reputation while ensuring long-term operational success.

Risk management is only effective when tracked through key performance indicators (KPIs). Hotels measure incident frequency rates, restaurants monitor compliance audit scores, and venues track response times to security alerts. These data points help improve safety protocols and enhance guest confidence.

Managing risk extends beyond safety and security—it also protects operations from disruption. From vendor delays to inventory shortages, the next section on supply chain and procurement management will explore how effective sourcing and logistics strategies keep hospitality businesses running smoothly.

THINK LIKE A MANAGER

A restaurant guest experiences a severe allergic reaction during dinner.

1 **Immediate action**: How do you ensure guest safety?

2 **Incident follow-up**: What should you document?

3 **Future prevention**: What quick actions will reduce future risks?

Reflect

Have you observed effective emergency handling in hospitality? What stood out?

Supply chain and procurement management: The backbone of hospitality operations

Picture this: You're enjoying breakfast at a luxury resort—freshly baked croissants, locally sourced honey, and organic coffee from a sustainable, fair-trade farm. What seems like a simple pleasure is the result of a carefully orchestrated supply chain, from sourcing ingredients to coordinating deliveries and managing inventory.

Supply chain and procurement management are the backbone of hospitality operations, ensuring that the right products arrive at the right place, at the right time, and at the right cost. Without them, even the best-planned guest experiences could fall flat.

Supply chain and procurement management: What's the difference?

In hospitality, supply chain and procurement management work together to ensure businesses have the right products and services at the right time, quality, and cost. Without a well-managed supply chain, hotels might run out of linens, restaurants could face ingredient shortages, and event venues might not receive critical equipment on time. These functions are essential for effective operations, cost efficiency, and guest satisfaction.

A simple way to think about this relationship is to compare it to running a restaurant kitchen. Procurement is like selecting the best ingredients—choosing suppliers, negotiating contracts, and making purchases. Supply chain management, on the other hand, ensures those ingredients make it from farm to table—overseeing transportation, inventory, and distribution. Both functions play a critical role: procurement ensures businesses source quality products at competitive prices, while supply chain management ensures those products are delivered efficiently and consistently.

Without strategic procurement and supply chain management, hospitality businesses risk delays, inflated costs, and service disruptions. A well-managed supply chain not only controls expenses; it supports sustainability initiatives, enhances brand reputation, and improves overall efficiency, making it a core function in successful hospitality operations.

Why supply chain and procurement matter in hospitality

Effective supply chain and procurement management are critical to ensuring seamless operations and exceptional guest experiences in the hospitality industry. A well-structured supply chain allows businesses to control costs, maintain quality standards, enhance efficiency, and support sustainability initiatives while mitigating risks.

One of the key advantages of strong supply chain management is *cost control*. By leveraging strategic sourcing and bulk purchasing, hospitality businesses can negotiate better pricing, reduce unnecessary expenses, and improve profit margins. Managing costs effectively ensures that businesses can reinvest in guest experiences, facility improvements, and employee development.

Equally important is *quality assurance*, as reliable suppliers ensure that hotels, restaurants, and entertainment venues receive high-quality products consistently. Whether sourcing luxury linens, fresh ingredients, or high-tech event equipment, strong vendor partnerships help maintain service standards that guests expect. Procurement teams carefully select suppliers based on factors including quality, reliability, and ethical sourcing to contribute to a positive and consistent brand experience.

Operational efficiency is another major benefit of a well-managed supply chain. Just-in-time delivery prevents inventory shortages and reduces waste by ensuring that supplies arrive exactly when needed. This approach is particularly important in food and beverage operations, where perishable ingredients must be managed carefully to minimize spoilage and maintain freshness. In the event industry, timely deliveries of lighting, décor, and audiovisual equipment ensure seamless event execution.

Sustainability has become an increasing priority across hospitality segments, making ethical sourcing and responsible procurement essential. Businesses that prioritize local partnerships and eco-friendly suppliers reduce transportation emissions and support sustainable practices. By integrating sustainability into supply chain decisions, such as using biodegradable packaging, sourcing organic produce, or selecting energy-efficient appliances, hospitality brands can appeal to environmentally conscious consumers and reduce their ecological footprint.

Beyond cost savings and efficiency, risk management plays a crucial role in supply chain operations. Supply chain disruptions, whether due to natural disasters, transportation delays, or vendor shortages, can significantly impact business operations. By diversifying suppliers, developing contingency plans, and implementing real-time tracking systems, businesses can mitigate these risks and maintain operational stability. Marriott International, for example, has developed a sourcing strategy that prioritizes local farmers for fresh produce. This initiative supports local economies and reduces transportation emissions, ensuring that the company upholds both sustainability and quality standards. By forming strong, reliable partnerships with suppliers, Marriott minimizes the risk of supply chain disruptions while maintaining its commitment to fresh, high-quality ingredients for its guests.

By mastering supply chain and procurement strategies, hospitality leaders can ensure their businesses remain competitive, resilient, and capable of delivering outstanding service. These functions are more than just logistical processes—they're the foundation for efficient, cost-effective, and sustainable hospitality operations.

Key concepts in supply chain and procurement management

Sourcing and vendor selection

Sourcing is the foundation of procurement, ensuring that businesses select suppliers who meet standards for quality, price, reliability, and sustainability. It's similar to choosing the right ingredients for a large-scale catering event—suppliers must be carefully vetted to ensure consistency, ethical practices, and cost efficiency.

Best practices in sourcing include establishing clear vendor evaluation criteria, which assess suppliers based on price, quality, reputation, and sustainability commitments. The request for proposal process allows businesses to compare multiple suppliers transparently, ensuring the best value for goods and services. Preferred supplier agreements help secure discounts, service guarantees, and long-term stability in procurement. For example, Compass Group, a global leader in food service management, has developed a supplier diversity initiative to source fresh produce, dairy, and other ingredients from local farmers and minority-owned businesses. This approach not only ensures quality and sustainability; it also strengthens community partnerships while reducing supply chain vulnerabilities.

Inventory management

Inventory management plays a crucial role in balancing supply and demand while minimizing waste. Whether managing linen stock at a luxury resort or perishable ingredients at a corporate cafeteria, businesses must track inventory efficiently to avoid shortages or excess stock.

A par stock system ensures that minimum inventory levels are maintained to meet operational demands. The FIFO method helps prevent waste, particularly in food service operations, by ensuring that older products are used first. Many hospitality businesses now use inventory tracking systems such as barcode scanning and real-time data analytics to monitor stock levels accurately and reduce the potential for human error. For instance, Sodexo, a global facilities and food services provider, utilizes cloud-based inventory systems across its dining operations to track ingredient usage and minimize food waste. This approach improves cost control, reduces environmental impact, and ensures that menu offerings remain fresh and high quality.

> **THINK LIKE A MANAGER**
>
> You are the general manager of a restaurant, and your profit margins are falling. Which cost control areas would you address first—labor, inventory, or marketing—and why?

Logistics and distribution management: Delivering on time, every time

Logistics and distribution management focus on getting supplies where they need to be on time and in peak condition. This involves coordinating transportation, warehousing, and last-mile deliveries to ensure uninterrupted service. Whether it's delivering uniforms to a stadium's concession staff or transporting high-end kitchen equipment to a cruise ship, logistics play a crucial role in supply chain success.

Centralized warehousing consolidates supplies in a single location to streamline distribution, reducing costs and improving efficiency. Many hospitality businesses partner with third-party logistics providers to manage transportation and warehousing, allowing them to focus on service delivery rather than supply chain operations.

Additionally, real-time tracking technologies, including GPS and IoT devices, provide businesses with live updates on shipments, improving reliability and reducing delays.

Sustainable procurement practices: Sourcing responsibly

Sustainable procurement is becoming an industry standard, as businesses recognize the importance of reducing environmental impact and supporting ethical sourcing. Hospitality organizations are increasingly prioritizing local, fair trade, and eco-friendly sourcing strategies to align with consumer demand and meet corporate social responsibility goals.

Local sourcing helps reduce carbon emissions associated with long-distance transportation while supporting regional economies. Many businesses also commit to fair trade products, ensuring that suppliers adhere to ethical labor and environmental standards. Eco-friendly packaging solutions, such as biodegradable containers and reusable service ware, further contribute to sustainability initiatives.

Measuring supply chain success

To determine if your supply chain is running efficiently, track the key metrics in Table 5.3.

As future leaders, your ability to manage these threads with care and precision will be the invisible art that shapes every guest experience. Whether responding to

Table 5.3 Typical supply chain KPI metrics

Key performance indicator	Definition	Example
Cost savings	Reduction in purchasing costs through better vendor management	A hotel saves 10% annually by switching to bulk sourcing.
Order accuracy rate	Percentage of orders delivered correctly and on time	A spa achieves a 98% order-accuracy rate by using barcode tracking.
Supplier lead time	Average time for suppliers to fulfill orders	A resort reduces lead times by 15% by using local vendors.
Inventory turnover	How quickly inventory is sold and replaced	A restaurant increases inventory turnover by 20% through just-in-time ordering.
Sustainability metrics	Percentage of local, organic, and/or eco-friendly products sourced	A cruise line achieves 80% eco-friendly product sourcing.

disruptions or adopting emerging technologies, mastering supply chain management will empower you to lead with efficiency, resilience, and purpose.

Effective supply chain management not only ensures operational efficiency; it also directly supports sustainability initiatives. Next, we'll explore how sustainability creates long-term value for hospitality and tourism businesses.

Sustainability and environmental management: Building a greener future

The greenest building is the one that is already built.

—US Green Building Council

Hospitality and tourism sustainability aligns closely with the United Nations Sustainable Development Goals (UN SDGs), a globally recognized framework aimed at promoting sustainable development through environmental stewardship, social responsibility, and economic viability (United Nations, 2015). By addressing all three pillars, hospitality and tourism businesses create balanced, sustainable, and resilient operations for the future.

Sustainability isn't just about the environment—it's about people, profit, and planet; a concept known as the triple bottom line (TBL) framework.

Theoretical framework integration: Triple bottom line

The TBL framework, developed by John Elkington in 1994, provides a comprehensive approach to evaluating business success beyond financial performance. This framework emphasizes three interconnected pillars: *people*, *profit*, and *planet*, ensuring that businesses operate sustainably and balance social, economic, and environmental responsibilities.

In the hospitality industry, the people aspect focuses on fair labor practices, ethical sourcing, and supporting local communities, such as partnering with regional farmers or ensuring suppliers adhere to fair trade standards. The profit component highlights cost-saving strategies through energy efficiency, responsible procurement, and waste reduction, which ultimately contribute to long-term financial stability. Finally, the planet pillar prioritizes environmental responsibility by, for example, reducing emissions, minimizing food and water waste, and incorporating sustainable materials and energy efficiency into operations. By adopting the TBL framework, hospitality businesses can enhance their sustainability efforts and have a positive social impact while maintaining profitability, ensuring a thriving future for both the industry and the communities it serves.

Why sustainability matters in hospitality

Sustainability in the hospitality industry is more than an environmental initiative—it is a strategic driver of business success. Implementing sustainable practices reduces operational costs, enhances brand reputation, and ensures long-term viability. According to Booking.com (2024), 83 percent of global travelers agree that sustainable travel is important to them.

The business case for sustainability in hospitality is compelling. Cost savings are achieved through energy-efficient systems, water conservation measures, and waste reduction strategies, directly impacting the bottom line. Embracing eco-friendly practices provides a competitive advantage, attracting the growing segment of eco-conscious visitors. This alignment with guest values fosters brand loyalty, as consumers increasingly support businesses that demonstrate environmental responsibility. Moreover, sustainable operations promote long-term viability by ensuring compliance with evolving environmental regulations and mitigating risks associated with resource scarcity. By integrating sustainability into their core strategies, hospitality businesses not only meet current market demands but also contribute to a more sustainable future, securing their position in an increasingly eco-aware industry.

Core areas of sustainability in hospitality operations

Sustainability in hospitality extends beyond environmental responsibility—it's a strategic approach that enhances efficiency, reduces costs, and meets growing consumer demand for eco-conscious services. From energy conservation to sustainable sourcing, businesses across the industry are implementing initiatives that benefit both the planet and their bottom line.

Energy efficiency: Reducing costs and carbon footprints

Energy is one of the greatest expenses in hospitality operations, making energy efficiency a crucial component of sustainability. Smart energy practices lower costs and reduce carbon footprints. Many hospitality businesses are adopting technologies such as motion sensors, smart thermostats, and LED lighting to optimize energy use. Renewable energy sources including solar panels, wind turbines, and geothermal heating provide long-term savings while decreasing reliance on fossil fuels. Additionally, green building design that incorporates features such as natural lighting and energy-efficient HVAC systems helps reduce overall consumption.

REAL-WORLD EXAMPLE:
INDUSTRY SPOTLIGHT Marina Bay Sands: Solar energy leadership

In 2017, Marina Bay Sands in Singapore installed a 145 kWp rooftop solar power system on its iconic Sands SkyPark, collaborating with sustainability partners Conergy and Asiatic Engineering. This high-profile installation, one of Singapore's most notable urban solar projects, comprises 536 solar panels spanning 880 square meters. Annually, the solar array generates approximately 187 MWh of energy, significantly reducing the resort's carbon footprint by around 70 tonnes of CO_2 per year (Asiatic Engineering, 2017; Conergy, 2017).

By integrating renewable energy solutions early into its operations, Marina Bay Sands has demonstrated industry-leading commitment to sustainability, showcasing how environmental initiatives can enhance both operational efficiency and long-term business success. The project shows how major hospitality businesses can successfully embed renewable energy into their infrastructure, benefiting the environment while maintaining profitability and guest experience (Marina Bay Sands Singapore, 2021).

Water conservation: Managing a critical resource

Hospitality businesses consume significant amounts of water, from guest showers to laundry services and landscaping. Efficient water management practices can lead to substantial cost savings while preserving a critical resource. Low-flow fixtures, including water-saving showerheads, toilets, and faucets, help reduce consumption without compromising guest experience. Greywater recycling systems repurpose wastewater for irrigation and other non-potable uses. Smart irrigation systems use sensors to adjust watering based on weather conditions, preventing waste and promoting sustainable landscaping.

Waste management: Reducing environmental impact

The hospitality industry generates substantial waste, from food scraps to packaging materials. Effective waste management strategies focus on reducing, reusing, and recycling. Food waste management programs, such as composting and donating excess food, help divert waste from landfills while supporting communities. Many businesses are eliminating single-use plastics in favor of biodegradable or reusable alternatives. Comprehensive recycling programs would ensure that paper, glass, and plastics are properly sorted and repurposed, further reducing environmental impact.

> **THINK LIKE A MANAGER**
>
> Your hotel's food waste is increasing, and guests are noticing. What sustainable initiatives would you implement to reduce waste without compromising service?

Sustainable sourcing: Promoting ethical and local supply chains

The way hospitality businesses source their products directly impacts the environment and local economies. Sustainable sourcing emphasizes responsible production, smaller carbon footprints, and more ethical labor practices. Many hospitality brands prioritize local and seasonal ingredients to minimize food miles and support regional farmers. The purchase of certified fair-trade products, such as coffee, tea, and linens, ensure ethical sourcing and better conditions for producers. Additionally, eco-friendly amenities, including biodegradable toiletries and sustainably produced linens, enhance sustainability efforts while aligning with guest expectations.

Achieving recognized sustainability certifications assists hospitality businesses in setting goals, measuring progress, and communicating their commitments to stakeholders. In the US, the LEED certification recognizes sustainable building design and energy efficiency. The Green Key Certification promotes eco-friendly practices within the hospitality industry.

REAL-WORLD EXAMPLE:
INDUSTRY SPOTLIGHT Compass Group: Sustainability in action

In its 2023 sustainability report, Compass Group, the world's largest food-service company, highlighted significant achievements in sustainability across its global operations. It successfully reduced its direct greenhouse gas emissions by 12 percent compared to its 2019 baseline. Additionally, the group introduced advanced food-waste-tracking technologies in approximately 8,000 locations worldwide and donated around 1.6 million meals to communities in need.

Compass demonstrated its financial commitment to sustainability by allocating £689 million in sustainable bond proceeds to support climate and environmental projects. These efforts align closely with nine of the UN SDGs, reflecting the company's ambitious goal to achieve net-zero emissions by 2050 through its Planet Promise initiative.

Furthermore, Compass emphasizes local sourcing strategies, promotes plant-based menu options, and prioritizes responsible procurement practices, significantly enhancing its environmental and community resilience (Compass Group, 2024).

Measuring and reporting sustainability performance

Sustainability is more than a business practice—it's a promise to future generations. Hospitality leaders make choices that will define their organization's success and its impact on the world. By championing sustainable operations, sourcing responsibly, and driving innovation, they create lasting value for the business, its guests, and the planet. Tracking KPIs ensures that sustainability efforts drive real results, as in the examples in Table 5.4.

> **Reflect**
>
> Why do you think tracking sustainability metrics (such as energy per occupied room) is essential for hospitality managers? How could these numbers guide decisions on future eco-friendly initiatives?

Sustainability goes beyond operations—it extends to the facilities that house them. From energy-efficient HVAC systems to smart building technologies, facilities management plays a vital role in sustainable guest-centric operations. Let's go on to explore how effective facilities and asset management keep hospitality businesses efficient, safe, and profitable.

Table 5.4 Typical sustainability KPIs

Key performance indicator	Definition	Example
Energy usage per occupied room	Measures improvements in energy efficiency	Smart thermostats reduce energy use by 15%
Water consumption per guest night	Tracks conservation efforts	Low-flow fixtures reduce water use by 20%
Waste diversion rate	Percentage of waste diverted from landfills	Event venues recycle 85% of concert waste
Carbon footprint per room night	Measures greenhouse gas emissions	Cruise lines reduce emissions by switching to cleaner fuels

Facilities and asset management: Preserving the foundations of hospitality

Imagine stepping into a luxury hotel lobby: polished marble floors gleam under soft lighting, lush greenery softens the space, and the temperature is perfectly controlled. Every element may seem effortless, yet behind this experience is an intricate system of maintenance, technology, and long-term asset planning.

Facilities and asset management is the backbone of operational excellence in hospitality, ensuring that physical structures, equipment, and essential services remain in peak condition. More than just fixing problems as they arise, this function is about prevention, preservation, and long-term investment.

Why facilities and asset management matter

From HVAC systems and elevators to commercial kitchens and digital security networks, well-executed facilities management ensures safety, efficiency, and cost-effectiveness. A single system failure, whether a malfunctioning refrigerator in a commercial kitchen or an elevator breakdown in a high-rise hotel, can disrupt operations, increase expenses, and impact guest satisfaction.

A well-executed facilities and asset management strategy extends the life of infrastructure, reduces operational costs, and enhances the guest experience. Hospitality businesses rely on this function to:

- **Ensure guest satisfaction**: Clean, well-maintained environments create positive experiences.
- **Increase operational efficiency**: Preventative maintenance minimizes downtime and costly emergency repairs.
- **Maintain safety and compliance**: Adhering to building codes and health regulations prevents legal risks.
- **Support sustainability goals**: Energy-efficient systems lower environmental impact and utility costs.
- **Protect asset value**: Proactive maintenance extends the lifespan of expensive equipment and infrastructure.

For example, Sodexo, a global leader in facilities management, oversees stadiums, healthcare facilities, and corporate buildings, ensuring that its properties remain energy-efficient, well-maintained, and compliant with industry regulations.

THINK LIKE A MANAGER

Your hotel is receiving complaints about slow elevator service. How would you identify the problem and improve the guest experience while controlling costs?

Key concepts in facilities and asset management

Facilities and asset management is not just about fixing problems—it is about long-term investment in infrastructure. A single system failure can disrupt operations, impact guest satisfaction, and cost thousands of dollars in emergency repairs, whereas strategic facilities management ensures the seamless operation of physical assets, from buildings to critical equipment.

Preventative maintenance: Stopping problems before they start

Preventative maintenance is a proactive approach that stops minor issues from escalating into major, costly repairs. Just as regular oil changes keep a car running smoothly, routine maintenance of critical systems helps hospitality businesses avoid downtime, reduce costs, and extend asset lifespans.

Hotels, resorts, restaurants, and event venues implement preventative maintenance across a variety of systems:

- **HVAC systems:** Regular inspections and cleanings improve efficiency, reducing energy waste and preventing system failures.
- **Plumbing infrastructure:** Detecting and fixing small leaks prevents water damage that could impact entire sections of a building.
- **Electrical systems:** Regular checks reduce fire hazards and ensure reliable power distribution.
- **Elevators and escalators:** Working with external providers ensures equipment is inspected and operates smoothly for guest safety.
- **Kitchen equipment:** Routine servicing prevents sudden breakdowns that could disrupt food service.

For example, a minor leak in a hotel's cooling system might seem insignificant at first. However, if left unresolved, it could lead to a full HVAC system failure, resulting in a $50,000 replacement fee. A scheduled inspection could have identified and resolved the issue for a fraction of the cost.

Asset tracking and life-cycle management: Maximizing investments

Hospitality businesses own and manage thousands of assets, from room furnishings and commercial kitchen appliances to security cameras and fitness center equipment. Effective asset tracking and life-cycle management help businesses optimize usage, extend asset longevity, and prevent unnecessary expenditures.

Asset tracking ensures hospitality businesses maintain equipment efficiently, reducing unnecessary replacements and improving budgeting. By monitoring asset lifespans, companies prevent downtime and optimize maintenance schedules.

Energy and resource management: A smart investment

Sustainability initiatives such as water conservation and waste reduction were covered earlier, but facilities management also plays a central role in energy efficiency. A strategic approach to energy management helps businesses cut costs, optimize operational resilience, and meet rising sustainability expectations from guests, investors, and regulators.

Optimizing energy and resource usage in hospitality facilities include:

- **Building automation systems:** Smart controls to regulate HVAC, lighting, and security systems for maximum efficiency.
- **Energy-efficient equipment:** Investing in low-energy appliances, LED lighting, and motion-sensor technology to significantly reduce power usage.
- **Heat recovery systems:** Capturing and reusing waste heat from kitchens, laundry operations, and industrial boilers to minimize overall energy demand.
- **Renewable energy integration:** Increasing investments in solar panels, wind turbines, and geothermal heating to supplement traditional energy sources.

For example, Compass Group has implemented energy-monitoring technology across multiple global sites, enhancing its ability to manage and reduce electricity consumption without impacting operational effectiveness (Compass Group, 2024).

THINK LIKE A MANAGER

You're the facilities director for a convention center with a limited budget. A recent audit highlights three issues:

1 Aging HVAC system, which runs inefficiently, raising energy costs by 20 percent.

2 Elevator malfunctions: Guests report occasional delays, but no major failures yet.

3 Roof leak in an infrequently used meeting room, but delay could cause costly damage.

You can only address one this quarter. Which do you prioritize, and why?

The role of facilities and asset management in long-term success

A well-managed facilities and asset strategy ensures that hospitality businesses operate efficiently, meet compliance requirements, and protect long-term investments. By proactively maintaining infrastructure, optimizing asset usage, and implementing energy-efficient solutions, hospitality leaders can reduce costs, improve guest satisfaction, and future-proof operations.

Measuring success in facilities and asset management

To ensure facilities and assets are maintained efficiently, businesses track KPIs that monitor cost, efficiency, and system longevity (Table 5.5).

Facilities and asset management is more than just maintenance and repairs—it's about strategic planning, technology integration, and sustainability. Facilities and asset management ensure business longevity, cost savings, and seamless operations.

Table 5.5 Tracking typical facilities and assets KPIs

Key performance indicator	Measurement goal
Work order completion time	Average time to resolve maintenance issues (e.g. target: 45 minutes)
Energy efficiency per occupied room	Measures energy use relative to occupancy (e.g. reduce use by 20%)
Water efficiency per guest night	Tracks water conservation success (e.g. reduce water use by 30%)
Asset utilization rate	Measures efficiency of asset use (e.g. track gym equipment usage for upgrades)

> **Key takeaways**
>
> - **Financial management**: Establishes financial stability through budgeting, cost control, and cash flow management, ensuring long-term business viability and reinvestment in guest experiences.
> - **Revenue and yield management**: Maximizes profitability by leveraging dynamic pricing, demand forecasting, and inventory optimization to align pricing strategies with market conditions.
> - **Risk management and compliance**: Mitigates financial, operational, and reputational risks through proactive safety measures, legal compliance, and emergency preparedness strategies.
> - **Supply chain and procurement management**: Ensures seamless operations by optimizing sourcing, vendor relationships, inventory control, and logistics while integrating sustainability into procurement strategies.
> - **Facilities and asset management**: Extends asset lifespan, reduces operational costs, and enhances efficiency through preventive maintenance, strategic energy management, and technology-driven asset tracking.

Looking ahead

This chapter has provided a foundational understanding of essential business functions within the hospitality industry. As we move on to the next chapter, on career exploration, you'll discover how these operational areas connect to potential career paths and opportunities in hospitality and tourism.

References

Accor (2020) *Accor Ethics and Corporate Social Responsibility Charter*. hera.accor.com/static/media/ACCOR_Ethics_and_Corporate_Social_Responsibility_Charter_20_ENG.f98ff6ec.pdf (archived at https://perma.cc/S3WA-GKX6)

Asiatic Engineering (2017) Asiatic constructs solar PV systems on Marina Bay Sands. asiaticgroup.com.sg/news-and-events/asiatic-march2017.html (archived at https://perma.cc/658P-5DNY)

Barney, J. (1991) Firm resources and sustained competitive advantage, *Journal of Management*, 17 (1), 99–120.

Booking.com (2024) *2024 Sustainable Travel Report*. gstc.org/booking-sustainable-travel-report-2024 (archived at https://perma.cc/N55G-DCLV)

Compass Group (2024) *Sustainability Report 2023*. compass-group.com/content/dam/compass-group/corporate/sustainability/updates-2024/cgplc_sustainability_report_2023.pdf (archived at https://perma.cc/E5K3-55UG)

Conergy (2017) Conergy brings solar power to Marina Bay Sands; reduces carbon footprint, Blueleaf Energy, September 25. blueleafenergy.com/press/conergy-brings-solar-power-to-marina-bay-sands-reduces-carbon-footprint (archived at https://perma.cc/HR4G-ZJTC)

Elkington, J. (1994) Towards the sustainable corporation: Win-win-win business strategies for sustainable development, *California Management Review*, 36, 90–100.

Hilton Hotels & Resorts (2024) *Hilton 2023 Annual Report*. stories-editor.hilton.com/wp-content/uploads/2024/04/Hilton2023AnnualReport.pdf (archived at https://perma.cc/CY6J-LYZX)

Hyatt Hotels (2015) Hyatt notifies customers of malware incident. newsroom.hyatt.com/news-releases?item=123450 (archived at https://perma.cc/758M-BLA2)

IAAPA (International Association of Amusement Parks and Attractions) (n.d.) *Ride Safety Report*. iaapa.org/safety/ride-safety-report (archived at https://perma.cc/DH6M-RPKR)

Kimes, S.E. (1989) Yield management: A tool for capacity—constrained service firms, *Journal of Operations Management*, 8 (4), 348–63.

Marina Bay Sands Singapore (2021) *Responsible Business Highlights 2021*. marinabaysands.com/sustainability/performance-highlights-2021.html (archived at https://perma.cc/X3MJ-27NA)

Marriott International (2024) *Annual Report 2023*. marriott.gcs-web.com/static-files/ac930e85-f477-4fa8-b873-bf4d2e09ca33 (archived at https://perma.cc/G4HP-TF77)

United Nations (2015) *Transforming Our World: The 2030 Agenda for Sustainable Development*. sdgs.un.org/2030agenda (archived at https://perma.cc/L6SN-6W2T)

Von Neumann, J. & Morgenstern, O. (1944) *Theory of Games and Economic Behavior*. 2021. Princeton, NJ: Princeton University Press.

Career exploration in hospitality and tourism 6

LEARNING OBJECTIVES

- Explore diverse career paths across hospitality and tourism sectors, including lodging, events, managed services, travel, entertainment, and emerging fields.
- Identify and explain key transferable skills gained through hospitality education and their relevance to careers within and beyond the industry.
- Examine professional development opportunities, such as certifications, internships, mentorships, and associations.
- Reflect on personal strengths and goals to develop a focused and actionable career exploration plan in hospitality and tourism.
- Articulate the role of networking in career development and create a professional elevator pitch for industry engagement.

Introduction: Envisioning your future in hospitality

Imagine yourself leading the guest experience team for a major league sports stadium during the championship finals. Picture orchestrating seamless hospitality, from VIP suites and player dining to engaging thousands of fans through innovative entertainment, interactive technology, and inclusive practices that ensure all guests feel welcome. Or perhaps you envision yourself coordinating sustainability initiatives for an international festival, crafting immersive experiences that connect diverse cultures while protecting the environment. Maybe your passion lies in promoting a cultural destination, where your strategic tourism marketing boosts economic development and helps preserve cherished heritage sites. Or your ambition could be launching an innovative travel app that transforms tourism, making travel more accessible, sustainable, and personalized.

These scenarios provide just a glimpse into the dynamic and rewarding career opportunities that await you in the hospitality and tourism industry—an industry projected to employ nearly 348 million people globally by the end of 2024, contributing approximately $11.1 trillion, or 10 percent of global GDP (WTTC, 2023b). For example, in the US, the travel industry directly employs 8 million people and supports nearly 15 million jobs, representing nearly a quarter of all employment nationwide (US Travel Association, 2023). Similarly, the UK's hospitality industry directly employs over 3.2 million individuals, making it the country's third-largest private-sector employer (UKHospitality, 2023).

Your exploration of hospitality careers directly builds upon the foundational skills you've gained in previous chapters. In Chapter 2, you discovered how human interaction, empathy, and emotional intelligence form the heart of every successful hospitality professional. As Goleman (1995) emphasized, emotional intelligence significantly predicts workplace success, particularly in fields driven by human relationships and guest interactions. Hospitality, inherently centered on people, is uniquely suited for individuals who excel at understanding and responding to human needs.

Chapter 3 highlighted cultural responsiveness, emphasizing the importance of creating welcoming spaces that resonate with global audiences. As hospitality businesses increasingly serve guests from around the world, professionals who understand and appreciate cultural differences stand out. Deloitte (2018) underscores that organizations fostering culturally aware leadership significantly enhance team performance, decision-making, and collaboration.

Building further, Chapters 4 and 5 introduced core business functions such as operational management, financial planning, revenue management, risk management, and sustainability. For instance, Marriott strategically utilizes operational efficiency and revenue management, achieving annual revenues exceeding $20 billion globally (Marriott International, 2023). These core business fundamentals prepare you for leadership roles in operations, strategy, or entrepreneurship within hospitality.

At its core, hospitality uniquely combines human connection, operational expertise, and global perspectives. Understanding guest needs, anticipating desires, and consistently exceeding expectations ensure that hospitality careers are not simply jobs—they're pathways toward personal growth, meaningful interactions, and impactful leadership. Career exploration matters because hospitality offers unparalleled opportunities for diverse experiences and meaningful contributions. Hospitality professionals positively impact lives daily through exceptional service, sustainable practices, innovation, and cultural exchange.

This chapter aims to ignite your curiosity by providing a view of career opportunities across key industry segments—such as lodging, events, managed services, cruising, club management, and other, emerging, fields. As you engage with professional insights, you'll understand how to pursue meaningful careers aligned with your personal values and professional aspirations. Your hospitality journey is full of opportunity, purpose, and the potential to make lasting, meaningful connections.

> **Reflect**
>
> As you begin your exploration, consider what excites you most about a career in hospitality and tourism. How do you envision making an impact through your work? Your hospitality career journey begins today—filled with possibility, purpose, and the potential for meaningful connections and lasting impact.

Building bridges: Transferable skills and cross-sector opportunities

Picture this: You're managing a busy dinner shift at a popular restaurant. A server calls in sick, a supplier is running late, and a guest has a last-minute allergy request. Despite the pressure, you stay calm, adjust the floor plan, communicate clearly with your team, and personally check in with the guest to ensure their needs are met. These moments might feel routine in hospitality, but they build a powerful toolkit of skills that can unlock doors far beyond the front of house.

Throughout earlier chapters, we explored the foundational skills that define great hospitality professionals. Now it's time to activate those skills; to apply them across different segments of hospitality and even into entirely new industries. Hospitality doesn't limit your path—it expands it.

The power of transferability

You may be wondering, "If I start my career in a hotel, am I locked into hotels forever?" Or, "If I study hospitality, am I limited to restaurants or resorts?" The answer is a resounding no, and that's the true power of hospitality: it builds skills that move with you. Hospitality is a dynamic industry where people regularly develop both business expertise and people-focused abilities. These two strengths together are incredibly valuable—not just in hotels or events, but in nearly every sector of today's economy.

Think of transferable skills as your professional toolkit. The more you build it, the more adaptable you become. You might begin in a front-of-house restaurant role, grow into a leadership position at a conference center, and eventually lead a guest experience team at a global tech firm or healthcare system. What connects each step is your ability to lead, adapt, solve problems, and connect with people from all walks of life.

This matters now more than ever. Today's employers want team members who can think strategically, manage operations, and respond with empathy. These are the very skills you've been developing throughout your hospitality education and experiences. By learning to recognize them, communicate them, and apply them in new settings, you gain flexibility, mobility, and long-term success.

Transferability across industries

Skills gained through hospitality and tourism education—such as communication, empathy, adaptability, cultural competence, and operations management—are highly valued across various sectors. These human-centered and service-oriented competencies help graduates in diverse roles in industries seeking flexibility, innovation, and interpersonal expertise.

In healthcare, for example, hospitality and tourism professionals often thrive in patient experience roles, hospital concierge services, and healthcare logistics. These positions draw on guest service competencies, such as empathy, responsiveness, and operational coordination (Huang et al., 2021).

In technology, customer success managers, user-experience support specialists, and onboarding coordinators appreciate professionals trained in hospitality and tourism who can quickly adapt and prioritize user needs—skills ingrained in these fields. In education, professionals in student services, alumni engagement, and international program support use their cultural responsiveness, event coordination, and community-building—all key strengths developed in hospitality and tourism education (Deloitte, 2018). In nonprofit and community organizations, roles in outreach, fundraising, and volunteer coordination require robust leadership, stakeholder engagement, and logistical planning, which are fundamental to hospitality and tourism management, especially within event and guest service contexts. In retail and consumer goods, hospitality and tourism professionals can excel in store management, brand experience strategy, or consumer engagement, applying their deep understanding of service delivery, team leadership, and operational planning. In digital platforms, such as travel apps or experience marketplaces, professionals from hospitality and tourism backgrounds are highly valued for their skills in personalizing service, managing user experiences, and swiftly adapting to evolving customer preferences.

CAREER SPOTLIGHT
Heather Buck, senior system director of food and nutrition services, OhioHealth

Heather Buck brings a distinctive combination of culinary innovation, operational leadership, and genuine hospitality to healthcare. With nearly 15 years in upscale restaurant leadership, she has developed deep expertise in delivering guest-centric dining experiences, building high-performing teams, and setting standards of culinary excellence.

Transitioning her extensive hospitality background into healthcare, Buck now strategically oversees food and nutrition operations across OhioHealth's extensive hospital system. Recognizing that hospital dining presents unique challenges and opportunities, she emphasizes:

> Patients in hospitals are often in vulnerable states. While some have the freedom to enjoy varied menu items and even desserts, others require strictly controlled diets, leaving no room for flexibility. Our responsibility is to deliver not just nutritional excellence but also personalized care that respects each patient's dietary needs and enhances their overall experience.

Under Buck's leadership, OhioHealth's dining services have undergone a transformative journey, evolving from ranking in the bottom 2 percent nationally in patient satisfaction scores to consistently achieving exceptional results. By implementing hospitality-driven service standards, focusing on operational excellence, and training teams to meet the nuanced needs of hospital dining, Buck and her team have significantly enhanced patient satisfaction and nutritional outcomes.

Reflecting on her transition from hospitality to healthcare, Buck emphasizes the critical role of operational agility and empathy, stating:

> Transitioning into healthcare dining presented distinct challenges, but also tremendous opportunities to positively influence patient well-being. Hospitality and empathy go hand-in-hand—this is especially true in healthcare, where a thoughtfully prepared meal can profoundly impact a patient's day and overall recovery experience.

Buck's leadership exemplifies the impactful transferability of hospitality expertise into healthcare environments, highlighting the growing recognition of hospitality professionals in advancing patient satisfaction, operational quality, and nutritional excellence in hospitals.

Transferability within hospitality

Transferable skills not only facilitate moves into other industries; they are essential for career growth within hospitality and tourism itself. The field's fluidity allows professionals to explore diverse segments, roles, and specialties, continually drawing on their existing expertise.

For example, a restaurant manager experienced in operations and guest service might transition smoothly into managing a stadium or large event venue, applying similar logistics at a broader scale. A hotel general manager could move into cruise operations or assume leadership in club management or managed services, utilizing familiar financial, human resources, and guest satisfaction strategies. Similarly, an event planner skilled in logistics and stakeholder communication could effectively shift into destination marketing, tourism development, or guest experience strategy for attractions and theme parks. These career transitions illustrate the versatility of hospitality and tourism professionals, highlighting opportunities to build upon foundational skills and expand across industry segments.

CAREER SPOTLIGHT

Zach Clapper, general manager of facility operations for Aramark Facilities Management at Red Rocks Park and Amphitheatre and the Denver Coliseum

Hospitality management alumnus Zach Clapper has built an impressive career marked by versatility and progressive leadership roles across hospitality, tourism, events, and entertainment. Currently serving as general manager of facility operations at Red Rocks Park and Amphitheatre and the Denver Coliseum, Clapper oversees operations, landscaping, maintenance, and security for these iconic Colorado venues. Previously, as director of operations, he successfully managed logistical complexities, facility enhancements, and guest experiences.

Clapper's diverse industry journey includes impactful roles at prestigious organizations such as Disney, where he was a guest experience manager at Animal Kingdom at Walt Disney World Resort, refining service standards at one of the world's most visited attractions. He also contributed to operational success and event planning at Columbus Zoo and Aquarium, Cedar Fair Entertainment Company (Cedar Point), and SeaWorld Parks and Entertainment.

He credits internships, experiential learning, and early-career roles as essential foundations for professional growth, emphasizing their significance in discovering career passions and developing industry expertise:

> Casting a wide net and obtaining diverse experience throughout all facets of the hospitality industry very early on is a great way to set yourself up for success later in your career. Exposure to different people, practices, and ideas can really open your eyes to opportunities in the future and allow you to take things from each role and use them to craft your own personal brand of leadership going forward.

Making the connection

Knowing your skills are transferable is the first step. The next is learning how to clearly communicate that value to others—in résumés, cover letters, interviews, and during networking conversations. Employers want to see how your experience solves *their* problems, in *their* language. When describing your skills:

- Adjust your terminology to suit the audience (for example "guests" may become "clients," "patients," or "users" depending on the context).
- Focus on outcomes. What improvements or impact did you create?
- Be specific. Tell stories that showcase adaptability, leadership, or results.

This kind of storytelling helps employers see your hospitality background not as a limitation, but as a strategic advantage.

> **INTERACTIVE EXERCISE**
> Map your transferable skills
>
> Take a few minutes to reflect on your recent academic, internship, or work experience in hospitality. Then walk through the following steps:
>
> 1. List three transferable skills you've developed.
> 2. Describe a specific situation where you applied each skill.
> 3. Identify at least one career field or industry where that skill would be valuable beyond hospitality.
> 4. Write a bridge statement that connects your hospitality experience to a role outside the industry.
>
> For example: "During my internship at a convention hotel, I led daily stand-up meetings to align the team, troubleshoot challenges, and improve service delivery. That experience taught me how to lead under pressure, communicate across departments, and manage real-time problem solving—skills I can bring to a project coordination role in healthcare or nonprofit management."

Your hospitality education doesn't just prepare you for one job; it prepares you for a resilient, adaptable, and fulfilling career. The interpersonal, analytical, and operational skills you've developed are assets in any setting. As seen in Chapters 2 and 3, these are the very capabilities that drive meaningful guest experiences, build inclusive teams, and ensure strong business outcomes.

Now you've learned how to activate those skills—how to name them, connect them to broader career goals, and present them confidently across industries or segments. Whether you choose to grow within hospitality or explore new pathways, your ability to lead with empathy, solve complex challenges, and deliver value makes you highly competitive in today's job market.

Let's explore how the skills and experiences you've developed can come to life across the many segments of hospitality and tourism. From lodging and events to managed services, recreation, and beyond, these pathways offer countless opportunities to apply your strengths, pursue your passions, and shape a career that's uniquely yours. Your journey is just beginning, and the skills you've built in hospitality will take you farther than you think.

Exploring the segments: Where will your career take you?

Hospitality and tourism offer a remarkable range of careers, each aligned with your passions, strengths, and ambitions. Whether you're drawn to guest-facing service, creative experiences, data analysis, or sustainability, there is a place for you in this industry.

This section introduces key industry segments and the diverse career opportunities they offer. As you read, consider how your personal strengths, experiences, and goals might align with these pathways, and how the transferable skills you've developed can be applied within and beyond each segment.

Lodging: More than just a place to stay

One of the most foundational sectors in the field, lodging plays a pivotal role in hospitality and tourism, creating environments where comfort, connection, and care can shape unforgettable guest experiences. Whether it's a boutique hotel in an iconic city or an eco-friendly resort on a secluded beach, lodging touches every aspect of hospitality, generating over $1.3 trillion annually worldwide (Statista, 2025).

Lodging as a hub for core business functions

As we discussed in Chapters 4 and 5, the lodging sector uniquely brings together every core business function within hospitality, such as operations, finance, marketing, human resources, procurement, sustainability, and risk management. Lodging professionals gain comprehensive experience by applying these foundational skills at both the property level (managing daily guest experiences) and above-property levels (developing corporate strategy and global initiatives). See Table 6.1.

Table 6.1 Career pathways snapshot: Lodging

Role	Impact you'll make
Hotel general manager	Lead overall hotel operations, guest service, team development, and strategy implementation.
Revenue management analyst	Optimize profitability through data-driven pricing strategies, market analysis, and forecasting to maximize hotel performance.
Director of operations	Oversee departments such as front office and housekeeping to enhance guest experiences.
Sales and marketing director	Develop marketing strategies, foster client relationships, and drive revenue growth.
Director of finance	Manage budgets, financial forecasts, cost control, and strategic financial planning.
Procurement manager	Source quality supplies sustainably and cost-effectively, supporting operational excellence.
Sustainability manager	Lead initiatives that benefit guests, communities, and the environment.
Director of security	Ensure comprehensive safety and security plans for guests, employees, and assets.
Chief engineer	Oversee facility maintenance and infrastructure, ensuring guest comfort and operational safety.

Many lodging professionals grow into above-property corporate or regional roles, influencing entire hotel brands and global strategies, including areas such as:

- brand strategy and development
- global revenue management
- learning and development
- sustainability and social responsibility.

In later chapters, we'll dive deeper into the lodging sector, exploring operations, marketing, sustainability, and more, to fully understand and prepare for these rewarding career paths.

Food and beverage: Beyond the menu

While lodging offers an immersive experience in operations, leadership, and guest engagement, food and beverage (F&B) careers offer their own unique rhythm—fueled by creativity, precision, and the joy of shared meals. Whether serving a gourmet dinner, leading a stadium's concessions program, or curating luxury dining on a cruise ship, F&B professionals shape how people gather, celebrate, and connect. Let's explore what this flavorful, fast-paced segment has to offer.

Food and beverage is an essential, vibrant segment within hospitality and tourism. Globally, foodservice generates trillions annually, and the US restaurant industry alone was projected to surpass $997 billion in 2023 (National Restaurant Association, 2023). Yet, the heart of F&B is far richer than its revenue—it's about crafting memorable experiences, bringing people together, and infusing daily moments with connection, creativity, and joy.

Where creativity meets operational excellence

Food and beverage seamlessly integrates core hospitality functions such as operations, finance, procurement, marketing, and sustainability. Professionals in this segment balance artistic expression with precise management of resources, delivering unforgettable guest experiences even in fast-paced, high-volume settings (Table 6.2).

Food and beverage is where hospitality's emotional intelligence, creativity, and operational skills converge. It's your opportunity to lead, innovate, and leave lasting impressions, one meal, event, or concept at a time.

Table 6.2 Career pathways snapshot: Food and beverage

Role	Impact you'll make
Executive chef	Lead culinary innovation, menu creation, and kitchen operations excellence.
Restaurant manager	Direct service operations, manage teams, budgets, and deliver exceptional guest dining.
Beverage director/ sommelier	Curate beverage programs that enhance guest experiences through creativity and storytelling.
Catering and banquet manager	Plan and execute memorable events, managing logistics, staffing, and guest satisfaction.
Food and beverage director	Oversee multi-outlet operations, maintain quality standards, and optimize profitability.
Pastry chef	Design and produce innovative desserts with precision and creativity.
Sustainability manager	Develop and implement environmentally sustainable practices within food and beverage operations.
Director of security	Safeguard guests, staff, and facilities through rigorous safety and security protocols.
F&B consultant/ entrepreneur	Advise or launch restaurant concepts and culinary ventures, applying operational expertise.

> **IMAGINE YOUR IMPACT**
>
> Picture yourself...
>
> - Launching a sustainable restaurant concept that redefines local dining
> - Managing the culinary experience at a prestigious international event
> - Leading beverage innovation for a global resort brand
>
> As you continue this textbook journey, future chapters will provide a deeper exploration of F&B, including restaurant operations, culinary innovations, beverage management, and the latest trends shaping this dynamic segment.

Managed services: Diverse opportunities, endless impact

While F&B blends creativity and operational expertise, managed services extend hospitality principles beyond traditional boundaries, delivering excellence across diverse environments, from corporate offices and stadiums to healthcare and education.

Managed services providers, including Sodexo, Compass Group, and Aramark, for example, bring hospitality excellence into specialized settings such as hospitals, universities, sports arenas, and corporate campuses. Valued at approximately $299 billion globally in 2023—and projected to reach $731 billion by 2030 (Grand View Research, 2023)—this sector offers significant growth opportunities for hospitality professionals.

In this field, you'll blend hospitality fundamentals with specialized skills in facilities management, operations, nutrition, event planning, and customer experience. Your hospitality expertise—such as communication, empathy, and responsiveness—becomes essential in creating positive experiences beyond traditional settings.

Managed services demonstrate hospitality's versatility. Professionals in this area directly enhance daily experiences in healthcare, education, corporate workplaces, and events, transforming routine interactions into meaningful moments. If you're driven by variety, specialized roles, and opportunities to apply your skills in innovative environments, managed services offer a rewarding career path (Table 6.3).

Table 6.3 Career pathways snapshot: Managed services

Role	Impact you'll make
General manager (managed services)	Lead service excellence across diverse sectors like healthcare, corporate, and education settings.
Food and nutrition services director	Manage nutritional operations, quality standards, and guest satisfaction.

(continued)

Table 6.3 (Continued)

Role	Impact you'll make
Facilities manager	Oversee building management, safety compliance, and operational efficiency.
Sustainability manager	Develop sustainable service practices across managed environments.
Client relationship manager	Build strategic partnerships, ensuring client satisfaction and retention.
Event and catering director	Coordinate specialized events within managed environments like stadiums and corporate facilities.
Human resources manager	Lead recruitment, training, employee engagement, compliance, and organizational culture initiatives.
Social media and communications manager	Manage digital content strategy, social media engagement, brand reputation, and internal/external communications.
Finance and operations manager	Oversee financial management, strategic budgeting, procurement, forecasting, and operational efficiency.
Technology solutions manager	Lead integration of innovative technology to streamline operations, enhance guest experiences, and improve service delivery.

CAREER SPOTLIGHT
Hannah Pierce, sales coordinator, Lucas Oil Stadium

Hannah Pierce exemplifies proactive leadership and professional engagement as a graduate who strategically pursued leadership opportunities and industry experiences throughout college. By managing student-led events and serving in roles such as operations manager for signature program events, she developed transferable skills in event management, strategic communication, and collaborative teamwork. Her dedication demonstrates that leadership is not defined by title but by actively seeking opportunities to contribute, collaborate, and excel, ultimately setting herself apart professionally post-graduation:

> Prioritizing empathy and humility while pursuing new opportunities and learning from leaders who are willing to share their knowledge with the next generation during my time in college helped set the groundwork and prepared me for continued success throughout my career. Systems and operations can be learned with time, but the ability to lead and work well with others while remaining open to growth and development will set you apart and allow you to thrive in any position, company, or industry.

Events: Creating unforgettable moments

Just as managed services extend hospitality into diverse environments, the events segment showcases the industry's unique ability to turn creativity and organizational skills into powerful, memorable experiences. Whether it's coordinating international conferences, festive celebrations, elegant weddings, or strategic corporate gatherings, event professionals unite people through shared moments, emotion, and connection.

The global events industry is thriving—projected to reach approximately $2.05 trillion by 2032 (Allied Market Research, 2023). Professionals in this segment bring people together through meticulously planned corporate meetings, vibrant festivals, personal celebrations, and milestone events. If you enjoy coordinating complex logistics, designing creative experiences, and building meaningful connections, the events sector offers countless opportunities.

Where creativity meets operational excellence

Events careers uniquely combine creativity, strategic thinking, and detail-oriented planning. You'll rely on operational skills such as logistics coordination, risk management, budgeting, and stakeholder communication, transforming visions into reality and creating lasting memories for diverse audiences (Table 6.4).

Table 6.4 Career pathways snapshot: Events

Role	Impact you'll make
Entrepreneur/CEO	Launch and lead innovative event-focused businesses, driving strategy and guest experiences.
Corporate event planner	Coordinate high-profile meetings, conferences, and product launches, managing logistics and vendor partnerships.
Wedding and special events planner	Coordinate high-profile meetings, managing logistics and partnerships.
Venue events manager	Manage venue bookings, event logistics, and operational coordination.
Destination events manager	Develop events enhancing tourism, cultural exchange, and economic growth.
Nonprofit and fundraising event coordinator	Organize impactful events, build donor relationships, and manage strategic fundraising initiatives.
Experiential marketing specialist	Design immersive brand experiences, connecting businesses to audiences creatively.
Convention center manager	Coordinate large-scale conventions, trade shows, exhibitors, and facility logistics.
Virtual and hybrid events coordinator	Manage digital and blended events, ensuring seamless technology integration.
Festival and entertainment event manager	Plan and execute festivals and entertainment events, overseeing talent, safety, and production.

Events professionals have the unique opportunity to craft meaningful, memorable experiences—moments that resonate long after the event concludes. Whether you're managing large-scale festivals or intimate celebrations, an ability to blend creativity with meticulous planning will leave lasting impressions and build stronger communities.

> **CAREER SPOTLIGHT**
> Lucretia Williams, president and CEO, Distinct Event Planning
>
> Lucretia Williams is a dynamic entrepreneur who turned her passion for hospitality into a powerful brand. As the founder and CEO of Distinct Event Planning, she leads a boutique firm known for executing culturally inclusive, high-impact events for corporate and nonprofit clients. With a strong foundation in relationship-building and a commitment to excellence, Williams has built a reputation for transforming visions into memorable guest experiences. Her journey reflects the heart of modern hospitality entrepreneurship—blending creativity, strategic growth, and community-centered values. Her story shows that, with vision, resilience, and genuine service, entrepreneurs can create lasting impact in the hospitality industry:
>
> > In hospitality entrepreneurship, your brand is only as strong as the relationships you build. Lead with integrity, serve with heart, and stay consistent—because repeat business is built on trust, not trends.

Recreation and entertainment: Making fun a profession

Just as events create powerful shared experiences, the recreation and entertainment segment offers careers centered around joy, wonder, and engagement. From theme parks and sports arenas to cruising, casinos, and museums, this exciting segment brings hospitality to life through storytelling, creativity, and immersive experiences.

In 2023, the US amusement and theme park industry generated approximately $28.4 billion (Statista, 2023, 2024). Meanwhile, Tokyo Disneyland attracted 15.1 million visitors, ranking fourth worldwide, while Tokyo DisneySea welcomed 12.4 million guests, placing seventh. In Europe, Disneyland Paris drew about 9.9 million visitors, underscoring the industry's international appeal and career opportunities (TEA/AECOM, 2024).

Recreation and entertainment uniquely blend hospitality fundamentals—guest service, operations management, and safety awareness—with creativity and story-telling. If you're drawn to high-energy environments where each day is unique, this segment offers abundant career possibilities (Table 6.5).

Table 6.5 Career pathways snapshot: Recreation and entertainment

Role	Impact you'll make
Guest experience manager	Monitor and enhance guest satisfaction, implement feedback-driven improvements, and lead service-excellence initiatives.
Theme park operations manager	Manage daily operations, guest experiences, safety, staffing, and ride maintenance to ensure visitor enjoyment.
Casino operations manager	Oversee gaming operations, hospitality services, regulatory compliance, entertainment offerings, and risk management.
Museum director	Curate engaging exhibits, manage daily operations, foster community relationships, and lead educational initiatives to enhance cultural relevance.
Sports venue guest experience manager	Coordinate guest services at sporting events, managing ticketing, crowd flow, concessions, VIP experiences, accessibility, and safety protocols.
Theater operations director	Lead venue operations for performing arts, oversee production schedules, audience engagement, ticketing, venue maintenance, and community outreach.
Zoo and aquarium hospitality manager	Direct visitor services, events, educational programs, vendor partnerships, sustainability practices, and operational safety in zoological or marine facilities.
IT and technology manager	Lead technology integration, digital guest experiences, and operational tech support, ensuring seamless, secure, and innovative visitor engagement.
Social media and digital marketing manager	Manage digital platforms, content creation, influencer partnerships, and social media engagement to build excitement and visitor loyalty.
Human resources manager	Oversee staffing, employee engagement, training, workplace culture, and compliance to ensure positive staff experiences and exceptional guest service.
Finance and revenue manager	Direct budgeting, forecasting, ticket pricing, revenue management, and financial planning to ensure sustainable growth and operational efficiency.

This segment allows you to shape experiences that inspire, educate, and delight. Recreation and entertainment careers uniquely combine creativity, operational skill, and guest-focused storytelling to positively impact lives and communities.

Club management: Building community through personalized experiences

Just as recreation and entertainment venues engage guests through immersive experiences, the club management segment excels at fostering meaningful relationships, personalized service, and exclusive community connections.

Club management offers a distinctive hospitality experience in, for example, golf, yacht, athletic, and social clubs, combining exclusivity, personalized service, and community-building. In the US, the private club industry alone generates approximately $32.6 billion annually (CMAA, 2023). Globally, the Club Managers Association of Europe unifies 13 national associations and represents over 4,000 members across 40 countries, spanning Europe, the Middle East, and North Africa (CMAE, 2024). These figures illustrate club management's strong presence and professionalization across multiple international markets.

Professionals in club management leverage hospitality expertise—relationship building, personalized service, and operational excellence—to cultivate environments where members feel welcomed, connected, and deeply valued, wherever they are in the world (Table 6.6).

Table 6.6 Career pathways snapshot: Club management

Role	Impact you'll make
General manager (country or golf club)	Lead overall club operations, hospitality services, financial management, staff development, member engagement, and strategic planning.
Membership director	Manage member recruitment and retention, marketing strategies, personalized services, and events to foster an engaged membership community.
Athletic director	Coordinate fitness programs, manage facilities, promote wellness initiatives, and enhance member experiences through dynamic programming.
Yacht club operations manager	Oversee marina services, amenities, sailing events, waterfront dining, safety protocols, and operational excellence for boating enthusiasts.
Social club manager	Lead upscale urban or private clubs, managing dining experiences, member events, entertainment programming, and community-building.
Finance and operations director	Direct budgeting, capital investments, procurement, financial forecasting, and strategic operations for long-term sustainability.

(continued)

Table 6.6 (Continued)

Role	Impact you'll make
Events and catering director	Oversee event planning, catering, weddings, and private events, enhancing club revenue and guest satisfaction.
Director of food and beverage	Manage culinary operations, dining services, menu design, and beverage management, integral to a club's member experience.
Facilities and grounds manager	Ensure the maintenance, aesthetics, safety, and sustainability of club buildings, grounds, golf courses, or recreational facilities.

Club management uniquely prioritizes personalized hospitality, relationship-driven service, and community engagement. It provides meaningful opportunities to directly impact members' experiences, build lasting relationships, and lead within prestigious environments.

Cruising: Hospitality on the high seas

Just as club management emphasizes tailored experiences and community connections, the cruise industry takes personalized hospitality to the open seas, combining travel, entertainment, and cultural exploration into unforgettable voyages.

Cruising uniquely integrates all major segments of hospitality—lodging, food and beverage, events, recreation, entertainment, and supply chain—into one dynamic experience. This $155 billion global industry supports nearly 1.2 million jobs worldwide (CLIA, 2023), offering exciting opportunities to professionals who thrive in vibrant, fast-paced environments. Whether managing onboard guest experiences, orchestrating memorable dining, coordinating shore excursions, or leading sustainability initiatives, cruising provides a distinct setting to leverage your hospitality skills (Table 6.7).

Cruising offers professionals the unique ability to blend hospitality expertise with global travel, cultural engagement, and operational innovation. If you envision yourself leading dynamic teams aboard luxury ships, exploring international destinations, or shaping unforgettable guest memories, cruising is an exceptional segment to explore.

Table 6.7   Career pathways snapshot: Cruising

Role	Impact you'll make
Cruise director	Manage onboard entertainment, activities, and guest experiences.
Food and beverage director	Oversee culinary operations, dining experiences, and team leadership onboard.
Chief sustainability officer	Lead company-wide sustainability initiatives, environmental strategies, and social responsibility programs across operations.
Talent development and training manager	Design and implement training programs, professional development pathways, and foster inclusive, engaged workplace cultures.
Shore excursions manager	Coordinate memorable and enriching guest excursions at ports.
Entertainment director	Develop and manage diverse onboard entertainment offerings.
Director of security	Ensure passenger safety through rigorous onboard and port security protocols.
Revenue and sales director	Develop strategic sales initiatives to maximize profitability across the fleet.
Engineering and maintenance director	Oversee technical vessel operations, maintenance, and efficiency.

Travel and tourism: Gateway to global exploration

Stepping off the cruise ship onto shore brings us into the broader world of travel and tourism, a sector that invites professionals to create inspiring journeys, foster global connections, and design innovative experiences for travelers everywhere. Just as cruising combines hospitality with exploration at sea, travel and tourism careers blend guest service with adventure, cultural immersion, and sustainable innovation on a global scale.

Travel and tourism careers empower hospitality professionals to create meaningful journeys and connect global communities. With a global economic impact of nearly $9.9 trillion annually (WTTC, 2023a), this sector relies on innovative professionals skilled at combining guest service, cultural responsiveness, and strategic operations. Whether promoting destinations, crafting adventure itineraries, or pioneering travel technology, professionals in this field have the power to shape how people explore the world.

Travel and tourism careers enable hospitality professionals to make a global impact through cultural exchange, sustainable development, and personalized guest experiences. Professionals in this sector not only influence how travelers see the world—they actively shape the future of travel by prioritizing innovation, sustainability, and meaningful human connections (Table 6.8).

Supply chain and vendors: Powering hospitality's engine

Behind every memorable travel experience lies a hidden world of logistics, coordination, and strategic partnerships. From managing global procurement for hotel amenities to ensuring timely delivery of fresh ingredients for cruise dining, the supply chain and vendor management segment powers the hospitality engine. Let's move behind the scenes to discover how careers in supply chain and vendor management enable excellence across all areas of hospitality and tourism.

Exceptional hospitality experiences rely on the strength of their supply chains. Whether it's sourcing high-quality ingredients for a fine dining establishment, procuring eco-friendly products for sustainable resorts, or managing advanced technology platforms for global hotel brands, supply chain and vendor professionals directly influence operational success, sustainability efforts, and guest satisfaction.

Supply chain management and vendor relations drive every hospitality segment, from sourcing ingredients for fine dining, procuring sustainable amenities for hotels, managing logistics for events, to ensuring seamless operations for cruise lines and resorts. Professionals skilled in strategic sourcing, negotiation, financial oversight, and operational efficiency are essential in powering exceptional guest experiences behind the scenes (Table 6.9).

Table 6.8 Career pathways snapshot: Travel and tourism

Role	Impact you'll make
Destination marketing director	Promote global destinations, attracting visitors and supporting communities.
Adventure tourism operator	Design sustainable, immersive outdoor travel experiences.
Travel technology entrepreneur	Innovate digital platforms and tools that enhance guest travel experiences.
Tour operations director	Oversee complex travel logistics, ensuring seamless global tours.
Destination experience manager	Create authentic visitor experiences supporting cultural engagement and local communities.
Corporate travel manager	Manage corporate travel logistics, balancing quality, compliance, and cost-efficiency.
Sustainable tourism coordinator	Drive sustainability initiatives, supporting environmental conservation and local economies.

Table 6.9 Career pathways snapshot: Supply chain and vendors

Role	Impact you'll make
Supply chain director	Oversee sourcing, logistics, vendor management, and product quality.
Sustainability solutions manager	Develop, implement, and maintain eco-friendly supply chain practices.
Technology solutions manager	Integrate innovative tech solutions to enhance operations efficiency.
Procurement manager	Lead strategic purchasing processes, ensuring cost and quality efficiency.
Vendor relations manager	Build and sustain effective supplier relationships and partnerships.
Security and compliance manager	Ensure rigorous safety, security, and compliance standards across supply chain activities.
Finance and procurement manager	Direct financial management and strategic resource allocation within the supply chain.
Engineering and maintenance director	Manage infrastructure reliability, compliance, and energy efficiency.

Professionals in supply chain and vendor management don't just enable great hospitality experiences—they actively shape the future of the industry. This career path offers an opportunity to drive innovation, champion sustainability, and strategically influence how hospitality organizations operate at every level. Your decisions directly enhance the guest experience, improve operational outcomes, and support long-term growth.

Gaining real-world experience: Internships, employment, and practical learning

You've now explored diverse hospitality segments, each offering unique opportunities aligned with your strengths, skills, and passions. But how do you turn these career aspirations into reality? The next step is actively investing in your professional growth.

In this section, you'll learn how certifications, internships, mentorship programs, and industry engagement can sharpen your skills, build your credibility, and accelerate your journey from student to successful hospitality professional.

Your journey from classroom theory to real-world practice is vital to a successful hospitality career. Internships, part-time jobs, and industry roles offer unmatched opportunities to apply what you've learned, develop essential skills, and build meaningful professional relationships. Think of each role—from serving guests at a restaurant to assisting at a hotel front desk—as a stepping stone on your professional journey. These experiences provide practical insights, strengthen your résumé, and significantly boost your career readiness upon graduation.

Internships: Opening doors to professional opportunities

Internships immerse you in real-world industry settings, providing specialized training and firsthand exposure to potential career paths. Consider the leading hospitality internship programs included in Table 6.10.

Remember: Structured internships will not only develop your professional skills but also help you discover your passions and strengths within hospitality.

Table 6.10 Internship examples

Role	Experience you'll gain
Marriott International	Voyage program: Structured leadership training and mentorship across hotel operations.
Hilton	Early talent programs: Diverse internships in operations, finance, culinary, and sales.
Disney	Disney College program: Immersive internships building foundational skills and global connections.
Delta Air Lines	Internships emphasizing aviation hospitality, customer experience, and operations management.
MGM Resorts	College programs: Practical experience in guest services, hotel operations, and internal management.
Sodexo	Internships, co-ops, and apprenticeships in culinary arts, hospitality, and managed services.
Yum! Brands	Leadership internships in restaurant operations, finance, marketing, and sustainability.
Royal Caribbean	Summer internship: Ten-week immersive experience in hospitality operations, marketing, and entertainment at sea.
NetJets	Internships in luxury aviation hospitality, including guest services, operations, and marketing.

> **REAL-WORLD EXAMPLE:**
> **INDUSTRY SPOTLIGHT** Disney internships: Diverse opportunities, global impact
>
> Imagine interning at the place where storytelling comes to life—where hospitality, creativity, and innovation converge. Disney's globally recognized internship programs span diverse hospitality and tourism disciplines, providing exceptional real-world experience.
>
> Whether your passion is culinary arts, guest relations, entertainment management, technology, sustainability, or event planning, Disney offers internships designed to build the professional skills, confidence, and global perspective essential for today's interconnected industry.
>
> Disney interns benefit from immersive experiences including (Disney, n.d.):
>
> - **Professional and personal development**: Structured training in financial literacy, emotional intelligence, sign language basics, improvisation, and career readiness—skills empowering your professional and personal growth.
>
> - **Behind-the-scenes learning**: Insight into operational excellence at iconic Disney attractions, highlighting logistics and innovative guest experiences.
>
> - **Endless Possibilities series**: Direct engagement with Disney executives and industry experts through sessions such as Career Spotlights, Culinary Conversations, and Tech Behind the Dreams, providing mentorship and networking opportunities.
>
> - **Multi-Week Learning series**: Structured courses like Leadership 101, The Magic of Storytelling, and Exploring Disney Hospitality, earning credentials including the Mouster's Certificate.
>
> These internships provide practical, professional experiences and foster cultural intelligence, adaptability, and a global mindset—qualities highly valued by employers across the international hospitality landscape.
>
> Disney internships shape professional identities characterized by creativity, excellence, and meaningful human connections. The skills and insights gained from these experiences are universally transferable, preparing you to excel wherever your hospitality journey takes you.

Everyday roles, extraordinary skills

In addition to internships, experience in everyday roles, such as restaurant servers, hotel receptionists, event staff, and customer support specialists, provide invaluable professional development. These positions build real-world operational knowledge, cultural responsiveness, adaptability, and guest-service excellence—skills that employers deeply value. When employers see these roles on your résumé, they recognize your ability to thrive in fast-paced environments, solve problems effectively, and deliver exceptional guest experiences.

Taking the next steps: Global opportunities await

Your professional journey extends far beyond structured programs or initial roles. The hospitality industry spans continents, cultures, and segments, offering countless opportunities for career growth and global experiences. The following suggestions could broaden your professional exploration:

- **Visit global hospitality career websites**: Explore early-career pages of leading hospitality companies, identifying structured internships, graduate roles, and leadership programs.
- **Leverage international job platforms and networks**: Use platforms like LinkedIn, Hosco, or regional job sites to discover internship and employment opportunities.
- **Join professional associations**: Become a member of international associations that offer valuable certifications, resources, and networking opportunities.

INTERACTIVE EXERCISE
Mapping your hospitality future

This exercise encourages you to reflect on the skills you've gained so far and helps you to strategically plan your hospitality career. You've already had a look at segments like lodging, events, food and beverage, cruising, recreation, managed services, club management, travel and tourism, and supporting roles—each offering unique career possibilities. This activity sets the foundation for deeper exploration.

Step 1: Reflect on your strengths

Identify three key skills or knowledge areas you've developed in this course (such as emotional intelligence, cultural responsiveness, operations management).

Step 2: Identify your interests

Think about the hospitality segments introduced briefly in this chapter. (Later chapters will cover these in greater depth.) Which hospitality segment(s) currently excite you most, and why?

- Preferred segment(s):
- Reason for interest:

Step 3: Set goals

Based on your strengths and interests, set one short-term (1–2 years) and one long-term (5–10 years) career goal. These goals may evolve as you learn more.

- Short-term goal:
- Long-term goal:

Step 4: Explore professional opportunities

Review the list of structured internships and early-career programs in Table 6.10. Select one program that aligns with your goals.

- Chosen program/internship:
- Briefly explain how this specific opportunity could help you achieve your career goals:

Step 5: Action plan

List three specific steps you'll take within the next three months to move closer to your short-term career goal.

Reflect

- How have the hospitality skills you've gained so far increased your confidence in pursuing your career pathway?
- As we prepare to explore each hospitality segment in greater depth later in this book, what specific topics or questions are you most curious to learn more about?

Networking and industry engagement

Building professional relationships: The power of connection

Industry estimates suggest that up to about 85 percent of jobs are filled through networking or personal connections (LinkedIn, 2023). This means your ability to build meaningful relationships is as vital to your hospitality career as the skills you've developed in class. Effective networking isn't about simply collecting business cards—it's about forming genuine connections, exchanging ideas, and creating professional relationships that can guide and accelerate your career growth.

Imagine attending your first hospitality or tourism conference and meeting a senior executive from Marriott or a prominent global tourism board. A casual conversation could lead to invaluable career advice, mentorship, or even your first industry role. Moments like these demonstrate how networking can transform your career path, bringing clarity and confidence as you navigate your professional journey.

Professional associations: Your gateway to the hospitality community

Joining professional associations allows you to access a global network, learn industry insights, and open doors to career opportunities. Consider exploring the impactful associations listed in Table 6.11.

Many associations offer discounted student memberships, making it easier to begin building your professional network early. Additionally, consider engaging with professionals virtually through LinkedIn, industry forums, or webinars, allowing you to build relationships regardless of geographic location.

Table 6.11 Professional associations

Association	Who should join	Key benefits
American Hotel and Lodging Association (AHLA)	Lodging professionals	Training, networking, advocacy
Meeting Professionals International (MPI)	Event management professionals	Professional certification, global networking
Club Management Association of America (CMAA)	Private club management	Specialized training, networking opportunities
Club Managers Association of Europe (CMAE)	Private club management (Europe, Middle East, North Africa)	Industry education, international networking, career resources
Cruise Lines International Association (CLIA)	Cruise industry careers	Industry connections, specialized certifications
Professional Convention Management Association (PCMA)	Meetings and conventions professionals	Resources, global networking, development

Industry events: Expanding your professional horizons

Attending hospitality industry events, ranging from major international conferences to local career fairs, provides critical networking opportunities, exposure to emerging industry trends, and direct engagement with industry leaders. The following are notable global events you might explore:

- **International Meetings Exchange (IMEX):** Leading international conference focused on events and conventions, fostering global networking.
- **Hospitality Industry Technology Exposition and Conference (HITEC):** World's largest hospitality technology event, showcasing innovation and industry trends.
- **National Restaurant Association (NRA) Show:** Premier event for food and beverage professionals, highlighting industry innovations.
- **Global Gaming Expo (G2E):** Premier global event for gaming, entertainment, and hospitality professionals.
- **Boutique Design New York (BDNY):** International hospitality design trade fair focusing on trends and creativity in lodging and hospitality spaces.
- **IAAPA Expo:** Global attraction industry event showcasing innovations in theme parks, attractions, and visitor experiences.

Remember, many smaller, regional events also provide targeted, meaningful connections to local industry professionals, helping you build relationships closer to home. Consider this student's perspective:

> Attending HITECH conference was an incredible opportunity to experience hospitality technology up close, connect with industry professionals, and gain valuable insight into my career direction. I highly recommend it to any hospitality student interested in innovation and the future of the industry.
>
> —*Fares Allahyani, hospitality management student*

Networking with authenticity: How to make lasting impressions

Authenticity is at the core of effective networking. Genuine interactions create stronger, lasting relationships. When you secure meetings or engage with professionals, approach these conversations with sincerity, clear goals, and thoughtful questions that demonstrate your genuine interest.

Sample networking questions

- What inspired you most on your journey to your current role?
- What early career steps made the biggest difference for you?
- How do you see this hospitality segment evolving in the next five years?
- What advice would you offer someone entering your area of hospitality?

INTERACTIVE EXERCISE
Crafting your elevator pitch

Imagine you're attending your first industry networking event. You spot an executive from your dream hospitality company and have a brief moment to introduce yourself. How do you make that first impression count?

Craft a concise, genuine elevator pitch (approximately 30–60 seconds) that naturally conveys:

- **Who you are**: Briefly introduce your education and specific area of interest.
- **Your authentic motivation**: Share why hospitality excites you.
- **Your unique strengths**: Mention two or three core skills or personal qualities relevant to hospitality.
- **What you're seeking**: Clearly state your objective for the interaction: advice, mentorship, internship opportunities, or simply career insight.

Genuine example elevator pitch

"Hello, I'm Alex Taylor, studying hospitality management at The Ohio State University. Events fascinate me because I love creating meaningful moments that impact people's lives. I thrive in solving problems, enjoy working with diverse teams, and excel in managing details behind the scenes. I'd genuinely appreciate your insight or advice on navigating the industry, particularly any tips you might have about internship opportunities with Marriott."

Reflect and improve

- Which parts of your pitch best reflect your genuine passion and strengths?
- How can you stay authentic while clearly communicating your professional goals?
- Which hospitality strengths naturally emerge when you speak confidently?

Mentorship: Accelerating your career growth

Mentorship is one of the most powerful, yet often overlooked, opportunities available to hospitality students and young professionals. A mentor is more than an advisor—they are a trusted guide who provides personalized insights, industry knowledge, emotional support, and career guidance. Research highlights that mentorship significantly enhances career satisfaction, advancement, and professional confidence, particularly for those entering new fields or navigating career transitions (Eby et al., 2013). Effective mentoring relationships can profoundly shape your career trajectory, offering invaluable perspectives that classrooms alone cannot provide.

Why mentorship matters: Insights from research

According to Eby et al. (2013), mentees consistently report higher levels of career satisfaction, increased confidence, better networking opportunities, and faster professional growth compared to peers without mentors. Mentors can also provide psychological support, helping mentees build resilience, navigate organizational culture, and manage the stressors associated with career uncertainty. Importantly, mentorship helps to set clearer professional goals and identify actionable strategies to achieve them, significantly impacting overall career outcomes and success.

Formal mentorship programs: Structured opportunities

Many hospitality organizations offer structured mentorship programs, often integrated into internships or early-career positions:

- **Disney's college program:** Pairs students directly with experienced mentors, helping participants successfully navigate hospitality operations, career decisions, and professional development.
- **Hyatt's global mentorship initiative:** Connects early-career hospitality professionals with senior executives, facilitating accelerated career growth and internal promotions.
- **Sodexo's leadership development program:** Provides structured mentoring tailored to managed services, healthcare, education, and corporate hospitality, significantly enhancing leadership skills and career pathways.

Informal and university-based mentorship opportunities

Mentorship doesn't always have to be part of a structured industry program. Often, informal mentorship opportunities can be just as powerful. Your university or hospitality program may have faculty mentors, alumni mentorship programs, or industry advisory boards where professionals volunteer their time specifically to support student career growth.

Informal mentorship relationships often develop organically through networking or university events, allowing for authentic, personalized connections. You can proactively seek mentors among professors, guest speakers, or hospitality professionals you meet at career fairs, alumni events, or through LinkedIn connections.

Navigating mentorship: Getting the most from your mentorship experience

To fully benefit from mentorship, approach it proactively and with clear intentions. The following steps can help you navigate and maximize your mentorship experience:

1 **Clarify your goals:** Before reaching out to a mentor, reflect on what specific guidance or insights you're seeking. Clear goals help your mentor provide tailored support.

2 **Choose the right mentor:** Look for mentors whose career paths, values, or skills align with your professional aspirations. Compatibility and trust are key for a productive mentoring relationship.

3 **Respect your mentor's time:** Be mindful of your mentor's schedule, always arriving prepared for meetings. Come equipped with thoughtful questions and discussion topics to guide your conversations.

4 **Be open and responsive:** Listen actively, demonstrate willingness to learn, and be open to constructive feedback. Mentorship thrives on honest, authentic dialogue.

5 **Maintain regular communication:** Regular check-ins, whether monthly or quarterly, keep the relationship active, meaningful, and mutually beneficial.

Questions you might ask your mentor

- What career steps or experiences most significantly shaped your professional growth?
- How have you navigated challenging workplace scenarios?
- What advice would you give someone starting out in your specific hospitality sector?
- What skills or experiences do you think are most important for career advancement in hospitality?

Looking forward: Turning connections into career opportunities

Your professional network will grow significantly throughout your hospitality journey. Start early, approach relationships with sincerity, and actively engage with industry professionals through associations, events, and mentorship programs. These connections don't merely advance your career—they shape it, guiding you toward opportunities aligned with your passions and strengths.

Remember: Your network is more than a collection of contacts—it's your professional community, supporting you, inspiring you, and opening doors you might not even know existed.

Conclusion: Shaping your unique hospitality journey

Hospitality and tourism offer extraordinary opportunities to build careers that resonate deeply with your passions, strengths, and aspirations. Throughout this chapter, you've explored diverse pathways across lodging, events, managed services, cruising, and beyond, discovering how the skills you acquire in hospitality can seamlessly transfer across sectors, enhancing your professional adaptability and growth.

By proactively pursuing certifications, structured mentorships, internships, and meaningful networking opportunities, you're taking essential steps toward crafting a career that is not only successful but personally fulfilling. Your hospitality journey is uniquely yours. Continuously embrace curiosity, genuine connections, and lifelong learning to unlock opportunities that align with your purpose and allow you to make a meaningful, lasting impact.

> **Reflect**
>
> - What immediate next step will you take today toward your hospitality career goals?
> - How will you continue leveraging your transferable skills beyond this chapter?
>
> The hospitality world awaits—where will your career take you?

> **Key takeaways**
>
> - **Expansive career opportunities**: Hospitality and tourism offer diverse career pathways across segments including lodging, food and beverage, managed services, events, recreation and entertainment, club management, cruising, travel, and tourism, and supporting fields such as supply chain and vendor management.
> - **Transferable skills across industries**: The core skills developed in hospitality—including adaptability, emotional intelligence, cultural responsiveness, leadership, and operational management—are highly valued and broadly applicable, enhancing your career flexibility within and beyond hospitality.
> - **Structured professional development**: Pursuing industry certifications, internships, mentorship opportunities, industry employment, and involvement in professional associations are crucial steps to gaining practical experience, building credibility, and advancing professionally.
> - **Networking as a career accelerator**: Creating authentic professional relationships through industry events, associations, mentorship, and meaningful personal connections significantly broadens career possibilities and accelerates advancement opportunities in hospitality and tourism.
> - **Communicating your professional value**: Clearly articulating your transferable skills, crafting an impactful "elevator pitch," and effectively leveraging professional networks positions you for career success, enabling you to confidently showcase your unique value to future employers.

Looking ahead

In Chapter 7, which focuses on managed services, you'll explore hospitality beyond traditional hotels and restaurants, diving deeper into sectors such as healthcare, education, corporate dining, and venue management. You'll discover how the skills you've developed translate effectively into these specialized service environments and learn about career paths and strategic opportunities in this dynamic segment of hospitality.

References

Allied Market Research (2023) *Events Industry Market by Type, Revenue Source, Organizer, and Region: Global Opportunity Analysis and Industry Forecast, 2023–2032*. alliedmarketresearch.com/events-industry-market-A06262 (archived at https://perma.cc/V6TD-SJCQ)

CLIA (Cruise Lines International Association) (2023) *2023 State of the Cruise Industry Report*. cruising.org/resources/2023-state-cruise-industry-report (archived at https://perma.cc/RJK2-YFPK)

CMAA (Club Management Association of America) (2023) *Private Club Industry Economic Impact Report*. cmaa.org/media/01hnzs2i/economic-impact-report_executive-summary.pdf (archived at https://perma.cc/JB7M-Y8K9)

CMAE (Club Managers Association of Europe) (2024) What we do. cmaeurope.org/aboutus/what-we-do (archived at https://perma.cc/5KF7-VUTP)

Deloitte (2018) The diversity and inclusion revolution: Eight powerful truths. *Deloitte Review*, 22. deloitte.com/content/dam/insights/us/articles/4209_Diversity-and-inclusion-revolution/DI_Diversity-and-inclusion-revolution.pdf (archived at https://perma.cc/C597-Y8QK)

Disney (n.d.) *Disney Programs: Experiential learning*, sites.disney.com/disneyprogramsexperience (archived at https://perma.cc/X246-78FV); *Disney Careers*, disneycareers.com/en/students-and-recent-graduates (archived at https://perma.cc/ZD7G-YCPC)

Eby, L.T., Allen, T.D., Hoffman, B.J., et al. (2013) An interdisciplinary meta-analysis of the potential antecedents, correlates, and consequences of protégé perceptions of mentoring. *Psychological Bulletin*, 139 (2), 441–476. https://doi.org/10.1037/a0029279

Goleman, D. (1995) *Emotional Intelligence: Why It Can Matter More Than IQ*. New York: Bantam Books.

Grand View Research (2023) *Managed Services Market Size, Share & Trends Analysis Report, 2023–2030*. grandviewresearch.com/industry-analysis/managed-services-market (archived at https://perma.cc/V4QF-4LH8)

Huang, A.Y., Fisher, T., Ding, H., & Guo, Z. (2021) A network analysis of cross-occupational skill transferability for the hospitality industry, *International Journal of Contemporary Hospitality Management*, 33 (12), 4215–4236. doi.org/10.1108/IJCHM-01-2021-0073 (archived at https://perma.cc/YP6X-8MUR)

LinkedIn (2023) *Hospitality Industry Trends and Insights*. business.linkedin.com/talent-solutions (archived at https://perma.cc/RPN7-JS4H)

Marriott International (2023) *Annual Report 2023*. marriott.gcs-web.com/static-files/b82978a6-9d28-4e38-9855-fc4ae2cebe11 (archived at https://perma.cc/X47J-YV7U)

National Restaurant Association (2023) *2023 State of the Restaurant Industry Report*. restaurant.org/research-and-media/media/press-releases/2023-national-restaurant-association-state-of-the-industry-report-a-new-normal (archived at https://perma.cc/5PJW-M2SG)

Statista (2023) U.S. amusement park industry market size 2022–2023. statista.com/statistics/1174515/amusement-park-industry-market-size-us (archived at https://perma.cc/A3SF-R6LF)

Statista (2024) Amusement park industry market size in the United States from 2011 to 2024. statista.com/statistics/1174515/amusement-park-industry-market-size-us (archived at https://perma.cc/A3SF-R6LF)

Statista (2025) Market size of the hotel and resort industry worldwide from 2013 to 2023. statista.com/statistics/1186201/hotel-and-resort-industry-market-size-global (archived at https://perma.cc/U4UJ-FWNC)

TEA/AECOM (2024) *Global Attractions Attendance Report 2023*. aecom.com/theme-index (archived at https://perma.cc/FCX3-PZ3V)

UKHospitality (2023) *UK Hospitality Economic Impact Report*. ukhospitality.org.uk/insight/economic-contribution-of-hospitality (archived at https://perma.cc/WSY3-VFCR)

US Travel Association (2023) *The State of the Travel Industry*. ustravel.org/sites/default/files/2023-04/answersheet_2023_final.pdf (archived at https://perma.cc/HEP3-FHCN)

WTTC (World Travel & Tourism Council) (2023a) *Global Economic Impact Report 2023*. wttc.org/research/economic-impact (archived at https://perma.cc/6ZXC-PJ3G)

WTTC (2023b) Travel & tourism set to break all records in 2024, reveals WTTC. wttc.org/news-article/travel-and-tourism-set-to-break-all-records-in-2024-reveals-wttc (archived at https://perma.cc/N2JL-6YCR)

Managed services in hospitality 7

LEARNING OBJECTIVES

- Define managed services and identify their unique characteristics within the hospitality industry.
- Explain the historical evolution of managed services and how they have become integral to contemporary hospitality operations.
- Analyze managed services across various sectors, including healthcare, education, business and industry, leisure, sports, military, and government.
- Demonstrate understanding of key operational considerations, including budgeting, menu planning, sustainability, and compliance with industry regulations.
- Explore how technology and innovation are shaping the future of managed services.

Introduction

Imagine stepping into a vibrant university dining hall in London, buzzing with energy as students swap stories and enjoy globally inspired dishes, each carefully customized through cutting-edge AI. Visualize walking through the bright corridors of a state-of-the-art Sydney hospital, where sustainably sourced meals designed for recovery also reflect a deep commitment to our planet. Or picture yourself grabbing a quick yet delicious lunch at a trendy corporate café in the heart of New York City, where menus are crafted not just to nourish but to energize and inspire creativity. These distinct experiences all have one thing in common—they exemplify the dynamic world of managed services.

While food and beverage services are central, managed services also encompass facilities management, housekeeping, maintenance, security, and other tailored support services. Managed services provide customized food, beverage, and support services directly at client locations, from bustling campuses to high-tech offices and healthcare facilities. Unlike traditional hotels and restaurants, managed services excel by adapting specifically to the unique needs of institutions and their diverse communities (Jones and Lockwood, 2018). Throughout this chapter, you'll explore how managed services influence daily life globally, transform industry operations, and innovate using sustainability and technology to shape hospitality's future.

Understanding managed services: Serving two audiences

Managed services providers operate uniquely within the hospitality industry because they must simultaneously satisfy two distinct audiences: their direct client (such as a university, hospital, or corporation) and their client's guests (students, patients, employees, or visitors). Unlike traditional hospitality settings, providers must carefully balance the expectations, preferences, and requirements of these two groups, delivering tailored services that achieve the client's organizational goals while aiming for an exceptional experience for the end user.

For instance, a managed services company operating dining facilities at a university must meet the university administration's goals of cost efficiency, sustainability, and nutrition, while also ensuring students have diverse, delicious meals conveniently available. This dual responsibility is central to the managed services model and shapes every aspect of the service planning, execution, and innovation you'll explore throughout this chapter.

Historical evolution of managed services

The managed services field has deep historical roots, significantly shaped by the demands of large-scale operations throughout history. One of the earliest examples dates back to ancient Rome, where military campaigns necessitated efficient food provision for vast armies on the move. Organized catering systems emerged to ensure that soldiers received adequate nutrition during long campaigns, marking one of the earliest forms of institutionalized managed services (Tannahill, 1988).

Fast-forward to the American Civil War. The immense logistical challenge of feeding large groups of soldiers spurred 19th-century innovations that set foundational standards for contemporary managed service models. The complexity and scale of this endeavor highlighted the importance of structured foodservice management, influencing subsequent institutional practices, particularly in the military and government sectors (Shrader, 1997).

The early 20th century saw educational institutions and hospitals begin outsourcing their food and support services, driven by the need for greater efficiency and specialization. Notable milestones include the establishment of Aramark in 1929, originally founded as a vending service in the US, which evolved rapidly to become a global leader in managed services (Aramark, 2023). Sodexo, founded in France in 1966, began by providing catering services to institutions before expanding globally into healthcare, education, and corporate sectors, illustrating the worldwide adoption of managed services practices (Sodexo, 2023). Compass Group began in 1941 as Factory Canteens, providing foodservices to wartime factory workers in the UK. Through strategic acquisitions and expansions, Compass Group has grown significantly to become one of the largest global providers of foodservice and support services across various sectors, including healthcare, education, and corporate environments (Compass Group, n.d.a).

The era after World War II witnessed significant expansion, driven by economic growth, technological progress, and changing social expectations regarding food quality, nutrition, and convenience. Managed services providers began incorporating systematic approaches, rigorous standards, and professional management practices that mirrored corporate operations, aligning closely with the evolving demands of their diverse clientele (Davis and Stone, 2020).

Today, managed services continue to grow, propelled by advances in technology, sustainability initiatives, and increasingly sophisticated consumer expectations. Providers are harnessing AI for menu customization and sustainability-driven procurement practices, transforming how managed services are delivered worldwide.

Throughout this chapter, you'll explore how managed services operate across key sectors, examine critical operational elements such as budgeting and regulatory compliance, and consider the significant influence of technological advances.

Managed services across key sectors

Managed services play an essential role across diverse sectors, each with unique operational requirements and client needs. This section explores some of the most prominent sectors globally, highlighting key features, trends, and operational insights.

Healthcare

In healthcare, hospitality meets compassion. Managed services providers don't just feed patients—they actively contribute to healing and wellness. Imagine autonomous robots smoothly navigating hospital halls to deliver perfectly portioned meals, improving safety and delighting patients. At UCSF Medical Center in California, these robotic assistants, affectionately named TUGs, ensure timely and hygienic meal delivery, while dietitians use digital apps connected to patient records to personalize nutritional care (Smith, 2023). It's hospitality at its most meaningful: where every bite matters.

This intersection of hospitality and healthcare highlights the critical role managed services play in patient recovery and satisfaction. Providers meld high-quality service with specialized care, positively influencing patients' physical health and their emotional well-being and overall experience. Operating across hospitals, clinics, and senior living communities worldwide, providers such as Sodexo adhere to strict hygiene, nutritional, and safety standards mandated by organizations like the NHS in the UK and the CDC in the US (Cousins et al., 2019). For instance, Sodexo's tailored foodservices are contributing to improved patient outcomes at over 3,000 healthcare facilities globally, demonstrating just how impactful hospitality excellence can be in healthcare environments.

> **THINK LIKE A MANAGER**
>
> You manage foodservices at a busy hospital. Choose one technology or sustainability practice from this section and briefly explain how it improves patient experience and supports nutritional goals.

Nutrition and wellness initiatives form integral components of healthcare managed services. Providers collaborate closely with dietitians and medical teams to ensure meals align with clinical objectives, accommodate dietary restrictions, and promote healthier lifestyles. Programs such as "farm-to-hospital" emphasize sustainable, locally sourced ingredients to enhance meal quality, support patient recovery, and benefit local communities environmentally and economically (Practice Greenhealth, n.d.).

REAL-WORLD EXAMPLE:
INDUSTRY SPOTLIGHT Enhancing patient recovery at Cleveland Clinic, Abu Dhabi

At Cleveland Clinic, Abu Dhabi, Sodexo introduced personalized menu planning integrated with patient health records, culturally tailored meal options, and sustainable sourcing practices. These innovations—reflective of Sodexo Healthcare's global patient dining model—improved patient satisfaction scores substantially and contributed to faster recovery times, demonstrating the profound impact of nutritional care and personalized service within healthcare environments (Sodexo Healthcare, 2024).

Education sector

Campus dining has come a long way from mystery meat Mondays. Today's students expect convenience, variety, and sustainability—and managed services providers deliver. Take The Ohio State University, where Starship robots zip across campus, delivering freshly prepared meals directly to students. Initiatives like the Zero Waste Campus program at the University of California further highlight students' and staff members' growing demand for eco-friendly practices, showcasing dining halls as centers for sustainable innovation.

These innovations underscore how managed services are essential to enhancing student experiences on campuses globally. Beyond just meals, providers create comprehensive environments that support academic success, student wellness, and overall quality of life. From dining halls to facility management and even security services, companies such as Compass Group and Aramark help campuses worldwide to meet evolving student expectations through thoughtful, integrated services.

Consider the wide variety of hospitality opportunities available within educational settings, whether you're physically on a campus or exploring these possibilities remotely. Food, beverage, and nutritional services are central to educational institutions—spanning dining operations, catering, nutrition planning, sustainability programs, and culinary innovation—making this sector dynamic and impactful. Additionally, educational environments often include facilities management, housekeeping, event coordination, lodging and conference services, recreation and athletic venues, healthcare clinics, transportation, and sometimes even airports. These diverse functions may be managed directly by university employees or outsourced to specialized management companies such as Aramark, Compass Group, or Sodexo. This structure demonstrates the broad scope of hospitality careers available, whether working within a university itself or as part of a managed services provider partnering with educational institutions.

These diverse hospitality functions are increasingly enhanced by emerging technologies, significantly transforming the educational managed services landscape. Autonomous delivery robots—such as those by Starship Technologies—are already widely utilized on US campuses including Purdue University and George Mason University, and have expanded significantly into broader city environments in the UK, notably Cambridge, Leeds, and Milton Keynes, reflecting strong potential for future campus adoption. Additionally, mobile dining platforms like Grubhub Campus in the US, and Uni Food Hub across UK and Australian universities, enable students to browse menus, place orders, manage dietary preferences, and schedule pickups, further enhancing responsiveness and personalization in campus hospitality.

Companies such as Aramark and Compass Group manage dining services for thousands of educational institutions, emphasizing nutritional balance, menu variety, and cultural inclusivity, effectively supporting diverse student populations. Various sustainability initiatives also shape educational managed services, with practices such as waste reduction, composting, and local sourcing becoming increasingly common.

REAL-WORLD EXAMPLE:
INDUSTRY SPOTLIGHT Autonomous food delivery at The Ohio State University

In August 2021, The Ohio State University introduced a fleet of over 100 autonomous food delivery robots to meet growing student demand for convenient and efficient campus dining options. Students, faculty, and staff place orders through the Grubhub mobile app, and robots deliver meals directly to designated campus locations. The initiative now averages more than 1,000 deliveries per day, significantly reducing wait times, streamlining operations, and enhancing the overall campus dining experience (Hendrix, 2025).

INTERACTIVE EXERCISE
Campus dining innovation proposal

- In a small group, create a basic proposal for enhancing a university's dining program through managed services. Your goal is to improve:
  - Student satisfaction (consider menu variety, convenience, and dietary needs)
  - Nutritional health (balanced menus, healthy eating options)
  - Environmental sustainability (waste reduction and eco-friendly practices)
- Use examples from the chapter (such as mobile ordering apps, autonomous delivery robots, composting, and local sourcing).
- Be ready to share your proposal briefly, clearly explaining your ideas and why they would benefit students and the campus community.

Leisure, sports, and entertainment

Going to the big game or a concert now means more than just watching the action—it means enjoying exceptional hospitality. Venues worldwide are embracing innovations like cashier-free checkout stands, AI-powered ordering kiosks, and sustainability practices. Seattle's Climate Pledge Arena, for example, features Amazon's Just Walk Out technology, where grabbing snacks is as easy as picking them up and walking away—no lines, no delays, just easy enjoyment. Providers such as Levy Restaurants turn stadiums and arenas into culinary hotspots, transforming entertainment venues into comprehensive hospitality destinations.

These advanced hospitality experiences highlight how essential managed services have become to leisure, sports, and entertainment. Managed services now go beyond just providing refreshments—they can offer thoughtfully curated, diverse food and beverage experiences tailored specifically to each event and audience. Whether at packed sports stadiums in the US, iconic concert venues like the O2 Arena in London, or bustling Asian theme parks such as Tokyo Disneyland or Universal Studios Singapore, managed services deliver hospitality that perfectly complements and enhances the excitement of the main event.

> **THINK LIKE A MANAGER**
>
> You're managing foodservices at a popular local stadium. Outline two strategies you would use to ensure high-quality guest experiences, manage operational efficiency, and incorporate sustainable practices.

Technology-driven innovations such as cashierless concession stands are becoming increasingly prevalent, exemplified by Amazon's Just Walk Out at Seattle's Climate Pledge Arena. Guests can select food and beverages without checkout delays, enhancing convenience and customer satisfaction. Additionally, AI-powered ordering kiosks and facial-recognition payment technologies, used extensively in stadiums across China and South Korea, offer personalized, frictionless service, reflecting broader global hospitality trends.

Levy Restaurants, a subsidiary of Compass Group, operates premium dining experiences at renowned venues like Wembley Stadium in London and Staples Center in Los Angeles. The focus on locally sourced ingredients, innovative menus, and sustainable practices enhances the spectator experience and the venue's reputation. Sustainability initiatives, including compostable packaging and reduced waste strategies, were prominently featured during the Tokyo 2020 Olympics, setting global benchmarks for environmentally responsible event catering (Tokyo Organising Committee, 2021).

REAL-WORLD EXAMPLE:
INDUSTRY SPOTLIGHT   The culinary transformation at Tottenham Hotspur Stadium

When Tottenham Hotspur Stadium opened in London in 2019, it set a new global standard for managed services in sports venues. Operated by Levy UK + Ireland, the stadium includes over 60 unique food and beverage outlets, from street food crafted by local artisans to upscale dining in luxury suites, featuring neighborhood breweries and regional ingredients. Sustainability is central, with extensive recycling programs and no single-use plastics. This innovative approach has increased fan engagement and positioned the venue as a global model for stadium hospitality (Compass Group UK, n.d.b).

INTERACTIVE EXERCISE
Beyond food and beverage: Exploring managed services

- Think about attending a major sporting event or concert. In addition to food and beverage, identify at least three managed services essential to the event's success. For each service:
  - Clearly state the service (such as security, cleaning, technology, crowd management, parking, sustainability practices).
  - Explain why it matters (how does it improve the experience for both guests and the hosting client?).
  - Suggest a company (like Aramark, Sodexo, or Compass Group) or type of organization that could realistically provide this service.
- Be ready to briefly share your ideas, highlighting the diverse roles managed services play beyond catering.

Business and industry

Corporate dining today is a far cry from the bland cafeterias of the past. It has evolved into a dynamic space driving employee satisfaction, wellness, and creativity. Companies such as Google have transformed workplace dining into vibrant social hubs, offering culinary events, interactive cooking classes, and globally inspired menus—each meal becoming a moment for collaboration and innovation. Automated micro-markets and digital wellness platforms further ensure employees feel energized, valued, and connected throughout their workday.

This evolution illustrates how managed services have become integral to shaping workplace culture and enhancing productivity within the business and industry sector. Leading providers now offer highly customized dining experiences, comprehensive facility management, and tailored wellness programs that directly align with the shifting expectations of a diverse global workforce. Innovations including 24/7 sensor-based micro-markets allow employees constant access to fresh meals and snacks, while integrated wellness apps track nutritional intake and encourage healthier choices, further promoting employee well-being and engagement.

> **THINK LIKE A MANAGER**
>
> You manage dining services for a global tech company. How would you use employee feedback and new technology to keep menus fresh, meet diverse preferences, and support sustainability goals? Briefly outline your strategy.

REAL-WORLD EXAMPLE:
INDUSTRY SPOTLIGHT   Google's workplace dining: Beyond the cafeteria

At Google's headquarters in Mountain View, California, Compass Group transforms traditional corporate dining into a vibrant, community-focused experience. Employees enjoy complimentary meals featuring global cuisines, healthy options, and sustainably sourced ingredients. Interactive culinary events, cooking classes with professional chefs, and educational sustainability initiatives add educational value, enhance employee satisfaction, and contribute to a well-being and collaborative workplace culture. This innovative approach can boost morale and turn everyday meals into meaningful opportunities for engagement, creativity, and productivity (Compass Group, n.d.a).

> **INTERACTIVE EXERCISE**
> Corporate café challenge
>
> - In a small group, create a basic managed services plan for a company's employee café. Focus on:
>   - **Menu choices**: Foods appealing to diverse employee tastes and dietary needs.
>   - **Employee engagement**: Ways to keep employees involved and excited about dining options (such as special food events, themed days).

- o **Efficiency and convenience**: Simple ideas to streamline ordering and reduce wait times.
- o **Sustainability**: Practical suggestions for eco-friendly practices like waste reduction or local sourcing.
- Use examples from this chapter (perhaps digital ordering platforms, wellness-focused menus, or compostable packaging).
- Briefly share your ideas, clearly highlighting how they enhance employee satisfaction and support sustainability.

Military and government

In military and government settings, managed services deliver reliability under pressure. They don't just meet but consistently exceed rigorous nutritional standards and logistical requirements, ensuring troops and government personnel receive appropriate, balanced, nutritious meals whether stationed at remote outposts or bustling urban centers. Innovations such as deployable kitchens powered by renewable energy and RFID-enabled supply chains highlight how managed services providers maintain smooth operations, prioritize sustainability, and ensure mission readiness in even the most challenging environments.

Operating successfully in this sector demands meticulous attention to detail, stringent compliance with safety and nutritional standards, and exceptional logistical capabilities. Providers like Aramark and Sodexo excel in meeting these specialized demands by delivering comprehensive, reliable meal and facility management solutions globally. For example, deployable kitchen units, used by US and NATO forces, are equipped with advanced solar-powered systems, water purification devices, and sustainable food preparation methods, enabling quality meal provision even in remote or crisis scenarios.

REAL-WORLD EXAMPLE:
INDUSTRY SPOTLIGHT   Optimizing operational efficiency at Fort Bragg, US

Aramark's partnership with Fort Bragg, one of the largest US military bases, demonstrates the strategic role of managed services in supporting operational readiness. Through comprehensive meal planning, streamlined logistics, and strict compliance with nutritional guidelines, Aramark significantly enhanced service delivery efficiency and troop satisfaction. Sustainability initiatives, such as waste reduction programs and sustainable sourcing, further improved the base's environmental impact.

The examination of managed services across diverse sectors underscores their pivotal role in addressing sector-specific needs, from patient nutrition and student wellness to employee productivity and guest satisfaction. Each sector reveals distinct operational demands and opportunities, reinforcing the need for a robust understanding of operational considerations. The following sections will explore critical operational elements such as budgeting, menu planning, regulatory compliance, and sustainability, which are essential for effective management across these varied contexts.

Applying core business functions in managed services

In Chapters 4 and 5, we explored fundamental business functions essential to the hospitality industry, such as finance, risk management, operations, and service excellence. Managed services uniquely integrate these functions by delivering customized hospitality solutions directly at client sites. For example:

- **Finance and budgeting**: Managed services require precise budgeting and careful financial oversight due to contractual constraints and cost-efficiency requirements. Providers can utilize financial analytics to forecast demand, manage food costs, and maximize efficiency, ensuring financial sustainability without compromising service quality.
- **Risk and compliance**: Compliance management, from food safety regulations (FDA, FSA) to ISO standards, is critical in managed services. Providers systematically mitigate operational risks through meticulous training, rigorous audits, and real-time monitoring of standards, ensuring consistent safety and service reliability across locations worldwide.
- **Service and operations**: Managed services depend on seamless operations, from procurement and logistics to meal preparation and delivery. Providers strategically manage supply chains, inventory, and staffing across diverse client environments, be it hospitals, universities, or corporate cafeterias, to consistently deliver tailored, high-quality experiences.
- **People management**: Exceptional guest experiences in managed services depend significantly on people management. Companies invest heavily in employee training, emphasizing adaptability, cultural competency, and responsiveness, enabling staff to exceed expectations across diverse sectors and cultures.

This integration of core functions demonstrates how managed services represent the practical intersection of foundational business disciplines, emphasizing operational excellence and strategic adaptability.

Operational considerations: A more conversational approach

Operational excellence in managed services isn't just about managing budgets—it's about balancing creativity, compliance, and sustainability to achieve results. Providers look to strategically forecast demand, optimizing inventory to reduce waste without sacrificing quality. Menu planning becomes an art form, blending nutrition, cultural sensitivity, and culinary trends into meals that delight and nourish diverse audiences worldwide.

Compliance isn't just a checklist—it's a critical part of trust in hospitality. Managed services providers navigate complex standards, from FDA food safety regulations in the US to stringent ISO standards internationally, ensuring guests always dine safely and confidently.

Sustainability transforms operations, too. Providers increasingly source locally, choose eco-friendly packaging, and prioritize energy-efficient and waste-reduction technologies, proving hospitality can both serve and protect our planet.

Budgeting and cost management

Sound budgeting and cost management strategies are central to successful managed services operations. Providers must balance financial constraints with delivering high-quality services, carefully managing resources to optimize performance. For example, Compass Group employs sophisticated forecasting methods to anticipate demand and efficiently manage inventory, significantly reducing food waste and controlling costs.

In healthcare settings, budgeting complexities include the requirements of nutritional quality and patient-specific dietary requirements. Aramark's collaboration with healthcare institutions demonstrates how predictive analytics can optimize meal production, manage labor costs, and precisely control portions, contributing both to patient satisfaction and cost efficiency (Aramark, 2023).

Educational institutions also require meticulous budgeting, particularly in university environments with diverse student populations. Sodexo's partnership with universities worldwide highlights strategic sourcing of local ingredients and streamlined inventory management to maintain cost-effectiveness without compromising meal quality or variety (Sodexo, 2024c).

Once budgeting frameworks are in place, managed services providers turn their attention to another critical element—menu planning.

Menu planning and nutritional considerations

Menu planning in managed services goes beyond culinary creativity, requiring thoughtful consideration of nutritional requirements, dietary restrictions, cultural preferences, and operational feasibility. In healthcare, precise nutritional planning directly impacts patient recovery and wellness. Sodexo's integration of dietitian-led meal planning at the Mayo Clinic exemplifies this approach, offering customized menus that enhance patient outcomes and satisfaction.

In educational settings, menus must accommodate a wide variety of dietary preferences and cultural backgrounds. At Oxford University in the UK, Compass Group successfully developed menus reflecting global cuisine trends and diverse dietary needs, enhancing student satisfaction and cultural inclusivity.

Corporate dining environments require menus that promote wellness and productivity. As we have seen, Google's workplace dining strategy, managed by Compass Group, includes nutritionally balanced, globally inspired meals, supporting employee health, engagement, and productivity.

Regulatory compliance

With thoughtfully planned menus established, maintaining rigorous compliance with industry regulations is the next key step. Adherence to regulatory standards is paramount in managed services, particularly regarding food safety, nutrition, and environmental responsibility. In the US, managed service providers must comply with FDA regulations, which involve stringent food handling practices, nutritional labeling, and allergen management (FDA, 2024). Similarly, the UK's Food Standards Agency (FSA) imposes rigorous standards on food preparation and nutritional quality in educational and healthcare facilities, requiring meticulous compliance records and regular inspections from providers (FSA, n.d.). Globally, ISO standards such as ISO 22000 provide comprehensive frameworks ensuring consistency and reliability across international operations, demonstrating providers' commitment to high-quality service delivery and regulatory compliance (ISO, 2023).

Beyond compliance, integrating sustainability throughout operations facilitates long-term success and positive impacts.

Sustainability in sourcing and operations

Sustainability practices significantly influence operational decisions, consumer perceptions, and viability. Providers increasingly prioritize eco-friendly sourcing, waste reduction, and sustainability certifications to align with global environmental goals.

Sodexo, for example, has implemented extensive sustainability initiatives, including sourcing locally produced, organic ingredients and deploying advanced waste-reduction technologies. These practices improve service quality, reduce environmental impact, and support corporate social responsibility. Compass Group's global sustainability strategies feature comprehensive waste management programs and substantial investments in plant-based menu development, aligning operational practices with consumer expectations for sustainability.

> **INTERACTIVE EXERCISE**
> Elementary school managed services
>
> - Imagine you're responsible for improving managed services at a local elementary school. Your goal is to introduce healthier meals and enhance sustainability, but stay within a tight budget. Develop a simple plan covering:
>   - **Menu improvements**: Child-friendly, nutritious options appealing to young students.
>   - **Sustainability efforts**: Practical ideas suitable for elementary schools (such as reducing food waste, recycling programs).
>   - **Cost management**: Ideas to keep costs affordable without sacrificing quality.
> - Be ready to share your plan, clearly explaining how your ideas support both students and the environment, using examples and concepts from this chapter.

Technology and innovation: Directly engaging guests

From robot servers in Japan's elderly care facilities to AI-driven menus at the Cleveland Clinic, managed services exemplify hospitality's intersection with technological innovation. Automated check-ins, digital menus, and contactless payments have rapidly evolved from conveniences into consumer expectations. Further developments such as blockchain transparency for supply chains and smart kitchen technologies reducing food waste underscore technology's role in shaping sustainable, efficient hospitality.

These rapid technological changes are actively reshaping the hospitality workforce and influencing industry dynamics. Future hospitality professionals are likely to encounter technology-driven solutions such as automated services, robotics, and AI platforms more regularly, meaning familiarity and comfort with these tools will become increasingly valuable.

Rather than fully replacing human interaction, these technologies will complement professionals' skills, enhancing service efficiency and personalization. New roles will likely emerge around overseeing technological integration, managing sustainability initiatives through data-driven practices, and leveraging digital innovations to meet evolving guest expectations. Preparing to adapt to and collaborate with these technologies can significantly enhance career opportunities within the hospitality and managed services sectors.

AI-driven personalized menu planning and dietary management

Artificial intelligence has revolutionized managed services, particularly in sectors requiring precise dietary management, such as healthcare and education. AI-powered platforms utilize advanced data analytics and predictive modeling to maximize operational efficiency and offer customized meal solutions in which nutrition is optimized. For example:

- In healthcare, personalized dietary management significantly improves patient recovery and satisfaction. For example, Compass Group's deployment of AI-driven dietary software at the Cleveland Clinic enables real-time adjustments to patient menus based on clinical data, dietary requirements, and patient preferences, resulting in better clinical outcomes and enhanced patient experiences.
- Internationally, hospitals in Singapore are utilizing sophisticated AI in nutritional management systems that integrate patient health data and dietary needs to generate personalized menus. This approach has dramatically improved patient satisfaction and accelerated recovery, positioning Singaporean hospitals among global leaders in technology-driven patient care.
- In the education sector, universities are increasingly engaging in international alliances focused on leveraging AI technology to enhance operations and sustainability. For instance, Imperial College London recently joined an international AI alliance aimed at fostering collaborative research and innovation, which can potentially benefit diverse aspects of university-managed services, including dining, resource management, and operational efficiency (Imperial College London, 2023).

Automated and contactless services post-pandemic

The Covid-19 pandemic significantly accelerated the adoption of contactless and automated technologies across managed services, permanently shifting consumer expectations and operational practices. Digital and automated solutions have become essential for maintaining hygiene standards, enhancing convenience, and improving guest experiences worldwide:

- Globally renowned airports, such as Dubai International and Heathrow in the UK, have incorporated automated check-ins, digital menu ordering systems, and robotic food delivery systems. These innovations improve operational efficiency and customer satisfaction while addressing hygiene and safety concerns, creating a secure and comfortable environment for travelers (Dubai Airports, 2024; Heathrow Airport Holdings, 2024).

- In corporate environments, automation has streamlined dining services by enabling employees to pre-order meals through digital platforms. These systems reduce wait times, improve service flow during peak periods, and create a more convenient and productive dining experience for employees.
- In Japan, automation is increasingly prevalent in elderly care facilities, where robotic systems deliver meals efficiently, safely, and consistently. These innovations directly address labor shortages while ensuring a positive experience and nutritional well-being of the aging population.

Sustainability innovations: Technology in action

Technological advances are also pivotal in sustainability efforts within managed services, with innovative solutions for tracking and reducing food waste, optimizing supply chains, and ensuring responsible sourcing.

For example:

- **Smart kitchen technologies** are being developed to combat food waste by using IoT sensors and data analytics to monitor freshness, predict spoilage, and optimize portion sizes. Research shows such systems can reduce food waste by 20–30 percent while improving efficiency and sustainability in large-scale food operations (Saleem et al., 2025).
- Sodexo has committed to halving food waste by 2025 through its "WasteWatch powered by Leanpath" program, which uses **digital tracking** to measure and analyze food waste across thousands of sites globally. In Australia, it pairs this with IoT temperature-monitoring systems and surplus food partnerships such as Yume to reduce spoilage and redirect edible surplus food (Sodexo, 2024a).
- **Blockchain technology** is being adopted globally to improve transparency, traceability, and supply chain sustainability. According to the World Economic Forum (2024), blockchain can help reduce food waste by enabling real-time tracking from farm to table, improving environmental, social, and governance (ESG) outcomes.

Future-focused innovation

Looking forward, technology continues to evolve, promising new opportunities for managed services. Developments such as virtual kitchens, automated nutritional tracking tools, and next-generation IoT-enabled facility management are emerging. These innovations have the potential to further redefine operational standards, elevate guest experiences, and drive sustainable outcomes worldwide.

> **THINK LIKE A MANAGER**
>
> Imagine you're organizing foodservices for a large international event. You want to use technology (such as mobile ordering, contactless payments, or automated kiosks) to improve service.
>
> - Which technology would you choose, and why?
> - How would you make sure technology helps guests without sacrificing friendly, personal service?
>
> Clearly explain your decisions, using examples from this chapter to support your ideas.

While technological advances bring substantial operational benefits to managed services, providers must thoughtfully navigate ethical considerations associated with these innovations. Institutions such as Imperial College London highlight the importance of international collaboration in AI research, underscoring the need to establish stringent protocols for data privacy, particularly when implementing AI systems across sensitive areas like healthcare and educational settings (Imperial College London, 2023).

Furthermore, as automated and digital services become prevalent, ensuring equitable access across diverse populations is essential to avoid unintentionally excluding individuals less familiar with or without access to advanced technologies. Finally, maintaining a balance between automation and personalized, human-centric services remains crucial; overly automated systems can potentially diminish the warmth, responsiveness, and human connection fundamental to hospitality.

Managed service providers should adopt transparent data practices, ensure technology is accessible to all users, and balance automation thoughtfully with human interaction to sustain genuine hospitality alongside operational efficiency.

> **INTERACTIVE EXERCISE**
> Technology in action
>
> - In a small group, choose one technology discussed in this chapter (perhaps delivery robots, AI-driven menus, or mobile ordering apps). Briefly discuss and answer these questions:
>   - How could this technology improve guest experiences in managed services?
>   - What are some possible challenges with using this technology?
> - Be prepared to briefly share your answers, using examples from hospitality settings you're familiar with and/or from this chapter.

Introduction to Hospitality and Tourism Management

The rapid evolution of technology has undeniably reshaped operational practices, customer experiences, and sustainability efforts within managed services. These developments are not isolated but significantly contribute to broader economic, social, and cultural dynamics globally. In the final section, we will examine the global impact of managed services, highlighting economic contributions, employment trends, cultural influences, and the importance of strategic global partnerships.

Reflect

- Which hospitality technologies discussed in this chapter excite or intrigue you the most, and why?
- How comfortable do you feel working alongside technology-driven tools like AI or automated services?
- What steps could you take now to improve your comfort and skills in using these emerging technologies?

Global impact and scope: A more storytelling tone

As we have seen, managed services aren't just about good food—they encompass a wide range of customized solutions including facilities management, housekeeping, event coordination, and more. Employing millions worldwide and contributing billions to the global economy, this diverse sector shapes cultures, economies, and social practices around the world. Strategic alliances between hospitality giants and technology leaders spark innovation, while emerging markets like India, Brazil, and the UAE highlight the sector's dynamic growth potential. In each region, managed services uniquely adapt to client needs, reflecting local tastes, operational standards, and community values—demonstrating hospitality's universal yet flexible impact.

> In hospitality and managed services, we shape culture and create meaningful change for our people and our consumers, every day. It's a privilege—and a responsibility—to lead with both strategy and empathy, making a real impact in communities around the world.
>
> —*Annick de Vanssay, group chief human resources officer*

Economic contribution and workforce data

Globally, managed services represent a major contributor to hospitality's economic footprint:

- Global GDP contribution: Approximately $300 billion annually (WTTC, 2024).
- US employment: 5 million jobs in managed foodservices (National Restaurant Association, 2024).
- UK employment: Approximately 1.7 million jobs (UKHospitality, 2023).
- Emerging markets employment (Grand View Research, 2024):
    o India: Over 2 million in institutional catering.
    o Brazil: Around 1.3 million jobs.

This robust economic presence highlights the substantial role managed services play in global hospitality.

Market size and projected growth

The global managed services market continues to grow robustly, driven by outsourcing trends, cost efficiencies, and expectations for higher-quality, personalized services. The worldwide contract catering market is expected to reach around $321 billion in 2025, with growth continuing at a compound annual growth rate (CAGR) of about 6 percent through 2032 (Coherent Market Insights, 2024).

The Asia-Pacific region demonstrates particularly strong growth potential due to increased outsourcing by corporations, educational institutions, and healthcare facilities. Emerging markets such as China and India are forecast to drive much of this expansion, reflecting rising middle-class incomes and increased demand for outsourced food and support services in healthcare and education. From 2024 to 2030, Brazil's managed services market is expected to grow at a CAGR of 14.8 percent, reaching $20.2 billion by 2030. In Mexico, the hospitality sector is projected to grow at a CAGR of 7.74 percent from 2025 to 2032, driven by expanding tourism infrastructure, which may contribute to the growth of managed services in the region (Verified Market Research, 2024).

Social and cultural influences

Managed services providers significantly influence social and cultural trends, responding to diverse global consumer expectations. Providers adapt their offerings to local tastes, dietary trends, and sustainability practices, enhancing social and cultural integration.

In corporate environments, culturally inclusive menus are becoming standard practice. For example, Sodexo and Compass Group design menus to reflect diverse culinary traditions, catering to dietary practices such as halal, kosher, vegetarian, and vegan diets across their global operations.

Providers also actively support healthier lifestyles. Sodexo's global nutritional education programs have been implemented in educational institutions in countries including France, Brazil, China, and South Africa, with the aim of improving local dietary habits and promoting healthier food choices.

Strategic alliances and global partnerships

Strategic alliances and partnerships enable managed services providers to operate effectively across borders, enhance service quality, and drive sustainability and technological innovation. For example, Compass Group's strategic alliances with international technology firms have enabled innovative digital ordering and inventory management systems worldwide. Its partnership with Microsoft facilitated the global rollout of AI-driven predictive analytics software, improving supply chain efficiency and customer service across international operations.

Sodexo's global sustainability collaboration with the World Resources Institute (WRI) significantly enhanced its sustainable sourcing and reduced food waste across operations in Asia, Africa, and South America, aligning operational practices with global environmental targets and consumer expectations (Sodexo, 2024b; WRI, 2024).

Reflect

Hospitality's global influence

- Reflecting on the global impact of managed services, consider how hospitality practices can shape local economies, cultural exchanges, and social dynamics. Which aspects resonate most strongly with you, and why?
- How can awareness of global trends and diverse cultural needs enhance your effectiveness as a hospitality professional?
- What actions can you take now to better understand global hospitality perspectives and prepare yourself for working within an increasingly interconnected world?

Emerging markets spotlight

Emerging markets such as Africa and the Middle East represent significant growth opportunities for managed services providers. For instance, the UAE has rapidly expanded its managed services sector, particularly within airports and luxury hospitality environments. Dubai International Airport, one of the world's busiest, uses managed services to deliver tailored, culturally sensitive dining experiences to over 80 million travelers annually (Dubai Airports, 2024).

In Africa, managed services have become integral to growing educational, healthcare, and corporate sectors, with South Africa leading the way. Contract catering and facility management services across major cities such as Johannesburg and Cape Town have grown significantly, driven by increased corporate investments and public-sector outsourcing (Credence Research, 2024).

Alongside significant growth opportunities, managed services providers in emerging markets face several notable challenges. Complex regulatory frameworks in countries such as India, Brazil, and South Africa often require specialized local expertise, careful compliance management, and effective stakeholder engagement to navigate successfully. Additionally, adapting to diverse cultural tastes and dietary preferences can prove demanding; providers must carefully tailor menus and service practices to meet unique local needs, which demands considerable research, flexibility, and community engagement. Logistical challenges, particularly in regions with less developed infrastructure, may complicate supply chains, leading to difficulties sourcing high-quality, consistent ingredients and implementing sustainability initiatives effectively. To address these challenges, managed services providers must foster strategic local alliances, invest in robust market research, and develop adaptable operational frameworks capable of addressing the diverse, dynamic environments inherent in emerging markets.

INTERACTIVE EXERCISE
Emerging markets reflection

Select one emerging market region (such as Asia-Pacific, Latin America, Africa, or the Middle East) and reflect briefly on these questions:

- Why might emerging markets be particularly attractive for managed services providers?
- What general cultural or operational factors might managed services providers need to consider when entering these markets?
- How could hospitality leaders effectively adapt their managed services to meet the diverse needs of these regions?

Career pathways in managed services: Property, above-property, and corporate levels

Expanding on the career exploration in Chapter 6, managed services offer dynamic professional opportunities across multiple organizational levels, including property-level roles (directly onsite), above-property positions (regional or multi-unit oversight), and corporate leadership roles (strategic management and global direction). Understanding these distinctions provides insight into the breadth of career options and professional growth within managed services.

> Over the course of my 30 years in the managed services industry, I have been able to build a diverse set of skills through career progression with roles within properties, regional and division leadership positions, as well as corporate strategic roles supporting the business. The ability to develop both business acumen and strategic thought leadership across those roles enables me to understand the challenges facing our business operators and to help create solutions that are scalable and sustainable. I believe that my success across my career has been directly related to the dynamic roles and experiences that the industry has afforded me.
>
> —Molly Kurth, SVP, corporate HR, learning and talent development, Compass Group North America

Property-level careers (onsite roles)

Property-level positions involve daily management and direct oversight of managed services at specific client sites, such as a hospital, university, stadium, or corporate cafeteria. Professionals at this level focus on operational execution, customer satisfaction, and compliance.

Example roles

- **Site manager or director:** Directly oversees daily operations, staffing, and client relationships. Responsible for quality assurance, financial management, regulatory compliance, and customer service at the property level.
- **Executive chef:** Leads culinary operations, menu planning, nutritional management, food safety, and sustainability initiatives onsite, directly influencing client satisfaction and operational excellence.
- **Facilities manager:** Manages physical infrastructure, safety protocols, and compliance standards at the client location, ensuring seamless service and efficient operation.

Above-property careers (regional or multi-unit roles)

Above-property roles manage multiple client sites or an entire geographic region, requiring strategic planning, consistency of standards, operational oversight, and effective management across diverse locations.

Example roles

- **District or regional manager:** Oversees multiple property-level managers, ensuring operational consistency, adherence to corporate standards, financial efficiency, and strategic client relationships across several managed service locations.
- **Regional nutrition and wellness manager:** Directs nutritional programs, compliance with dietary guidelines, and wellness initiatives across multiple healthcare or educational facilities, ensuring quality and consistency regionally.
- **Regional sustainability coordinator:** Implements company-wide sustainability initiatives across multiple client sites, standardizing best practices, managing local sourcing strategies, and monitoring regional environmental impact.

Corporate-level careers (strategic and global roles)

Corporate-level roles involve strategic decision-making, global innovation, and organizational leadership, often at a national or international scale. These positions focus on strategic direction, resource allocation, corporate partnerships, innovation, and global sustainability practices.

Example roles

- **Vice president of managed services operations:** Leads strategic direction, financial planning, and global operational initiatives across sectors, ensuring alignment with organizational goals and industry trends.
- **Global director of innovation and technology:** Guides the integration of emerging technologies (AI, robotics, blockchain) across global operations, shaping innovation strategies and enhancing competitive advantage.
- **Chief sustainability officer:** Develops and implements global sustainability strategies, partnering with international organizations, suppliers, and clients to meet environmental goals and enhance corporate social responsibility.
- **Senior vice president of human resources:** Oversees global talent acquisition, retention, training, and development strategies across managed services. Responsible for establishing inclusive workplace practices, advancing DEIBA (diversity, equity, inclusion, belonging, and accessibility) initiatives, driving

organizational culture, and ensuring leadership development aligns with strategic objectives. This role is critical for building and maintaining a motivated, skilled workforce and fostering organizational success across diverse geographic regions.

Professional development across levels

Professionals across these levels benefit from targeted professional development:

- **Property-level:** Specialized certifications in food safety (such as ServSafe), culinary skills, facility management, compliance training, and operational excellence.
- **Above-property:** Advanced training in multi-unit leadership, project management (for example PMP qualification), strategic communication, sustainability certifications (such as LEED), and regulatory compliance standards.
- **Corporate level:** Executive development programs, global leadership training, advanced analytics, innovation management, sustainability strategy, and strategic partnership management.

INTERACTIVE EXERCISE
Exploring career paths in managed services

- In a group, select two of the following organizational levels discussed in this chapter:
  - Property-level (for example site manager, executive chef)
  - Above-property level (for example regional manager, sustainability coordinator)
  - Corporate-level (such as VP of operations, chief sustainability officer, senior VP of HR)
- Research real job postings from managed services companies such as Compass Group, Aramark, or Sodexo. For each organizational level:
  - Identify one management-level role currently available.
  - Summarize the main responsibilities of this role.
  - List two to three key skills required for success.
  - Suggest ways someone could develop these skills (training, experience, education).
  - Share one reason why this management role is important to the company's overall success.
- Be prepared to briefly share your findings, clearly explaining how these roles contribute to hospitality operations and career growth opportunities.

> **Key takeaways**
>
> - **Dynamic role of managed services**: Managed services deliver customized, client-centered hospitality solutions beyond traditional food and beverage, impacting sectors such as healthcare, education, corporate environments, leisure, sports, military, and government. Recognizing their dual-customer model (clients and end-users) is essential for effective management.
> - **Evolution and significance**: Understanding the historical evolution, from ancient Roman military logistics to today's sophisticated, technology-driven operations, provides valuable insight into managed services' ongoing importance and adaptability within the global hospitality landscape.
> - **Operational excellence and sustainability**: Successful managed services strategically balance budgeting, menu planning, compliance with industry regulations (FDA, FSA, ISO standards), and sustainability initiatives. This strategic balance emphasizes financial acumen, operational efficiency, regulatory adherence, and environmental responsibility.
> - **Influence of technological innovation**: Keeping pace with technological changes, including AI-driven dietary management, automation, robotics, and blockchain-enabled transparency, is critical for operational efficiency and client and guest satisfaction, and for achieving sustainability objectives within managed services globally.
> - **Career paths and organizational structures**: Understanding distinct organizational levels, including property-based roles, regional oversight, and corporate leadership, supports targeted career exploration, skill development, and professional advancement across diverse roles within the managed services industry.
> - **Global impact and professional development**: Leveraging global employment trends, strategic partnerships, and professional resources (such as industry associations, certifications, and structured training programs) positions you effectively for global career opportunities and leadership roles in the rapidly expanding managed services sector.

Looking ahead

In Chapter 8, you'll learn about events within hospitality and tourism, examining their economic significance, historical evolution, emerging industry trends, inclusive event planning strategies, organizational structures, and diverse career opportunities within this dynamic sector.

References

Aramark (2023) *Annual Report 2023*. aramark.gcs-web.com/static-files/f86f1d3f-f6a2-4830-b6ef-4c1e0395fd47 (archived at https://perma.cc/G4JZ-G44W)

Coherent Market Insights (2024) Contract catering market size, share, trends, growth and forecast 2024–2032. coherentmarketinsights.com/market-insight/contract-catering-market-3342?utm_source (archived at https://perma.cc/7PMG-ADET)

Compass Group (n.d.a), compass-group.com. See *Sports & Leisure, Education*, and *Food Services* (or relevant), and *Our heritage*. (archived at https://perma.cc/82HD-BD2Z)

Compass Group UK (n.d.b) *Levy UK + Ireland at Tottenham Hotspur Stadium*. compass-group.co.uk/about-us/our-work/levy-uk-tottenham-hotspur (archived at https://perma.cc/82HD-BD2Z)

Cousins, J., Foskett, D., Gillespie, C., & Rippington, N. (2019) *Food and Beverage Management: For the Hospitality, Tourism and Event Industries* (4th edn). Oxford: Goodfellow Publishers.

Credence Research (2024) *South Africa Managed Services Market Report*. credenceresearch.com/report/south-africa-managed-services-market (archived at https://perma.cc/YS68-VJV9)

Davis, B. & Stone, S. (2020) *Food and Beverage Management: An Innovative Approach*. London: Routledge.

Dubai Airports (2024) *Dubai Airports fact file*. media.dubaiairports.ae/dubai-airports-main-fact-file (archived at https://perma.cc/G5KK-GQQK)

FDA (Food and Drug Administration) (2024) *Guidance and Regulation (Food and dietary supplements)*. fda.gov/food/guidance-regulation-food-and-dietary-supplements (archived at https://perma.cc/6VEG-EZFG)

FSA (Food Standards Agency) (n.d.) *Food Safety and Hygiene*. food.gov.uk/food-safety-and-hygiene (archived at https://perma.cc/BUZ6-N4XL)

Grand View Research (2024) *Brazil Managed Services Market Size Report, 2024–2030*, grandviewresearch.com/horizon/outlook//managed-services-market/brazil (archived at https://perma.cc/357V-A2KK); *India Managed Services Market Size & Outlook, 2023-2030*, https://www.grandviewresearch.com/horizon/outlook/managed-services-market/india?utm_source (archived at https://perma.cc/2ST8-96EF)

Heathrow Airport Holdings (2024) *Annual Report and Financial Statements 2023*. heathrow.com/content/dam/heathrow/web/common/documents/company/investor/reports-and-presentations/annual-accounts/airport-holdings/2023_FY_HAHL_ARA_Final.pdf (archived at https://perma.cc/LFA5-TF9L)

Hendrix, S. (2025) Ohio State students embrace rovers for campus food delivery, March 19. *The Columbus Dispatch*. dispatch.com/story/news/education/2025/03/19/ohio-state-students-embrace-rovers-for-campus-food-delivery/82328637007 (archived at https://perma.cc/9P4W-HYB2)

Imperial College London (2023) Imperial joins international AI alliance to accelerate innovation. imperial.ac.uk/news/250038/imperial-joins-international-ai-alliance (archived at https://perma.cc/4A2U-8JRB)

ISO (International Organization for Standardization) (2023). *ISO 22000:2018 – Food safety management systems – Requirements for any organization in the food chain*. iso.org/standard/65464.html (archived at https://perma.cc/7PXH-L8ZK)

Jones, P. & Lockwood, A. (2018) *Hospitality Operations: A Systems Approach*. Oxford: Routledge.

National Restaurant Association (2024) *US foodservice industry employment statistics*. restaurant.org/research-and-media/research/industry-statistics/national-statistics (archived at https://perma.cc/K2T7-3C8H)

Practice Greenhealth (n.d.) *Sustainable procurement*. practicegreenhealth.org/topics/sustainable-procurement/sustainable-procurement (archived at https://perma.cc/FG8Y-UC5H)

Saleem, M.A., Mohammed, M., Khan, M.N.U., Saranya, M., Mohankumar, N., & Ashwini, B. (2025) Advanced IoT-Embedded Culinary Intelligence using RNN model for smart kitchen solutions with food waste reduction features, *Proceedings of the 11th International Conference on Communication and Signal Processing (ICCSP)*, IEEE, pp. 1275–1280.

Shrader, C.R. (ed.) (1997) *United States Army Logistics, 1775–1992: An Anthology*. Washington, DC: Center of Military History, US Army. history.army.mil/Portals/143/Images/Publications/Publication%20By%20Title%20Images/U%20Pdf/cmhPub_68-1.pdf (archived at https://perma.cc/VE9R-RJW6)

Smith, T. (2023) Robots are taking over UCSF Hospital – And that's a good thing, April 21. *Bay Area Telegraph*. bayareatelegraph.com/2023/04/21/robots-are-taking-over-ucsf (archived at https://perma.cc/4TTL-3JQE)

Sodexo (2023) *Financial Results and Publications*. sodexo.com/investors/financial-results-and-publications/financial-results (archived at https://perma.cc/VVF7-GC9Q)

Sodexo (2024a) Reducing food waste, us.sodexo.com/corporate-responsibility/impact-on-environment/reducing-food-waste?utm_source (archived at https://perma.cc/5JJ6-4NVA); Reducing food waste: One plate at a time with Yume, au.sodexo.com/insights/case-studies/2025/reducing-food-waste-with-yume?utm_source (archived at https://perma.cc/628V-6ZUM)

Sodexo (2024b) *Serving those who serve in the U.S. Government and military*. us.sodexo.com/industry/government (archived at https://perma.cc/EX6S-MMHS)

Sodexo (2024c) *Sustainability and Social Responsibility Reports*. us.sodexo.com/inspired-thinking/corporate-responsibility/reports/sustainability-social-responsibility (archived at https://perma.cc/AH9W-YQ6C)

Sodexo Healthcare (2024) *Patient dining services*. https://us.sodexo.com/industry/healthcare (archived at https://perma.cc/9TKL-NB3C)

Tannahill, R. (1988) *Food in History*. New York: Crown Publishers.

Tokyo Organising Committee (2021) *Sustainability Post-Games Report: Tokyo 2020*. library.olympics.com/Default/doc/SYRACUSE/1327958/sustainability-post-games-report-tokyo-2020-the-tokyo-organising-committee-of-the-olympic-and-paraly?_lg=en-GB (archived at https://perma.cc/E8B2-D44H).

UKHospitality (2023) *The Economic Contribution of the UK Hospitality Industry*. ukhospitality.org.uk/insight/economic-contribution-of-hospitality (archived at https://perma.cc/GV7G-MQTK)

Verified Market Research (2024) *Mexico Hospitality Market Size and Forecast*. verifiedmarketresearch.com/product/mexico-hospitality-market (archived at https://perma.cc/7KTG-TNS7)

World Economic Forum (2024) How blockchain tracks food across the supply chain and saves lives, August 12. weforum.org/stories/2024/08/blockchain-food-supply-chain/?utm_source (archived at https://perma.cc/6VCR-QDJ8)

WRI (World Resources Institute) (2024) Sourcing "better" meat entails significant tradeoffs, WRI analysis finds (press release), April 16. wri.org/news/release-sourcing-better-meat-entails-significant-tradeoffs-wri-analysis-finds (archived at https://perma.cc/8Q8P-6MFP)

WTTC (World Travel & Tourism Council) (2024) *Economic Impact Reports*. wttc.org/research/economic-impact (archived at https://perma.cc/YV56-6DW7)

Events   8

LEARNING OBJECTIVES

- Define events and event management, highlighting their role within hospitality and tourism.
- Explore the historical evolution of events and their transformation into sophisticated experiences.
- Identify different event categories and analyze their economic and cultural contributions.
- Explain the event planning process using the inclusive event planning framework.
- Examine emerging trends in events, including technology, sustainability, and inclusivity.
- Analyze real-world scenarios illustrating best practices in event management.

Introduction: What is event management?

Imagine attending a vibrant cultural festival in Rio de Janeiro, where rhythmic music and vivid colors unite visitors from around the world. Or picture yourself at Quebec City's Winter Carnival, strolling through snowy streets alive with ice sculptures, music, and joyful festivities. Perhaps you envision the excitement of Oktoberfest in Munich, where cultural traditions, lively music, and spirited celebrations draw crowds eager to experience Bavarian charm. These compelling gatherings highlight the dynamic world of events—an essential sector within hospitality and tourism. But what exactly defines an event, and what does event management entail?

An event is a carefully planned public or private gathering designed to meet specific objectives, such as celebrating milestones, sharing knowledge, or fostering community connections. Event management involves the strategic application of project management principles to effectively plan, coordinate, and evaluate events. Key responsibilities in this process include theme development, budgeting, venue selection, vendor coordination, marketing, risk management, and post-event evaluation (Cvent,

2025). Ultimately, successful event management ensures seamless experiences that fulfill their intended purposes and create lasting impressions.

Events serve crucial social, economic, and cultural purposes. They facilitate networking, education, and cultural exchange, while economically stimulating local communities by boosting tourism and creating jobs. High-profile events like the Olympic Games or Coachella exemplify this by significantly benefiting regional economies and promoting global visibility.

In hospitality and tourism, events are intertwined with the sectors of lodging, dining, travel, and recreation. Successful events often rely on hotels for guest accommodation, restaurants for catering services, and efficient travel logistics. Conversely, hospitality businesses regularly depend on events to increase occupancy rates and enhance revenues.

Moreover, events are strategic tools for corporate branding, customer engagement, and community enrichment. Whether launching new products, hosting industry conferences, or organizing cultural celebrations, effective event management strengthens relationships, boosts brand recognition, and promotes inclusivity. In today's landscape, technology and sustainability have become integral to event design. From virtual access and real-time engagement tools to eco-conscious menus and zero-waste goals, event planners are embracing innovation and responsibility to meet evolving guest expectations.

Understanding event management is essential for hospitality professionals. It requires critical skills in project management, marketing, financial oversight, and logistical coordination. Equipped with these skills, professionals can create impactful experiences tailored to diverse audiences and client expectations.

In this chapter, you'll explore event management's evolution, categories, operational frameworks, and emerging trends. Through these insights, you'll be prepared to excel in this dynamic and continually evolving field.

Historical overview and evolution of events

Events have played a pivotal role throughout human history, evolving dramatically over time to reflect societal, technological, and cultural changes. From early communal gatherings and celebrations to today's sophisticated global events, the journey of event management mirrors the development of civilization itself.

Historically, events served predominantly religious or seasonal purposes. Ancient civilizations, including those of Egypt, Greece, and Rome, regularly hosted festivals to worship deities, celebrate victories, and mark agricultural cycles. For example, the ancient Olympic Games in Greece not only showcased athletic excellence but also promoted unity and peace among city-states.

The medieval period introduced events that facilitated commerce and cultural exchange, such as fairs and markets. These gatherings, held regularly in European towns, became essential centers of trade, communication, and social interaction, laying the foundation for modern conventions and trade shows.

The Industrial Revolution significantly transformed event management by enabling mass transportation and communication. This period witnessed the emergence of world exhibitions like London's Great Exhibition in 1851 and Chicago's World Fair in 1893, which drew millions of domestic and international visitors and highlighted global industrial developments and cultural diversity. The 19th century also marked the revival of the Olympic Games, with the first modern Olympics in Athens in 1896. This revival underscored how historical events could be adapted and expanded into globally significant gatherings.

The 20th century saw a rapid evolution in the scale and sophistication of events. Advances in transportation and broadcast technology enabled events such as the Olympic Games and FIFA World Cup to reach global audiences, enhancing their cultural impact and economic significance. These large-scale events not only promoted international understanding but also stimulated substantial economic activity through tourism, infrastructure development, and job creation.

> **THINK LIKE A MANAGER**
>
> Imagine you're organizing a modern re-creation of the original Olympic Games. What historical elements would you preserve, and how would you adapt the event for today's global audience?

In recent decades, technological innovations have profoundly reshaped event management. The rise of the internet, digital communication tools, and social media platforms, such as Instagram, LinkedIn, and TikTok, have enabled event organizers to engage with global audiences instantly and efficiently. For example, platforms like Zoom and Hopin allowed major conferences, including the 2021 Consumer Electronics Show, to pivot to virtual formats during the Covid-19 pandemic, expanding their reach to thousands of additional participants worldwide who might not otherwise have attended. Similarly, social media-driven engagement during festivals like South by Southwest (SXSW) and Coachella has extended attendee interaction, with real-time audience feedback and enhanced overall event visibility. Alongside technological innovation, sustainability has emerged as a defining consideration in modern event management that shapes decisions around venue choice, material use, energy consumption, and community impact.

As global travel and communication have accelerated, the scope and complexity of event management has expanded. Planners today must consider international audiences, cultural norms, and multilingual needs, requiring inclusive, globally aware practices. Recognizing this historical evolution provides hospitality professionals with essential insights into contemporary event management. Today's sophisticated events reflect centuries of innovation, adaptation, and growth, positioning event management as a dynamic and influential field within hospitality and tourism.

> **Reflect**
>
> - Think about an event you've attended or studied. How has its history shaped the experience attendees have today?
> - Identify at least one historical factor or trend that significantly influenced how this event evolved into its current form.

Events across key sectors

Events are powerful engines driving economic growth, brand visibility, cultural expression, and community engagement. While distinct from each other, events deeply integrate across diverse sectors—hospitality, tourism, business, and beyond. From corporate conferences and global festivals to intimate weddings and sporting events, each sector uniquely leverages events to achieve strategic goals and create meaningful experiences.

This section explores how different segments integrate events into their operations, strategies, and identities. Each area has its own unique event types, planning needs, logistical demands, and target audiences, yet all share a common thread: the potential of events to create meaningful impact and memorable experiences.

Hospitality and tourism

Events are deeply embedded within the hospitality and tourism industries, driving visitation, stimulating local economies, and elevating guest experiences. From global festivals to intimate celebrations, events boost occupancy, support local vendors, and strengthen destination branding. As explored earlier, events serve purposes well beyond celebration—shaping economies, elevating brand identity, and building lasting community connections.

Hotels and resorts: Setting the stage for events

Hotels and resorts serve as versatile backdrops for a wide range of events, combining refined hospitality, seamless logistics, and inspiring settings to bring experiences to life. These venues offer both the physical space and the service expertise needed to transform a gathering into a memorable occasion.

Corporate retreats and conferences often unfold in well-appointed meeting rooms and flexible indoor-outdoor spaces, where professionals network, collaborate, and strategize against backdrops of serene beaches, vibrant cityscapes, or tranquil mountain ranges. Weddings and social celebrations shine in elegant ballrooms adorned with soft lighting, floral arrangements, and personalized details, from custom menus to thoughtful guest amenities, creating unforgettable moments for hosts and guests.

Hotels and resorts are also ideal venues for brand activations and marketing events, offering rooftop terraces, VIP suites, and luxury amenities for exclusive product launches, influencer campaigns, and curated guest experiences. Expansive exhibition halls and conference centers within large hotel properties accommodate trade shows and industry conventions, providing immersive environments for business exchange, learning, and innovation.

Prestigious galas and fundraising events take center stage in grand venues known for impeccable service, gourmet cuisine, and polished programming, inspiring both celebration and generosity. Cultural and seasonal celebrations further transform public spaces into festive, immersive environments with themed décor, live entertainment, and culinary specialties that reflect the local culture and seasonal spirit.

Collectively, these event types highlight the essential role hotels and resorts play as active hosts and creative partners. By managing and orchestrating events on-site, lodging venues boost brand equity, generate substantial revenue, and build lasting guest relationships. For example, Atlantis Paradise Island Resort in the Bahamas hosts large-scale corporate retreats, destination weddings, and exclusive brand launches that contribute directly to increased occupancy, dining revenue, spa use, and leisure activity engagement. These events not only fill rooms but also position resorts as destinations, driving repeat visitation and long-term loyalty (Atlantis Bahamas, n.d.).

Food and beverage: Enhancing culinary experiences

Culinary events play a crucial role in elevating hospitality offerings by showcasing regional gastronomy and creating memorable dining experiences that drive guest engagement. From chef-hosted tasting menus and themed dining nights to expertly curated wine or cocktail pairings, restaurants and private dining venues use events as platforms for creativity and brand differentiation. Catering services also shine in this segment—at weddings, gala dinners, and corporate functions—providing substantial revenue streams and visibility for local culinary talent. These experiences are not just meals—they are immersive expressions of place, culture, and hospitality. Food events such as the Melbourne Food & Wine Festival attract over 250,000 attendees annually, benefiting local economies and reinforcing the value of destination gastronomy (Melbourne Tourism, 2024).

Destination management and tourism organizations

Destination management organizations leverage events strategically to enhance destination branding, extend visitor stays, and generate year-round economic activity. Cultural and heritage festivals celebrate regional traditions, drawing global travelers and promoting cross-cultural understanding. Seasonal attractions such as holiday markets, themed food festivals, and community-wide celebrations create compelling reasons for repeat visitation and local pride. Brazil's iconic Rio Carnival, for instance, generates over $1 billion in economic activity each year, significantly boosting local tourism, hospitality, and international visibility (Rio Carnival, 2025). Sports tourism also plays a significant and vital role, with events like marathons, international competitions, and national championships attracting participants and spectators and filling hotels and restaurants.

Convention and exhibition centers: Economic powerhouses

Convention and exhibition centers serve as anchor institutions for business events, hosting large-scale trade shows, expos, and professional conferences that drive substantial economic activity. Trade shows and expos facilitate international commerce, providing platforms for product launches, networking, and industry collaboration. Meanwhile, professional conferences bring together researchers, thought leaders, and corporate professionals to share knowledge and spark innovation. Participating venues demand robust hospitality support systems, from lodging and catering to logistics and guest services. The Dubai World Trade Centre, for example, contributes approximately $3.3 billion annually to the city's economy, exemplifying how such venues are essential to business tourism (Dubai World Trade Centre, 2024).

Recreation and entertainment venues: Creating memorable experiences

Recreational and entertainment venues transform events into immersive, emotionally charged experiences that captivate guests and fuel tourism. Sports and entertainment arenas deliver electric atmospheres during international concerts, sporting events, and televised spectacles, all of which significantly benefit surrounding hotels, restaurants, and transportation providers. Theme parks like Disneyland and Universal Studios go a step further by hosting signature seasonal events, such as Halloween horror nights or holiday parades, that generate brand loyalty and repeat visitation. These experiences blend storytelling, hospitality, and spectacle to position venues as iconic destinations. Disney's special events, for instance, contribute to an annual economic impact exceeding $8.5 billion in the Orlando region alone (Visit Orlando, 2024).

Transportation and luxury travel: Enhancing visitor journeys

Transportation hubs and luxury travel providers are increasingly using events as strategic tools to enrich traveler experiences and foster high-end brand loyalty. Airports and cruise terminals now host cultural exhibits, destination showcases, and interactive installations that reflect local hospitality and welcome travelers with a sense of place. At the luxury end, private aviation services such as NetJets and elite yacht charters are known for hosting refined onboard events, ranging from exclusive culinary showcases to executive networking sessions. These curated experiences reinforce brand identity while delighting high-value guests. During the Monaco Yacht Show, for example, visitors aboard luxury yachts are treated to live music and personalized dining as part of an immersive brand activation. The event draws approximately 30,000 affluent visitors annually, significantly boosting luxury hospitality and tourism revenue in the region (Monaco Yacht Show, 2024).

> At NetJets, events are integral to our brand ethos, enabling us to foster deeper connections and deliver unmatched personalized experiences. Our carefully curated events—from exclusive onboard culinary experiences to high-touch client networking gatherings—serve as a powerful platform to showcase our commitment to excellence, build enduring client relationships, and distinguish our service in the luxury travel sector.
>
> —*Brittany Francis, executive vice president, owner services, NetJets*

Corporate and business

While hospitality-focused events drive visitation and enrich guest experiences, corporate and business events strategically leverage gatherings to achieve distinct commercial and marketing goals. Collectively known as MICE (meetings, incentives, conferences, and exhibitions), these events, including conferences, trade shows, product launches, and executive retreats, allow businesses to showcase innovations, strengthen professional networks, and engage stakeholders effectively. For instance, the Consumer Electronics Show (CES) in Las Vegas annually attracts over 175,000 global professionals and generates more than $300 million in local economic activity, benefiting the hospitality sector through hotel occupancy, dining, and transportation (CES, n.d.).

The strategic importance and broader economic impact of MICE events on the hospitality sector have been widely recognized (Cvent, 2024b; EHL Insights, 2020). MICE events significantly impact hospitality businesses by driving substantial revenue and enhancing destination reputation. The structured nature of these gatherings often requires specialized venues, tailored services, and meticulous event planning, underlining their importance in the broader hospitality and tourism landscape.

REAL-WORLD EXAMPLE:
INDUSTRY SPOTLIGHT   Salesforce Dreamforce Conference

Dreamforce 2024 generated significant economic benefits for its host city, San Francisco, with estimates ranging from $93 million to $100 million in local economic activity (Anand, 2024; Pena, 2024).

Arts, culture, and entertainment

Beyond business objectives, events in the arts, culture, and entertainment sectors foster creativity, storytelling, and cultural heritage. Festivals, theater productions, and art exhibitions attract diverse audiences, inspire community engagement, and enhance local economies through tourism.

Events within arts, culture, and entertainment play a vital role in enriching cultural experiences, showcasing artistic talent, and stimulating economic development. Festivals, theater productions, and art exhibitions not only enhance community engagement but also significantly attract regional, national, and international visitors.

The Venice Biennale, a major international arts exhibition in Italy, attracts more than 600,000 visitors every year, providing substantial economic benefits and cultural prestige for Venice. Effective management includes coordinating diverse international participants, extensive venue preparations, and high-profile media coverage (Harris, 2024).

REAL-WORLD EXAMPLE:
INDUSTRY SPOTLIGHT   Edinburgh Fringe Festival

The Edinburgh Fringe Festival is the largest arts festival globally, annually hosting over 3,000 performances across more than 300 venues. It attracts nearly 3 million attendees each year, significantly impacting Edinburgh's local economy, driving hospitality and tourism, and reinforcing Scotland's cultural prominence worldwide (Edinburgh Fringe, 2025).

Sports and recreation

Just as cultural events enhance artistic communities, sporting events serve as powerful catalysts for economic growth, community spirit, and international visibility. From local tournaments to global championships, sporting events require extensive planning, logistical coordination, and careful management.

The FIFA World Cup, for example, consistently attracts billions of global viewers, generating substantial economic impacts, infrastructure investments, and boosting tourism significantly in host countries. The 2022 World Cup in Qatar contributed an estimated $17 billion to the local economy (FIFA, 2023).

**REAL-WORLD EXAMPLE:
INDUSTRY SPOTLIGHT** Super Bowl LVII

Super Bowl LVII, hosted in Glendale, Arizona, attracted over 70,000 attendees and generated approximately $500 million in economic impact. Operational complexity included rigorous crowd control measures, extensive security logistics, media broadcasting requirements, and high-stakes vendor management, underscoring sports events' multifaceted planning needs (City of Glendale, 2023).

Healthcare and wellness

Events in healthcare and wellness sectors play essential roles in advancing medical knowledge, promoting public health initiatives, and fostering global health collaborations. Conferences, symposiums, and expos facilitate critical professional exchanges and health advocacy.

The American Heart Association's Scientific Sessions, for example, attract approximately 15,000 healthcare professionals annually, driving important collaborations and advances in cardiovascular health research and treatment (AHA, n.d.).

Government and civic engagement

From healthcare innovation to democratic engagement, government and civic events play pivotal roles in public awareness, diplomatic relations, and civic education. These events require rigorous adherence to protocol, security management, and meticulous logistics.

For example, the United Nations General Assembly, held annually in New York, involves complex planning, including international diplomatic protocols, comprehensive security arrangements, and logistical coordination for thousands of delegates and international media (United Nations, 2023).

**REAL-WORLD EXAMPLE:
INDUSTRY SPOTLIGHT**   COP28 Climate Summit

COP28, the UN Climate Change Conference in the UAE, involved over 200 countries and operated with a budget exceeding $100 million. Effective event management entailed extensive international cooperation, diplomatic protocol adherence, security measures, sustainability practices, and precise logistical arrangements, facilitating global environmental policy dialogues (UNFCCC, 2023).

Nonprofit and philanthropy

Just as government events facilitate international dialogue, nonprofit events play crucial roles in advocacy, fundraising, and community engagement. Such events require strategic planning to maximize impact, volunteer involvement, and effective community messaging.

The Susan G. Komen Race for the Cure events have engaged millions globally, raising over $2 billion for breast cancer research and awareness initiatives, emphasizing the event's significant role in public health advocacy (Komen, 2024).

**REAL-WORLD EXAMPLE:
INDUSTRY SPOTLIGHT**   American Cancer Society's Relay for Life

Relay for Life events involve more than 2 million participants annually, raising over $6 billion since their inception. These events, held as a series of community-driven gatherings organized locally, underscore their critical role in community engagement, fundraising, and public health advocacy (American Cancer Society, 2024).

Education

Moving from nonprofit advocacy to educational empowerment, academic events foster knowledge dissemination, institutional branding, and community relationships. Academic conferences, commencement ceremonies, and recruitment fairs require meticulous coordination and inclusive planning.

For example, the annual NAFSA Conference & Expo for international educators attracts over 10,000 attendees globally, significantly influencing international education policies, partnerships, and academic practices (NAFSA, n.d.).

REAL-WORLD EXAMPLE:
INDUSTRY SPOTLIGHT   Harvard University Commencement

Harvard's Commencement annually hosts around 32,000 guests, contributing significantly to local economic activity and institutional prestige. Operational management involves meticulous logistical planning, extensive security measures, accommodation coordination, and comprehensive event-day execution to ensure a memorable experience (Harvard University, n.d.).

Marketing, media, and PR

Events in marketing, media, and public relations sectors strategically amplify brand visibility and customer engagement. Experiential campaigns, brand activations, and media events rely on creative planning and precise execution.

The Cannes Lions International Festival of Creativity attracts approximately 15,000 advertising and communications industry leaders annually, significantly influencing global advertising trends and creative strategies (Cannes Lions, n.d.).

Real estate and development

> Real estate events are a powerful tool for connection and growth. Beyond celebrating key milestones, they play a vital role in fostering resident retention, attracting new prospects and strengthening community ties. These shared experiences create a sense of place and belonging, transforming properties into thriving neighborhoods where people feel connected, valued and inspired to call "home."
>
> —*Kari Derryberry, director of events and programming, Crawford Hoying*

From brand visibility in marketing to investor engagement in real estate, events strategically highlight property developments and stimulate market interest. Groundbreaking ceremonies, investor showcases, and property launches require detailed staging and precise logistics.

For example, MIPIM, the world's largest real estate event, attracts over 20,000 global property professionals each year, significantly influencing international real estate investment trends (MIPIM, n.d.).

REAL-WORLD EXAMPLE:
INDUSTRY SPOTLIGHT   CBRE investor showcase events

CBRE, a global commercial real estate services and investment firm, regularly hosts events that influence multimillion-dollar investment decisions. These presentations strategically showcase property developments through meticulous staging, targeted audience management, and precise logistical planning, directly impacting global real estate markets (CBRE, n.d.).

Inclusive event planning framework

Across every segment explored, whether hospitality and tourism, corporate, or arts and entertainment, events serve as a unifying force that connects people, places, and purpose. While each industry brings its own objectives, scale, and audience, successful event planning shares common threads: intentional design, thoughtful execution, and a focus on the guest or participant experience. Now that we've explored how different sectors use events to create impact, let's turn to how hospitality professionals can intentionally plan events that are inclusive, accessible, and aligned with core values.

Have you ever attended an event that felt genuinely welcoming, accessible, and memorable? The inclusive event planning framework guides and supports hospitality professionals to consistently create these meaningful experiences. Grounded in industry best practices and inclusivity principles, this comprehensive model emphasizes strategic clarity, audience understanding, proactive and intentional inclusivity, and thoughtful execution (Figure 8.1).

> The Inclusive Event Planning Framework helped me see event operations through a new lens. Planning events for people with different accessibility needs—such as mobility, sensory sensitivities, or language barriers—has supported my ability to consider a diverse range of individuals and their needs in hospitality and everyday settings.
>
> —*Sophia Troutman, hospitality management student*

Figure 8.1 Inclusive event planning framework

1. Discovery and analysis

Effective event planning begins by deeply understanding your audience and clearly defining event objectives. During this initial phase, systematically gather essential information about your attendees, including demographics, cultural backgrounds, accessibility needs, and expectations. Utilize tools such as surveys, historical attendance data, social media listening, and direct stakeholder conversations to collect comprehensive insights.

Early identification of potential risks, including budget constraints, venue limitations, and safety considerations, enables proactive management. Additionally, 75 percent of event professionals prioritize risk management and compliance as critical elements in their event strategies, emphasizing proactive management of potential risks, including budget constraints, venue limitations, and safety considerations (Cvent, 2024a).

2. Strategic planning

Strategic planning provides a clear roadmap, aligning event objectives with broader organizational or community goals within the clearly defined vision of the client. Effective planning involves setting measurable goals, defining priorities, establishing timelines, and allocating resources efficiently. When events are closely aligned with organizational strategy, they are more likely to achieve higher levels of relevance, engagement, and satisfaction among participants. Clearly define team roles and responsibilities, develop comprehensive contingency plans, and document your strategic objectives meticulously. Transparent communication enables smooth coordination among stakeholders, sponsors, and attendees, promoting effective collaboration and successful outcomes. An experienced planner will leverage their expertise to suggest engaging or accommodating elements that encourage the client to thoughtfully consider inclusivity and attendee engagement, always guided by and respectful of the client's vision and understanding of their audience.

3. Theme development

An impactful theme is the anchor and central narrative of your event. It clearly communicates the event's purpose, provides coherence across all elements, and acts as a filter guiding every decision, from design and décor to content, messaging, and speaker selection. Themes shape expectations, immediately signaling the "why" behind the event.

A thoughtfully selected theme ensures attendees instantly understand the event's core message and purpose. When themes are clearly communicated, participants are more likely to recognize relevance and value, which strengthens engagement. Themes guide branding, content creation, event messaging, and even logistical choices, creating cohesive, immersive experiences rather than disconnected activities.

4. Creative and inclusive design

Inclusive design transforms your event theme into a set of welcoming, accessible experiences for every visitor, regardless of physical, cognitive, cultural, or sensory abilities. For example, approximately 80 percent of individuals without hearing impairments regularly use captioning for enhanced clarity, underscoring how inclusive features benefit everyone (3Play Media, 2023).

Key inclusive considerations include:

- Clear, universally understandable signage (for example, use of universally recognized symbols, multilingual directions, Braille translations)
- Multilingual and accessible materials (event information provided digitally and in print, materials translated into multiple languages, easy-read formats for guests with cognitive disabilities)

- Sensory-friendly and quiet spaces (designated calm/quiet rooms, sensory-friendly lighting, reduced noise levels for guests sensitive to sensory stimulation)
- Captioning and sign language interpretation (real-time captioning benefiting both hearing-impaired guests and non-native speakers; captions improve content retention for all attendees)
- Flexible layouts and adaptive seating arrangements (wheelchair-accessible seating, seating variations for guests with different mobility needs or comfort preferences, open spaces to accommodate assistive devices or service animals)
- Inclusive communication strategies (promoting event details using multiple platforms to reach diverse audiences, ensuring inclusive language and imagery across promotional materials, training staff on respectful and clear communication)
- Religious and cultural accommodations (prayer rooms, scheduling mindful of religious observances, culturally respectful event dates)
- Dietary accommodations and transparent food labeling (clearly marked halal, kosher, vegan, gluten-free options)
- Mobility and transportation considerations (accessible shuttles, convenient drop-off points, barrier-free navigation pathways)

Considerately designed events significantly enhance attendee comfort, enjoyment, and participation—in environments where everyone feels genuinely welcomed and valued.

> **THINK LIKE A MANAGER**
>
> You're organizing a 500-person conference at a major hotel venue. The planning committee includes diverse stakeholders with varying access needs and cultural backgrounds. You've been tasked with ensuring the event design reflects the organization's values of inclusivity and wellness.
>
> What are three specific features or practices you would implement to ensure the event is welcoming, accessible, and inclusive for all attendees—without compromising on creativity or brand image?

5. Detailed planning and logistics

Detailed logistical planning ensures smooth, successful event execution. Develop precise operational plans and budgets covering all anticipated costs, including venue fees, catering, entertainment, accessibility accommodations, marketing expenses, and contingency funds. Without meticulous preparation, even small oversights in logistics can quickly escalate into major challenges, underscoring the necessity of careful planning.

Clearly documented responsibilities, timelines, vendor agreements, and regulatory compliance requirements mitigate operational risks. Comprehensive staff and volunteer training ensures everyone understands their roles, inclusivity standards and expectations, and crisis management protocols.

6. Marketing, promotions, and invitations

Strategic marketing effectively communicates your event's value, accessibility features, and inclusive commitments to diverse audiences. Utilize inclusive messaging, multilingual communication, and accessible digital formats across social media, websites, emails, and print materials to broaden attendee reach.

Events with clearly articulated inclusivity measures foster a stronger sense of belonging, which ensures all participants feel welcomed and valued. By anticipating diverse needs, such as accessibility accommodations, cultural considerations, dietary requirements, and gender-inclusive practices, planners create environments where attendees can fully engage. This improves the participant experience and strengthens the event's reputation as a space that reflects care, equity, and professionalism.

7. Coordination and execution

Effective coordination ensures detailed plans translate smoothly into real-time success. Efficient event-day management involves clearly structured communication, immediate issue resolution, real-time logistics oversight, and seamless guest experiences.

Event management tools, such as mobile apps, digital schedules, and real-time communication platforms, support teams to streamline execution and swiftly respond to operational challenges. Proactive, thorough coordination helps manage guest flow, vendor activities, accessibility accommodations, emergency preparedness, and technical support, delivering reliable, high-quality event experiences.

8. Evaluation and feedback

Comprehensive evaluation is crucial for continuous improvement and long-term success. Systematically collect structured feedback through surveys, interviews, stakeholder debriefings, and attendance metrics. Effective post-event evaluation allows planners to pinpoint areas for improvement, helping future events achieve higher satisfaction rates and operational efficiency.

Utilizing models such as Kolb's (1984) experiential learning cycle—encompassing concrete experience, reflective observation, abstract conceptualization, and active experimentation—supports ongoing learning. Events employing structured feedback loops show a 40 percent greater improvement in attendee satisfaction over successive events (PCMA, 2024), highlighting the benefit of evaluation for continuous event improvement.

9. Legacy and community impact (optional)

Outstanding events often produce lasting positive impacts beyond immediate outcomes. Look to clearly define, measure, and communicate your event's long-term economic, social, cultural, or environmental legacies. Demonstrating long-term impacts can significantly increase stakeholders' and community support, strengthening credibility and fostering goodwill.

Legacy planning includes long-term sustainability initiatives, ongoing community engagement, educational contributions, and lasting behavioral or social changes among attendees. Highlighting your event's enduring contributions supports future stakeholder investment, increases community engagement, and elevates the event's broader significance.

A checklist for the full framework is given in Figure 8.2.

Figure 8.2 Inclusive event planning framework checklist

Inclusive event planning framework checklist

- [x] **Discovery and analysis**
  - Identify audience needs (accessibility, culture, logistics).
  - Gather data (surveys, stakeholder input).
- [x] **Strategic planning**
  - Set goals, timeline, and contingency plans.
  - Align with organizational values and stakeholders.
- [x] **Theme development**
  - Craft a theme that reflects a purpose and drives decisions.
  - Apply theme consistently across all elements.
- [x] **Creative and inclusive design**
  - Consider signage, dietary needs, mobility access.
  - Incorporate captioning, quiet rooms, inclusive visuals.
- [x] **Detailed planning and logistics**
  - Assign roles and budgets.
  - Confirm vendor compliance and accommodations.
- [x] **Marketing and communication**
  - Use inclusive language and representative imagery.
  - Promote accessible features.
- [x] **Coordination and execution**
  - Real-time issue resolution and guest experience.
  - Staff training on inclusion and roles.
- [x] **Evaluation and feedback**
  - Collect feedback from all stakeholders.
  - Apply lessons to future planning.
- [x] **(Optional) Legacy and communication impact**
  - Plan for long-term benefit, sustainability, and reporting.

THINK LIKE A MANAGER
Crisis scenario

During a large community event, a major weather disruption forces a last-minute venue change. You've already committed to sustainability and accessibility standards in your original plan.

- How would you adapt quickly while maintaining your core event values?
- Which parts of your inclusive event planning framework would guide your response?

INTERACTIVE EXERCISE
Inclusive event planning at your organization

Approach this task thoughtfully, creatively, and practically. Your careful planning will directly translate into events that foster inclusivity, align with your organization's core values, engage stakeholders effectively, and deliver meaningful experiences for all participants.

Practice applying the inclusive event planning framework to design (or enhance) a small-scale event within your school, workplace, or community organization, ensuring alignment with organizational values, stakeholder expectations, accessibility, and belonging.

- Select one of the following options (note that for clarity and practicality, your event should have fewer than 300 attendees):
  a) Choose an existing event at your organization (for example, student club social, guest speaker series, workplace training session, community fundraiser) and enhance it using inclusive event planning principles.
  b) Create a new, small-scale event specifically designed to align with and highlight the core values of your organization or community.
- Clearly outline your inclusive event plan by addressing each of the following structured steps. Develop an inclusive event outline clearly addressing:

  1 Discovery and audience analysis

  o *Audience identification*: Who specifically is your event designed for? Identify key audience segments (students, employees, community members, and so on).

- *Accessibility needs*: Clearly list at least two specific accessibility or inclusivity needs your audience might have (such as dietary restrictions, mobility access, cultural or religious accommodations).
- *Data collection*: Briefly explain how you'll gather accurate and relevant information about audience needs (perhaps short surveys, focus groups, interviews, social media engagement).

2 **Connecting with organizational values and stakeholders**
- *Organizational values*: Identify two core values of your school, workplace, or community organization (such as diversity, sustainability, wellness). Clearly explain how your event specifically embodies and promotes these values.
- *Stakeholder goals*: List two key stakeholders (organizational leaders, department heads, community members, attendees). Briefly describe their goals or expectations and explain how your event addresses and aligns with these objectives.

3 **Theme development and inclusive design**
- *Event theme*: Clearly present your event's theme, describing why it effectively communicates the event's purpose, supports organizational values, and provides a clear, cohesive experience for attendees.
- *Inclusive elements*: Detail two specific inclusive design elements or activities you'll incorporate (such as sensory-friendly spaces, multilingual signage, religious accommodation areas like prayer rooms, clearly marked dietary options).

4 **Planning and logistics**
- *Logistics*: Give two logistical details directly linked to inclusivity and accessibility (accessible venue pathways, provision of accessible transportation, sign language interpretation availability, and so on).
- *Budgeting*: Clearly identify one budget consideration essential for inclusivity (such as costs associated with hiring interpreters, closed captioning services, providing assistive technology).

5 **Marketing and communication**
- *Inclusive marketing strategies*: Clearly outline two strategies you'll use to effectively market and communicate your event's inclusivity efforts (inclusive and representative visuals, multilingual or plain-language promotional materials, targeted outreach to diverse groups).

6 **Coordination, execution, and evaluation**
   - *Execution planning:* Briefly describe your approach to ensuring effective day-of-event coordination (detailed run schedules, clearly assigned staff roles, real-time communication strategies).

7 **Feedback and continuous improvement**
   - Identify one practical method you'll use to gather attendee feedback after the event (such as short online surveys, in-person interviews, suggestion boxes).
   - Clearly explain how you'll analyze and apply this feedback to continuously enhance inclusivity and overall event effectiveness for future planning.

- Draw up a concise and structured summary (two to three pages) clearly outlining your inclusive event plan. Prepare a brief informal presentation highlighting key inclusive strategies, organizational value alignment, stakeholder engagement, and anticipated logistical challenges with your proposed solutions.
- **Select or create an event**: Choose an event idea that is both meaningful and practical for your group.
- **Clearly define team roles**: Clearly assign roles within your team (audience researcher, logistics coordinator, stakeholder liaison, marketing specialist, evaluation coordinator, and so on) to streamline efficiency and ensure thorough planning.

Emerging trends in events

As the event industry evolves, professionals must stay attuned to emerging trends that reflect global values, sustainability, and technological innovation. Shifting audience expectations are transforming how events are imagined and executed, requiring experiences that are not only well-organized, but also immersive, inclusive, and impactful. Whether planning a music festival, leadership summit, or international trade show, understanding emerging trends is essential to designing meaningful experiences.

Importantly, these trends represent broader shifts in values and strategy rather than short-term fads. While technologies and tools may change, the themes of personalization, access, sustainability, and community connection are likely to remain relevant. Still, professionals must stay curious and proactive as the industry continues to evolve.

Event professionals are encouraged to regularly read industry publications, such as those from Skift Meetings, PCMA, and Cvent, participate actively in professional associations, and attend educational events to stay informed about industry innovations, emerging trends, and audience preferences. According to Cvent (2024a), 79 percent of planners view events as significantly more valuable compared to other sales, marketing, or business initiatives, underscoring the importance of a clear understanding of audience needs for enhancing event outcomes.

Immersive and experiential design

Modern audiences crave more than information—they seek *experience*. An immersive event design taps into the senses and emotions of guests, in environments that foster deep engagement.

From sensory lounges and light shows to interactive installations and themed spaces, event planners are leveraging creative storytelling to make events unforgettable. VR/AR tools allow guests to explore venues, try products, or attend sessions in fully digital formats.

Hybrid and phygital events

The Covid pandemic accelerated the rise of hybrid events, which blend physical and digital components to enhance accessibility, flexibility, and global reach. Taking this concept further, "phygital" events integrate physical environments with digital tools, offering easy transitions between in-person and virtual experiences. These events often feature live-streamed panels with real-time Q&A, digital networking lounges, on-demand content libraries, and AR wayfinding apps that enrich both engagement and user experience. As technology continues to shape event planning, hybrid formats are no longer seen as temporary solutions but as industry standards—72 percent of event organizers now report that hybrid capabilities are a permanent expectation (Skift Meetings, 2024).

Purpose-driven and inclusive programming

Today's attendees increasingly expect events to reflect their values, leading to a rise in mission-aligned programming that centers on equity, inclusion, social impact, and community building. Inclusive event design goes beyond intent—it requires thoughtful planning that accounts for diverse identities and needs. This includes curating diverse speaker lineups, providing closed captioning and sign language interpretation, offering gender-neutral bathrooms, and designing sensory-friendly environments. Ensuring culturally respectful content is also critical to fostering a sense of belonging among attendees. Festivals like the Oska Bright Film Festival in the UK spotlight neurodivergent filmmakers, setting an example for inclusive representation.

Similarly, the Sundance Film Festival offers captioned virtual screenings and BIPOC filmmaker showcases to broaden access and amplify underrepresented voices (Sundance Institute, n.d.).

Sustainability and climate-conscious planning

As climate concerns rise, sustainability has become a central focus in event planning. Planners are rethinking every aspect of the event life cycle to minimize environmental impact and model responsible practices. Common strategies include using compostable and reusable materials, selecting plant-based catering, reducing printed materials or going entirely paperless, choosing venues with LEED certifications, and offering carbon offset options to attendees. One notable example is Fuji Rock Festival in Japan, which has implemented a zero-waste strategy by using reusable dishware and organizing volunteer-led recycling education—reducing landfill waste by over 50 percent (Fuji Rock Festival, 2025). Reflecting a wider shift in the industry, 76 percent of planners now say sustainability goals directly influence their vendor and venue decisions (Event Industry Council, 2023).

AI, smart tech, and personalization

Artificial intelligence and smart technologies are revolutionizing how events are planned, managed, and experienced. AI tools are often used to generate personalized attendee schedules based on individual interests, match participants for networking opportunities, translate sessions in real time, and deliver automated customer support via chatbots. Wearables like smart badges and RFID wristbands track attendee movements across event spaces, providing real-time insights into foot traffic, popular booths, and session engagement. These data points help organizers refine event design, improve flow, and create more customized experiences.

> **THINK LIKE A MANAGER**
>
> How could AI tools help you tailor an event to the preferences of different guest segments in real time?

Wellness integration

Wellness has emerged as a core component of the modern attendee experience, evolving from a luxury into a standard expectation. Today's events increasingly incorporate stretch breaks, guided meditation, nutritious catering options, mental health resources, and designated quiet or decompression zones. These offerings support physical and emotional well-being while improving attendee satisfaction and engagement. The PCMA Convening Leaders conference exemplifies this trend by including yoga sessions, guided journaling activities, and a dedicated Rest and Recharge Lounge to help participants maintain energy and focus throughout the event (PCMA, 2024).

Festivalization and edutainment

The line between entertainment and education is blurring as event planners borrow from the high-energy format of festivals to reimagine traditional conferences. This trend—often called "festivalization"—infuses events with music, food trucks, pop-up activations, interactive art, and surprise performances to boost engagement and emotional resonance. These vibrant environments promote learning through experience and social connection, transforming passive participation into active exploration. The South by Southwest (SXSW) festival is a leader in this space, blending concerts, comedy, TED-style talks, and workshops to present a cross-industry creative knowledge exchange in a celebratory festival format.

Micro-events and curated experiences

In contrast to sprawling mega-conferences, many planners now favor micro-events—smaller, curated gatherings designed to foster intimacy and meaningful connection. These include executive retreats, invite-only product demos, and VIP networking dinners that target specific audiences with personalized content and experiences. Micro-events allow brands and organizations to go deeper rather than broader, building trust, loyalty, and long-term relationships through high-impact, high-touch engagement.

Creative venues and local experiences

Today's events are breaking free from traditional ballrooms. Unique venues like rooftop gardens, museums, greenhouses, and industrial warehouses offer unexpected and memorable backdrops for experiences.

Pairing events with local culture, such as farm-to-table dining or regional entertainment, adds authenticity and sense of place. As an example, the Global Wellness Summit in Tel Aviv has hosted events in art galleries, local markets, and historic neighborhoods, offering immersive cultural context.

> **THINK LIKE A MANAGER**
>
> Which emerging trend do you believe will have the most lasting impact on the event industry? Why? Consider recent events or examples from this chapter to support your perspective.

Emerging event trends reflect a desire for meaningful, inclusive, and connected experiences. However, trends are continually developing in response to changing technologies, global conditions, and audience expectations. While many of the trends outlined here are expected to influence event design for the foreseeable future, professionals must stay informed and agile as the industry continues to shift.

For example, technology is increasingly supporting sustainable practices, from digital ticketing and AI-optimized scheduling to carbon-tracking software that helps planners quantify and reduce environmental impact. Planners are increasingly challenged to balance technology, human needs, and social responsibility, making innovation not just a goal but a necessity. Whether large or small, events that align with contemporary values and adapt creatively to change are more likely to leave a lasting impression.

> **Reflect**
>
> - Which emerging trend discussed in this chapter, such as sustainability, technology, or inclusivity, do you find most important or impactful for the future of event management? Why?
> - Provide an example of how this trend could positively transform a real-world event you're familiar with or would like to plan.

Event management structures: Models, partnerships, and integrated approaches

Event management structures vary based on an organization's size, ownership model, and operational priorities. Some venues, such as convention centers, arenas, and stadiums, use multi-vendor partnerships, where specialized providers manage services including catering, audiovisual production, security, and operations. This model offers flexibility and deep expertise, but can involve complex coordination.

Conversely, vertically integrated models are managed by a single company that oversees multiple aspects of the event life cycle, including venue operations, catering, rentals, décor, and full-scale planning. This structure provides greater control, cohesive branding, streamlined communication, and often higher profitability, especially in destination resorts and large hotel chains with in-house event teams.

Structural preferences also vary by region. In North America and Europe, multi-vendor partnerships are most common. Asia, the Middle East, and Latin America tend to favor integrated or bundled service models, often managed by government-affiliated organizations or large corporations. Understanding these global differences is part of the cultural adaptability required in international event careers.

Whether you aspire to work in a hotel's in-house events team, join a global agency, or manage operations for a stadium or cultural venue, knowing how events are structured behind the scenes will help you find the roles that best fit your strengths and goals. Table 8.1 summarizes key models of event management, along with representative examples of each in action.

Career pathways within event management structures

The type of event management structure you choose to work within significantly influences your daily responsibilities, career trajectory, and advancement opportunities. Career paths within event management can vary widely, from roles in large, multinational organizations to positions in SMEs or entrepreneurial ventures. Table 8.2 illustrates typical pathways in various organizational settings.

Table 8.1 Common event organizational structures in practice

Model	Description	Examples
Venue-based management (multi-vendor model)	Multiple specialized vendors manage distinct services like catering, audiovisual, and security, requiring extensive coordination.	Javits Center (NY), ExCeL London (UK), Greater Columbus Convention Center (OH), Mercedes-Benz Stadium (GA)
Integrated management (single entity model)	One company manages all event elements (planning, ticketing, operations), allowing streamlined decision-making.	Coachella (USA), Glastonbury Festival (UK), Summer Sonic (Japan)

(continued)

Table 8.1 (Continued)

Model	Description	Examples
Vertically integrated event firms	Companies begin with one core service (such as catering) and expand to own venues and manage events end to end.	Cameron Mitchell Premier Events (USA), Wolfgang Puck Catering (USA), MCI Group (global)
Agency-based event management	Agencies manage logistics, branding, and experiences on behalf of clients, especially for large corporate or global events.	Freeman (global), George P. Johnson (USA), BCD Meetings & Events (global), Pico Group (Asia)
Hotel-based event management	Hotels internally manage all event aspects: venue, catering, guest rooms, and audiovisual services.	Marriott, Hilton, Hyatt, IHG (global)
Entertainment and sports venue operations	Blended management structures using internal teams and external partners for hospitality and premium services.	Madison Square Garden (NY), OVG (global), AEG Worldwide (global), Accor Arena (Paris)

Table 8.2 Career pathways within event management

Organizational setting	Typical entry-level roles	Advancement opportunities
Venue-based management (such as convention centers, arenas)	• Catering assistant • Concessions staff • Venue operations assistant	• Executive chef • Director of F&B • Regional director of operations • VP of venue services
Integrated festival/event company	• Food vendor coordinator • Logistics intern • Guest services assistant	• Director of experience • Culinary program director • VP of festival operations • Co-founder/owner
Vertically integrated event firm (such as catering plus venues plus rentals)	• Event services coordinator • Rental fulfillment • Culinary assistant	• Director of catering • Head of culinary innovation • Managing partner • CEO

(continued)

Table 8.2 (Continued)

Organizational setting	Typical entry-level roles	Advancement opportunities
Agency-based event firm	• Event assistant • Project coordinator • Onsite logistics support	• Senior producer • Strategy director • VP of brand events • Agency principal
Hotel-based event team	• Banquet server • Event sales assistant • F&B attendant	• Director of catering and events • Director of F&B • Area hotel general manager • VP of operations
Entertainment or sports venue	• Concessions host • Premium lounge server • Fan experience associate	• Premium hospitality manager • Director of guest experience • VP of culinary services • Head of venue hospitality
Dedicated F&B or catering organizations	• Culinary apprentice • Catering driver • Setup crew	• Executive chef • Director of culinary operations • Regional catering director • Chief culinary officer

Additionally, professionals often progress from roles within larger, established organizations or SMEs (such as Marriott, Levy Restaurants, and Freeman) to launching their own independent event management businesses. Venue size and complexity further influence the organizational structure and operational strategy. Larger venues like stadiums and convention centers often integrate extensive internal teams with numerous external vendors, whereas smaller venues or SMEs typically collaborate closely with selected key service providers. Understanding these variations can help aspiring professionals strategically navigate their career development within the dynamic events industry.

> **INTERACTIVE EXERCISE**
> Analyzing a cross-sector career path
>
> Review the following spotlight story on Molly Kurth, then complete Table 8.3 to analyze how different aspects of her journey align with key concepts from this and previous chapters.

Table 8.3 Career path analysis

Category	How does Molly Kurth's career illustrate this?
Industry segments	For example, managed services, sports and entertainment, education, corporate dining
Event disciplines	For example, operations, HR, guest experience, marketing, logistics
Core service elements	For example, catering, venue strategy, talent development
Transferable skills	For example, communication, leadership, adaptability, strategic thinking

Reflecting on Molly Kurth's career will help you to better understand how different industry segments, event disciplines, service areas, and transferable skills work together to support professional growth in the hospitality and events industry.

Optional extension

Choose another leader in the hospitality or events industry (such as Marriott or Freeman), smaller boutique event planning organizations, or independent event management companies. Research their career path and fill in the same chart. Compare the similarities and differences in roles, segments, and skill development. Consider exploring paths that involve progressing from roles within larger companies to founding one's own event planning business.

CAREER SPOTLIGHT

Hospitality in action: From student catering manager to senior VP, Molly Kurth, Compass Group

Molly Kurth's hospitality journey began as a student catering manager with Marriott Management Services, managing event setup, staffing, and guest experiences on campus. Over the years, she advanced through operational and strategic leadership roles across industry-leading companies including Marriott, Sodexo, and Compass with roles in Levy and Chartwells, as well as enterprise-level positions. Along the way, she gained expertise in operations, sales, marketing, communications, business strategy, hospitality innovation, and talent development.

Her career includes roles as vice president of NCAA Operations at Levy, where she developed national strategies to elevate the fan experience, and division president of Chartwells, where she led business strategy and team development. Today, she serves as senior vice president of HR, learning, and talent development at Compass Group USA, one of the world's largest managed services companies.

With over 300,000 associates and services delivered at over 10,000 client locations across the US, Compass Group touches nearly every facet of hospitality, including sports and entertainment, healthcare, higher education, and corporate services. In this role, Kurth helps shape the future of hospitality by developing people-first strategies that support talent across all levels of the industry.

Key takeaway

Kurth's path illustrates how hospitality professionals can grow from hands-on roles to executive leadership through curiosity, collaboration, and strategic thinking. Her career demonstrates the power of cross-functional expertise across food and beverage operations, sales and marketing, people development, and change management—and how managed services companies offer meaningful, scalable career paths for aspiring leaders.

Reflect

- Which aspects of Molly Kurth's experience are most relevant or appealing to your own career goals?
- How can transferable skills allow hospitality professionals to seamlessly move across different industry segments and roles?
- Identify a specific industry segment and role combination you would most like to pursue, and briefly explain why.

Getting started in your career exploration

Now that you understand the various organizational structures, event trends, and potential career paths within the events industry, it's time to actively explore your career opportunities. This section offers resources spanning US, UK, and global markets to help you begin your career exploration journey effectively.

Join professional associations

Professional associations offer valuable opportunities for networking, career development, continuing education, and professional recognition. Many provide free or heavily discounted memberships for students, giving you access to exclusive events, job boards, and industry insights. Joining these associations early in your career can help you build connections, explore career paths, and stay informed about trends in the events industry.

Explore the following curated list of regional and global associations:

Global

- **International Live Events Association (ILEA)**—ileahub.com: A global community for live event professionals, focused on collaboration and education.
- **Meeting Professionals International (MPI)**—mpi.org: The largest international association for meeting and event professionals.
- **International Association of Exhibitions and Events (IAEE)**—iaee.com: Supports professionals involved in exhibitions and trade shows worldwide.
- **Professional Convention Management Association (PCMA)**—pcma.org: Offers education and networking for professionals in meetings and conventions.
- **International Congress and Convention Association (ICCA)**—iccaworld.org: Specializes in global association meetings and convention management.

US

- **National Association for Catering and Events (NACE)**—nace.net: Serves professionals in catering, event planning, and hospitality.
- **Events Industry Council (EIC)**—eventscouncil.org: Establishes standards and certifications for the global events industry.

UK and Europe

- **Association of Event Organisers (AEO)**—aeo.org.uk: Represents companies that organize trade and consumer events.
- **Meetings Industry Association (MIA)**—mia-uk.org: Offers accreditation, training, and best practice resources for meetings professionals.
- **European Major Exhibition Centres Association (EMECA)**—emeca.eu: Represents leading exhibition venues across Europe.

Asia-Pacific

- **Asia Pacific Incentives and Meetings Event (AIME)**—aime.com.au: A premier networking and trade event for Asia-Pacific meeting and event professionals.

- **Meetings & Events Australia (MEA)**—mea.org.au: Supports the professional development of event practitioners in Australia.

Equipped with these valuable resources and practical strategies, you can proactively explore the dynamic world of event management. Remember that each career path is unique, so continually engage with industry professionals, stay informed about emerging trends, and seek opportunities to build experience and connections. The resources provided here offer a robust foundation to support your ongoing professional development and success in the global events industry.

> Bookmark company career pages and follow their LinkedIn profiles to stay updated on seasonal and long-term hiring trends.

Key takeaways

- **Dynamic role of events**: Events are powerful engines of economic, cultural, and social impact, serving critical roles within hospitality and tourism, and extending into sectors such as corporate, arts and entertainment, sports, healthcare, nonprofit, education, marketing, real estate, and government.
- **Evolution and significance**: Understanding the historical evolution of events, from ancient cultural celebrations to today's sophisticated global events, offers valuable insight into their ongoing importance and dynamic adaptation within global hospitality practices.
- **Inclusive event planning**: Implementing the inclusive event planning framework ensures events are strategically designed, accessible, welcoming, and impactful. This approach emphasizes comprehensive audience understanding, strategic alignment, intentional inclusivity, logistical precision, and continuous improvement through structured evaluation and feedback.
- **Emerging industry trends**: Staying informed about emerging event trends—such as immersive experiences, hybrid and virtual event formats, sustainability practices, AI-driven personalization, wellness integration, and purposeful inclusivity—is essential for organizing innovative, relevant, and successful events.
- **Career paths and organizational structures**: Understanding various organizational models—including venue-based, integrated festival management, vertically integrated firms, agency-based companies, hotel event teams, and entertainment venues—enables targeted career exploration and strategic professional growth in the diverse events industry.

- **Global professional development resources**: Leveraging professional associations, targeted job resources, strategic networking opportunities, and structured career exploration activities significantly accelerates your professional development and positions you effectively for global career opportunities within events and hospitality.

Looking ahead

In Chapter 9, on tourism, you'll discover how tourism interconnects with hospitality, examining its economic significance, historical development, key segments, and emerging trends. Explore how tourism destinations strategically leverage hospitality services and events to attract and retain visitors, and learn about diverse career pathways within the vibrant and globally impactful tourism sector.

References

3PlayMedia (2023) *Accessibility and online video statistics*. 3playmedia.com/accessibility-online-video-stats (archived at https://perma.cc/8LGC-RSK6)

American Cancer Society (2024) Celebrating 40 Years of Relay for Life. acsresources.org/relayforlife/40yearsofimpact (archived at https://perma.cc/TZ97-9L4R)

AHA (American Heart Association) (2024) *Scientific Sessions*. professional.heart.org/scientificsessions (archived at https://perma.cc/F5BP-GPKR)

Anand, P. (2024) Benioff on bringing Dreamforce back to SF: "If all goes well, why not?", *The San Franciso Standard*, September 17. sfstandard.com/2024/09/17/benioff-bringing-dreamforce-back-to-san-francisco (archived at https://perma.cc/7644-FHKQ)

Atlantis Bahamas (n.d.) *Meetings and events*. atlantisbahamas.com/meetings (archived at https://perma.cc/E69P-AXZZ)

Cannes Lions (n.d.) *Festival*. canneslions.com/festival (archived at https://perma.cc/PQY3-PCZ5).

CBRE (n.d.) *Events & Presentations*. ir.cbre.com/events-presentations/events (archived at https://perma.cc/8SK3-GNDG)

CES (n.d.) *Consumer Electronics Show*. ces.tech (archived at https://perma.cc/8YJY-QWQF)

City of Glendale (2023) Super Bowl LVII generates $1.3 billion economic impact for Arizona. glendaleaz.com/news/what_s_new/super_bowl_l_v_i_i_economic_impact (archived at https://perma.cc/7LFK-UZE4)

Cvent (2024a) 116 event statistics shaping the industry in 2025 (blog), March 27. cvent.com/en/blog/events/event-statistics (archived at https://perma.cc/X3TL-GK2V)

Cvent (2024b) What Is MICE? Your guide to meetings, incentives, conferences, and exhibitions (blog), February 26. cvent.com/en/blog/hospitality/what-is-mice (archived at https://perma.cc/R9EK-S347)

Cvent (2025) What is event management? An ultimate guide? (blog), March 12. cvent.com/en/blog/events/what-is-event-management (archived at https://perma.cc/T7SV-JNV2)

Dubai World Trade Centre (2024) DWTC set to welcome over 3.6 million attendees in 2024. dwtc.com/en/press/dwtc-attendees-in-2024 (archived at https://perma.cc/UH35-L536)

Edinburgh Fringe (2025) *Our review of the year*. edfringe.com/about-us/the-fringe-society/our-review-of-the-year (archived at https://perma.cc/8GZ9-7PU7)

EHL Insights (2020) What is MICE? (Meetings, incentives, conferences & exhibitions), August 20. hospitalityinsights.ehl.edu/what-is-mice (archived at https://perma.cc/53ME-6KL9)

Event Industry Council (2023) *Sustainability and Events Study*. eventscouncil.org/Sustainability (archived at https://perma.cc/7PTT-JD5K)

FIFA (2023) *FIFA World Cup Qatar 2022 Sustainability Report: Economic Impact*. https://inside.fifa.com/tournament-organisation/world-cup-2022-sustainability-report (archived at https://perma.cc/KS9E-QS6D)

Fuji Rock Festival (2025) *Festival Echo: Fuji Rock with the Forest*. en.fujirockfestival.com/2024/0607b (archived at https://perma.cc/8GEC-RZ7F)

Harris, G. (2024) Venice Biennale reveals 2024 visitor figures, *The Art Newspaper*, November 25. theartnewspaper.com/2024/11/25/venice-biennale-reveals-2024-visitor-figures (archived at https://perma.cc/VR88-XD3W)

Harvard University (n.d.) *Harvard University Commencement*. commencement.harvard.edu (archived at https://perma.cc/39LD-BNQJ)

Kolb, D.A. (1984) *Experiential Learning: Experience as the Source of Learning and Development*. Englewood Cliffs, NJ: Prentice-Hall.

Komen (2024) *Susan G. Komen Race for the Cure*. komen.org/raceforthecure (archived at https://perma.cc/Z3UG-MVSZ)

Melbourne Tourism (2024) *Melbourne Food & Wine Festival Annual Impact Report*. melbournefoodandwine.com.au (archived at https://perma.cc/Q9F3-2J4X)

MIPIM (n.d.) *MIPIM: The global urban festival*. mipim.com (archived at https://perma.cc/A67V-LQRF)

Monaco Yacht Show (2024) The Monaco Yacht Show: A tribute to innovation and excellence (press release), October 23. monacoyachtshow.com/en/the-monaco-yacht-show-2024-a-tribute-to-innovation-and-excellence (archived at https://perma.cc/CS74-YHYP)

NAFSA (n.d.) *Conferences*. nafsa.org/conferences (archived at https://perma.cc/E2AS-FVQS)

PCMA (2024) *2024 PCMA Convening Leaders*. pcma.org/event/2024-pcma-convening-leaders (archived at https://perma.cc/GQL9-T5H5)

Rio Carnival (2025) Economic and tourist impacts of Rio Carnival 2026. https://www.rio-carnival.net/en/impactos-economicos-e-turisticos-do-carnaval-do-rio-2026/ (archived at https://perma.cc/BT5S-4DSR)

Pena, L. (2024) A look into how Dreamforce changed SF for the better during its 4-day conference, ABC7 News, September 20. abc7news.com/post/dreamforce-2024-how-conference-changed-san-francisco/15327493/#:~:text=Dreamforce%20is%20set%20to%20bring,money%20outside%20of%20the%20hotels (archived at https://perma.cc/C52W-M8YR)

Skift Meetings (2024) *Skift Meetings Megatrends 2024*. meetings.skift.com/reports/skift-meetings-megatrends-2024 (archived at https://perma.cc/4PCT-JV7M)

Sundance Institute (n.d.) *Equity, impact and belonging*. sundance.org/programs/outreach-and-inclusion (archived at https://perma.cc/8WZG-8EL9)

UNFCCC (2023) COP28: What was achieved and what happens next? unfccc.int/cop28/5-key-takeaways (archived at https://perma.cc/BZC6-V835)

United Nations (2023) High-Level Week 2023. un.org/en/high-level-week-2023 (archived at https://perma.cc/J6JJ-47JW)

Visit Orlando (2024) Central Florida's tourism industry hits record $92.5 billion in economic impact (blog), August 23. visitorlando.org/about/corporate-blog/post/central-floridas-tourism-industry-hits-record-925-billion-in-economic-impact (archived at https://perma.cc/E723-2BB3)

The tourism industry 9

> **LEARNING OBJECTIVES**
>
> - Describe the historical development and key milestones shaping the modern tourism industry.
> - Analyze tourism's economic, cultural, and environmental impacts using real-world examples.
> - Identify key tourism segments, including leisure, business, cultural, ecotourism, and niche markets, highlighting their distinct characteristics.
> - Evaluate factors influencing traveler behavior and decision-making processes in tourism contexts.
> - Discuss sustainable tourism principles and practices, emphasizing their importance in balancing economic growth with environmental and cultural preservation.
> - Connect core hospitality and tourism concepts to practical career opportunities, highlighting essential skills and professional pathways within the tourism sector.

Introduction: Tourism as a global industry

Imagine backpacking through Europe's historic cities, feeling the energy of iconic music festivals like Glastonbury or Coachella, sampling street food in Tokyo's vibrant neighborhoods, or marveling at Dubai's futuristic skyline. These diverse experiences capture the essence of tourism: a dynamic, globally interconnected industry that thrives on human interaction, cultural exchange, innovation, and sustainability.

As noted in earlier chapters, tourism significantly influences global economies, cultures, and environments. It was projected to generate a remarkable $11.1 trillion globally in 2024, directly supporting nearly 348 million jobs worldwide and surpassing pre-pandemic employment levels (WTTC, n.d.). Beyond economic benefits, tourism fosters cross-cultural understanding, sustainable growth, and meaningful international collaboration, reinforcing its global interconnectedness.

Every year, curiosity, adventure, business, education, and the simple desire for new experiences drive millions to explore unfamiliar places. Tourism intricately weaves together hospitality, transportation, attractions, events, and managed services, creating a collaborative ecosystem where each sector supports and enriches the others. As you'll discover throughout this chapter, tourism thrives most when this network operates sustainably, innovatively, and inclusively, prioritizing responsible growth and universal accessibility.

Furthermore, tourism plays a critical role in raising cultural and environmental awareness. It provides a valuable platform for regions around the globe to celebrate and, if care is taken, protect their unique traditions, histories, and natural beauty. When it supports conservation and sustainable practices, tourism helps preserve destinations' authenticity and vitality, ensuring their continuation for future generations.

In this chapter, you'll explore tourism's fascinating history, analyze its wide-ranging economic and cultural impacts, identify key trends shaping its future, and uncover rewarding career paths available within this exciting and evolving industry.

Historical development and evolution of tourism

The roots of tourism extend deep into history, reflecting humanity's enduring curiosity and desire to explore beyond familiar boundaries. Early tourism revolved around spiritual journeys, with pilgrims traveling significant distances to sacred locations such as Mecca, Rome, Jerusalem, and Varanasi. These pilgrimages represented some of the earliest structured tourism activities, blending spirituality with cultural discovery.

The medieval era expanded travel significantly along the Silk Road, a vast network connecting Asia, the Middle East, and Europe. Although intended primarily for commerce, the Silk Road facilitated leisure and educational travel, allowing travelers to exchange goods, ideas, and cultural practices.

During the Renaissance, global exploration surged dramatically. Iconic explorers such as Marco Polo, Vasco da Gama, and Ferdinand Magellan documented extensive travels, profoundly influencing future generations' desire for exploration. These journeys expanded global horizons and created early foundations for destination marketing and cultural tourism.

The Industrial Revolution brought transformative advances in transportation—steamships and railways—broadening travel accessibility beyond wealthy elites. The 18th and 19th centuries popularized the Grand Tour among affluent Europeans, directly influencing modern educational and cultural tourism (Towner, 1985).

Seaside resorts and spa towns sprang up, planting seeds for today's wellness and leisure tourism.

Further transport developments reshaped tourism throughout the 20th century. Automobiles sparked domestic tourism growth, giving families unprecedented freedom. Subsequently, commercial aviation drastically reduced global travel time, setting the stage for mass international tourism.

The economic boom after World War II accelerated tourism. Destinations including Disneyland and Mediterranean resorts became symbols of leisure tourism, driven by affordability and advances in air travel. Packaged tours and charter flights, pioneered notably by Thomas Cook, democratized travel by making international experiences accessible to millions. Cruise tourism evolved significantly, with about 30 million travelers annually choosing cruise vacations by 2020, highlighting enormous career opportunities and economic impacts (CLIA, 2020).

Technological advances in recent decades, particularly the internet, smartphones, and social media, have transformed traveler behavior. Today's tourism landscape emphasizes personalized experiences, sustainable practices, and cultural immersion, influenced by events such as the Covid pandemic, which underscored digital adoption and health-conscious travel (Figure 9.1).

In response to growing environmental awareness in the late 20th century, ecotourism and sustainable travel emerged prominently, emphasizing responsible exploration of natural environments and local community engagement (Honey, 2008). Recent decades have seen the rise of digital nomadism and remote-work tourism, driven by technological innovation and changing work cultures, creating new career paths in tourism and hospitality management.

Looking ahead, tourism will continue to evolve in response to shifting consumer preferences, technological developments, and sustainability priorities. Understanding this historical evolution helps hospitality students appreciate current tourism dynamics and equips them to anticipate future industry transformations.

Economic, community, and global impact

Tourism profoundly shapes economies, communities, and international relationships. Central to understanding tourism's economic power is the concept of the multiplier effect, where tourist spending creates cascading benefits—direct, indirect, and induced—throughout local and global economies (Figure 9.2).

Economic impact

Tourism serves as a critical revenue generator, supporting employment, fostering business growth, and prompting infrastructure enhancements worldwide.

Figure 9.1 Milestones in tourism history: How and why the industry evolved

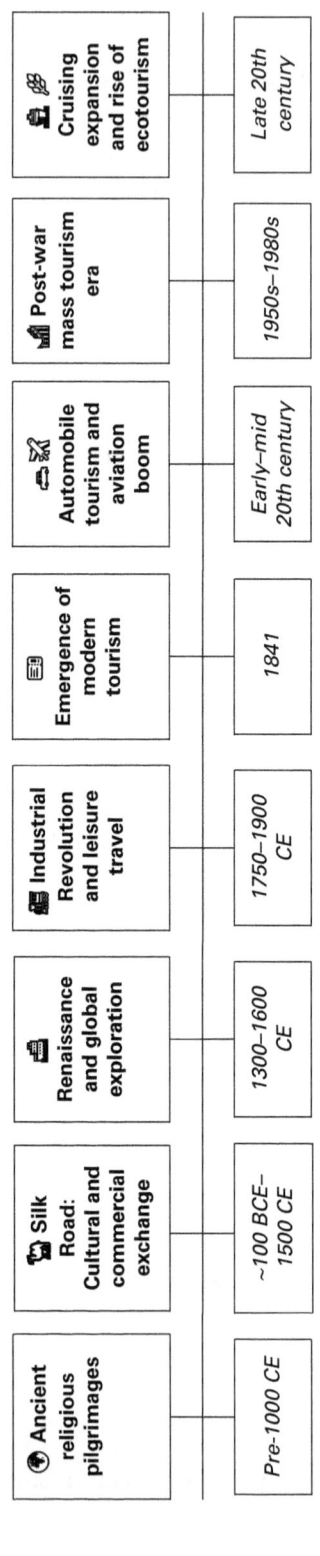

International events vividly exemplify this power. For instance, the Tokyo 2020 Olympics generated approximately $15 billion despite Covid restrictions, and the Paris 2024 Olympics similarly drove significant economic benefits—between €6.7 and €11.1 billion—particularly benefiting local communities like Seine-Saint-Denis (IOC, 2024). Major cultural events like these offer excellent demonstrations of tourism's economic power.

REAL-WORLD EXAMPLE:
INDUSTRY SPOTLIGHT Taylor Swift's *Eras* world tour: Illustrating the multiplier effect

In 2023–2024, music icon Taylor Swift captivated millions globally with her groundbreaking *Eras* tour. Beyond cultural impact, the tour offers an excellent demonstration of the multiplier effect—highlighting how initial visitor expenditures create extensive economic benefits that ripple throughout the economy.

Direct impact

Swift's three-night run in Philadelphia materially lifted local tourism activity. The Federal Reserve (2023) reported that May 2023 was the strongest month for hotel revenue in Philadelphia since the Covid pandemic, attributing the surge in large part to the concerts, alongside increased spending at local businesses.

Indirect impact

This surge in tourism spending led local businesses to elevate their own economic activity. Hotels replenished inventories, restaurants purchased locally sourced ingredients, and transportation companies expanded staffing, thereby spreading economic gains broadly throughout the community.

Induced impact

With boosted revenues, employees and business owners gained additional disposable income, enabling them to spend further within the local economy. This cycle of spending on retail, entertainment, and services further reinforced economic vitality.

Similar benefits were clear during Swift's concerts at Wembley Stadium in London, generating over £200 million in visitor spending (Murray, 2024). Such events significantly highlight tourism's capacity to bolster economies locally and globally.

Figure 9.2 Tourism's multiplier effect: Ripple model

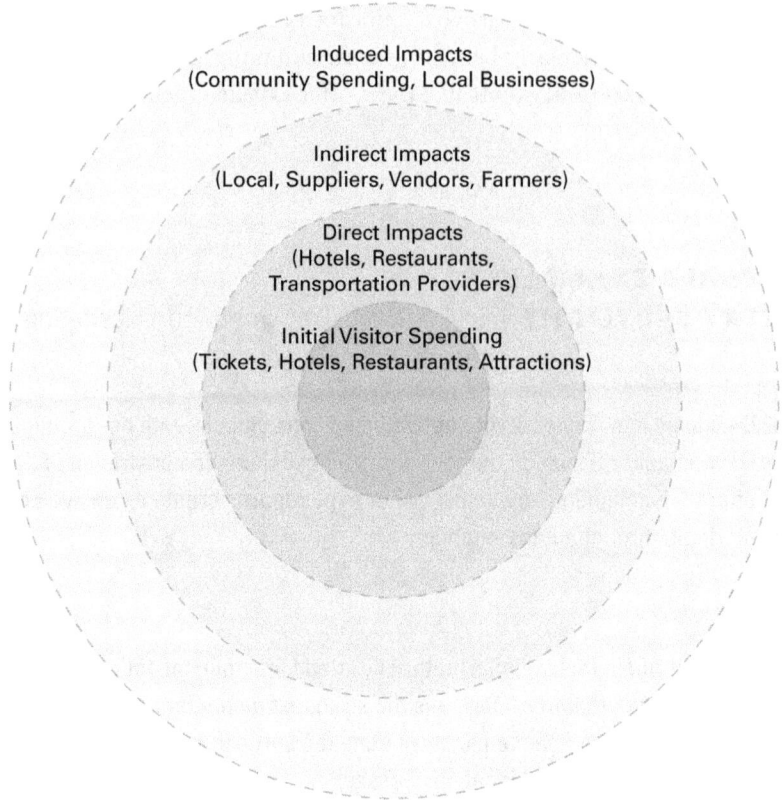

Community impact

Tourism also positively transforms communities by enhancing critical infrastructure such as airports, roads, public transport, and sanitation systems, thereby significantly improving residents' quality of life. In Bali, Indonesia, tourism-driven development has developed infrastructure, with benefits to residents and visitors.

However, unmanaged tourism growth can lead to challenges such as overcrowding, loss of housing among local residents, and cultural commodification as seen in locations like Venice and Majorca. Effective solutions, including visitor management systems, controlled entry fees, and cultural preservation initiatives, help ensure tourism's benefits outweigh its risks, preserving the unique qualities that attract travelers in the first place.

Additionally, tourism revenues often directly support environmental conservation and heritage preservation. In Rwanda, mountain gorilla tourism generates substantial income that directly funds conservation projects and local community initiatives, demonstrating tourism's potential to positively intertwine economic and environmental objectives.

REAL-WORLD EXAMPLE:
INDUSTRY SPOTLIGHT Experience Columbus

Experience Columbus exemplifies modern tourism management through innovative marketing, inclusivity, accessibility, and sustainability initiatives. The organization strategically positions Columbus, Ohio, as a vibrant destination for meetings, conventions, and leisure travel, highlighting diverse neighborhoods, thriving culinary experiences, and extensive hospitality amenities. Central to its approach are comprehensive DEIBA efforts, ensuring all visitors feel welcome and represented. Its Green Meetings program promotes eco-friendly practices such as waste reduction, sustainable sourcing, and energy efficiency, significantly lowering tourism's environmental impact.

Economically, Experience Columbus effectively demonstrates tourism's multiplier effect, creating widespread benefits for local businesses, employment, and community pride. It serves as a powerful model for integrating strategic planning, inclusiveness, and sustainability to create meaningful visitor experiences and lasting community impact.

> At Experience Columbus, we believe inclusivity, accessibility, and sustainability aren't just important—they're essential for creating vibrant, welcoming communities that thrive economically and culturally. Innovative destination marketing allows us to share Columbus' authentic story globally, ensuring tourism positively benefits both visitors and residents alike.
>
> —*Brian Ross, president and CEO, Experience Columbus*

Global impact

On a global scale, tourism encourages cross-cultural dialogue, international cooperation, and educational growth beyond traditional classrooms. By respectfully experiencing diverse cultures firsthand, travelers can foster mutual respect and global solidarity. Educational tourism initiatives, such as study abroad programs and cultural exchanges, aim to significantly enhance participants' global awareness, empathy, and personal development.

Tourism strongly aligns with global sustainability and conservation goals, evident through successful ecotourism practices in countries such as Costa Rica and Bhutan, where tourism revenue directly supports environmental protection, sustainable community livelihoods, and ecological stewardship.

REAL-WORLD EXAMPLE:
INDUSTRY SPOTLIGHT   Rwanda's mountain gorilla tourism: Transforming communities and conservation

In Rwanda, mountain gorilla tourism exemplifies tourism's potential to sustainably uplift local communities. Visitors to Volcanoes National Park not only experience profound wildlife encounters but directly contribute to economic prosperity, conservation, and social infrastructure. Tourism revenue—totaling approximately $107 million annually—funds vital community initiatives, including local schools, healthcare facilities, and anti-poaching programs (Flowers, 2020). This integrative model demonstrates how thoughtful tourism can positively intertwine economic growth, environmental stewardship, and enhanced community well-being.

INTERACTIVE EXERCISE
Maximizing economic impact

This activity will help you understand practical strategies that can enhance tourism's multiplier effect.
  Imagine your city is hosting a major international cultural festival attracting visitors worldwide.

- Identify three strategies your city could implement to maximize visitor spending in lodging, dining, and retail sectors.
- Clearly outline how you would communicate these strategies to local businesses to ensure widespread economic benefits.

Key tourism segments

Tourism is a diverse industry composed of distinct segments, each catering to specific traveler interests, motivations, and preferences. Understanding these segments allows tourism professionals to craft targeted experiences, effectively manage resources, and anticipate evolving traveler expectations.

Leisure tourism

Leisure tourism is the most common segment, characterized by travel primarily undertaken for relaxation, recreation, and entertainment. Leisure travelers typically seek enjoyable experiences away from routine life, including beach vacations, cultural activities, theme parks, and cruises. Popular global destinations include Hawaii's idyllic beaches, Spain's vibrant island of Ibiza, the luxury resorts of the Caribbean, and cultural hubs in the Mediterranean such as the French Riviera and the Greek Islands.

In 2023 alone, Hawaii received approximately 9.5 million visitors, generating over $19 billion in revenue, clearly demonstrating leisure tourism's substantial economic impact (State of Hawai'i DBEDT, 2024). Within leisure tourism, sub-segments like adventure and wellness tourism have significantly expanded. Adventure tourism attracts those seeking excitement through activities such as hiking in New Zealand, skiing in Canada's Rocky Mountains, diving in Australia's Great Barrier Reef, or wildlife safaris in Kenya's Maasai Mara. Wellness tourism emphasizes health and rejuvenation, offering experiences like spa retreats in Bali, yoga centers in India, and holistic healing resorts in Sedona, Arizona. Globally, wellness tourism grew to approximately $830 billion in 2023, underlining its rising popularity (Global Wellness Institute, 2024).

Business tourism

Business tourism encompasses travel undertaken for professional purposes, including meetings, conferences, exhibitions, and incentive travel. This segment significantly contributes to tourism revenue, as business travelers often spend more per day than leisure tourists. Major cities such as New York, London, Singapore, and Dubai dominate this segment due to their advanced infrastructure, international connectivity, and status as global business hubs.

Las Vegas, for instance, hosts approximately 24,000 conventions and meetings annually, directly contributing over $11 billion to the local economy (LVCVA, 2024). Similarly, Barcelona has strategically positioned itself as a major European business tourism destination, drawing significant economic benefits from hosting international conventions and exhibitions.

Incentive travel, a component of business tourism, rewards employees or business partners for achieving specific goals or milestones. Companies often choose luxury destinations and unique experiences to motivate and retain their top talent, blending business networking with leisure opportunities, thereby benefiting both participants and hosting destinations economically and socially.

Cultural and heritage tourism

This tourism segment centers on visitors' interests in exploring historical sites, museums, cultural festivals, and local traditions. Cultural tourists seek deep connections with destinations through immersive experiences. The United Nations Educational, Scientific, and Cultural Organization (UNESCO) World Heritage sites such as Machu Picchu in Peru, the Great Wall of China, and the Colosseum in Rome attract millions annually. Machu Picchu, for instance, welcomed roughly 1.5 million tourists in 2023, contributing essential funding for preservation efforts and local economic development (Statistica, 2024b). (You'll learn more on World Heritage tourism later.)

Cultural festivals, such as India's vibrant Holi celebrations, Brazil's Rio Carnival, and Japan's Cherry Blossom Festival, are also significant attractions, drawing global audiences eager to experience local culture authentically. These events can stimulate local economies, support cultural preservation, and foster intercultural understanding.

> **INTERACTIVE EXERCISE**
> Designing a cultural tourism itinerary
>
> Select a culturally rich destination not previously highlighted in this chapter. Develop a detailed three-day itinerary featuring authentic local experiences, cultural practices, and heritage sites. Clearly explain how your itinerary embodies cultural tourism principles and benefits visitors and host communities economically, culturally, and socially.

Ecotourism and sustainable tourism

> We're at a pivotal moment in hospitality and tourism—an industry uniquely positioned to protect natural resources, uplift communities, and shape global behavior. No other sector blends consumption with such deep dependence on a healthy planet. The most forward-thinking brands have already embraced sustainability not just as a responsibility but as a strategic advantage: reducing costs, generating revenue, and deepening guest loyalty. Travelers are paying close attention—and those who wait to catch up will find themselves left behind. The future of hospitality is sustainable. And it's already here.
>
> —*Amy Wald, founder and president, Greenluxe*

When you imagine your ideal vacation, do you envision relaxing in a luxury eco-resort surrounded by lush rainforests, or exploring stunning wildlife reserves where your visit actively contributes to conservation? Welcome to the world of ecotourism—travel that prioritizes environmental protection, meaningful education, and genuine benefits to local communities.

Costa Rica exemplifies successful ecotourism, generating over $1.5 billion annually, funding extensive wildlife conservation and community projects. Visitors enjoy eco-adventures that directly contribute to protecting the ecosystems they explore (Loss, 2019).

Whether trekking through rainforests or kayaking among tranquil mangroves, sustainable tourism experiences directly fund critical conservation efforts and benefit local communities. It's about a thoughtful balance that enhances local culture, promotes community well-being, and preserves natural beauty, no matter where you travel. Bhutan, for instance, takes sustainability to heart. This Himalayan gem carefully controls visitor numbers, focuses on quality experiences, and channels tourism revenue directly back into environmental protection and local community projects.

REAL-WORLD EXAMPLE:
INDUSTRY SPOTLIGHT Iceland's model of sustainable tourism

Iceland might conjure images of glaciers and volcanic landscapes, but it's also setting a global benchmark in sustainable tourism. In the 12-month period up to early 2025, revenue from foreign tourists reached 621.4 billion ISK (about US $4.8 billion). This tourism model rooted in environmental stewardship alongside economic vitality—eco-friendly hotels, nearly 100 percent renewable electricity, and deliberate infrastructure and site-protection strategies—shows how tourism and thriving ecosystems can coexist harmoniously (Statistics Iceland, 2025).

Niche, special interest, and remote-work tourism

Understanding and clearly differentiating these more unusual segments enables tourism professionals to strategically target marketing campaigns, develop tailored visitor experiences, and effectively respond to evolving travel behaviors and preferences.

Niche tourism

This explicitly caters to specialized traveler interests and preferences, offering highly tailored and meaningful travel experiences. It's a clear example of how tourism continuously evolves to meet diverse traveler motivations and needs.

Culinary tourism

Tourism centered on food has surged in popularity globally, with travelers actively seeking authentic local food experiences. Approximately 81 percent of travelers cite unique culinary offerings as a major motivator for destination selection, with renowned culinary destinations including Italy, France, and Japan (World Food Travel Association, 2024).

Medical tourism

Traveling abroad explicitly for medical treatments or healthcare procedures is another growing segment. Popular destinations include Thailand, India, and Turkey, seen to have high-quality and cost-effective healthcare services, attracting millions of travelers annually seeking affordable, specialized medical care.

Sports tourism

Tournaments and championships attract travelers interested in participating in or spectating major sporting events. Iconic events like Wimbledon, the Masters golf tournament, and Formula 1 races significantly boost local economies by attracting dedicated sports enthusiasts from around the globe.

Astrotourism

Astrotourism is an emerging niche. It explicitly draws travelers interested in astronomy and stargazing. Prime astrotourism destinations include Iceland and Chile's Atacama Desert, offering clear skies and specialized infrastructure to create exceptional astronomical experiences.

Voluntourism

This is growing steadily as travelers actively combine leisure with meaningful volunteer work. This approach allows visitors to travel economically and engage in community development and conservation efforts, promoting responsible tourism practices that positively impact local communities.

Digital nomadism and remote work tourism

Linked to business travel, these have rapidly expanded as global connectivity enables professionals to seamlessly blend work and travel. In 2023 alone, over 35 million digital nomads significantly reshaped tourism economies, especially in vibrant cities like Lisbon (Portugal), Bali (Indonesia), and Tallinn (Estonia), known for their appealing lifestyles, affordability, and robust digital infrastructures (Statistica, 2024a).

Customer behavior and traveler influences

Understanding customers' behavior and the factors influencing travelers' decisions is essential for tourism professionals to attract, satisfy, and retain visitors. Traveler choices are influenced by an interplay of psychological, cultural, economic, technological, and environmental factors, each shaping unique travel patterns and preferences.

Psychological factors

Psychological factors, including motivations, perceptions, attitudes, and emotions, directly shape travelers' decisions. Motivations can range from relaxation or adventure to personal growth and meaningful social interactions. For instance, thrill-seekers might choose challenging treks in Patagonia or wildlife safaris in Tanzania, while relaxation-focused travelers often prefer leisurely stays at luxurious Maldives resorts or on Caribbean cruises.

Recent studies illustrate shifting traveler priorities. According to the Global Wellness Institute (2024), wellness tourism reached $651 billion in 2023 and is projected to grow at an average annual rate of 16.6 percent through 2027, making it one of the fastest-growing segments in global travel. McKinsey (2024) notes that 82 percent of US consumers consider wellness a top or important priority, pointing at significant potential for wellness-oriented travel, particularly in major tourism markets like the United States.

Positive perceptions—often shaped by memorable experiences, effective marketing campaigns, and personal recommendations—drive repeat visitation. Emotional connections formed through meaningful experiences strengthen traveler loyalty, reinforcing the role of tourism professionals in creating memorable, emotionally resonant experiences.

Cultural influences

Cultural background profoundly influences traveler expectations, behaviors, and preferences. Individuals from collectivist cultures (such as Japan or China) often favor structured group experiences with shared interactions, while travelers from individualistic cultures (like the US or Australia) frequently prefer independent and personalized travel experiences.

Generational differences further shape these cultural expectations. Younger travelers (Generation Z, millennials) increasingly prioritize authentic cultural experiences and immersive interactions with local communities. Expedia's 2024 report highlights that today's young travelers—particularly Gen Z—actively seek destinations that offer meaningful engagement with diverse cultural and indigenous traditions (Expedia, 2024a).

Additionally, addressing cultural sensitivities, including Halal dining, prayer facilities, and culturally respectful hospitality, enables destinations to appeal to diverse international markets and demonstrate cultural inclusivity and awareness.

> **THINK LIKE A MANAGER**
> Cultural inclusion
>
> Imagine managing tourism at a diverse destination.
> - Identify one strategy to ensure tourism is culturally inclusive.
> - Briefly explain how you would engage local stakeholders to support this strategy.

Economic factors

Travelers' economic considerations, including disposable income, currency exchange rates, and perceived value, significantly impact destination choices and travel behaviors. Economic fluctuations, such as recessions, rising inflation, or currency instability, often prompt travelers to shift toward domestic tourism or more affordable international destinations.

Price sensitivity distinctly varies across segments. Luxury travelers prioritize exclusivity, comfort, and personalized services, often remaining less sensitive to price changes. Conversely, budget-conscious travelers consistently seek affordable packages, promotional offers, and value-oriented experiences.

Technological influences

Technological developments fundamentally reshape how travelers research, plan, book, and share travel experiences. Online platforms, mobile apps, and digital booking tools provide travelers with greater information, comparison capabilities, flexibility, and convenience. Social media platforms—particularly Instagram and TikTok—significantly drive destination choices, notably influencing traveler preferences and expectations. According to Statista (2024c), 75 percent of travelers report that social media influences their travel destination decisions, surpassing traditional media such as TV and print.

Digital technologies, including AI-driven platforms and personalized planning tools, are becoming central to transforming the tourism experience, facilitating tailored recommendations, streamlined bookings, and improved customer engagement. VR and AR technologies also increasingly enhance how travelers preview and anticipate experiences, shaping preferences and expectations, especially among younger generations and travelers with specific accessibility needs.

Environmental influences

As highlighted earlier, growing environmental awareness significantly impacts traveler decisions. Climate conditions, seasonal travel patterns, and sustainability concerns profoundly shape destination choices. For instance, ski resorts experience seasonal peaks in winter, while warmer coastal destinations attract significant visitation during summer months.

Environmental incidents, such as wildfires or pollution events, also notably affect visitation trends. Increasingly, travelers demand sustainable accommodations and environmentally responsible tourism practices. Booking.com's 2024 sustainable travel report found that 83 percent of travelers consider sustainable travel important, although only 45 percent make it a key factor when booking.

Impact of global events

Global events, including geopolitical developments, disease, and major international cultural and sporting events, have significant impacts on traveler behaviors. The Covid pandemic reshaped global traveler priorities toward health, safety, travel insurance, and flexible booking options—preferences that persist beyond the immediate crisis.

Conversely, major global events, like the FIFA World Cup, Olympics, or major cultural festivals, stimulate international travel and cultural exchange. As mentioned earlier, the Paris 2024 Olympics, for example, significantly boosted local tourism spending by approximately 30 percent, demonstrating powerful economic and socio-cultural ripple effects (IOC, 2024).

Future trends in consumer behavior

Emerging trends indicate a growing preference for personalized, authentic, and immersive travel experiences aligned closely with individual lifestyles and values. Travelers increasingly seek meaningful experiences such as wellness retreats, immersive culinary adventures, authentic cultural interactions, and impactful volunteer tourism activities.

According to Deloitte's 2024 *Travel Outlook*, immersive travel experiences using VR and AR technologies will increase by approximately 35 percent annually over the next five years, driven significantly by younger travelers seeking accessible, inclusive, and enriching travel experiences.

Tourism professionals who proactively adapt to evolving traveler behaviors and expectations will be uniquely positioned to effectively engage diverse market segments, enhance visitor satisfaction, and sustain destination competitiveness.

> **INTERACTIVE EXERCISE**
> Analyzing traveler decisions
>
> This activity offers insights into psychological, cultural, economic, and technological factors influencing traveler decisions.
>
> 1 Choose one of these traveler segments:
>   o Gen Z adventure travelers
>   o Digital nomads
>   o Luxury travelers
> 2 Clearly identify:
>   o Psychological motivations and emotional appeals driving their destination choices
>   o Cultural expectations and sensitivities important for this segment
>   o Economic factors influencing their decisions
>   o Technological tools they utilize for planning, booking, and sharing their travel experiences
> 3 Briefly describe strategies you would implement as a tourism manager to specifically attract, satisfy, and retain this segment.
> 4 Summarize your approach clearly in a concise written analysis or short presentation.

Sustainable tourism and ecotourism

Have you ever considered the broader impacts your travels might have, not just on your own experiences but on the communities and environments you visit? That's the question at the heart of sustainable tourism and ecotourism. Such an approach aims to ensure that tourism delivers real benefits to local people and protects our planet's incredible natural wonders.

Understanding sustainable tourism

At its core, sustainable tourism is about balance. It means creating memorable travel experiences that boost local economies, explore and protect natural environments, and enjoy and respect cultural traditions—without compromising the ability of future generations to enjoy these same opportunities.

The picturesque country of Slovenia, for example, has become a global leader in sustainable tourism by investing in eco-friendly accommodations, emphasizing local sourcing, and integrating extensive conservation efforts into its tourism strategy. In 2024, Bela Krajina, Brežice, Jeruzalem, Ljubljana, Miren-Kras, and Rogla-Pohorje were featured in the world's Top 100 Green Destinations Stories, highlighting community-driven initiatives that connect tourism with environmental stewardship. This recognition reflects Slovenia's long-term commitment to sustainability and illustrates how thoughtful policies can shape tourism experiences that benefit both visitors and local communities (Government of Slovenia, 2024).

> Sustainability isn't an add-on—it's a core business strategy. In hospitality, embedding sustainability into finance, procurement, and infrastructure isn't just responsible—it's smart business. Leaders who understand the triple bottom line don't just reduce harm—they uncover opportunities to innovate, cut waste, and drive long-term value, building resilient, future-ready operations.

—*Christy Cook, CEO, InvestHER Strategies, and CSO, 4xi Global Consulting*

Exploring ecotourism: Traveling responsibly

Ecotourism takes sustainable travel one step further by focusing specifically on responsible trips to natural areas, often with educational elements. The goal? To conserve the environment and directly improve the lives of local people alongside the travel experience.

Costa Rica has become the poster child of successful ecotourism, dedicating nearly 25 percent of its land to protected natural reserves. Visitors can explore dense rainforests and stunning coastal ecosystems, knowing their adventures directly support conservation efforts and community well-being (Visit Costa Rica, 2023).

Protecting the environment: Why it matters to travelers

Responsible tourism emphasizes travelers' active role in making choices that positively impact destinations. Many of today's travelers care deeply about environmental sustainability. According to the 2024 Booking.com *Sustainable Travel Report*, 67 percent of travelers say that witnessing sustainable practices while traveling inspires them to adopt similar habits in their daily lives, showing how sustainability in tourism extends its impact well beyond the trip itself (GSTC, 2024). Whether it's staying at an eco-lodge powered by solar energy or booking a hotel that reduces waste and conserves water, eco-conscious choices are becoming mainstream.

As we have seen, Rwanda's mountain gorilla tourism offers a great illustration. This remarkable conservation program generated around $107 million in 2019, with revenues supporting anti-poaching efforts, habitat protection, and local schools (Flowers, 2020). Travelers here aren't just visitors—they're partners in conservation.

Cultural connections: Inclusive tourism experiences

Sustainable tourism isn't just about nature—it's also about protecting cultures and traditions. Community-based tourism is one way to ensure local people directly benefit from tourism, giving them control over how their stories and heritage are shared. One inspiring example is Ban Talae Nok village in Thailand. Here, locals lead cultural experiences that are enriching for visitors: imagine cooking traditional meals together or learning village crafts firsthand. The income generated supports local healthcare, education, and infrastructure, demonstrating tourism's incredible potential to empower communities socially and economically.

Young travelers, especially Gen Z and Millennials, increasingly value cultural immersion and engagement with local communities. Expedia's *Inclusive Travel Insights* (2022) highlights that inclusivity and authentic local experiences are now important travel criteria for many consumers. For younger generations, travel isn't just about sightseeing—it's about genuine connection and positive impact.

Making tourism accessible and economically sustainable

Sustainable tourism also means making travel accessible to people across diverse economic backgrounds, ensuring everyone can experience the world responsibly. New Zealand offers a compelling case study. In the year ending March 2024, overseas visitor arrivals reached 3.2 million. Total tourism expenditure rose to a record NZD 44.4 billion, with NZD 16.9 billion generated by international visitors. The industry directly supported 182,727 jobs and, when indirect roles are included, employed 303,420 people—around one in nine New Zealanders (Tourism New Zealand, 2024).

Challenges in sustainable tourism: The road ahead

Despite the positives, sustainable tourism isn't without its challenges. Popular destinations such as Venice and Santorini have struggled with overtourism, threatening local communities and ecosystems. To tackle these issues, destinations are adopting smart strategies, such as visitor quotas, entry fees, and responsible travel campaigns, to try to make tourism sustainable for the long term.

There's still work to be done educating travelers and businesses about sustainable practices. For example, Trip.com's 2024 *Sustainable Travel Consumer Report* found that nearly half of travelers admit they aren't entirely clear on what "sustainable travel" really means. Clearly, awareness is crucial—and we can all play a role in spreading the word.

THINK LIKE A MANAGER
Promoting sustainable tourism

Imagine you're leading tourism operations at a destination that is facing sustainability challenges, such as environmental degradation or community resistance to tourism growth.

- Identify one actionable strategy you'd implement to enhance sustainability at your destination.
- Briefly explain how you would gain support from local stakeholders (residents, businesses, local government) to ensure successful implementation.

The future: Sustainability meets innovation

Technology is set to play a big role in making sustainable travel easier and more accessible. Imagine using an app to see how crowded an attraction is in real-time, or exploring sensitive natural habitats through VR before visiting responsibly in person.

Deloitte's 2024 *Tourism Outlook* predicts that innovations such as AI-driven visitor management platforms and sustainability analytics will dramatically reshape the industry. Younger travelers, who often lead the way in embracing technology, are expected to drive these innovations and need to help in ensuring tourism evolves responsibly.

As future tourism professionals, you'll have the exciting responsibility—and opportunity—to design experiences that balance profitability, environmental stewardship, and community empowerment. Together, we can shape tourism into a force for lasting good.

UNESCO World Heritage and tourism

Have you been so fortunate as to stand in awe beneath the intricate architecture of the Taj Mahal, wandered through the ancient ruins of Machu Picchu, or snorkeled along Australia's breathtaking Great Barrier Reef? These aren't just spectacular destinations—they're UNESCO World Heritage sites, globally recognized treasures of our planet's rich cultural and natural diversity.

UNESCO carefully selects these remarkable locations for their outstanding universal value, placing them under special protection to preserve their stories and beauty for future generations. As of 2025, 1,248 World Heritage sites exist worldwide, spanning 972 cultural sites, 235 natural sites, and 41 mixed sites across 170 countries (UNESCO, 2025). Each site is a doorway into unique histories, cultures, and ecosystems, inspiring millions of travelers each year to explore and learn.

These prestigious designations aren't just about attracting visitors—they can also significantly boost local economies and fuel important preservation projects. For instance, Cambodia's awe-inspiring Angkor temple complex welcomed over 2 million international visitors annually in pre-pandemic years, generating significant funds for extensive conservation work and support for local communities (B2B-Cambodia, 2024).

Yet, as popularity grows, many UNESCO sites face tough challenges. Venice, the iconic city of canals, has grappled with overtourism, leading to environmental damage and overcrowding. Similarly, the Great Barrier Reef faces critical threats from climate change and over-visitation, prompting innovative management and protection strategies to safeguard its delicate ecosystems.

Managing tourism at fragile World Heritage sites

Some of the world's most treasured UNESCO sites, such as the Galápagos Islands and Bhutan's Tiger's Nest monastery, have learned to carefully balance visitor access with environmental responsibility. These destinations use visitor quotas, educational programs, and strict regulations to ensure tourists leave only positive footprints and help to protect sites for decades to come. Imagine exploring the Galápagos with a trained guide who helps you deeply understand the wildlife and landscapes and ensures that your visit actively contributes to conservation and local well-being.

When thoughtfully managed, visits to World Heritage sites can deliver great economic and social benefits. Take Petra in Jordan, which generates around $800 million annually through tourism revenue, contributing to local infrastructure, schools, and crucial conservation projects (Jordan Tourism Board, 2024). Similarly, communities around Luang Prabang in Laos directly benefit from UNESCO designation, supporting local artisans and small businesses, ensuring tourism creates lasting positive impacts.

Looking ahead, innovative technologies, such as VR experiences, are enhancing visitors' appreciation while reducing their environmental impact. Imagine touring ancient ruins through augmented reality before you even arrive, deepening your understanding and excitement for your actual visit.

Ultimately, preserving these invaluable sites is a shared responsibility. As future travelers and/or tourism professionals, your role is vital. By choosing and enabling responsible travel options, respecting local guidelines, and promoting sustainable practices, you actively help protect these extraordinary places, ensuring they remain vibrant, inspiring destinations for generations to come.

Exploring iconic World Heritage sites

Some UNESCO sites have become synonymous with global travel, drawing visitors eager to experience history, culture, and natural beauty firsthand. India's majestic Taj Mahal attracted nearly 8 million annual visitors pre-pandemic, significantly boosting Agra's economy. Similarly, Machu Picchu in Peru attracts approximately 1.5 million visitors annually, directly funding heritage conservation and community development through its UNESCO designation (Statista, 2024b).

In Europe, Paris showcases several iconic UNESCO sites, including the Palace of Versailles, Notre-Dame Cathedral, and the banks of the Seine, which attract tens of millions annually and reinforce France's global tourism appeal. Meanwhile, the US boasts notable sites such as Yellowstone National Park, the Statue of Liberty, and Independence Hall, each holding immense cultural and historical significance. Yellowstone alone welcomes over 4 million visitors each year, underscoring its role in both tourism and conservation (Statista, 2024b).

Challenges and pressures facing World Heritage sites

UNESCO sites attract millions of global visitors annually, providing substantial economic and cultural benefits. However, increased tourism also introduces considerable challenges, including overcrowding, environmental degradation, infrastructure strain, and negative impacts on local communities. Successfully managing these pressures requires strategic, integrated approaches, including visitor regulation, sustainable funding mechanisms, education, and rigorous compliance oversight. Two prominent examples—Venice, experiencing overtourism, and Australia's Great Barrier Reef, coping with visitation pressures compounded by climate change—clearly illustrate the complexities and practical considerations involved in sustainably managing high-profile World Heritage locations.

Venice has long struggled with overtourism, regularly attracting more than 20 million visitors annually, significantly overwhelming local infrastructure and negatively impacting residents' quality of life (NPR, 2024; Reuters, 2024). In April 2024, the city piloted a €5 entry fee for day-trippers (later extended into 2025) and an increased €10 fee for arrivals booked within four days of travel on 54 peak dates between April and July (NPR, 2024; Reuters, 2024). The program introduced a digital QR-code booking system, capped guided tours at 25 people, banned amplified speakers, and exempted residents, overnight guests, and students (Reuters, 2024). The 2024 pilot reportedly raised approximately €2.4 million; however, initial assessments indicate visitor numbers on charged days actually rose by approximately

7,000, and enforcement has been inconsistent, with relatively few active compliance checks (Business Insider, 2025).

Australia's Great Barrier Reef similarly faces mounting pressures from climate change and year-round tourism. According to the Great Barrier Reef Marine Park Authority (GBRMPA, 2024), the region sees roughly 1.6 million tourist visits annually, translating to approximately 2.3 million visitor-days. Management strategies implemented to address these pressures include:

- Zoning and permit limits to restrict access in sensitive reef areas
- A daily Environmental Management Charge directly funding reef conservation, compliance, and scientific research
- Eco-certification programs to promote sustainable practices among tourism operators, with high-standard operators benefiting from extended permits (CRC Reef Research Centre, 2014; GBRMPA, 2024)
- Mandatory environmental briefings in immersive visitor education aimed at encouraging responsible behavior (GBRMPA, 2024)
- Regular compliance oversight, including regulated vessel paths, waste management, and pollution-control protocols (CRC Reef Research Centre, 2014)

These multifaceted systems demonstrate how conservation and tourism can coexist within UNESCO World Heritage frameworks.

Sustainable management of World Heritage sites

Thankfully, well-implemented sustainable tourism practices significantly mitigate these pressures. UNESCO advocates for proactive management strategies such as visitor quotas, seasonal restrictions, timed entry systems, and targeted educational programs.

As highlighted previously in our ecotourism discussion, the Galápagos Islands and Bhutan's Tiger's Nest monastery exemplify UNESCO sites successfully integrating tourism with ecological responsibility and cultural preservation, protecting their unique identities while providing extraordinary visitor experiences.

Economic and community benefits of World Heritage tourism

When managed responsibly, tourism at World Heritage sites can profoundly benefit communities. Visits to Jordan's ancient city of Petra generate approximately $800 million annually, directly supporting conservation, infrastructure, and community livelihoods (Jordan Tourism Board, 2024). Likewise, Luang Prabang in Laos demonstrates how UNESCO designation empowers local artisans and small businesses, ensuring tourism directly contributes to local well-being and cultural preservation.

The future of Word Heritage sites: Innovations and opportunities

The future for World Heritage locations is promising, with innovative digital technologies set to enhance visitor experiences while minimizing environmental impact. Imagine exploring a virtual reconstruction of Rome's Colosseum before visiting, enhancing your understanding and appreciation. UNESCO continues to actively promote advanced digital visitor management solutions, sustainable infrastructure, and robust educational programs to protect these irreplaceable sites for future generations.

> **THINK LIKE A MANAGER**
> Addressing overtourism challenges
>
> You manage a popular but overcrowded UNESCO site (Cinque Terre in Italy, for instance).
>
> - Identify one immediate solution you could implement to reduce overcrowding while preserving revenue.
> - Briefly explain how you would effectively communicate this solution to visitors.

Emerging trends in tourism

Have you ever thought about what future travel experiences might look like? The tourism industry continuously evolves, shaped by innovative technologies, shifting traveler expectations, and global developments. While we've previously explored key trends such as sustainable tourism, technological advances, and digital nomadism (see earlier sections in this chapter), let's now focus specifically on some fresh, compelling trends transforming how we travel today.

Bleisure travel: Blending business and leisure

Imagine extending your next business trip to explore local markets, enjoy a beach resort, or hike scenic trails after your meetings conclude. Welcome to bleisure travel, where business trips and leisure activities meld into one experience. Recent research indicates nearly 89 percent of business travelers now embrace this trend, reshaping the tourism landscape worldwide (Statista, 2023).

Cities such as Dubai and Singapore have become bleisure hubs by thoughtfully combining professional facilities with leisure opportunities. Business hotels now regularly feature vibrant coworking spaces, culturally enriching city tours, or relaxing spa treatments tailored specifically to busy professionals. This fusion not only improves traveler satisfaction but significantly boosts local economies.

REAL-WORLD EXAMPLE:
INDUSTRY SPOTLIGHT   Dubai: The ultimate bleisure destination

Dubai strategically attracts business travelers with state-of-the-art convention facilities and luxury hotels, combined with leisure activities like desert safaris, cultural excursions, and world-class shopping experiences. This model drives increased visitation and robust economic impact year-round.

"Last chance" tourism: Experiencing endangered wonders

Have you ever felt an urgency to visit a destination before it disappears? That's the driving force behind "last chance" tourism, where travelers prioritize visiting locations threatened by environmental changes, such as Antarctica's melting glaciers, the rapidly shrinking Great Barrier Reef, or the vulnerable Amazon rainforest.

While this trend raises awareness about urgent environmental issues, it also presents ethical dilemmas. As we have seen with, for example, UNESCO heritage sites, increased visitation can accelerate environmental degradation unless carefully managed. Consequently, such destinations are implementing strict visitation controls, robust environmental guidelines, and educational programs that balance traveler curiosity with critical sustainability goals.

REAL-WORLD EXAMPLE:
INDUSTRY SPOTLIGHT   Great Barrier Reef: Balancing visitation and conservation

Australia's Great Barrier Reef, facing severe threats from climate change, has adopted stringent visitor guidelines and eco-friendly tourist practices. While travelers can continue to enjoy guided snorkeling and diving, they simultaneously learn about conservation and support efforts to safeguard this iconic natural wonder and precious element of the Earth's ecosystems.

Social media's influence on tourism choices

Beyond environmental concerns, another compelling force reshaping travel decisions is the powerful influence of social media. As highlighted in "Technological influences" earlier, 75 percent of travelers report that social media influences their destination choices, surpassing traditional media (Statista, 2024c). Younger travelers, particularly Gen Z and millennials, actively seek destinations featured prominently on platforms such as Instagram and TikTok, confirming these platforms as powerful drivers of tourism preferences. Destinations increasingly leverage these platforms to craft appealing narratives, capturing traveler interest through highly shareable experiences.

REAL-WORLD EXAMPLE:
INDUSTRY SPOTLIGHT Paris's social media boost from *Emily in Paris*

After Netflix's hit series *Emily in Paris* aired, interest in visiting Paris surged significantly, with online searches for travel to Paris increasing by nearly 50 percent (ETIAS, 2024). The popularity of the series prompted the emergence of specialized tourist offerings, including themed walking tours, fashion events, and culinary experiences especially designed for fans eager to replicate and share their experiences on social media (Forbes, 2024; *Le Monde*, 2024). Despite some local concerns about overtourism, the city's hospitality and retail sectors have benefited substantially, illustrating the influential role pop culture can play in tourism marketing strategies if acted upon promptly.

Health, safety, and travel confidence

Travelers today continue to prioritize health and safety on their visits, especially following the Covid pandemic. An Expedia (2024b) report notes that 84 percent of global travelers carefully evaluate health standards, cleanliness, and safety protocols when planning trips.

In response, destinations and tourism providers offer transparent hygiene ratings, contactless check-ins, and digital health apps that provide real-time safety updates. Such measures restore traveler confidence, attract cautious travelers, and differentiate proactive destinations, becoming central to maintaining competitive advantage in the global tourism market.

Rediscovering local and regional tourism

On the other hand, why travel halfway around the world when there's incredible beauty and adventure right in your own backyard? Global uncertainty and increased sustainability awareness have sparked renewed interest in local and regional tourism. The World Travel & Tourism Council (2024) reports domestic tourism spending reached $5.3 trillion globally in 2024, highlighting a meaningful shift toward localized experiences.

Countries like Japan, with its highly successful "Go To Travel" campaign, encouraged citizens to rediscover local heritage, culture, and natural attractions. This approach stimulated local economies, strengthened community pride, and fostered deeper cultural appreciation among travelers.

> **THINK LIKE A MANAGER**
>
> Imagine your local community has untapped tourism potential.
>
> - Design an engaging promotional campaign encouraging residents to explore nearby attractions.
> - Identify key selling points, develop catchy messaging, and clearly articulate how your campaign benefits local businesses, communities, and travelers.

Inclusive tourism: Welcoming every traveler

Inclusivity matters more than ever. Destinations increasingly embrace inclusive tourism practices, ensuring accessibility and meaningful experiences for travelers of all ages, abilities, economic backgrounds, and cultural identities. Tourism professionals should actively create barrier-free environments, accessible accommodations, inclusive tours, and culturally sensitive experiences, promoting tourism as a universally welcoming activity.

REAL-WORLD EXAMPLE:
INDUSTRY SPOTLIGHT   Barcelona's commitment to accessibility

Barcelona has become a global leader in accessible tourism, offering comprehensive accessibility guides, specialized city tours, and adapted public transport options. The city's proactive efforts significantly boost its global reputation as a welcoming, inclusive destination for travelers with diverse needs.

Brief review of previously explored trends

We've detailed sustainability, technology, and digital nomadism earlier in the chapter, so it's helpful to briefly highlight their ongoing significance:

- **Sustainability:** Travelers worldwide increasingly choose eco-friendly accommodations and responsible experiences.
- **Technology:** Innovations like AI-driven trip planners and immersive AR/VR experiences continue to reshape tourism, enhancing personalization and accessibility.
- **Digital nomadism:** Growing numbers of remote-working professionals now significantly influence destination infrastructure and community dynamics.

These trends remain crucial, shaping tourism strategies and informing innovative industry practices.

> **INTERACTIVE EXERCISE**
> Tourism trends pitch
>
> This activity applies current tourism trends to rejuvenate a destination's visitor appeal.
>
> 1 Identify a tourism destination currently experiencing declining visitation or needing revitalization (for example Atlantic City or Marseille).
>
> 2 Drawing on emerging trends discussed in this chapter (such as wellness tourism, hybrid experiences, immersive technology), propose two or three innovative tourism experiences that aim to attract and engage new visitor segments.
>
> 3 Clearly outline how each of your proposed experiences addresses contemporary traveler preferences and can effectively boost the destination's appeal.
>
> 4 Summarize your recommendations clearly and present your rationale through a concise pitch or brief class discussion.

Careers in tourism: Pathways and opportunities

Building upon earlier career discussions, this section specifically highlights distinctive career pathways within the tourism industry. Tourism is a diverse, rapidly evolving sector offering a broad array of professional roles, from visitor-focused frontline positions to strategic roles guiding entire tourism regions. This exploration will help you identify pathways aligned with your passions and strengths (Figure 9.3).

Studying tourism has significantly shaped my worldview and deepened my understanding of global hospitality. By exploring diverse cultures through each lesson and applying that knowledge in real-world interactions, I have gained a deep appreciation for the power of creating bridges between cultures through personalized and inclusive service. Each lesson and each experience continues to fuel my passion for the hospitality and tourism industry and has inspired me to pursue a career where I can meaningfully connect with guests from all cultures and backgrounds.

—*Sophia Peacock, hospitality management student*

Frontline tourism careers

Frontline tourism roles offer direct, rewarding interactions with travelers, shaping memorable experiences and delivering personalized service. Travel consultants, for example, craft individualized itineraries tailored precisely to visitors' preferences. Tour guides enrich visitor experiences with engaging narratives and local insights, sharing deep cultural and historical knowledge. Visitor information specialists provide travelers with accurate and helpful guidance, enhancing their overall experience.

Destination marketing and promotion

Professionals specializing in tourism marketing and promotion, such as those working in convention and visitors bureaus, uniquely contribute to destination growth by creatively showcasing tourism experiences. Destination marketing specialists develop strategies leveraging digital media and storytelling to highlight destinations' distinctive features, including local culture, natural attractions, or niche experiences. Public relations managers extend destination appeal by building positive media relations and effectively managing destination narratives, ensuring tourism locations maintain attractive, accurately presented, and engaging public images.

Sustainable and community-based tourism

Tourism careers in sustainability and community engagement focus specifically on enhancing the environmental, social, and cultural impacts of tourism activities. Sustainability consultants advise tourism operators and destinations on responsible practices, guiding eco-certification processes, resource conservation, and community engagement strategies. Community-based tourism managers develop and oversee tourism programs that directly benefit local populations, empowering residents economically and culturally. Ecotourism specialists similarly design travel experiences focused explicitly on ecological education, responsible travel, and conservation.

Tourism research and strategic planning

Careers in tourism research and strategic planning involve in-depth market analysis, economic impact studies, and future-focused planning. Tourism research analysts provide vital data-driven insights into visitor behavior, economic trends, and tourism performance to inform strategic decisions. Strategic planners leverage this information, formulating long-term development plans that maximize tourism potential sustainably. Economic analysts evaluate and communicate tourism's direct economic contributions, offering valuable evidence for policy-making and investment decisions.

Essential skills and competencies for tourism professionals

Tourism professionals across all roles benefit significantly from strong interpersonal skills, cultural awareness, adaptability, and creative problem-solving. In today's digitally driven environment, proficiency with tourism-specific digital tools, analytics, and strategic thinking is critical. An unwavering commitment to ethical leadership and sustainability also remains central to successful, responsible tourism practice.

Education, certification, and professional development

Formal education, professional certifications, and practical experience form a powerful combination that can significantly advance your tourism career. A degree in a field such as Tourism and Hospitality Management, Marketing, Business Administration, or Environmental Studies offers a foundational understanding essential for professional growth. Earning industry-recognized credentials, such as the Certified Travel Associate (CTA) or Sustainable Tourism Professional (STP), further distinguishes your expertise and commitment to the tourism field.

Gaining practical experience through internships, volunteer roles, and study-abroad programs would also prove invaluable, providing hands-on learning that builds essential skills and expands your professional network.

Join professional associations

Professional associations are valuable resources for career development, networking, continuing education, and gaining industry recognition. Many offer free or discounted student memberships, giving you access to exclusive events, job boards, and the latest industry insights. Engaging with associations early can accelerate your professional growth, deepen your industry understanding, and open doors to meaningful career opportunities.

The following is a curated list of important tourism-focused associations to explore.

Global

- **World Tourism Organization (UNWTO)**—unwto.org: Provides global leadership and research on sustainable tourism practices.
- **World Travel & Tourism Council (WTTC)**—wttc.org: Advocates for sustainable and inclusive growth in tourism globally.
- **Destinations International**—destinationsinternational.org: Offers professional development and resources specifically for destination marketing and management professionals.
- **International Ecotourism Society (TIES)**—ecotourism.org: Specializes in promoting responsible, sustainable tourism practices worldwide.

US and Canada

- **US Travel Association (USTA)**—ustravel.org: Supports US tourism growth through advocacy, networking, and research.
- **Tourism Industry Association of Canada (TIAC)**—tiac-aitc.ca: Represents and supports Canada's tourism sector, offering professional networking opportunities and advocacy.

Europe

- **European Travel Commission (ETC)**—etc-corporate.org: Promotes tourism to Europe through research and marketing initiatives.
- **European Cities Marketing (ECM)**—europeancitiesmarketing.com: Supports urban tourism professionals with resources and best practices.

Asia-Pacific

- **Pacific Asia Travel Association (PATA)**—pata.org: Facilitates sustainable tourism growth in the Asia-Pacific region through networking, events, and research.
- **Australian Tourism Export Council (ATEC)**—atec.net.au: Advocates for and supports Australian tourism operators through networking and education.

Niche tourism associations

- **Adventure Travel Trade Association (ATTA)**—adventuretravel.biz: Dedicated to adventure tourism professionals, offering targeted resources and networking opportunities.
- **International Festivals & Events Association (IFEA)**—ifea.com: Provides networking, resources, and professional development for event-focused tourism professionals.

Figure 9.3 Tourism industry career pathways

Tourism Industry Career Pathways

Senior/Executive Roles

- Chief Tourism Officer or Tourism Director
- Vice President of Destination Marketing
- Tourism Development Director
- Head of Global Partnerships
- Regional Director of Tourism Policy and Planning
- CEO or Founder
- Senior Sustainable Tourism Strategist
- Head of Research and Innovation
- Executive Director of National or State Tourism Office

Mid-Career Roles

- Destination Marketing Coordinator
- Tour Operations Manager
- Product Development Manager
- Sustainable Tourism Consultant
- Cruise Excursion Manager
- Guest Relations Assistant
- Transportation Guest Services Agent
- Cultural or Heritage Interpreter
- Event Assistant
- Ecotourism Assistant Guide
- Travel Sales Associate

Entry-level Roles

- Visitor Services Representative
- Travel Agent/Consultant Assistant
- Tour Guide or Local Guide
- Guest Relations Assistant
- Tour Guide or Assistant Guide
- Guest Relations Assistant
- Transportation Guest Services Agent
- Event Assistant
- Ecotourism Assistant Guide
- Travel Sales Associate

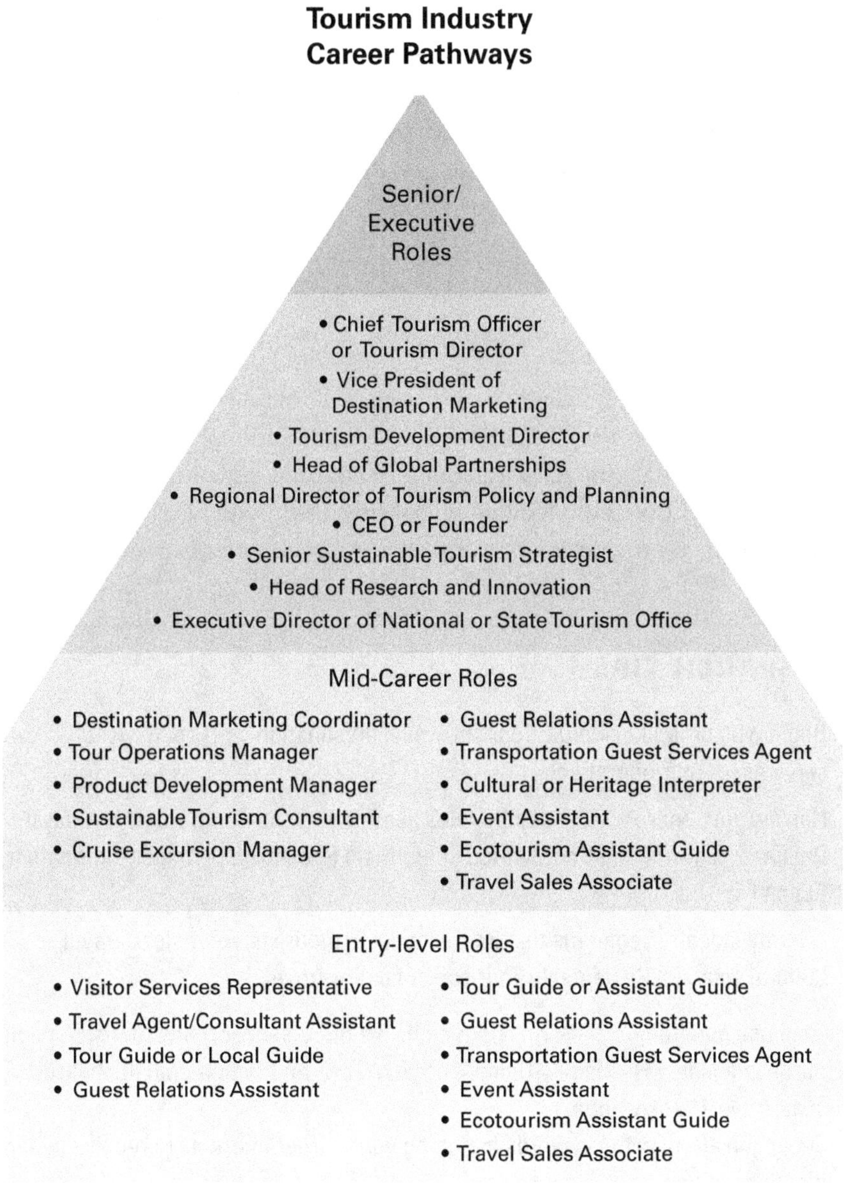

Job search resources: Finding your path in the tourism industry

After identifying key associations for building your professional network and industry knowledge, your next step is to explore job opportunities in tourism.

Actively searching job websites and company career pages is one of the most effective ways to discover internships, part-time roles, and full-time opportunities within the tourism industry. While the following suggestions are not exhaustive, they offer a strong starting point for your search.

Be sure to regularly check the career sections of prominent tourism-related employers, such as major tour operators (Intrepid Travel, TUI Group, G Adventures), airlines and cruise lines (BA, Delta Airlines, Emirates, Royal Caribbean), and destination marketing organizations (VisitBritain, Tourism Australia, VisitCalifornia).

Looking ahead

In Chapter 10, on lodging, you'll explore one of hospitality's foundational sectors. You'll examine lodging's evolution, its diverse organizational structures, service innovations, operational strategies, emerging trends, and wide-ranging career opportunities. You'll discover how lodging intersects closely with tourism, managed services, and events to provide comprehensive, memorable guest experiences.

JOB SEARCH TIPS

- Begin with broad keywords: Tourism, travel, destination marketing, visitor services, or tour operations.
- Narrow your search with specific roles like Travel Consultant, Tourism Analyst, Destination Marketing Coordinator, Ecotourism Specialist, or Visitor Information Specialist.
- Filter by industry segments that interest you: Ecotourism, Adventure Travel, Cultural Tourism, Sustainable Tourism, or Luxury Travel.

You can use general job platforms (Indeed, LinkedIn, Glassdoor) and tourism-specific resources including Hospitality Online and Hcareers, and region-specific boards such as Travel Weekly Jobs.

Set up job alerts with keywords matching your career interests to receive instant notifications of new opportunities.

Key takeaways

- **Global economic and cultural influence**: Tourism significantly boosts economies, enriches cultural exchange, and strengthens global connections, shaping communities worldwide.

- **Historical foundations**: Understanding tourism's evolution, from ancient pilgrimages and explorations to today's mass travel and digital nomadism, shows its dynamic adaptability and growth.

- **Diverse tourism segments and traveler behavior**: Clearly differentiating segments (leisure, business, cultural, ecotourism, niche markets) and analyzing traveler motivations helps tourism professionals strategically manage and market destinations.

- **Commitment to sustainability**: Sustainable tourism and ecotourism practices effectively balance economic development with environmental conservation and cultural integrity, ensuring long-term destination resilience.

- **Innovation and emerging trends**: Awareness of trends like bleisure travel, inclusive tourism, immersive technology, and social media-driven choices empowers industry professionals to proactively innovate and develop visitor experiences.

- **Rewarding career pathways**: Tourism offers diverse, globally impactful careers, requiring strategic thinking, cultural intelligence, commitment to sustainability practices, technological proficiency, and continuous professional growth.

References

B2B-Cambodia (2024) Angkor Wat retains status as global tourist attraction; international visitor numbers still lag behind pre-pandemic levels, June 2. b2b-cambodia.com/news/angkor-wat-retains-status-as-global-tourist-attraction-international-visitor-numbers-still-lag-behind-pre-pandemic-levels/?utm_source (archived at https://perma.cc/C876-E22Y)

Booking.com (2024) *Sustainable Travel 2024*. news.booking.com/download/904910bb-db77-4886-9ead-accbf87ad891/sustainabletravelreport2024.pdf (archived at https://perma.cc/NCW8-NDMJ)

Business Insider (2025) Venice doubles its last-minute "tourist tax"—with other cities looking to copy its approach to overtourism, February 11. businessinsider.com/overtourism-venice-doubles-last-minute-tourist-tax-other-cities-follow-2025-2 (archived at https://perma.cc/7Z84-JPDY)

CLIA (Cruise Lines International Association) (2020) *2020 Global Passenger Report*, cruising.org/resources/clia-global-passenger-report-2020 (archived at https://perma.cc/FW2A-ZCVP); *The Economic Contribution of the International Cruise Industry Globally in 2019*, europe.cruising.org/wp-content/uploads/2021/08/Global-Cruise-Impact-Analysis-2020-V1.0-1.pdf (archived at https://perma.cc/DXB4-C52Z)

CRC Reef Research Centre (2014) *Marine Tourism Impacts and Their Management on the Great Barrier Reef*. Townsville: CRC Reef Research Centre.

Deloitte (2024) *2024 Travel Outlook*. deloitte.com/content/dam/Deloitte/us/Documents/consumer-business/us-travel-hospitality-industry-outlook-2024.pdf (archived at https://perma.cc/2QML-5ETD)

ETIAS (2024) France's tourism industry gets boost from Netflix shows, January 29. etias.com/articles/pop-culture-boosts-french-tourism (archived at https://perma.cc/KH3K-7X3C)

Expedia (2022) *Inclusive Travel Insights Report*. go2.advertising.expedia.com/rs/185-EIA-216/images/_FINAL-InclusiveTravel_Whitepaper_2022.pdf?utm_source (archived at https://perma.cc/27FT-T3DM)

Expedia (2024a) Unpack '24: The Trends in Travel, https://partner.expediagroup.com/en-us/resources/research-insights/unpack-24-travel-trends-2024

Expedia (2024b) *The Path to Purchase: Understanding Traveler Behavior and Influences*. partner.expediagroup.com/en-us/resources/research-insights/path-to-purchase (archived at https://perma.cc/K3AQ-4CJ6)

Federal Reserve Bank of Philadelphia (2023) *The Beige Book: Summary of Commentary on Current Economic Conditions*. federalreserve.gov/monetarypolicy/files/BeigeBook_20230712.pdf?utm_source (archived at https://perma.cc/2B4J-ZLVD)

Flowers, J. (2020) Keeping the world's last mountain gorillas safe during Covid-19, AFAR, October 19. afar.com/magazine/gorilla-trekking-in-volcanoes-national-park-rwanda-during-covid-19 (archived at https://perma.cc/LE6Z-6K3B)

Forbes (2024) "Emily in Paris" tourism fuels local hostility as Season Four begins filming, February 13. forbes.com/sites/alexledsom/2024/02/13/emily-in-paris-tourism-local-hostility-as-season-four-begins-shooting (archived at https://perma.cc/MQ6H-4XVK)

GBRMPA (Great Barrier Reef Marine Park Authority) (2024) *Great Barrier Reef Outlook Report 2024*. elibrary.gbrmpa.gov.au/jspui/handle/11017/4078 (archived at https://perma.cc/MQ6H-4XVK)

Global Wellness Institute (2024) Wellness tourism. globalwellnessinstitute.org/what-is-wellness/what-is-wellness-tourism (archived at https://perma.cc/PW56-CD6A)

Government of Slovenia (2024) Inspiring green stories from Slovenia once again among the world's top 100, October 18. gov.si/en/news/2024-10-18-inspiring-green-stories-from-slovenia-once-again-among-the-worlds-top-100/?utm_source (archived at https://perma.cc/WK75-AF5G)

GSTC (Global Sustainable Tourism Council) (2024) *Booking.com Sustainable Travel Report 2024*. Global Sustainable Tourism Council. gstc.org/booking-sustainable-travel-report-2024/?utm_source (archived at https://perma.cc/KJ84-W3N3)

Honey, M. (2008) *Ecotourism and Sustainable Development: Who Owns Paradise?* (2nd edn), Washington, DC: Island Press.

IOC (International Olympic Committee) (2024) *IOC Final Report on Paris 2024*. library.olympics.com/Default/doc/SYRACUSE/3459871/ioc-final-report-on-paris-2024-international-olympic-committee?_lg=en-GB (archived at https://perma.cc/864J-R7LY)

Jordan Tourism Board (2024) Tourism sector thrives in 2023, contributes 14.6% to GDP despite challenges, Jordan News Agency, January 21. petra.gov.jo/Include/InnerPage.jsp?ID=56341&lang=en&name=en_news (archived at https://perma.cc/5NU5-CNRX)

Le Monde (2024) Netflix's "Emily in Paris" and "Lupin" drive Paris tourism, January 18. lemonde.fr/en/france/article/2024/01/18/netflix-s-emily-in-paris-and-lupin-drive-paris-tourism_6443181_7.html (archived at https://perma.cc/8B3N-6NDK)

Loss, L. (2019) Ecotourism in Costa Rica generates USD 1.4 billion a year, TourismReview News, November 11. tourism-review.com/ecotourism-in-costa-rica-developing-news11257 (archived at https://perma.cc/6XZZ-RLGB)

LVCVA (Las Vegas Convention and Visitors Authority) (2024) *Trends & Data: Research Reports*. lvcva.com/research (archived at https://perma.cc/RX7Q-S9D5).

McKinsey & Company (2024) Still feeling good: The US wellness market continues to boom. mckinsey.com/industries/consumer-packaged-goods/our-insights/still-feeling-good-the-us-wellness-market-continues-to-boom (archived at https://perma.cc/D6MU-D8EF)

Murray, A. (2024) Taylor Swift's Wembley concerts generate over £200 million for London's economy, BusinessLive, August 24. business-live.co.uk/economic-development/taylor-swifts-wembley-concerts-generate-29798540 (archived at https://perma.cc/NSE8-WB9G)

NPR (2024) Venice is charging day-trippers €5 to visit the city, April 25. npr.org/2024/04/25/1247162570/venice-entry-fee-day-trippers-tourists (archived at https://perma.cc/C4F9-GWQM)

Reuters (2024) Venice expands tourist entry fee system to include more days, October 24. reuters.com/world/europe/venice-expands-tourist-entry-fee-system-include-more-days-2024-10-24 (archived at https://perma.cc/8GSK-QJZG)

State of Hawai'i DBEDT (2024) *2023 Annual Visitor Research Report*. hawaiitourismauthority.org/media/13190/2023-annual-report-final.pdf (archived at https://perma.cc/8AGJ-DFUX)

Statista (2023) Travelers are keen to blend business with leisure. statista.com/chart/30139/travelers-extending-work-trips (archived at https://perma.cc/NN64-6KDB)

Statista (2024a) Digital nomads: Statistics and facts. statista.com/topics/9259/digital-nomads (archived at https://perma.cc/5J55-4YPA)

Statista (2024b) Number of visitors to Machu Picchu, Peru 2019–2023, statista.com/statistics/1082462/visitors-machu-picchu-peru (archived at https://perma.cc/Q6HZ-QCMA); Number of visitors to Yellowstone National Park in the U.S. 2008–2023, statista.com/statistics/254231/number-of-visitors-to-the-yellowstone-national-park-in-the-us (archived at https://perma.cc/T5TH-Z69L)

Statista (2024c) Social media use in travel and tourism: Statistics and facts. statista.com/topics/13406/social-media-use-in-travel-and-tourism (archived at https://perma.cc/L8YZ-VYD9)

Statistics Iceland (2025) Tourism short-term indicators in March 2025. statice.is/publications/news-archive/tourism/tourism-short-term-indicators-in-march-2025 (archived at https://perma.cc/L8YZ-VYD9)

Trip.com Group (2024) *Sustainable Travel Consumer Report*. images3.c-ctrip.com/marketing/grouptrip/Trip.com%20Group%20Sustainable%20Travel%20Consumer%20Report%202024-ENG.pdf?utm_source (archived at https://perma.cc/RFW9-W8XY)

Tourism New Zealand (2024) Tourism's contribution to New Zealand: Year ended March 2024. tourismnewzealand.com/insights/tourism-impact/?utm_source (archived at https://perma.cc/6WE6-J3FJ)

Towner, J. (1985) The Grand Tour: A key phase in the history of tourism, *Annals of Tourism Research*, 12 (3), 297–333.

UNESCO (2025) *World Heritage List*. whc.unesco.org/en/list/ (archived at https://perma.cc/T65Z-DXMD)

Visit Costa Rica (2023) *Sustainability: Protected areas. San José: ICT*. visitcostarica.com/sustainability?utm_source (archived at https://perma.cc/Z3Y9-566S)

World Food Travel Association (2024) *2024 State of the Food & Beverage Tourism Industry Annual Report*. worldfoodtravel.org/2024-state-of-the-industry-report-available (archived at https://perma.cc/TTY3-8Q5T)

WTTC (n.d.) *Travel & Tourism Economic Impact Research*. wttc.org/research/economic-impact (archived at https://perma.cc/UGM7-AHGF)

Lodging 10

LEARNING OBJECTIVES

- Define lodging and explain its integral role within hospitality.
- Trace lodging's historical evolution and key milestones shaping the industry.
- Classify primary lodging segments, clearly identifying their distinct characteristics and target markets.
- Explain and differentiate between hotel management, ownership, and branding/franchising.
- Evaluate critical industry trends impacting lodging, including sustainability, technological innovation, and experiential hospitality.
- Recognize essential operational functions within lodging and their application across the sector.
- Explore diverse lodging career opportunities, identifying roles, essential skills, and professional pathways.

Introduction: Lodging—Where hospitality meets home

Imagine stepping into the inviting lobby of a historic boutique hotel in London, warmly greeted by name and offered afternoon tea. Visualize yourself relaxing at a luxurious beachfront resort in the Caribbean, sipping a tropical drink while watching the sunset. Or perhaps you're arriving at an extended-stay hotel in San Francisco for a month-long project, feeling instantly at home with its residential-style amenities and personalized service. Each of these distinct scenarios captures the essence of lodging—a foundational pillar of the hospitality industry, focused on providing comfort, convenience, and memorable experiences tailored to guests' needs.

The lodging sector is a critical component of hospitality, encompassing diverse accommodations, including full-service hotels, select-service properties, luxury resorts, extended-stay facilities, and innovative alternative lodging solutions. While Chapter 1 introduced lodging's global significance within hospitality, this chapter provides a more detailed examination, featuring market data and regional insights.

For example, in 2024, the global accommodation market was valued at approximately $1.3 trillion, with projections indicating growth to $1.4 trillion by 2025 (The Business Research Company, 2025). According to the World Travel & Tourism Council (WTTC, 2024), the travel and tourism sector contributes over $10.9 trillion annually to the global economy and supports around 357 million jobs worldwide, with lodging representing a significant share of this impact.

Regionally, lodging's economic impact is equally substantial. In the US, hotels contribute nearly $900 billion to GDP and support about one in every 25 American jobs (about 8.3 million) as of early 2025 (AHLA, 2025). In the UK, the broader hospitality industry—which encompasses lodging, foodservices, and pubs—generated £62.5 billion in "gross value added" (approximately 2.8 percent of UK economic output) and employed around 2.8 million people as of June 2024 (UK Parliament, 2024). These figures highlight the industry's critical role in national economies, underscoring the importance of understanding local employment trends, economic contributions, and guest expectations. For hospitality professionals, awareness of this regional context helps in adapting service standards, staffing levels, and business strategies, setting the foundation for successful international careers and leadership roles.

Historically, lodging has evolved substantially, from early inns and guesthouses providing basic shelter to today's personalized boutique hotels, eco-friendly resorts, and technologically advanced accommodations that respond to modern traveler expectations. Understanding lodging's historical evolution, such as the rise of roadside motels alongside the automobile boom or the global expansion of hotel chains, helps explain today's diverse lodging landscape. These developments illustrate how hospitality continually adapts to technological changes, traveler expectations, and global trends, reflecting shifting preferences toward more personalized, authentic, and sustainable hospitality experiences.

Historical evolution of lodging

The concept of lodging dates back thousands of years, rooted in the basic human need for shelter while traveling. In ancient civilizations such as Egypt, Rome, and Greece, early inns and taverns provided simple accommodations for merchants, officials, and pilgrims navigating expansive trade and cultural routes. These early establishments offered basic necessities—shelter, food, and a place to rest—and were often strategically located near city gates or along well-traveled roads.

During the medieval period, lodging evolved in both function and form. Caravanserais—roadside inns designed for travelers in Asia, North Africa, and the Middle East—offered rest and safety along major trade routes like the Silk Road. In Europe, monasteries frequently provided lodging to pilgrims, sometimes at little or no cost, while independent inns became more common and sophisticated, offering meals and services to traveling merchants and wealthier guests.

The Industrial Revolution in the 18th and 19th centuries brought dramatic changes to the lodging industry, fueled by advances in transportation such as railways and steamships. As mobility increased, the demand for more and higher-quality accommodations surged, giving rise to grand hotels in major cities. Iconic properties like the Savoy in London and the Waldorf Astoria in New York set new standards in luxury and elegance, introducing modern conveniences and elevating expectations for comfort and personalized service.

In the early 20th century, the automobile revolution transformed the travel experience once again, especially in North America. Roadside motels and motor inns sprang up to accommodate travelers seeking convenience and affordability during long road trips. Following World War II, prosperity further diversified lodging options with the rise of large-scale resorts, budget hotels, and business-oriented properties designed to meet the growing needs of leisure travelers, families, and professionals.

The second half of the 20th century saw the global expansion of hotel chains, enabled by franchising, branding, and management contracts. Companies such as Marriott, Hilton, and InterContinental established worldwide networks of consistent, branded lodging options, giving travelers the confidence of familiarity regardless of destination.

In recent decades, digital innovation, shifting consumer expectations, and global trends have accelerated lodging industry evolution. Online travel agencies, dynamic pricing, and review platforms have transformed guest booking behaviors, making lodging choices more transparent and competitive. Alternative accommodation options, such as Airbnb and Vrbo, introduced new personalized and immersive lodging experiences, compelling traditional hotels to innovate. Today's lodging providers are responding by prioritizing sustainability, integrating smart technology, and enhancing experiential design, catering to travelers who value authenticity, personalization, and meaningful connections.

As lodging evolved, new property types emerged to meet travelers' increasingly diverse needs. This chapter illustrates how lodging adapts to lifestyle, purpose, and price point. It explores the historical foundations, distinct lodging segments, and operational frameworks of the industry, along with insights into current trends, business structures, and diverse career opportunities.

Reflect

- Consider the historical milestones that have shaped today's lodging industry.
- Identify one milestone you believe has most significantly impacted modern guest experiences. Explain why this development was especially influential, providing specific examples from hotels you've experienced or studied.

REAL-WORLD EXAMPLE:
INDUSTRY SPOTLIGHT   The rise of hotel franchising

After World War II, hotel franchising dramatically reshaped the lodging industry. Holiday Inn led the way by introducing standardized branding, consistent quality, and uniform guest experiences across independently owned properties, giving travelers confidence and familiarity wherever they traveled. This model quickly gained popularity, fueling significant growth among today's global hospitality leaders, including Marriott, Hilton, and IHG.

Franchising not only offered lucrative business opportunities for individual hotel owners—offering access to established brands, marketing resources, and centralized reservation systems—it also strengthened guest loyalty through consistency and trust. Today, franchising remains a core strategy driving expansion, profitability, and brand recognition across the global lodging industry.

Lodging segments

Lodging is wonderfully diverse, reflecting travelers' unique tastes, lifestyles, and purposes for travel. From vibrant urban hotels buzzing with energy to serene mountain resorts offering tranquility, each lodging segment delivers distinctive experiences tailored to specific guest needs. Hospitality professionals who clearly understand these segments can strategically design and deliver stays that are personalized, memorable, and aligned with distinct market expectations.

Understanding the wide variety of lodging options, from eco-lodges and boutique villas to hostels and cruise cabins, enables hospitality professionals to develop informed strategies that meet diverse guest expectations. Central to this understanding is recognizing how ownership, branding, and management structures directly influence the way lodging properties operate and position themselves in the market.

Full-service hotels: All-inclusive comfort

Picture a traveler stepping into the grand lobby of the Marriott Marquis in New York's bustling Times Square, welcomed by lively energy, refined décor, and expansive amenities. Full-service hotels generally offer extensive amenities, which often include multiple restaurants and bars, room service, fitness centers, pools, comprehensive meeting spaces, and concierge services. Specific offerings will vary by property, but, collectively, these amenities create a more comprehensive and convenient guest experience compared to select-service properties.

Select-service hotels: Smart, streamlined, and convenient

Imagine checking into the Courtyard by Marriott in Manchester, England, conveniently located near business parks and cultural attractions. You quickly settle into your well-appointed room, choose a complimentary breakfast in the sleek lobby, and plan your day. Select-service hotels provide targeted amenities, such as breakfast, fitness facilities, and limited meeting space, without the broader offerings of full-service properties.

Brands like Hampton by Hilton, Holiday Inn Express, and Courtyard by Marriott exemplify this segment, offering high-quality stays at accessible price points ideal for business professionals, families, and value-conscious travelers.

Luxury hotels and resorts

Luxury hotels deliver refined experiences through exclusivity, personalized service, and premium amenities, attracting guests seeking elevated stays. Iconic properties such as the Ritz-Carlton, Four Seasons Hotels and Resorts, and Dubai's Burj Al Arab embody luxury lodging, offering elegance, exceptional guest services, personalized attention, and exclusive amenities beyond those typically found in full-service hotels. The global luxury hotel market continues to grow, driven by increased demand for unique and meaningful high-end experiences (Statista, 2024).

Convention hotels: Epicenters of events and business

Picture the dynamic lobby of the Gaylord National Resort & Convention Center near Washington, DC, buzzing with meetings and conference attendees. Convention hotels like this are purpose-built to host large-scale events, offering expansive meeting spaces, cutting-edge audio-visual systems, on-site catering, and dedicated event staff.

Group and convention business is central to these properties' revenue strategies. As remote and hybrid work patterns are changing, face-to-face gatherings are experiencing renewed momentum. According to *The Wall Street Journal* (2024), group travel RevPAR—a key performance metric calculated by multiplying the ADR by the occupancy rate—rose 6.8 percent during the first eight months of 2024, outperforming leisure and transient segments. This underscores the continued significance of meetings, corporate retreats, and conferences for the hospitality industry.

Hotels like the Marriott Marquis, Hilton convention properties, and Gaylord Hotels illustrate how convention infrastructure, hospitality operations, and professional event planning converge, making group business not just a revenue stream but the core driver of profitability and identity.

Extended-stay hotels: Your home from home

Extended-stay hotels like Homewood Suites by Hilton in Toronto offer guests on long-term assignments or relocations home-like comfort and convenience. These properties feature spacious suites with fully-equipped kitchens, separate living areas, and laundry facilities—amenities typically not available in select-service or full-service hotels. They consistently maintain higher occupancy rates compared to traditional hotels. For instance, extended-stay hotels achieved a 72.7 percent occupancy rate in late 2024, significantly above the general hotel average (The Highland Group, 2025). Brands such as Residence Inn by Marriott, Staybridge Suites by IHG, and Hyatt House excel in this segment.

Alternative accommodations and specialized lodging segments

The lodging industry extends far beyond traditional hotels, encompassing a vibrant range of accommodations that align with travelers' unique preferences, values, and lifestyles. From home-like vacation rentals to themed resorts, alternative and specialized lodging options offer distinct experiences that meet the needs of evolving travel behaviors.

Alternative accommodations: Living like a local

Many travelers today crave authenticity, trading predictable hotel rooms for charming Parisian apartments perched above lively cobbled streets, or serene villas hidden in Bali's lush jungles. Thanks to platforms like Airbnb, Vrbo, and Booking.com, it's easier than ever to explore new places with the comfort and flexibility of a resident. By choosing these accommodations, visitors don't just observe—they immerse themselves, savoring everyday life in a way that locals might.

This segment has grown rapidly. Airbnb has grown to have over 8 million active listings in more than 150,000 cities across over 220 countries and regions, and has welcomed over 2 billion guest arrivals since its founding (Airbnb, 2025). This rapid growth reflects travelers' increasing preference for authenticity, space, and cost-effectiveness, particularly for group and extended stays. The global vacation rental market, valued at approximately $90 billion in 2024, continues to expand significantly, driven by digital platforms and evolving traveler preferences for home-style, private accommodations. This market now comprises an estimated 10–13 percent of the overall global lodging demand (Grand View Research, 2023).

Casino hotels: Entertainment and excitement under one roof

Casino hotels blend lodging with vibrant nightlife, world-class entertainment, and immersive gaming experiences. Think of Caesars Palace or the Bellagio in Las Vegas, where guests enjoy fine dining, headline performances, and dynamic casino floors, all within a single property.

The global casino hotel market is forecast to be worth approximately $157 billion in 2025 and to surpass $200 billion by 2030, according to projections published by Mordor Intelligence (2024). These properties attract leisure travelers, event attendees, and international tourists seeking all-in-one experiences.

All-inclusive resorts: Seamless leisure experiences

All-inclusive resorts simplify the vacation planning process by bundling accommodations, meals, drinks, entertainment, and activities into one upfront price. Guests at properties like Sandals Resorts or Club Med enjoy worry-free relaxation in beautiful destinations with unlimited options at their fingertips.

These resorts have surged in popularity following the pandemic. In sun-and-sand destinations like Mexico and the Dominican Republic, occupancy soared to around 77 percent, outperforming traditional leisure hotels in recovery (JLL, 2022). Meanwhile, travel advisors report a 324 percent year-over-year growth in bookings for major all-inclusive brands in 2024, driven notably by Gen Z travelers seeking convenience and value (Business Insider, 2024).

Bed and breakfasts: Intimate, personal hospitality

A weekend at a cozy farmhouse in Tuscany might start with homemade pastries, rich espresso, and warm conversations about local vineyards and hidden villages. Bed and breakfast providers (B&Bs) offer travelers the chance to experience personalized hospitality, thoughtfully prepared meals, and intimate, inviting surroundings, often tucked away in historically significant or scenic locations.

Though smaller in scale, B&Bs captivate travelers eager to slow down and savor authentic local experiences. Many now blend traditional charm with contemporary comforts, often at a lower price, making them especially appealing to couples and solo travelers who value genuine connections and memorable hospitality.

Timeshare and vacation ownership: Familiarity meets flexibility

Timeshares offer travelers the best of both worlds: consistent, familiar accommodations alongside the freedom to explore new destinations through global exchange programs. Brands like Marriott Vacation Club and Wyndham Destinations use flexible, points-based systems to balance reliable comfort with adventurous variety.

Especially popular with multigenerational families and frequent leisure travelers, timeshares provide long-term access to high-quality vacation stays. The American Resort Development Association (ARDA, 2024) reports that over 9.9 million owners in the US alone enjoy the benefits of timeshare, contributing to annual sales surpassing $10.5 billion.

Hostels: Social, budget-friendly stays

Hostels offer more than just affordable lodging—they're vibrant hubs for young travelers, backpackers, and adventure-seekers on a budget looking to meet new people and share experiences. With communal kitchens, shared rooms, and organized social activities, hostels foster a dynamic atmosphere ideal for building friendships and exploring destinations together.

Today, more than 17,700 hostels in 179 countries are listed worldwide, welcoming guests into social and budget-friendly environments (Hostelworld Group, 2024). Leading operators enhance this experience by combining boutique-style designs with digital conveniences. Generator Hostels is known for its contemporary, stylish approach to hostel accommodations, operating in major European and US cities, while, Hostelling International operates a global network of over 2,500 hostels across nearly 60 countries, offering travelers reliable and socially engaging accommodations (Hostelling International, 2024).

Eco-hotels and sustainable lodging: Hospitality with a purpose

Sustainability is transforming hospitality as eco-hotels and green resorts increasingly integrate energy-saving technologies, waste-reduction practices, locally sourced products, and engaging environmental education programs into their guest experiences. Innovative brands like 1 Hotels and Six Senses are proving that sustainability and luxury can coexist, appealing to travelers who want memorable stays that reflect their values. With eco-conscious lodging gaining momentum, travelers are clearly demonstrating that environmental responsibility is not just desirable—it's becoming essential to modern hospitality.

Cruise lines: Floating destinations

Cruise ships offer travelers a distinctive hospitality experience, combining accommodation, built-in dining, live entertainment, recreation, and transportation into one memorable journey. Leading operators such as Royal Caribbean, Norwegian, and MSC manage luxurious floating resorts, hosting thousands of guests with onboard restaurants, theaters, spas, fitness facilities, and diverse activities, all while exploring multiple global destinations.

From adventurous expedition cruises in remote waters to leisurely river voyages through historic cities, cruising appeals broadly—attracting families seeking convenience and amenities, as well as solo travelers looking for immersive, culturally rich experiences. As the cruise segment grows, it also navigates sustainability challenges, prompting industry leaders to implement environmentally responsible technologies and practices.

> **Reflect**
>
> - Think about a lodging segment that interests you the most, whether luxury hotels, extended-stay properties, or alternative accommodations. Why does this segment resonate with you personally or professionally?
> - How might understanding the unique attributes of your chosen segment help you design a memorable guest experience?

Hotel management, ownership, and branding: Understanding the structures

Have you ever wondered who owns your favorite hotel, or who ensures your stay runs smoothly behind the scenes? Most hotels involve three distinct but interconnected groups: the owner, the management company, and the franchisor (brand owner). The franchisor owns the overall brand (for example, Marriott International), while the brand itself is the specific identity under that franchisor (such as Moxy). According to Deloitte (2024), approximately 63 percent of rooms in major hotel chains globally operate under franchise agreements, highlighting the prevalence of these asset-light models.

> Clear delineation of ownership, management, and branding roles is fundamental to achieving operational excellence in hospitality. Each party brings distinct strengths—financial investment, daily operations, and brand equity—which together create an environment where guests experience consistency, quality, and value, no matter where they travel.
>
> —*Spiro Frangos, senior vice president, head of asset management, Rockbridge Holdings*

Hotel ownership: Investing in lodging assets

Owners are individuals or groups who purchase and maintain the physical hotel (the asset). They might be entrepreneurs, real estate developers, or investment firms. Their primary goal is to maximize their financial returns by ensuring the hotel is profitable, maintains value, and stays competitive.

Ownership structures can vary significantly. A small boutique hotel may have a single owner, whereas a larger hotel, such as a Marriott in Chicago, could be owned by an investment group like Rockbridge Holdings, which has invested in over 300 hotels worth more than $10 billion (Rockbridge, 2024). Real estate investment trusts (REITs), such as Host Hotels & Resorts, own numerous prominent hotels globally and earn income through strategic acquisitions and leasing.

Hotel branding and franchising: The power of recognition

Branding serves as a hotel's public identity and promise to its guests. Seeing a brand name like Moxy (owned by franchisor Marriott International), Hyatt, IHG, or Accor instantly signals a standard of quality, design, service, and value. Globally, branded rooms make up a significant majority of the market: 56.9 percent of hotel rooms worldwide carry a recognized brand, and 46.9 percent are franchised, meaning the franchisor (the company owning the brand) licenses the brand name to third-party operators (hotel owners) (Weinstein, 2024).

Through franchise agreements, property owners gain access to a brand's global reservation system, loyalty programs, and operational standards in exchange for fees. In turn, franchisors benefit from broader distribution, marketing support, and the assurance of consistency across properties—reinforcing guest trust and loyalty.

Key terms to understand here include:

- **Franchisor (brand):** The company owning the hotel brand (such as Marriott International) that allows the hotel owner to use their brand name and resources.
- **Franchisee (hotel owner):** The owner who pays to use the franchisor's brand, agreeing to uphold specified brand standards.

If both the franchisor and hotel owner agree the property aligns with the brand, they sign a franchise agreement. The franchisee pays the franchisor a percentage of total hotel sales (top-line sales) for access to these brand benefits.

Hotel management: Overseeing daily operations

While owners supply the capital and franchisors provide the brand, it is the management company that oversees the day-to-day running of the hotel. Management companies ensure that the property delivers consistent guest experiences, achieves operational efficiency, and meets financial targets.

These companies are responsible for staffing, training, payroll, purchasing, maintenance, guest services, food and beverage operations, and compliance with brand and legal standards. For example, large third-party operators such as Aimbridge

Hospitality and Interstate Hotels & Resorts manage hundreds of properties worldwide on behalf of owners.

In exchange for a base fee (usually a percentage of revenue) and often an incentive fee tied to profitability, management companies deliver professional expertise in operations and revenue optimization. They bring specialized knowledge in areas including revenue management, digital marketing, food and beverage innovation, and human resources—capabilities that individual owners might not be able to maintain in-house.

Some franchisors, such as Marriott and Hilton, also operate hotels directly through their own management divisions. However, independent third-party management firms have grown significantly, particularly in the US and Europe, where asset-light strategies dominate.

Ultimately, the management company acts as the bridge between owners (focused on financial returns) and franchisors (focused on brand integrity). Their success depends on balancing guest satisfaction with strong financial performance, ensuring the property remains competitive in a dynamic hospitality marketplace.

Visualizing the structure: The hospitality triangle

Imagine the hospitality structure as a collaborative triangle (Figure 10.1), illustrating how each group interacts and relies on each other for success:

- **Owner:** Owns the hotel, invests in the asset, and oversees overall financial performance. Owners negotiate franchise agreements directly with franchisors and select management companies to operate their hotels, ensuring strategic alignment and performance goals are met.
- **Franchisor (brand owner):** The company owning the hotel brand (such as Marriott), providing essential brand assets including recognition, reservation systems, marketing power, loyalty programs, and consistent standards. The franchisor collaborates closely with owners and management companies to ensure properties meet brand expectations, protecting and enhancing brand reputation.
- **Management company:** Manages daily hotel operations, staffing, guest services, and revenue management. It regularly communicates with the franchisor to maintain compliance with brand standards and with the owner to achieve financial and operational objectives.

This interconnected structure highlights the continuous partnership and mutual reliance required to successfully operate a hotel property.

Figure 10.1 The hospitality triangle

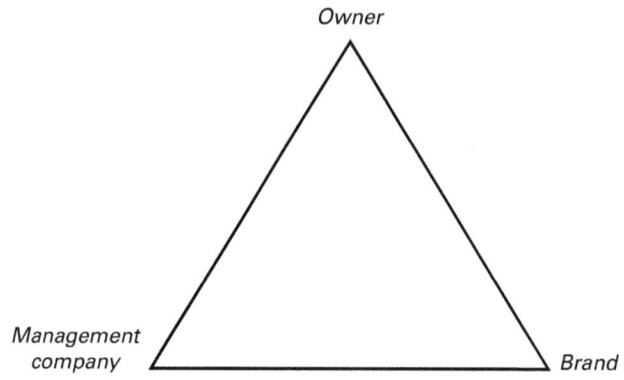

REAL-WORLD EXAMPLE:
INDUSTRY EXAMPLE   Noelle Hotel, Nashville, Tennessee

To understand how ownership, management, and branding structures intertwine seamlessly within hospitality, consider the Noelle Hotel in Nashville:

- **Owner**: Rockbridge Holdings—Responsible for financial investment and property value.
- **Brand**: Tribute Portfolio—The hotel's specific brand identity.
- **Franchisor (brand owner)**: Marriott International—Provides global reservation network, loyalty programs, and brand standards.
- **Management company**: Makeready—Oversees staffing, guest services, and daily operational management.

Each entity plays a crucial role by leveraging its expertise—financial investment, brand positioning, and operational excellence—to collectively ensure the hotel's success.

Reflect

- Reflect on your last hotel experience. Can you clearly identify the property's owner, management company, and brand affiliation?
- How do you think each of these entities influenced your stay, positively or negatively? Provide specific examples.

Why this matters: Building career awareness

Understanding hotel business structures is key to identifying where you may thrive in your own hospitality career. Those drawn to guest-facing roles and operational leadership might pursue positions with management companies. Individuals interested in real estate, finance, or investment may explore hotel ownership groups or REITs. Others may find their passion in branding, marketing, or customer loyalty programs within major hotel corporations.

INTERACTIVE EXERCISE
Who's behind the brand?

This activity explores the relationship between hotel ownership, management, and branding by investigating a real-world property.

Choose a hotel that interests you—this could be a local property you've visited, a hotel in a dream destination, or one affiliated with a global brand you admire. Then, use the hotel's website, LinkedIn, industry news websites (such as Hospitality Net, Hotel Management), or business databases to investigate the following:

1 **Hotel name and location**
   - What is the full name and address of the hotel you selected?

2 **Brand affiliation**
   - Who is the brand's parent company (perhaps Marriott, IHG, Hilton, Accor, Hyatt)?
   - Does the hotel's website mention affiliation with any loyalty or rewards programs? If so, what is the name of the program?

3 **Management company**
   - Who manages the day-to-day operations of the hotel?
   - Is it self-managed, part of a brand-managed property, or operated by a third-party management company (such as Aimbridge or Davidson Hospitality)?

4 **Ownership group**
   - Who owns the hotel? Is it a private owner, a real estate firm, or a hospitality investment company?
   - If applicable, name the ownership entity and share a fact about their portfolio.

5 **What surprised you?**
   - Reflect on something you discovered that challenged your assumptions about how hotels are structured.

Emerging trends and innovations in lodging

As the lodging industry evolves, professionals must anticipate what's next. This section highlights the trends that are shaping the guest experience and driving operational innovation worldwide.

Imagine checking into a hotel room personalized precisely to your preferences: automatically adjusted lighting, curated local experiences awaiting your arrival, and sustainability woven into the details of your stay. This isn't just the future of lodging—it's today's reality, driven by innovative trends reshaping hospitality around the globe. Today's hotels and alternative accommodations must innovate proactively to remain competitive, engaging, and relevant to travelers worldwide. Let's explore some of the most influential trends reshaping how guests experience lodging today, and how you, as a future hospitality professional, can anticipate and lead these exciting changes.

Sustainability and eco-conscious hospitality

Sustainability is no longer simply an optional amenity—it's a fundamental expectation reshaping the lodging industry. Many of today's travelers look beyond comfort and convenience, evaluating accommodations based on how they manage their environmental footprint, from innovative building designs that blend harmoniously with nature, to energy-efficient technologies, considerately curated guest amenities, and meaningful engagement with local communities. This shift toward conscious travel challenges hospitality operators not only to embrace sustainability but to integrate it genuinely at every guest touchpoint, reflecting a broader global movement toward mindful, purpose-driven hospitality.

Hotels are responding creatively, adopting practices such as waste reduction, water conservation, renewable energy use, and environmentally responsible construction. Brands like Six Senses Resorts exemplify this trend through on-site organic gardens, extensive solar energy provision, and ambitious zero-waste initiatives, proving sustainability and luxury can coexist seamlessly. Similarly, Marriott International has formally committed to achieving net-zero value-chain greenhouse gas emissions by 2050, guiding sustainability efforts across its global portfolio of managed and franchised properties (Marriott International, 2024). In Latin America, sustainability pioneers such as Inkaterra in Peru integrate ecotourism into luxury lodging, effectively balancing ecological conservation with premium guest experiences. At 1 Hotel Brooklyn Bridge, reclaimed wood furnishings, filtered water taps that minimize plastic waste, and rooftop gardens that enhance local biodiversity clearly demonstrate sustainability's compatibility with upscale comfort. These sustainability innovations significantly enhance the guest experience.

Trend focus: Technology integration and smart hotels

Sustainability is not the only transformative force shaping the lodging industry. As environmental responsibility redefines operational standards, technology simultaneously reshapes guest expectations, creating a dynamic intersection of digital innovation and hospitality excellence.

Because technology impacts nearly every aspect of the modern guest journey, this section takes a deeper dive into how hotels are integrating innovation across guest-facing and operational systems. From robotic luggage assistants to AI-powered revenue tools, technology is transforming how hotels operate, serve guests, and evolve.

According to Hospitality Net (2022), 73 percent of travelers expect hotels to offer contactless options, and over 40 percent prefer digital communication rather than phone or in-person interactions. The rise of phygital (physical plus digital) design is reimagining lodging to meet expectations for ease, personalization, and automation.

Across brands and property types, mobile check-in, digital keys, and app-based service requests have become standard. Luxury brands such as Four Seasons enhance guest experiences through in-room tablets that control lighting, food orders, and spa reservations. Voice-activated assistants like Amazon Alexa for Hospitality are featured in select Marriott and Wynn properties, while hotels in Asia increasingly employ facial recognition technology for easy and secure check-ins.

Behind the scenes, AI and machine learning optimize real-time pricing through systems like IDeaS and Duetto, maximizing occupancy and profitability. Chatbots manage a significant share of guest queries, freeing front-desk staff for personal interactions. Predictive maintenance tools alert engineering teams to potential equipment issues before they become problematic, and integrated energy management systems reduce environmental impacts by optimizing lighting, HVAC, and water use.

With these technological advances, data security remains a critical priority. Hotels are improving cybersecurity by adopting encrypted platforms, two-factor authentication, and compliance with data protection regulations such as the General Data Protection Regulation (GDPR) and other regional privacy laws. Additionally, many operators are carefully navigating the ethical use of AI, ensuring personalization efforts remain respectful, transparent, and free from algorithmic bias.

Experiential hospitality and authentic local experiences

Today's travelers are seeking more than just a place to sleep—they're looking for meaningful, memorable experiences that connect them to the people and culture of a destination. This desire for deeper engagement is fueling the rise of experiential hospitality, where every element of the stay, from design to dining to storytelling, provides a sense of place.

Boutique hotels often lead in this area. For example, each Hotel Indigo property is uniquely designed to reflect the character of its surrounding neighborhood, whether through curated local art, regional cuisine, or historical themes. Similarly, Kimpton Hotels host wine evenings and partner with local creatives and businesses to foster guest connection to the community. Even global brands are evolving: Marriott's Autograph Collection features independent properties with distinctive identities, and Hyatt's Unbound Collection focuses on storytelling-driven hospitality.

Platforms like Airbnb Experiences have also expanded how travelers engage with destinations, offering immersive activities such as culinary workshops, artisan tours, and cultural ceremonies led by locals. These hands-on experiences generate not only guest satisfaction, but strong emotional connections and word-of-mouth referrals.

For hospitality professionals, delivering experiential hospitality requires creativity, cultural curiosity, and a willingness to co-create with local communities. When done well, it turns a simple stay into a story worth remembering—and retelling.

THINK LIKE A MANAGER
Designing a local experience for guests

Your hotel is shifting toward a more experiential brand identity to appeal to today's travelers. You've been asked to recommend one guest experience that connects visitors to the local culture.

- What is one local or community-based experience you would integrate into the guest journey? How would you showcase it during the stay?
- Consider partnerships, storytelling, and sensory experiences. Think about operational coordination, guest communication, and brand reputation.

Wellness and mindfulness tourism: A growing force in lodging

As health and well-being become central to how people live, work, and travel, wellness tourism stands out as one of the fastest-growing segments in global hospitality. No longer confined to traditional spas, modern wellness offerings now include sleep optimization, stress reduction, mindfulness experiences, nutritional guidance, and active adventures. According to the Global Wellness Institute (2024), the wellness tourism market is expected to surpass $1 trillion in 2024 and continue climbing toward $1.4 trillion by 2027, driven by guests' preference for self-care and mental rejuvenation alongside traditional leisure activities.

Luxury wellness resorts such as Canyon Ranch and Miraval have redefined the category by offering holistic programs that combine fitness, nutrition, mindfulness, and personalized health coaching, thus transforming the notion of retreat into a comprehensive lifestyle reset. Brands like Westin Hotels & Resorts embed wellness into every stay through offerings including in-room fitness equipment, SuperFoodsRx menus, and wellness concierge services. Even midscale brands such as EVEN Hotels by IHG are fully designed around travelers' health needs, featuring natural sleep aids, hydration stations, and dedicated workout zones.

Wellness tourism is more than pampering—it reflects a societal shift toward balance, intentional living, and preventive health. By weaving wellness into the guest experience, even through simple touches like yoga mats, meditation app recommendations, or wholesome menu options, lodging providers can differentiate themselves in an increasingly competitive market.

For hospitality professionals, understanding wellness as a guest motivator is critical. Creating experiences that support physical vitality, mental well-being, and emotional renewal is no longer a luxury—it's a business essential.

Hybrid and flexible lodging models

Hotels increasingly cater to digital nomads, remote workers, and hybrid travelers through co-working spaces, high-speed Wi-Fi, flexible bookings, and amenities blending productivity and relaxation. CitizenM Hotels exemplifies this model, offering compact, tech-enabled rooms and stylish communal workspaces tailored for business travelers and digital nomads. Alternative accommodations similarly provide extended-stay discounts, comfortable workspaces, and residential amenities explicitly catering to remote professionals.

Central to delivering exceptional guest experiences in this diverse and dynamic lodging landscape is a foundational commitment to DEIBA.

Inclusive excellence in hospitality: A business imperative

Inclusive excellence isn't just about doing the right thing—it's about doing things better. In hospitality, where success depends on understanding, welcoming, and serving diverse guests, building an inclusive and equitable culture is not optional—it's a strategic advantage. Inclusive practices directly elevate guest experiences by equipping hospitality teams with the cultural competency and sensitivity needed to authentically engage diverse guests.

Companies that lead on inclusion consistently outperform peers. According to McKinsey (2023), organizations with greater diversity in leadership are 39 percent more likely to financially outperform their competitors. Inclusive organizations also report higher innovation rates, better employee retention, and greater guest satisfaction, making inclusive excellence not just ethical, but essential.

Hospitality leaders are embracing this imperative through initiatives that promote equitable opportunity, diverse representation, accessible design, and inclusive guest experiences. The following examples show how inclusive excellence is showing up across the industry.

Inclusive hiring and workforce development

- **Hyatt India's RiseHY** initiative provides job readiness and employment to "opportunity youth", training thousands of young adults from underserved backgrounds globally.
- **IHG's True Hospitality for Good** program supports skills-building, mentorship, and employment for underrepresented communities.
- **Marriott's Path to Leadership** program supports internal development of underrepresented talent at property and corporate levels.

Supplier diversity and ownership opportunities

- **Hilton's Supplier Diversity** program connects the company with women-, minority-, veteran-, and LGBTQ-owned businesses across its global supply chain.
- **Choice Hotels International** is recognized for its commitment to franchise ownership diversity, particularly among Black and Latino entrepreneurs through its Emerging Markets program.
- **Wyndham Hotels & Resorts** partners with diverse suppliers and entrepreneurs to expand ownership opportunities across underserved markets.

Accessibility and inclusive design

- **Scandic Hotels (Sweden)** leads Europe in accessible guest experience, offering digital hotel tours, tactile signage, vibrating fire alarms, and inclusive room design.
- **Disney Resorts** integrates sensory-friendly guides, wheelchair-accessible transportation, and assistive technology in all properties.
- **Accor Pacific** has partnered with Indigenous communities to train and employ local talent while adapting cultural design features and accessibility tools.

> I've always believed hospitality is about people first. Being able to create opportunities and advocate for belonging on a global scale has been one of the most meaningful parts of my journey. Hospitality truly thrives when everyone feels seen, valued, and cared for—investing in DEIBA initiatives not only strengthens our teams but also enriches the guest experience, turning ordinary stays into genuinely meaningful connections.
>
> —*Ronisha Goodwin, director, global human resources, Hyatt*

Inclusive leadership and belonging culture

- **Accor's RiiSE** gender-equity initiative spans 20 countries, fostering mentorship and inclusive leadership development through structured regional programs and formal mentoring circles (Accor, 2018).
- **Hyatt's RiseHY** initiative has significantly advanced employment opportunities for young people. Since its launch in 2018, Hyatt has provided job training, mentorship, and employment to more than 5,700 young people across over 400 hotels worldwide, with a goal of reaching 10,000 hires by 2025 (Hyatt, 2024).
- **IHG's True Hospitality for Good** invests in skills development, mentorship, and employment pathways through its global IHG Academy, significantly reducing employment barriers for underrepresented communities and promoting inclusivity and career growth.

Inclusive excellence improves team performance, sharpens cultural intelligence, expands customer reach, and future-proofs organizations against shifting market demands. In hospitality, where every guest interaction matters, inclusion isn't just behind the scenes—it's center stage.

Hotel organizational structure: Understanding executive leadership and operations

Having explored the diversity of lodging types and the major trends reshaping the industry, we now turn to the essential business and operational functions behind the scenes that ensure lodging excellence.

Behind every well-run hotel is an organized leadership structure that oversees strategic planning, daily operations, financial performance, guest satisfaction, and team culture. Understanding this structure helps aspiring hospitality professionals see where different business functions live, and where their own career paths might lead.

Most full-service hotels, resorts, and large urban properties are led by an executive committee (EC team)—a collaborative leadership group composed of the general manager and department heads across key disciplines.

- **General manager (GM):** The hotel's top leader, responsible for strategic direction, profitability, guest satisfaction, and overall team performance.
- **Director of operations/hotel manager:** Often second-in-command, this leader manages the day-to-day functioning of the property across rooms, food and beverage, engineering, and guest services.
- **Director of sales and marketing:** Leads all revenue-generating efforts, including group and transient sales, branding, partnerships, and digital marketing campaigns.

- **Director of finance:** Manages all financial operations—budgets, forecasts, payroll, audits, reporting, and regulatory compliance.
- **Director of human resources:** Oversees recruitment, training, performance management, employee engagement, benefits, and DEI initiatives.
- **Director of food and beverage:** Manages all culinary operations, including restaurants, bars, catering, banquets, and in-room dining, ensuring guest satisfaction and profitability.
- **Director of engineering:** Leads maintenance and physical plant operations, including sustainability initiatives, safety, and preventative upkeep.
- **Director of revenue management** (common in large hotels): Optimizes pricing, inventory, and distribution to maximize revenue based on data-driven demand forecasting.
- **Director of rooms** (in some properties): Oversees front office, housekeeping, guest services, and concierge operations to ensure seamless, service-driven stays.
- **Director of security and IT:** Oversees hotel safety, security protocols, guest and employee safety training, cybersecurity, data protection, and technology infrastructure.

In smaller or boutique hotels, many of these functions may be combined into broader roles, but the foundational structure remains: a leadership team working together to align strategy with daily execution.

By understanding how hotels are structured, hospitality students gain critical insight into how departments collaborate, where decisions are made, and how future leadership opportunities can evolve. Figure 10.2 gives an example of a typical full-service hotel organizational structure.

Core business and operational functions in lodging: The backbone of hospitality excellence

Delivering exceptional lodging experiences requires more than warm hospitality and elegant accommodation. Behind every seamless guest journey is an interconnected network of core business and operational functions—finance, operations, sales and marketing, risk management, and human resources—working together to drive service, satisfaction, and long-term business success.

Each of these functions directly influences guest satisfaction: finance and revenue management ensure guests perceive value; human resources nurture skilled,

Figure 10.2 Example full service hotel organizational structure

General Manager

- Director of Operations
  - Front Office Manager
    - Front Desk Supervisor
    - Shift Supervisor
  - Housekeeping Manager
    - Housekeeping Supervisor
    - Shift Supervisor
- Director of Sales and Marketing
  - Sales Manager
  - Marketing Manager
  - Coordinator/Administrative Assistance
- Director of Events
  - Catering Manager
  - Banquet Manager
  - Events Coordinator
- Director of Finance
  - Accounting Manager(s)
- Director of Human Resources
  - Human Resources Manager
  - Payroll Manager
  - Human Resources Coordinator
- Director of Food and Beverage
  - Restaurant Manager
  - In-Room Dining
  - Executive Chef
- Director of Engineering
  - Engineers
  - Maintenence Technicans
- Director of Revenue Mangement
  - Rooms Controller
  - Revenue Coordinator
- Director of Security and Information Technology (IT)
  - Security Manager
  - IT Manager

guest-focused employees; operations maintain the quality of the physical environment; and risk management fosters a secure, trusted stay.

Financial and revenue management: Stewardship for success

Financial management ensures lodging businesses operate efficiently and profitably. Through careful budgeting, forecasting, and expense control, properties allocate resources to maximize guest satisfaction and long-term growth. Revenue management teams closely monitor and adjust critical metrics such as ADR (the average revenue per rented room per day); occupancy (the percentage of available rooms sold); and RevPAR (calculated by multiplying ADR by occupancy rate).

Brands like Marriott and Hilton consistently refine revenue strategies to optimize RevPAR. Daily yield management, led by revenue teams, ensures properties strike the right balance between occupancy, rate, and profitability.

THINK LIKE A MANAGER
Prioritizing during staffing shortages

You manage housekeeping at a busy resort. A staffing shortage means several rooms won't be ready by the 3 p.m. check-in.

- What criteria determine room preparation priority?
- How will you clearly communicate delays to arriving guests?

Consider operational efficiency, guest satisfaction, and brand impact.

- What criteria would you use to decide which rooms to prioritize first?
- How would you communicate with arriving guests to manage expectations while maintaining service quality?

Think about operational coordination, guest communication, and brand reputation.

Front office and guest experience: Making the first impression

The front office serves as the heartbeat of guest interaction, setting the tone for the entire stay. Personalized welcomes, efficient check-ins, thoughtful service recovery, and culturally responsive interactions transform hotel stays from functional to unforgettable. Hotels like Moxy by Marriott reimagine front-office engagement with vibrant, interactive lobbies and mobile technologies that blend convenience with human warmth, aligning operational excellence with brand identity.

Housekeeping and facility maintenance: Details that define excellence

Meticulous housekeeping and proactive maintenance are vital to guest comfort and property preservation. Clean, fresh spaces convey trust and quality, while behind-the-scenes maintenance ensures seamless operations. Brands such as Four Seasons Hotels and Resorts ensure precision in housekeeping standards, while eco-luxury properties such as Six Senses integrate sustainability into linen management, energy systems, and facility upkeep, demonstrating that operational efficiency doesn't mean compromising environmental responsibility.

Sales, marketing, and guest engagement: Crafting loyalty through storytelling

Sales and marketing efforts connect hotels with targeted guest segments. Loyalty programs like Hilton Honors and Marriott Bonvoy drive guest retention through personalized rewards and exclusive experiences, while boutique hotels embrace local partnerships, unique narratives, and dynamic digital campaigns to foster emotional connections.

In an experience-driven market, effective marketing is not just about visibility—it's about resonance, helping brands speak to travelers seeking meaning, identity, and connection.

> **INTERACTIVE EXERCISE**
> Balancing operational complexity with premium guest experience
>
> You're the general manager of a large lifestyle resort hosting a multi-day corporate convention while also accommodating leisure travelers and families celebrating milestones. Your event services, food and beverage, and guest experience teams are stretched across competing priorities: VIP arrivals, banquet setups, late check-outs, and maintenance delays in one wing of the property.
>
> As the leader, how do you ensure each guest segment receives a seamless, high-quality experience?
>
> - Identify two immediate actions you would take to coordinate and unify your operations team.

- How would you communicate priorities to ensure consistent service across departments?
- What tools, cross-training strategies, or brand standards could help your team anticipate guest needs without compromising quality?

Try to think like a leader who understands how multiple departments must collaborate under pressure while maintaining hospitality excellence.

Food and beverage operations: Telling stories through cuisine

Exceptional dining enhances hotel stays by creating powerful sensory memories. Culinary programs at Kimpton Hotels highlight regional ingredients, telling the story of place through every dish. Similarly, luxury brands such as Mandarin Oriental deliver refined, globally inspired food and beverage experiences that reflect creativity, sustainability, and cultural immersion.

Food and beverage operations require a careful balance between culinary excellence and financial performance.

Safety, security, and risk management: Building guest confidence

Safety, while often invisible to guests, is foundational to trust and loyalty. Hotels like IHG's maintain rigorous health, safety, cybersecurity, and crisis management programs to protect guests, staff, and assets.

Risk management also includes regulatory compliance, from food safety to fire protection, accessibility standards, and data privacy laws such as GDPR. These efforts reinforce guest confidence and operational reliability.

Human resources and culture building: Empowering teams for excellence

Hospitality is powered by people. HR leaders recruit, develop, and retain diverse talent, shaping workplace cultures that emphasize inclusion, service excellence, and global awareness. Marriott's Voyage Global Leadership Development program exemplifies how leading companies can invest in developing the next generation of hotel professionals with both technical expertise and cultural competence.

Inclusive HR practices, embraced by brands like Accor, Hyatt, and Hilton, drive team cohesion, innovation, and the delivery of meaningful guest experiences.

Integration for seamless guest journeys

Each of these business and operational functions is interconnected. Financial management enables strategic investments in guest service. Marketing and sales attract the right guests. Operations deliver on brand promises. Risk management ensures safety and continuity.

Empowered hospitality teams bring every touchpoint to life. When these areas work in harmony, lodging professionals are able to create guest journeys that feel seamless, enriching, and unforgettable.

> **Reflect**
>
> - Which operational function discussed in this chapter (such as front office, revenue management, or food and beverage) do you think has the greatest impact on guest satisfaction?
> - Provide an example from your own experiences or observations to support your perspective.

Career pathways in lodging

Building on the broader hospitality career exploration introduced in Chapter 6, this section focuses on professional opportunities uniquely relevant to the lodging sector. Lodging careers span three primary tiers—property-level, above-property (regional), and corporate—each requiring specialized skills, industry certifications, and leadership development.

From hands-on guest service to global strategic leadership, lodging offers diverse pathways for rewarding, impactful careers.

Property-level careers (onsite roles)

Property-level roles offer dynamic opportunities to gain operational expertise, leadership skills, and guest service experience. In addition to executive leadership positions such as general manager and director of sales, hotels rely on a wide range of operational and mid-level professionals who support daily guest interactions and service excellence.

- **Guest services** careers include roles such as front-desk supervisor, guest relations manager, rooms controller, night auditor, and concierge, each shaping the arrival, departure, and overall stay experience.

- **Food and beverage** operations involve professionals like restaurant managers, banquet captains, beverage managers, sous chefs, and pastry chefs, who oversee dining outlets, events, and culinary storytelling.
- **Housekeeping and engineering** roles, including housekeeping supervisors, laundry managers, facilities supervisors, and maintenance technicians, maintain the physical comfort and aesthetic quality of properties.
- **Revenue management and sales** careers, such as revenue analysts, sales managers, and catering and events managers, drive property profitability through pricing strategies and relationship development.

Additional specialty roles like spa managers, recreation managers, retail managers, security supervisors, and executive assistants to general managers enhance the overall guest journey. Professionals in these roles build a strong operational foundation, often advancing into departmental leadership, executive committee membership, or regional oversight roles.

> Operational excellence begins with clear standards and a relentless focus on guest experience. It is a culture of accountability, empathy, and consistency. Even as technology transforms the industry, our commitment to empowering teams and delivering authentic service remains unchanged. The heart of hospitality is still human—anticipating needs, building trust, and creating moments that feel both memorable and personal. Great service isn't scripted—it's led by example.
>
> —Frank Chen, general manager, Hilton

Above-property careers (regional and multi-unit leadership)

Above-property careers focus on strategic leadership across multiple hotels or brands within a geographic region. These professionals ensure operational consistency, revenue growth, and service alignment across diverse properties.

Regional *directors of operations* oversee multiple general managers, aligning daily property performance with broader brand standards and financial goals. Regional *revenue managers* develop dynamic pricing and distribution strategies for multiple hotels, while area *directors of sales and marketing* coordinate cross-property sales campaigns and client relationship management.

Human resources and engineering leadership also expand at the regional level. Regional *HR directors* lead talent acquisition, professional development, and DEIBA initiatives across properties, while regional *engineering and facilities managers* oversee maintenance, sustainability, and risk management across geographically clustered hotels.

Above-property roles allow lodging professionals to influence multiple properties while managing complex teams, resources, and market strategies.

> **CAREER SPOTLIGHT**
> Lisa Timbo: Strategic leadership and community engagement
>
> Lisa Timbo's hospitality journey with Marriott International exemplifies strategic leadership, operational excellence, and meaningful community engagement. As the area general manager for Marriott properties in Chicago, she oversees multiple hotels, driving exceptional guest experiences, robust financial performance, and consistent brand excellence. Her distinguished career includes roles as market vice president and general manager, where she successfully optimized revenue, improved operational efficiencies, and championed talent development across Marriott's prominent brands, including JW Marriott and Renaissance Hotels.
>
> Timbo also demonstrates a deep commitment to her community, serving on the board of directors for Choose Chicago, Greater North Michigan Avenue Association, and Illinois Hotel Lodging Association, actively collaborating with local stakeholders to promote and sustain Chicago's dynamic hospitality industry. She says:
>
>> Hospitality leadership is about creating environments where both teams and guests thrive. Be genuine to guests and your team. The stronger leaders believe that being proactive in communication, knowing the importance of role modeling, and having a relentless pursuit of excellence will build a successful career but also meaningful relationships along the way.

Corporate-level careers (strategic and global leadership)

Corporate careers in lodging involve shaping global brand strategy, innovation, and growth across entire hotel groups or regions. These professionals focus on building competitive advantage, driving financial performance, and enhancing organizational excellence worldwide.

Vice presidents of global operations develop operational policy, oversee international performance metrics, and ensure brand consistency across continents. *Chief marketing officers* design global marketing campaigns, digital engagement strategies, and loyalty program innovations that resonate with diverse traveler markets.

Technology leadership roles, such as *chief technology officers*, manage digital infrastructure, cybersecurity initiatives, smart hotel innovations, and AI integration. Sustainability is also increasingly prioritized at the corporate level, with *chief sustainability officers* leading environmental and social responsibility strategies that align with brand values and guest expectations.

Corporate careers allow professionals to influence entire organizations, shape hospitality trends, and lead global innovation in the dynamic lodging industry. In addition to hands-on experience, certifications and executive development programs equip professionals with skills needed to advance across all lodging career tiers.

> **CAREER SPOTLIGHT**
> Ronisha Goodwin: From college intern to global HR leader
>
> Ronisha Goodwin began her hospitality career as a college intern. Through dedication, mentorship, and completion of Hyatt's Manager-in-Training program, she steadily advanced through HR and leadership roles. Prior to her current role, she led the execution of Hyatt's global DEI initiatives, helping embed inclusive practices across all properties.

Professional development across levels

Advancing within lodging careers requires continuous learning, professional certifications, and leadership development. Professional growth strengthens technical expertise, leadership capabilities, and strategic thinking at every level. Ongoing learning and skill development become increasingly important as professionals progress from operational roles into strategic leadership positions, enabling them to effectively navigate industry trends, drive innovation, and deliver consistent hospitality excellence.

At the property level, certifications such as the Certified Hotel Administrator (CHA), Certified Hospitality Supervisor (CHS), ServSafe Certification, and facilities management credentials validate operational excellence and leadership readiness. Above-property professionals enhance their skills with credentials such as Certified Hospitality Revenue Manager (CHRM), Project Management Professional (PMP), and Certified Hospitality Sales Professional (CHSP).

At the corporate level, executive education programs (such as Cornell University's General Managers Program), advanced analytics and digital leadership training, and sustainability strategy certifications strengthen strategic competencies and global leadership impact.

> **Reflect**
>
> - Which lodging career pathway (property-level, above-property, corporate) aligns most closely with your personal strengths and professional aspirations?
> - What skills or certifications will you pursue to advance along this career path?

Connecting career pathways to foundational hospitality concepts

Each level within lodging careers interconnects seamlessly with foundational hospitality principles previously discussed, such as exceptional guest service (Chapter 2), financial acumen (Chapter 5), cultural responsiveness (Chapter 3), sustainability practices (Chapters 1 and 6), and operational excellence (Chapter 5). Professionals across these roles collaborate strategically, applying interdisciplinary insights to consistently deliver high-quality lodging experiences, sustainable profitability, and industry leadership globally.

Professional certifications: Globally recognized hospitality credentials

Engaging with industry associations strengthens your professional network, increases access to opportunities, and improves your visibility within the global hospitality community.

Professional certifications from respected industry associations, such as the American Hotel & Lodging Educational Institute (AHLEI) and the Institute of Hospitality (UK), offer globally recognized credentials valuable across diverse hospitality markets. Achieving certification through these organizations enhances professional credibility, industry knowledge, and career opportunities. Examples include:

- **Certified Hotel Administrator (CHA)**: Validates advanced leadership competencies for general managers and hospitality executives globally (AHLEI).
- **Certified Hospitality Supervisor (CHS)**: Confirms proficiency in leadership, operational management, and team oversight skills for supervisory roles (AHLEI).
- **Institute of Hospitality Management Qualifications**: Offers multiple certification levels recognized internationally, demonstrating operational excellence, strategic leadership, and hospitality management expertise.

Industry associations and networking: Building meaningful connections

Actively engaging with hospitality industry associations and professional networks significantly strengthens career development and opens doors to new opportunities. These organizations offer certifications, advocacy, career tools, and a professional community dedicated to industry excellence:

- American Hotel & Lodging Association (AHLA): ahla.com
- International Hotel & Restaurant Association (IH&RA): ih-ra.org

- Institute of Hospitality (UK): instituteofhospitality.org
- Asian American Hotel Owners Association (AAHOA): aahoa.com
- European Hotel Managers Association (EHMA): ehma.com
- Hospitality Financial and Technology Professionals (HFTP): hftp.org

Regular participation in association conferences, webinars, workshops, and networking events helps you build industry knowledge, connect with mentors and peers, and discover new professional opportunities.

> **Key takeaways**
>
> - **Integral role of lodging**: Lodging is a foundational pillar of hospitality, encompassing diverse accommodations tailored to varied guest preferences, lifestyles, and travel motivations.
> - **Historical evolution and growth**: The lodging industry has significantly evolved through innovations in transportation, globalization, and technology, resulting in today's diverse and sophisticated global landscape.
> - **Lodging segments and specializations**: Key lodging segments include full-service hotels, select-service properties, luxury accommodations, resorts, convention hotels, extended-stay facilities, alternative accommodations, and specialized niche segments, each suited to distinct guest needs and market demands.
> - **Strategic business structures**: Successful lodging operations require an understanding of hotel management, ownership, branding, and franchising relationships, each influencing business strategy, financial performance, and daily operations.
> - **Emerging trends in lodging**: Major lodging trends include sustainability initiatives, technology integration, experiential hospitality, wellness-oriented stays, flexible and hybrid accommodations, and DEIBA practices, significantly reshaping the competitive landscape.
> - **Operational excellence**: Exceptional guest experiences rely on coordinated operational functions, including front office, housekeeping, food and beverage services, security, maintenance, and revenue management, supported by cultural responsiveness, sustainability, and technological innovation.
> - **Lodging career pathways**: Lodging offers dynamic career paths at the levels of property (onsite management), above-property (regional/multi-unit management), and corporate (global strategic leadership), each providing distinct professional growth opportunities and skill-building experiences.

- **Professional development and resources**: Ongoing professional growth through globally recognized certifications (such as AHLEI, Institute of Hospitality), active networking, and targeted job search strategies significantly enhance career opportunities within the lodging industry.

Looking ahead

Having explored the structure, trends, and career pathways within the lodging industry, we next turn to another essential hospitality pillar: the food and beverage segment. In the next chapter you'll discover how culinary innovation, operational excellence, and cultural storytelling converge to create exceptional guest experiences, and why food and beverage serve as powerful connectors and key value drivers in hospitality.

References

Accor (2018) Accor hotels launches RiiSE and renews its commitment to diversity and inclusiveness, Pressroom. https://press.accor.com/accorhotels-launches-riise-and-renews-its-commitment-to-diversity-and-inclusiveness?lang=en (archived at https://perma.cc/WG7H-J3DK)

AHLA (American Hotel & Lodging Association) (2025) AHLA President & CEO testifies before U.S. House Committee on Education and Workforce, February 26. ahla.com/news/ahla-president-ceo-testifies-us-house-committee-education-and-workforce (archived at https://perma.cc/9BPX-4S3X)

Airbnb (2025) *About us*. Airbnb Newsroom. news.airbnb.com/about-us (archived at https://perma.cc/V9RP-54UG)

ARDA (American Resort Development Association) (2024) *State of the Vacation Timeshare Industry: United States Study 2024 Edition*. ARDA International Foundation. arda.org/wp-content/uploads/2024/12/2024-state-of-industry-full-report.pdf (archived at https://perma.cc/B5XB-75NC)

Business Insider (2024) Gen Z is ushering in the allinclusive era, May 7. businessinsider.com/gen-z-trend-all-inclusive-resorts-luxury-convenience-mexico-2024-11 (archived at https://perma.cc/U9D6-4FCM)

Deloitte (2024) From uniformity to flexibility: The shifting landscape of hotel franchise operating models (blog), January 24. www.deloitte.com/uk/en/Industries/consumer/blogs/from-uniformity-to-flexibility.html (archived at https://perma.cc/324H-BMRG)

Global Wellness Institute (2024) *Global Wellness Economy Monitor 2024*. globalwellnessinstitute.org/industry-research/2024-global-wellness-economy-monitor (archived at https://perma.cc/8Q3S-2E3D)

Grand View Research (2023) *Vacation Rental Market Size, Share & Trends Analysis Report* grandviewresearch.com/industry-analysis/vacation-rental-market (archived at https://perma.cc/TA62-7JT4)

Hospitality Net (2022) 73% of travelers more likely to choose hotels offering self-service tech, February 18. hospitalitynet.org/news/4110830.html (archived at https://perma.cc/RP3X-GL6M)

Hostelling International (2024) *Our network of hostels*. hihostels.com/our-network-of-hostels (archived at https://perma.cc/FFJ3-9U5M)

Hostelworld Group (2024) *About Hostelworld Group*. partners.hostelworld.com/about (archived at https://perma.cc/8BQP-7N75)

Hyatt (2024) RiseHY program brings untapped talent into the hospitality industry, emphasizes retention and progressive skills training, March 20. newsroom.hyatt.com/news-releases?item=124476 (archived at https://perma.cc/EJ3D-JESA)

JLL (2022) *Americas All-Inclusive Resort Sector Trends & Outlook*. jll.com/en-us/insights/market-perspectives/americas-all-inclusive-resort-sector-trendsand-outlook (archived at https://perma.cc/KB4J-56TH)

Marriott International (2024) *Environmental, Social & Governance Global Progress*. serve360.marriott.com/wp-content/uploads/2024/07/2024ESGProgress.pdf (archived at https://perma.cc/2SAL-NAH7)

McKinsey & Company (2023) Diversity matters even more: The case for holistic impact, December 5. mckinsey.com/featured-insights/diversity-and-inclusion/diversity-matters-even-more-the-case-for-holistic-impact

Mordor Intelligence (2024) Global Casino Hotels Market–Size, Share, COVID-19 Impact & Forecasts (2025–2030) [report]. mordorintelligence.com/industry-reports/global-casino-hotels-market (archived at https://perma.cc/JL5K-GSCQ)

Rockbridge (2024) *Rockbridge Holdings homepage*. rockbridgecapital.com (archived at https://perma.cc/LGX8-DT3G)

Statista (2024) Luxury hotel market size worldwide 2021–2026. statista.com/statistics/1175289/luxury-hotel-market-size-worldwide (archived at https://perma.cc/464Y-N2PZ)

The Business Research Company (2025) *Hospitality Global Market Report 2025*. thebusinessresearchcompany.com/report/hospitality-global-market-report (archived at https://perma.cc/UEG8-T8NR)

The Highland Group (2025) *Extended-Stay Hotels Q4 2024 Performance Bulletin*. Asian Hospitality, December 31. asianhospitality.com/extended-stay-hotels-q4-2024-performance (archived at https://perma.cc/BA8H-Z9R3)

The Wall Street Journal (2024) Corporate retreats are back. Hotels are banking on it, October 14. wsj.com/business/hospitality/corporate-retreats-are-back-hotels-are-banking-on-it-6a08ad0b?mod=e2li (archived at https://perma.cc/3QKD-RQNG)

UK Parliament (2024) Support for pubs and the hospitality sector, Commons Library Briefing, October 21. commonslibrary.parliament.uk/research-briefings/cdp-2024-0132 (archived at https://perma.cc/BPP9-8GSR)

Weinstein, J. (2024) Hotels increasingly managed by third parties, *Hotel Investment Today*, December 4. hotelinvestmenttoday.com/Deals/Management/Hotels-increasingly-managed-by-third-parties (archived at https://perma.cc/T2GN-YAM6)

World Travel & Tourism Council (WTTC) (2024) Travel & Tourism Economic Impact Research 2024 – Global Summary, https://wttc.org/research/economic-impact (archived at https://perma.cc/CZ7U-KGFD)

The food and beverage industry 11

LEARNING OBJECTIVES

- Define the food and beverage (F&B) industry and explain its essential role in global hospitality and tourism.
- Summarize the historical evolution and significant milestones shaping the modern food and beverage industry.
- Identify and differentiate key restaurant segments, including full service, quick service, fast-casual, and fine dining.
- Gain foundational knowledge of beverage segments, including wine, beer, spirits, specialty coffees, and innovative non-alcoholic beverages.
- Discuss additional specialized F&B segments, including catering, managed services, and niche markets, emphasizing their operational distinctions.
- Evaluate critical trends influencing global F&B operations, including sustainability, technology, and experiential dining.
- Recognize diverse career opportunities within the food and beverage industry, including required skills, professional pathways, and opportunities for advancement.

Introduction: The universal language of food and beverage

Imagine yourself with your family spending a warm summer evening at the historic Burg Landshut in Germany's scenic Mosel Valley. Strings of softly glowing lights twinkle, casting a magical glow across vineyards stretching into the distance. A lively rhythm of music is heard, gently inviting guests onto the dance floor and infusing the night with joy. As you savor local Mosel wine paired with delicious regional dishes, the extraordinary power of food and beverages to transform ordinary settings into cherished lifelong memories becomes vividly apparent.

At its core, the F&B industry plays a pivotal role to global hospitality and tourism, transforming simple ingredients into lasting memories. From fine dining restaurants to vibrant street markets, this industry continuously informs global trends, consumer preferences, and societal values.

REAL-WORLD EXAMPLE:
INDUSTRY SPOTLIGHT   Cameron Mitchell: The power of "yes"

Cameron Mitchell, founder and CEO of Cameron Mitchell Restaurants, built a hospitality empire around a simple yet powerful philosophy:

"Yes is the Answer! What is the Question?"

This guiding principle demonstrates hospitality's true essence: prioritizing guests by anticipating needs, exceeding expectations, and embracing genuine care and flexibility.

Mitchell's milkshake moment

Early in his career, Mitchell and his family visited a restaurant where his son requested a milkshake, even though it wasn't listed on the menu. When the server initially said "no," Mitchell gently guided him toward a solution by pointing out that the restaurant offered a brownie à la mode—ice cream served with a brownie. Could they perhaps leave out the brownie, blend the ice cream with milk, and create a milkshake? With this suggestion, the server realized how he could indeed say "yes."

This simple interaction shaped Mitchell's vision of hospitality, realizing that exceptional service is about creatively removing barriers, not enforcing them. Special requests aren't always a sign of a "demanding" or "picky" guest; often, they reflect unique dietary needs, sensory sensitivities, or a genuine desire to fully enjoy the dining experience.

This chapter explores the historical evolution of food and beverage, its key operational segments, and essential industry trends, including sustainability, technological innovation, and experiential dining. You'll also gain insights into critical business functions, inclusive practices, and diverse career opportunities within this dynamic sector.

Welcome to the world of food and beverage, where every dish tells a story.

Reflect

- Think of a time when you or someone you know had a special request at a restaurant. How was it handled, and how did it impact your overall experience?
- How might adopting Mitchell's philosophy of saying "yes" influence the way you approach guest service, particularly in responding to unique or unexpected guest requirements?

Historical evolution of food and beverage

Ancient origins

Food and beverage establishments have historically served as vital social and cultural gathering places. Ancient taverns along the Silk Road in Asia, caravanserais in the Middle East, and roadside inns across medieval Europe offered nourishment and respite for weary travelers, establishing early foundations for hospitality as we know it today.

18th-century innovations

The modern concept of the restaurant emerged in 18th-century France, marking a departure from informal eateries. This era introduced structured dining etiquette, multiple distinct courses, and professional service standards. Parisian restaurants like Le Grand Véfour, established in 1784, became synonymous with luxury dining, elevating culinary experiences to an art form associated with social status and refinement. This sophisticated dining culture quickly spread across Europe and eventually reached other continents.

20th-century transformations

The 20th century brought profound changes driven by urbanization, globalization, and technological advances. The rise of casual dining democratized restaurant experiences, making them accessible to broader audiences. Quick-service and fast-casual concepts emerged to cater to increasingly busy lifestyles, exemplified by global brands like McDonald's, established in the mid-1950s, and Chipotle, founded in 1993, fundamentally shifting perceptions around convenience, affordability, and dining efficiency.

Technological advances such as refrigeration, microwave cooking, the automobile, and, later, digital ordering reshaped consumer behavior, leading to innovations such as drive-through establishments, home delivery, and convenience-oriented dining models.

Influential historical milestones in beverages

The beverage sector has experienced distinct historical milestones that illustrate critical turning points that continue to influence consumer behaviors, global hospitality practices, and industry innovation.

The 1920s Prohibition era in the US profoundly impacted spirits, beer, and cocktail culture, fueling innovation in clandestine cocktail bars (speakeasies) and popularizing spirits like gin and whiskey through "creative" distillation and mixology.

In the late 20th century, the craft beer movement emerged prominently in the 1980s, starting in the US and gradually spreading across the world. Small, independent breweries emphasized artisanal production, regional authenticity, and innovative flavors, significantly reshaping beer culture and consumer expectations.

Meanwhile, specialty coffee culture grew dramatically, driven by brands like Starbucks (founded in 1971) and the rise of independent coffeehouses promoting ethical sourcing, artisanal roasting techniques, and barista craftsmanship. This movement elevated consumer preferences for premium beverages, transforming coffee consumption into a sophisticated social experience.

Globalization and celebrity influence

Globalization expanded consumer tastes, introducing international cuisines into mainstream dining experiences. Celebrity chefs including Julia Child, Gordon Ramsay, and Massimo Bottura rose to prominence through television and digital media, influencing global culinary trends and increasing consumer enthusiasm for gourmet dining. Simultaneously, culinary tourism flourished as travelers sought the authentic, immersive food experiences they saw on TV and social media, from vibrant street food markets in Bangkok and Tokyo to renowned gastronomic tours across Italy and France.

21st-century trends: Digitalization and sustainability

In recent years, digital transformation has dramatically reshaped the industry. Technologies such as mobile apps, contactless payments, online delivery platforms, and virtual kitchens have revolutionized operational models and customer engagement. Sustainability has also emerged as a critical industry driver, with consumer demand for responsibly sourced ingredients, reduced food waste, and increased plant-based menu options shaping modern restaurant practices.

Today, the food and beverage industry remains a vibrant, dynamic sector, continually adapting to evolving tastes, societal shifts, and technological innovations. Its rich history demonstrates adaptability and creativity, promising continued growth and opportunities for meaningful experiences.

Key food and beverage segments

The global food and beverage industry consists of diverse segments, each uniquely aligned with consumer preferences, dining styles, and market trends. Recognizing these segments enables hospitality professionals to effectively target consumers, streamline operations, and create memorable guest experiences.

Full-service restaurants

Full-service restaurants warmly welcome guests with extensive menus, attentive table service, and an authentic passion for hospitality, creativity, and meaningful culinary experiences. This vibrant segment spans a delightful range, from casual dining spots known for imaginative yet approachable dishes—think Cooper's Hawk's innovative comfort foods or Bonefish Grill's fresh seafood—to beloved family-friendly establishments serving comforting, genuine fare like Maggiano's Little Italy and P.F. Chang's. At the fine-dining end, restaurants such as Fleming's Prime Steakhouse and Ruth's Chris Steak House craft memorable meals through careful culinary artistry and personalized hospitality.

Collectively, these restaurants form an essential and dynamic portion of the hospitality landscape. In the US alone, full-service restaurants generated an impressive $546.6 billion in sales in 2024, accounting for about 35.5 percent of total spending on meals purchased away from home (USDA, 2025). Similarly, in the UK, full-service restaurants earned approximately £23.3 billion in revenue in 2023–24, consistently attracting guests seeking authentic dining experiences and memorable occasions (IBISWorld, 2025). Successful operation in this segment requires passionate, attentive staff, creative menus that balance guest delight with profitability, and genuinely welcoming atmospheres that keep guests coming back.

Quick-service restaurants and fast food

Quick-service restaurants (QSRs), such as McDonald's, Subway, and KFC, maintain a strong global presence, generating approximately $311.5 billion in revenue in 2024, reflecting consistent industry growth worldwide (The Business Research

Company, 2024). Known for their streamlined menus and quick service, these restaurants efficiently cater to high volumes of customers across various international markets. Particularly successful in busy urban centers, transportation hubs, and popular tourist locations, QSRs frequently adapt menus creatively to local tastes and cultural preferences. Examples include vegetarian offerings in India or unique local specialties like Japan's Samurai Burger, highlighting the adaptability and cultural responsiveness essential to their global appeal.

Fast-casual restaurants

The fast-casual segment blends the convenience of fast food with the quality of casual dining, offering more customizable menus, fresh ingredients, and modern dining environments. Standout brands in this category include Chipotle and Shake Shack in the US, Nando's in the UK, and Vapiano in Germany. Globally, the fast-casual market was valued at around $209 billion in 2024, indicating its growing appeal to health-minded, convenience-seeking diners (Allied Market Research, 2020). These restaurants are reshaping the broader foodservice landscape, prompting traditional QSRs to introduce healthier, fresher, and ethically sourced options driven by consumer demand for transparency and customization.

Cafés and coffee shops

Cafés, coffee shops, and specialty beverage venues have become vital social hubs worldwide, offering more than just a drink—they might provide community, creativity, and comfort. Iconic brands like Starbucks and Panera Bread in the US, Costa Coffee and Pret A Manger in the UK, Café Coffee Day in India, Tim Hortons in Canada, and countless independent cafés illustrate the global breadth of this segment. In 2023, global coffee consumption reached 10 million tons (about 173 million 60 kg bags), signaling strong demand for premium beverages and café culture (International Coffee Organization, 2024). Meanwhile, the global café market was valued at around $299 billion in 2023, with expected growth as cafés serve remote workers, introduce innovative specialty drinks, and prioritize sustainability (Grand View Research, 2024). Operational trends in this space include accommodating digital nomads, developing eco-conscious beverage lines, and creating inviting, ambient spaces where customers feel at home.

Bars, lounges, and nightlife establishments

Bars, pubs, lounges, and clubs play a major role in urban tourism, offering beverages, entertainment, and vibrant social environments. The global alcoholic beverage market exceeded $1.62 trillion in 2024, suggesting a significant economic influence of nightlife venues (IMARC, 2024a). Rooftop lounges, such as Sky Bar in Bangkok, Ozone Bar in Hong Kong, and Cé La Vi in Singapore, offer expertly crafted cocktails, stylish ambiance, and breathtaking views to captivate both locals and visitors. Key operational considerations in this segment include managing peak-time crowds, ensuring strict compliance with alcohol regulations, and prioritizing guest safety.

Nutritional and managed services

Institutional dining spans services in schools, universities, hospitals, corporate offices, stadiums, and correctional facilities which are often managed by companies like Compass Group, Sodexo, and Aramark, with significant logistical scope and tight regulatory oversight. Compass Group alone serves around 5.5 billion meals annually across 40 or so countries, emphasizing the sector's scale and complexity (Compass Group, 2024). Globally, the contract catering and institutional foodservice market was valued at approximately $239 billion in 2024, with leading providers fueling both growth and innovation (Credence Research, 2025). Operational priorities in this segment include maintaining high nutritional and food safety standards, cost control through efficient logistics, ensuring consistent quality and service, and increasingly integrating sustainability practices into large-scale operations. (See Chapter 7 for further insights on managed services.)

Catering and event dining

Catering services deliver tailored on- and offsite dining for weddings, conferences, corporate events, and special occasions. Esteemed providers such as Levy, Wolfgang Puck Catering, and Relais & Châteaux are known for bespoke culinary experiences crafted to exacting client specifications. The global catering market was valued at approximately $288.8 billion in 2022 and is projected to reach $497.7 billion by 2032, showing its rapid expansion (Allied Market Research, 2023). Catering operations prioritize logistical efficiency, menu customization, culinary innovation, and strong client relationships, which are all essential for delivering seamless event experiences. (Detailed coverage of catering and event dining can be found in Chapter 8.)

Segment snapshot: Global foodservice industry

As mentioned, the global food and beverage industry comprises distinct segments, each addressing unique consumer needs:

- **Quick-service restaurants (QSRs)** lead the industry, generating approximately $406 billion globally in 2024 (Fortune Business Insights, 2024).

- **Full-service restaurants (FSRs)** represent a significant share, estimated around 35–40 percent of global foodservice market value, based on the global industry valuation of approximately $3.6 trillion (Technomic, 2024; USDA, 2025).
- **Fast-casual restaurants** stand out as one of the industry's fastest-growing segments, distinguished by higher-quality, customizable menu items often served in a convenient counter-service format (Investopedia, 2022).
- **Cafés and coffee shops** achieved a global market size of $298.7 billion in 2023, projected to continue to grow steadily as consumers increasingly seek premium beverages and café experiences (Grand View Research, 2024).
- **Nutritional and managed services** fall within the global contract catering market, valued at over $239 billion in 2024 (Credence Research, 2025).
- **Bars, lounges, and nightlife establishments** contribute notably within the larger alcoholic beverage market, valued at about $1.62 trillion in 2024 (IMARC, 2024a).

This overview highlights the dominance of QSR and FSR segments, along with substantial growth potential in fast-casual dining, café culture, and specialized hospitality markets. Each segment distinctly caters to evolving consumer demands for convenience, authenticity, quality, and innovation, reflecting the dynamic and multifaceted nature of the global food and beverage industry.

Understanding these segments empowers hospitality professionals to strategically position themselves, leverage emerging market opportunities, and shape compelling consumer experiences worldwide.

Specialized and niche food and beverage segments

In addition to mainstream segments, the food and beverage industry includes specialized and niche markets that reflect emerging culinary trends, innovative business models, and unique dining experiences. In these segments, hospitality businesses can differentiate themselves, cater to evolving consumer lifestyles, and capitalize on opportunities in a competitive global market.

Food trucks and street food markets

Food trucks and street food stalls are blossoming around the world, becoming vibrant hallmarks of urban culture. From the bustling night markets of Taipei and Bangkok—known for their electric atmosphere and authentic bites—to thriving food truck festivals across North America and Europe, this segment appeals to diners seeking convenience, affordability, and genuine culinary experiences. With lower start-up costs and full mobility, food trucks can easily pivot menus to align with emerging trends and prime locations.

In the US, IBISWorld (2024) estimates the food truck industry reached approximately $2.4 billion in 2024, reflecting continued consumer appeal and entrepreneurial growth. Meanwhile, the global street food market exceeded $249.6 billion in 2024, and is projected to grow at an 8.5 percent CAGR as demand for accessible, culturally rich street foods surges (Future Data Stats, 2024).

Operational advantages in this sector include lower investment requirements, the ability to move to high-traffic areas, and quick menu evolution to capture consumer interest.

Ghost kitchens and virtual restaurants

Ghost kitchens—dedicated commercial facilities that prepare delivery-only meals—are revolutionizing traditional restaurant models. Companies like CloudKitchens, Reef Kitchens, and Deliveroo Editions spearhead the trend by enabling restaurants and entrepreneurs to expand reach and optimize kitchen resources with less risk than physical locations. According to Euromonitor, the global ghost kitchen market is forecast to exceed $130 billion by 2030, supported by growing demand for convenience and digital ordering solutions (Van Rooyen, 2025). Earlier estimates even suggested the market could hit $1 trillion by 2030, capturing substantial shares of takeaway, ready meals, and dine-in channels (Restaurant Dive, 2020). There are employee rights issues to overcome in this area, but operational benefits of ghost kitchens include lower capital investment, full mobility, streamlined staffing, and rapid menu innovation, often critical for responding to shifting consumer trends.

Pop-up and experiential dining

Pop-up restaurants and experiential dining are gaining momentum globally, offering chefs a platform to test creative menus, generate immediate buzz, and forge direct connections with diners. The world's top culinary events, such as Madrid Fusion, Taste of London, and international pop-up series, demonstrate the power of immersive, temporary dining formats in building brand presence and delivering unique culinary narratives. Research confirms strong growth: in 2014 alone, pop-up restaurant activity soared by 82 percent worldwide (Taylor Jr. et al., 2018).

Experiential dining elevates meals into storytelling adventures, combining gastronomy with multisensory elements, from interactive theatrical settings to culture-rich tasting journeys, catering to guests seeking unforgettable, shareable experiences. Practically, pop-ups offer chefs lower initial costs, nimble menu development, and immediate customer feedback, making them ideal incubators for culinary innovation.

Culinary tourism and destination dining

Culinary tourism involves traveling primarily for memorable food experiences tied to local culture. Iconic examples include vineyard dining in Napa Valley, Bordeaux, or South Africa's Cape Winelands; Michelin-star restaurant tours across Europe and Asia; and immersive cooking classes in destinations like Tuscany, Kyoto, and Mexico City. Nearly 80 percent of leisure travelers learn about—and let food experiences shape—their travel decisions (Stone et al., 2021). Additionally, the global culinary tourism market was valued at approximately $1.09 trillion in 2024, with forecasts projecting it will reach $4.21 trillion by 2033, growing steadily at a CAGR of 14.5 percent (IMARC, 2024b).

Events like the EPCOT International Food & Wine Festival at Walt Disney World further demonstrate culinary tourism's global influence, celebrating international cuisines and fostering cultural exchange. Beyond dining, culinary tourism often enriches travel by deepening appreciation for local people, traditions, and environments, turning meals into transformative experiences.

Agrotourism and farm-to-table experiences

Agrotourism combines agricultural engagement with direct dining experiences, encouraging sustainability, supporting local economies, and offering rich educational tourism. Examples include farm stays in rural Italy, organic farm-to-table dinners in Sonoma County, California, and hands-on agrotourism experiences in New Zealand and France. A recent survey revealed that 60 percent of consumers globally prefer buying food sourced from their own country, underscoring strong demand for locally sourced ingredients and validating farmers' markets and agrotourism initiatives as economically and environmentally relevant (YouGov, 2022).

THINK LIKE A MANAGER
Farm-to-table experience

You are the manager of a restaurant exploring opportunities to integrate agrotourism and farm-to-table dining experiences into your current operations. Your goal is to provide guests with meaningful, authentic connections to local agriculture and sustainability practices.

- **Describe:** Outline your farm-to-table dining concept, including local farms or producers you would partner with and the key products you'd feature.
- **Engage:** List two engaging activities or features to deepen guests' appreciation for local farms and sustainable practices.
- **Promote:** Briefly describe how you would market this experience, emphasizing community involvement, sustainability, and uniqueness.

Think about operational coordination, guest communication, and brand reputation.

Specialty markets and gourmet food retail

Specialty markets and gourmet food halls—such as Eataly (Italy/US/global), Mercado San Miguel (Madrid), Harrods Food Hall (London), and Whole Foods Market (US)—blend retail and hospitality by offering carefully curated artisanal foods, premium ingredients, and culinary education. The global gourmet food market, spanning artisanal cheese, craft meats, specialty coffee, and organic wines, for example, reached almost $28 billion in 2023, and is expected to grow to around $58 billion by 2032 (Skyquest, 2025). Meanwhile, the broader luxury food market (which includes gourmet retail) is estimated at $195 billion in 2024, with forecasts exceeding $898 billion by 2034 (Market.us, 2025), driven by rising consumer demand for premium, authentic, and ethically sourced products.

These figures reflect increasing consumer desire for authenticity and sustainability, supported by government initiatives such as India's One District One Product and France's Label Rouge certifications, which boost artisan producers and preserve traditional craftsmanship. For hospitality professionals, this growth presents new avenues to engage consumers through curated retail experiences, such as in-store culinary demonstrations, sampling events, and farm-to-table partnerships in food halls and specialty markets.

Food and beverage operations on boats and cruises

Dining afloat uniquely combines culinary enjoyment with scenic exploration. Short-duration experiences, such as luxurious dinner cruises on London's Thames, sunset dining aboard traditional dhows in Dubai, and gourmet river cruises along Europe's Rhine and Danube, offer guests exceptional culinary experiences without overnight stays, focusing on sightseeing with fine dining. They require meticulous logistics, precise inventory management, and rigorous adherence to health, safety, and service standards.

Meanwhile, overnight cruise ships provide extensive dining operations, often featuring cross-cultural, international menus that enable passengers to experience diverse culinary traditions while sailing. According to TravelAge West (2023), major cruise lines invest over $2 billion annually in food and beverage operations, which underscores the critical role dining plays in guest satisfaction and repeat bookings. Luxury cruise operators increasingly integrate culinary programming, such as chef-led regional excursions and onboard cooking classes, to deepen guest connections with visited destinations (Barron's, 2024).

Customization and personalized dining options, including private chef services and tailored specialty menus, further differentiate luxury maritime hospitality, whether for short-duration dinner cruises or extended ocean voyages.

REAL-WORLD EXAMPLE:
INDUSTRY SPOTLIGHT Culinary cruising with Bateaux Parisiens

Imagine savoring gourmet French cuisine aboard a luxurious glass-enclosed boat gliding gently along the River Seine. Bateaux Parisiens offers guests exactly this experience: an extraordinary blend of fine dining, panoramic city views, and cultural immersion. Guests delight in signature dishes crafted by onboard chefs, perfectly complemented by carefully selected French wines.

Experiences such as these showcase culinary artistry and enrich guests' appreciation for Paris's vibrant history and the timeless charm of its riverside landmarks. They elevate guest satisfaction and influence repeat visitation, emphasizing the strategic importance of onboard dining excellence.

Key beverage segments

In addition to food, beverages represent a distinct and vital segment within the global hospitality industry, featuring unique market dynamics, consumer preferences, and operational intricacies. An independent exploration of beverages highlights strategic opportunities for hospitality professionals across production, distribution, retail, and experiential dimensions. See Table 11.1 for a snapshot.

Table 11.1 Snapshot of key beverage segments

Segment	Characteristics	Examples	Trends
Wine	Cultural heritage, culinary pairing, tourism-driven	Napa Valley, Bordeaux, Tuscany	Growth in vineyard tourism, sustainability, experiential tastings
Beer and craft brewing	Artisanal and sustainable production, regional/local authenticity, innovation	BrewDog, Stone Brewing, Mikkeller	Rapid global expansion, consumer demand for local, innovative flavors
Spirits and cocktails	Premium experiences, creative mixology, craft spirits	Artesian Bar (London), Licorería Limantour (Mexico City)	Premiumization, immersive experiences, craft distillation boom

(continued)

Table 11.1 (Continued)

Segment	Characteristics	Examples	Trends
Coffee and tea	Global café culture, increased demand for ethical sourcing, specialty beverages	Starbucks, Blue Bottle, Crimson Cup	Specialty segment growth, ethical sourcing, sustainability
Non-alcoholic beverages	Health-conscious, innovative, mindful consumption	Seedlip, GT's Kombucha, Bai, Lyre's	Increasing global demand, wellness orientation, sophisticated alcohol-free options

Alcoholic beverages

Alcoholic beverages significantly enhance hospitality experiences, from casual social gatherings to sophisticated culinary pairings. As previously noted, the global alcoholic beverage industry represents a substantial and economically influential sector. Within this category, specific beverage types—wine, beer, and spirits—each offer distinct opportunities in tourism, distribution, consumer engagement, and hospitality careers.

Wine

Wine represents cultural heritage, sophistication, and gastronomic refinement, deeply embedded within global hospitality traditions. Renowned wine regions, such as Bordeaux (France), Napa Valley (USA), Tuscany (Italy), Marlborough (New Zealand), and Barossa Valley (Australia), draw millions of visitors annually, all eager for authentic, immersive wine experiences. In Sonoma County alone, direct visitor spending from wine tourism was $2.3 billion in 2022, clearly demonstrating wine's significant economic influence (Sonoma County Economic Development Board, 2023).

Vineyards worldwide offer rich and engaging guest experiences, including picturesque guided walks between vines, interactive tastings led by passionate sommeliers, and educational workshops that vividly illustrate the winemaking process from grape to glass. These experiences deepen visitors' appreciation and enhance their understanding of wine's complexity and highlight each region's distinctive terroir.

Career opportunities in the wine industry extend far beyond traditional winemaking roles, encompassing viticulture, wine distribution, hospitality management, specialty retail, and sommelier services. Together, these positions create a dynamic employment ecosystem, offering hospitality professionals diverse and fulfilling career pathways.

REAL-WORLD EXAMPLE:
INDUSTRY SPOTLIGHT   Francis Ford Coppola Winery

Located in Sonoma County, Francis Ford Coppola Winery brilliantly fuses film, storytelling, and wine hospitality. Established by the acclaimed filmmaker, the winery offers guests immersive experiences that blend cinematic creativity with exceptional winemaking. Visitors enjoy engaging tours that explore Coppola's film history, intimate tastings led by enthusiastic hosts, and culinary pairings designed around the stories behind each bottle. Sustainability initiatives further enhance the narrative, showcasing how creativity and conscientious practices can harmoniously coexist.

Beer and craft brewing

Craft beer has significantly transformed global beer culture, emphasizing regional authenticity, innovative flavors, and artisanal brewing methods. Originating from small, independent breweries prioritizing quality, creativity, and community, the craft beer movement has surged across North America, Europe, Asia-Pacific, and Latin America. In 2024, the global craft beer market was valued at approximately $142.6 billion, with forecasts projecting substantial continued growth, driven by consumer enthusiasm for distinctive, locally produced brews (IMARC, 2024a).

Prominent breweries such as BrewDog (UK), Stone Brewing (US), Mikkeller (Denmark), and Hitachino Nest (Japan) exemplify craft beer's global appeal and cultural adaptability. Many craft breweries offer interactive brewery tours, educational tasting sessions, and vibrant community events, thus enriching guest experiences.

Career opportunities within craft beer span brewing science, brand marketing, logistics and distribution, hospitality management, retail, and beer education, highlighting craft beer's multifaceted role in global hospitality.

Spirits and cocktails

The resurgence of cocktail culture has elevated spirits into a dynamic hospitality segment characterized by creativity, innovation, and immersive engagement. Premium spirits and sophisticated mixology have become central to contemporary hospitality offerings, significantly influencing consumer preferences and industry growth. According to the International Wines and Spirits Record (IWSR, 2024), global spirits sales grew notably in value terms in 2023, driven by increasing demand for premium and craft spirits, alongside immersive cocktail experiences, despite global volume declines.

Celebrated cocktail establishments such as London's Artesian Bar, Singapore's Manhattan Bar, Mexico City's Licorería Limantour, and New York's The Dead Rabbit illustrate this global trend. These venues integrate storytelling, sensory-rich environments, and expertly crafted beverages into memorable guest experiences while encouraging responsible drinking.

The spirits sector offers diverse professional roles, including master distillers, skilled mixologists, beverage directors, spirits educators, brand ambassadors, distribution specialists, and hospitality consultants, each crucial for advancing this innovative and dynamic industry segment.

Non-alcoholic and wellness beverages

Non-alcoholic beverages represent one of the fastest-growing segments, meeting consumer demand for healthier and more mindful drinking options. According to NielsenIQ (2024), approximately 45 percent of global consumers actively seek premium and sophisticated non-alcoholic alternatives. This market includes alcohol-free spirits (Seedlip, Lyre's, Ritual Zero Proof), functional wellness beverages such as kombucha, vitamin-infused waters, probiotic drinks, and artisanal mocktails. The global non-alcoholic drinks market was valued at approximately $1.3 trillion in 2023 and was projected to reach roughly $2.9 trillion by 2035 (Allied Market Research, 2024).

INTERACTIVE EXERCISE
Beverage concept development

Design an innovative beverage concept for a hypothetical hospitality establishment. In your concept, clearly identify and describe:

- **Beverage category**: Specify your primary category (such as specialty coffee, craft cocktails, wellness beverages).
- **Target market**: Define your ideal customer demographics (age, lifestyle, preferences).
- **Unique selling points**: Explain what makes your beverage concept unique or appealing.
- **Operational considerations**: Outline key factors in production, sourcing, service, or staffing necessary to deliver this concept effectively.
- **Marketing strategy**: Suggest at least two strategic marketing approaches to attract and engage your target consumers.

Specialty coffee and tea

Specialty coffees and teas represent rapidly expanding beverage categories, driven by consumer preferences for high-quality, sustainably sourced, and expertly prepared beverages. As mentioned earlier, global coffee consumption highlights significant enthusiasm for artisanal beverages, creating robust opportunities for specialty offerings. Prominent specialty cafés and tea houses, including Starbucks, Blue Bottle Coffee, Costa Coffee, Gong Cha, and Chatime, distinguish themselves through, for example, wide ranges of ethically sourced products, skilled barista preparation, and innovative brewing techniques, and transform everyday beverages into engaging, sensory-rich experiences.

CAREER SPOTLIGHT
Greg Ubert, founder and president, Crimson Cup Coffee & Tea

Greg Ubert's twin passions for coffee and entrepreneurship have driven his successful career for over 30 years. In 1991, inspired by emerging café culture, he moved away from a promising career in computer software after graduating from Harvard University. He bought a small roasting machine, set up shop in a modest office, and began roasting coffee in his hometown.

The company name Crimson Cup, was inspired by the ripe red cherry of the coffee tree and Harvard's official color. From the outset, Ubert was guided by three core values: achieve results, have fun, and give back to the community. Under his leadership, Crimson Cup has grown into one of the most decorated coffee roasters in the US, winning prestigious awards such as the Golden Bean World Series Champion 2025, the Golden Bean North America Champion 2019, *Roast* magazine's Macro Roaster of the Year 2016 and multiple Good Food Awards. He notes:

> The specialty coffee and tea industry offers endless opportunities to create global impact—economically, environmentally, and socially. Building sustainable relationships with farmers worldwide has allowed us to elevate communities, improve livelihoods, and deliver outstanding quality. Pursuing excellence in coffee isn't just about brewing a great cup; it's about making a meaningful difference in people's lives.

Ownership, management, and branding in food and beverages

Ownership, management, and branding significantly shape the strategic direction and operational success of food and beverage establishments. Models range from independently owned businesses to multinational corporations and franchise operations, each offering distinct advantages and structures that cater to unique market dynamics and consumer expectations.

Independently owned establishments

Independent restaurants and bars often embody the personal vision and creative expression of their founders, chefs, or owners. These establishments succeed by emphasizing unique dining experiences, local authenticity, innovative culinary concepts, and personalized service. Independent establishments can often respond swiftly to changing market trends, consumer preferences, and local community needs, allowing them to thrive through agility and creativity. Many notable restaurants achieve recognition for their distinctive identity, such as renowned local fine-dining spots or innovative cocktail bars acclaimed within their communities.

Global restaurant groups and corporate ownership

Multinational restaurant corporations such as Yum! Brands (KFC, Pizza Hut, Taco Bell) and Darden Restaurants (Olive Garden, LongHorn Steakhouse) leverage substantial resources, centralized management systems, and global brand recognition to drive expansion and consistent experiences worldwide. Corporate ownership facilitates economies of scale, standardized operational practices, and streamlined quality control. For instance, Yum! Brands operated over 56,000 restaurants globally in 2024, demonstrating the extensive reach and operational capabilities achievable through corporate ownership.

Franchising and licensing models

Franchising offers independent entrepreneurs (franchisees) the opportunity to operate under established brand identities, leveraging the franchisor's (brand owner's) operational frameworks, marketing strategies, and business support systems. Renowned global brands such as McDonald's, Starbucks, and Subway use franchising extensively to scale rapidly, reduce direct capital expenditures, and maintain brand uniformity. Approximately 95 percent of McDonald's restaurants worldwide are franchise-operated, underscoring franchising as a powerful and scalable business model within the industry (McDonald's, 2025).

Management companies in food and beverage

Specialized management companies, including Compass Group, Aramark, and Sodexo, oversee food and beverage operations in settings such as hotels, resorts, stadiums, convention centers, and corporate facilities. These firms handle all operational aspects, from procurement, menu design, and staffing to training and compliance, enabling clients to focus on their primary business activities. Management companies provide operational efficiency, regulatory expertise, and consistent service delivery, particularly vital in complex, large-scale environments. (See Chapter 7 for a further exploration of managed services.)

Global branding and differentiation strategies

Successful global food and beverage brands strategically differentiate themselves through consistent quality, memorable consumer experiences, targeted marketing, and clear brand messaging. Brands like Starbucks adeptly combine consistent global branding with strategic local adaptations, such as unique beverages tailored to consumer tastes in China, Japan, and other regions. Increasingly, branding strategies emphasize sustainability, ethical sourcing, and corporate social responsibility to align with evolving global consumer expectations and enhance brand reputation.

REAL-WORLD EXAMPLE:
INDUSTRY SPOTLIGHT Starbucks' global brand and franchising model

Starbucks exemplifies an effective balance between company-owned and licensed stores, facilitating strategic global expansion. As noted in Starbucks' 2024 reports, the company operates over 40,000 locations across 86 countries, with approximately 48 percent licensed. This approach allows Starbucks to achieve rapid market entry, adapt flexibly to local consumer preferences, mitigate financial risks, and maintain brand integrity on a global scale.

Clearly differentiating and understanding these ownership, management, and branding strategies empowers hospitality professionals to strategically navigate opportunities within the global food and beverage landscape, positioning their businesses effectively for sustained growth, competitive advantage, and long-term success.

Key trends in the food and beverage industry

The global food and beverage industry continually evolves, shaped by shifting consumer preferences, technological advances, environmental concerns, and societal dynamics. Recognizing these trends is essential for industry professionals seeking competitive advantage, operational innovation, and sustained market relevance.

Sustainability and ethical dining

Sustainability and ethical sourcing have become pivotal considerations shaping consumer preferences and operational standards across the global food and beverage industry. Globally, around 78 percent of consumers say that a sustainable lifestyle is important to them (NielsenIQ, 2022), reflecting the broader shift toward eco-conscious decision-making that increasingly influences where and how people dine. Restaurants such as Blue Hill at Stone Barns in New York, and zero-waste pioneer Silo in London, exemplify this movement by embedding sustainability across their operations, from sourcing locally produced ingredients to implementing comprehensive composting and innovative waste management strategies. These practices enhance consumer loyalty, brand reputation, and operational efficiency, providing significant competitive advantages in an increasingly eco-conscious market.

Technological innovation and digital transformation

Technological advancements are significantly reshaping the global food and beverage industry, transforming operations, guest interactions, and consumer expectations. Digital solutions such as contactless ordering systems, mobile payments, interactive digital menus, and AI-driven personalized recommendations are becoming mainstream, improving both consumer convenience and operational efficiency. Robotics are increasingly prominent in kitchen and service operations, with examples ranging from robot-staffed restaurants to automated culinary.

In parallel, global food delivery platforms such as Uber Eats, Deliveroo, DoorDash, and Meituan have expanded at an unprecedented pace. The global online food delivery market, valued at $136 billion in 2021, is projected to reach approximately $365 billion by 2027, a robust annual growth rate of 18.6 percent

(Verified Market Reports, 2024). Innovative virtual brands such as Virtual Dining Concepts (MrBeast Burger) further demonstrate how digital transformation is reshaping consumer engagement and creating new revenue streams while redefining the boundaries of dining.

Experiential and immersive dining

Customers increasingly appreciate dining as a multisensory experience rather than merely sustenance. Immersive dining concepts integrate cuisine with storytelling, entertainment, and sensory elements to create deeply engaging experiences. Restaurants such as Sublimotion in Ibiza, Ultraviolet by Paul Pairet in Shanghai, and Alinea in Chicago, incorporate multimedia components—soundscapes, visual projections, aroma infusions, and interactive dining—to redefine traditional culinary experiences. Many diners now actively seek restaurants that deliver unique and memorable encounters, making experiential strategies a powerful way for hospitality leaders to differentiate their establishments and strengthen consumer loyalty.

Health, wellness, and dietary preferences

The global emphasis on health and wellness significantly influences food and beverage offerings. Consumers increasingly prefer plant-based, organic, and functional foods tailored to healthier lifestyles and specific dietary needs, including gluten-free, vegan, keto, and allergen-free diets. The global plant-based food market is projected to surpass $162 billion by 2030 (Bloomberg, 2021). Brands such as Beyond Meat, Oatly, and Impossible Foods have accelerated adoption of alternative proteins and animal-free options, reshaping menus worldwide. Restaurants such as Sweetgreen (US) and Leon (UK) illustrate mainstream adoption of wellness-driven menus, catering to health-conscious consumers and capturing market opportunities.

Post-pandemic health and safety standards

The Covid pandemic significantly shifted consumer expectations regarding health, hygiene, and safety standards in foodservice operations. Enhanced sanitation protocols, contactless service options, upgraded ventilation systems, and transparent health measures have become global industry benchmarks. Approximately 84 percent of consumers worldwide prioritize visible cleanliness when choosing dining establishments (Technomic, 2024). Restaurants globally have integrated rigorous cleanliness protocols and comprehensive staff training programs, maintaining consumer confidence in a post-pandemic landscape.

REAL-WORLD EXAMPLE:
INDUSTRY SPOTLIGHT   Sustainable dining innovations

Restaurants around the world continue to pioneer sustainability through innovative practices. Noma in Copenhagen, champions seasonal menus, local ingredient foraging, and zero-waste cooking methods. Similarly, Azurmendi near Bilbao, combines Michelin-starred culinary excellence with eco-friendly architecture and sustainability initiatives. These establishments demonstrate some of the significant opportunities available to restaurants in prioritizing sustainability and ethical practices, attracting discerning consumers in a globally conscious market.

Core business functions in food and beverage

Successful food and beverage operations depend on carefully coordinated core business functions, including food production, menu planning, service delivery, marketing, financial management, risk mitigation, and human resources. (Detailed exploration of these foundational concepts is in Chapters 5 and 6.) Mastery of these functions is essential for operational excellence, profitability, and sustainability in global F&B establishments.

Food production, procurement, and inventory management

Efficient food production starts with strategic procurement, rigorous inventory management, and precise demand forecasting. Operators must consistently maintain quality standards, minimize waste, control costs, and ensure timely product availability. Practices like just-in-time inventory management, vendor-managed inventory systems, and sustainable sourcing have become industry benchmarks. Implementing inventory management systems, along with waste tracking and menu engineering, can significantly reduce food waste and improve profitability. Advanced inventory software (such as Oracle MICROS, Toast, and Revel Systems) helps streamline these processes and optimize operational efficiency.

Menu engineering, pricing, and profitability

Menu engineering strategically balances ingredient costs, popularity, profitability, and presentation to maximize revenue and guest satisfaction. Managers often use frameworks like Kasavana and Smith's (1982) "stars, plow horses, puzzles, and dogs" to categorize menu items based on profitability and popularity. Pricing strategies such as psychological pricing, competitive pricing, and premium positioning further enhance perceived value and optimize revenue, directly influencing financial outcomes and operational effectiveness.

> **Think like a manager**
>
> You manage a popular global cuisine restaurant facing increased food costs and inventory management challenges.
>
> - Develop a strategy addressing procurement efficiency, food waste reduction, and cost control.
> - Evaluate technology or software solutions that could improve operational effectiveness and enhance profitability.

Service operations and front-of-house management

Exceptional service standards, rigorous staff training, efficient scheduling, and quality assurance systems are fundamental to front-of-house management. Superior guest experiences drive satisfaction, loyalty, and positive word-of-mouth marketing. Modern reservation platforms (such as OpenTable and Resy), table management tools, and digital ordering solutions improve convenience, operational responsiveness, and personalized guest interactions, thus improving service delivery.

Marketing, branding, and guest relationship management

Effective marketing and branding strategies differentiate food and beverage establishments in competitive global markets. Approaches include targeted digital marketing, social media engagement, compelling brand storytelling, loyalty programs, and personalized customer relationship management. Digital platforms like Instagram, TikTok, and Yelp significantly influence consumer choices and brand reputation. Various research has shown that the vast majority of global diners consult online reviews before selecting restaurants, which highlights the importance of robust online branding strategies.

Risk management, food safety, and regulatory compliance

Risk management in food and beverage involves stringent adherence to food safety standards, allergen management, liability reduction, and compliance with local and international regulations. Food safety incidents can significantly damage brand reputation and financial stability. Compliance with regulatory authorities such as the US Food and Drug Administration (FDA), European Food Safety Authority (EFSA), and local health departments is mandatory. Hazard Analysis and Critical Control Points systems are globally adopted practices to prevent contamination, manage allergens, and uphold rigorous food safety standards.

Human resources: Recruitment, training, and retention

Effective human resource practices—recruitment, training, retention, and career development—are crucial for consistent operational performance and high service standards. The hospitality industry faces significant challenges, including labor shortages and high turnover, emphasizing the need for strategic HR management. Leading global companies such as Marriott and Starbucks follow best practices through robust training programs, inclusive workplace cultures, and clearly defined career paths, improving employee satisfaction, operational efficiency, and competitive advantage.

> The most rewarding aspect of hospitality talent acquisition is creating meaningful connections—linking passionate individuals with opportunities where they can thrive, grow professionally, and enrich the community. In our industry, it's about more than filling positions or a transactional request; it's about transforming lives and careers to elevate the hospitality industry to a new level.
>
> —*Senior talent acquisition specialist, Cooper's Hawk Winery & Restaurants*

Inclusive practices in food and beverage

Inclusive practices are central to creating welcoming environments where guests feel valued and comfortable. Hospitality professionals worldwide recognize inclusivity's strategic importance in enhancing guest experiences, improving operational efficiency, and expanding market reach. Embracing inclusivity is not merely a matter of ethical responsibility—it is increasingly recognized as best practice in global hospitality management.

Accessibility in dining: A universal imperative

Inclusive dining begins with accessibility; ensuring that all guests, including those with disabilities or specific dietary needs, can enjoy seamless and comfortable dining experiences. Essential elements include barrier-free physical layouts, accessible seating, clearly marked pathways, and inclusive restrooms. Digital and printed menus that accommodate visual impairments (such as braille, large print, and high-contrast fonts) and accessible digital platforms further enable inclusivity.

As we age, visual and mobility impairments become increasingly common. According to the World Health Organization (2023), at least 2.2 billion people globally have vision impairments, most of whom are aged over 50; a demographic expected to grow significantly in coming decades. This adds emphasis to the need for establishments to proactively prioritize accessibility.

Sensory-friendly dining and inclusive design

Inclusive dining also accommodates individuals with sensory sensitivities, including those with autism, anxiety, and sensory processing disorders. Overly stimulating environments with loud noises, bright lights, or crowded spaces can be overwhelming and inhibit dining enjoyment. With autism diagnoses, for example, becoming more common (in about a third of US children say estimates from CDC, 2025), sensory-friendly approaches become more important.

Effective sensory-inclusive practices include designated quiet dining spaces, adjusted ambient lighting, reduced noise, sensory-friendly seating with increased personal space, and staff trained in awareness of and responsiveness to sensory sensitivities. Global examples like Chuck E. Cheese and AMC Theaters, which host sensory-friendly events, illustrate successful applications.

Cultural sensitivity and international guest services

With rising global mobility, hospitality establishments frequently serve culturally diverse guests. Effective operations incorporate multilingual staff training, culturally adaptive menu offerings, and sensitivity toward dietary and cultural traditions. Major hospitality hubs such as Dubai, London, and Singapore exemplify best practices in culturally sensitive guest services, and significantly enhance their global appeal.

Dietary inclusivity

Dietary inclusivity involves catering to diverse dietary needs, including gluten-free, vegan, vegetarian, allergen-sensitive, and religious dietary restrictions. Many of us have dietary preferences or restrictions that significantly influence our dining choices. Clear ingredient identification, thorough staff training, and flexible meal customization proactively enhance consumer trust and satisfaction.

Inclusive and equitable practices

Thoughtful integration of inclusive and equitable practices directly contributes to operational effectiveness, market reach, and employee retention. Practical initiatives include equitable recruitment, inclusive training, diverse supplier partnerships, and leadership practices that value diversity of thought and experience. Leading hospitality companies, such as Marriott and Hilton, demonstrate measurable outcomes from inclusive initiatives, including improved employee satisfaction and stronger consumer loyalty. Deloitte's (2022) insights survey notes 75 percent of diners prefer businesses visibly committed to inclusive practices.

Inclusive innovation and social responsibility

Forward-thinking hospitality businesses integrate inclusive innovation into operational models, directly impacting business performance and community perception. Emma's Torch (New York), combining culinary excellence with workforce training programs for refugees, or Dialogue in the Dark, offering immersive sensory dining experiences globally, exemplify how inclusive innovation can differentiate businesses competitively, enhance guest engagement, and positively contribute to communities.

Educational approaches: Experiential learning through community partnerships

Hospitality management educators collaborate with community organizations such as OCALI (Ohio Center for Autism and Low Incidence, a recognized leader in fostering inclusive environments), as well as national and global hospitality industry partners. OCALI provides free online training resources, including *Many Faces of Autism* and *Promoting Access for People Who are Deaf, Hard of Hearing, Blind, or Visually Impaired*. These resources equip students with foundational knowledge to effectively participate in immersive experiential learning opportunities such as "Dining in the Dark and Dim" and "Hospitality Listens."

Through these collaborations, students develop practical skills in creating sensory-friendly environments, managing diverse guest needs, and applying inclusive hospitality practices. Events like Dining in the Dark and Dim give students opportunities to serve guests who are visually impaired, enabling participants to experience firsthand the importance of accessibility in dining. Similarly, Hospitality Listens, established in 2012, provides sensory-friendly dining environments specifically designed for families affected by autism, teaching students to adjust environmental stimuli, train volunteers, and support guests effectively. These impactful events are executed with active involvement from hospitality industry experts, further enriching students' real-world learning.

> **INTERACTIVE EXERCISE**
> Inclusive practice scenario
>
> Select or create a hospitality scenario where inclusive practices (such as accessibility, dietary accommodations, cultural responsiveness, sensory-friendly initiatives) have significantly affected operational success and guest satisfaction. Then:
>
> - Clearly describe the scenario.
> - Analyze the impact on guests, staff, and overall operations.
> - Recommend two strategies to further improve inclusivity.

Food and beverage careers and professional development

The food and beverage industry offers diverse career pathways far beyond traditional operational roles. Opportunities span culinary arts, strategic leadership, marketing, technology, education, entrepreneurship, franchising, and consulting. Understanding these options helps aspiring professionals align their career choices with personal strengths and ambitions.

> **CAREER SPOTLIGHT**
> Frank Vizcarra: Unlocking human potential
>
> Frank Vizcarra's journey exemplifies the extraordinary power of resilience, mentorship, and visionary leadership. From his humble beginnings in Tijuana, Mexico, to becoming a global hospitality executive at McDonald's and a philanthropist, Vizcarra overcame significant barriers through determination and the critical support of mentors who believed in his potential. His career is a testament to hospitality's core promise of empowering individuals to achieve their fullest potential through authentic connections and unwavering encouragement:
>
>> People saw something in me that I couldn't yet see in myself. Their encouragement allowed me to overcome challenges I once thought impossible. True hospitality leadership is about recognizing potential in others and empowering them to unlock it. Now it's my turn to encourage others to discover what they're truly capable of.

Reflect

- Think about someone who has positively influenced your own professional or personal development through mentorship or support.
- How can you, as a future hospitality leader, actively empower others and help unlock their potential within your own teams and organizations?

Property-level careers

Property-level careers involve hands-on management of daily restaurant and hospitality operations, offering extensive guest interaction and operational expertise. Key roles include:

- **Restaurant manager:** Oversees service quality, staffing, inventory, and financial performance.
- **Executive chef:** Manages culinary teams, menu creation, food quality, and kitchen operations.
- **Beverage director/sommelier:** Curates beverage programs, procurement, training, and aims to elevate guest experiences.
- **Catering and events manager:** Coordinates specialized dining events, from menu planning to execution.

Corporate and above-property careers

Corporate careers focus on multi-unit oversight, strategic direction, and global organizational growth. For example:

- **Regional operations director:** Ensures brand consistency and profitability across multiple units.
- **Corporate chef/culinary director:** Oversees culinary programs and menu development across multiple properties.
- **Vice president of food and beverage:** Directs strategic planning, innovation, brand positioning, and overall operational excellence.

Entrepreneurship, franchising, and independent careers

Entrepreneurship enables individuals to set up innovative food and beverage businesses such as restaurants, cafés, breweries, or catering companies. Notable entrepreneurs, including José Andrés and Danny Meyer, illustrate how creativity, innovation, and strategic business management can result in internationally recognized brands.

Franchising allows entrepreneurs to manage operations under established brands, offering benefits including proven business models, operational support, and reduced risk. Prominent examples include franchises of global brands like Starbucks, Subway, or Dunkin'. Successful franchise ownership requires operational discipline, adherence to brand standards, and entrepreneurial vision.

Culinary education and professional development

Roles in culinary education and professional training include:

- **Culinary instructor/professor**: Educates future professionals in academic and culinary institutions.
- **Corporate trainer**: Conducts specialized training programs to enhance employee skills and effectiveness.
- **Curriculum developer**: Creates industry-aligned training materials and educational courses.

Marketing and communications

Marketing professionals drive brand visibility, customer engagement, and market positioning:

- **Brand manager**: Develops strategic branding initiatives and market positioning.
- **Digital marketing specialist**: Manages online marketing campaigns, social media, and guest engagement.
- **Public relations director**: Coordinates external communications, media relations, and promotional activities.

Sales, distribution, and supply chain

Careers ensuring efficient procurement, product distribution, and logistics include:

- **Distribution manager**: Oversees logistics, supplier relations, and product distribution.
- **Sales director**: Implements strategic sales plans and initiatives.
- **Supply chain analyst**: Optimizes purchasing, inventory management, and distribution efficiency.

Technology and innovation

Technological developments lead to dynamic roles within food and beverage, such as:

- **Technology consultant:** Advises on digital and technological solutions within F&B.
- **Data analyst:** Applies data analytics to improve guest experiences and operational efficiencies.
- **Innovation manager:** Leads initiatives focused on product and service innovation through technology.

Consulting and advisory services

Consultants provide specialized guidance to businesses seeking strategic growth and improved sustainability. For example:

- **Hospitality consultant:** Offers expertise in operations, menu design, and financial planning.
- **Sustainability advisor:** Guides businesses toward environmentally sustainable practices.
- **Beverage consultant:** Develops beverage programs, training, and operational excellence.

Beverage specialization

Specialized beverage careers include sommeliers, mixologists, coffee roasters, tea sommeliers, and innovators in wellness beverages, each requiring specialized certifications and professional expertise.

Career development and professional associations

Advancing your career in the dynamic food and beverage industry requires continuous professional development, making use of valuable industry resources, and actively engaging in networking opportunities.

Industry certifications and continuing education

Recognized certifications strengthen credibility, expand industry knowledge, and enable career progression opportunities. Prominent industry credentials include:

- **Certified Food and Beverage Executive (CFBE)**—ahlei.org: Validates advanced leadership and strategic skills in food and beverage management.
- **Certified Culinary Professional (CCP)**—iacp.com: Affirms culinary expertise, menu development, and kitchen leadership.
- **ServSafe Certification (National Restaurant Association)**—servsafe.com: Essential credential in food safety and sanitation.
- **Certified Sommelier (Court of Master Sommeliers)**—mastersommeliers.org: Globally recognized credential for wine professionals, focusing on wine service, tasting, and pairings.
- **Wine & Spirit Education Trust (WSET)**—wsetglobal.com: Structured courses in expertise in wine, spirits, and sake.
- **Cicerone Certification Program**—cicerone.org: Validates professional expertise in beer styles, service standards, and brewing knowledge.
- **Specialty Coffee Association (SCA)**—sca.coffee: Globally respected training programs in barista skills, coffee roasting, sensory analysis, and sustainable sourcing.

Professional associations: Building meaningful connections

Joining professional associations offers access to valuable career resources, industry insights, educational opportunities, and networking potential. Actively engaging with these groups enhances your visibility and fosters meaningful industry connections:

- National Restaurant Association (NRA)—restaurant.org
- American Culinary Federation (ACF)—acfchefs.org
- Society for Hospitality and Foodservice Management (SHFM)—shfm-online.org
- International Association of Culinary Professionals (IACP)—iacp.com
- Court of Master Sommeliers (CMS)—mastersommeliers.org
- Specialty Coffee Association (SCA)—sca.coffee

> **Key takeaways**
>
> - **Global importance of food and beverage**: The food and beverage industry significantly impacts hospitality, tourism, and cultural connectivity worldwide, serving as a universal platform for meaningful experiences, economic vitality, and community interaction.
> - **Historical development**: The industry has evolved profoundly from early taverns to sophisticated, modern dining concepts, demonstrating continuous adaptability to shifting consumer preferences, societal developments, and global culinary trends.
> - **Diverse operational segments**: Distinct restaurant segments (full service, quick service, fast-casual, cafés, fine dining) and specialized markets (food trucks, culinary tourism, cruises) cater strategically to varied consumer demands, operational models, and market positioning strategies.
> - **Comprehensive beverage insights**: A clear understanding of diverse beverage categories, including alcoholic beverages (wine, beer, spirits), specialty coffees and teas, and innovative non-alcoholic options, provides strategic opportunities across hospitality settings.
> - **Transformative industry trends**: Sustainability practices, technological innovations, and experiential dining significantly reshape global F&B operations, enhancing competitiveness, operational efficiency, and guest satisfaction.
> - **Inclusive and accessible hospitality**: Implementing inclusive practices, including sensory-friendly environments, cultural sensitivities, dietary accommodations, and accessible spaces, is essential for guest satisfaction, operational excellence, and market relevance.
> - **Expansive career pathways**: The food and beverage industry offers diverse, rewarding career opportunities in operational management, entrepreneurship, corporate strategy, technology, education, consulting, and beverage specialization. Understanding these paths and required competencies supports professional development and strategic career planning.

Looking ahead

In Chapter 12, on entertainment and recreation, you'll explore another dynamic and essential sector within hospitality and tourism. You'll examine the industry's evolution, including key milestones, organizational structures, strategic management practices, innovative trends, and inclusive approaches. You'll gain insights into diverse segments such as theme parks, gaming, sports venues, live entertainment, and recreational tourism. Additionally, you'll uncover expansive career opportunities, strategic considerations, and essential competencies necessary for professional success within this vibrant and rapidly evolving industry.

References

Allied Market Research (2020) Fast casual restaurant market to reach us $209.1 bn, globally, by 2027, PR Newswire, July 6. prnewswire.com/news-releases/fast-casual-restaurant-market-to-reach-209-1-bn-globally-by-2027-at-10-6-cagr-allied-market-research-301088253.html (archived at https://perma.cc/KL3E-6588)

Allied Market Research (2023) *Catering & Food Service Contract Market: Global Industry Trends, Share, Size, Growth, Opportunity and Forecast 2022–2032.* alliedmarketresearch.com/catering-and-food-service-contract-market A06609 (archived at https://perma.cc/4SX6-CKSD)

Allied Market Research (2024) Non-alcoholic Drinks Market Size, Share & Forecast 2023–2035, https://www.alliedmarketresearch.com/non-alcoholic-drinks-market (archived at https://perma.cc/G3Q7-56Z7)

Barron's (2024) Luxury cruises are riding the foodie wave, May 28. barrons.com/articles/cruises-for-gourmets-foodies-michelin-chefs-869fc24f (archived at https://perma.cc/ZTQ5-PVZG)

Bloomberg (2021) Plant-based foods market to hit $162 billion in next decade (press release, August 11. bloomberg.com/company/press/plant-based-foods-market-to-hit-162-billion-in-next-decade-projects-bloomberg-intelligence (archived at https://perma.cc/K6LW-YBWS)

CDC (2025) Data and statistics on autism spectrum disorder, May 27. cdc.gov/autism/data-research/index.html (archived at https://perma.cc/39NE-5KM2)

Compass Group (2024) *Annual Report 2024.* compass-group.com/en/investors/annual-report-2024.html (archived at https://perma.cc/Z3UZ-CAGU)

Credence Research (2025) *Catering and Food Service Contract Market, 2025–2032.* credenceresearch.com/report/catering-and-food-service-contract-market (archived at https://perma.cc/3RDW-JE5D)

Deloitte Digital (2022) *Authentically Inclusive Marketing: Global Marketing Trends.* https://www.deloittedigital.com/ce/en/insights/perspective/global-marketing-trends2.html?utm (archived at https://perma.cc/X9LG-4RZT)

Fortune Business Insights (2024) *Quick Service Restaurants Market Size & Trends Report, 2024–2032.* fortunebusinessinsights.com/quick-service-restaurant-market-106094 (archived at https://perma.cc/A2GM-2B7X)

Future Data Stats (2024) *Street Food Market Size & Industry Growth 2030.* futuredatastats.com/street-food-market (archived at https://perma.cc/6YJS-P7AU)

Grand View Research (2024) *Café Market Size, Share & Trends Analysis Report, 2023–2030.* grandviewresearch.com/industry-analysis/cafe-market-report (archived at https://perma.cc/QN5Y-25RL)

IBISWorld (2024) *Food Trucks in the US: Market Size Statistics*. ibisworld.com/united-states/market-size/food-trucks/4322 (archived at https://perma.cc/T26M-4JTG)

IBISWorld (2025) *Full-Service Restaurants in the UK: Market Research Report*. ibisworld.com/united-kingdom/market-research-reports/full-service-restaurants-industry (archived at https://perma.cc/EC5R-6B26)

IMARC (2024a) *Alcoholic Beverages Market: Size, Share, Trends and Forecast 2025–2033*, imarcgroup.com/alcoholic-beverages-market (archived at https://perma.cc/BSB3-2TF4); *Craft Beer Market Size, Share, Trends and Forecast, 2025–2033*, imarcgroup.com/craft-beer-market (archived at https://perma.cc/WU8M-7CSL)

IMARC (2024b) *Global Culinary Tourism Market Statistics, Outlook and Regional Analysis 2025–2033*. imarcgroup.com/culinary-tourism-market-statistics (archived at https://perma.cc/2A2K-CX5G)

International Coffee Organization (2024) *Coffee Report and Outlook December 2023, November 2024*, icocoffee.org/documents/cy2023-24/Coffee_Report_and_Outlook_December_2023_ICO.pdf (archived at https://perma.cc/CE9T-32P4); *Coffee Market Report – March 2024*, ico.org/Market-Report-23-24-e.asp

Investopedia (2022) Fast-food vs. fast-casual: What's the difference?, August 5. investopedia.com/articles/investing/020515/fast-food-versus-fast-casual.asp (archived at https://perma.cc/V7AP-BX8B)

IWSR (International Wines & Spirits Record) (2024) Global beverage alcohol market set for moderate recovery in 2025. theiwsr.com/insight/global-beverage-alcohol-market-set-for-moderate-recovery-in-2025-while-challenges-persist-in-2024 (archived at https://perma.cc/X6X9-CB56)

Kasavana, M.L. & Smith, D.I. (1982) *Menu Engineering: A Practical Guide to Menu Analysis*, Hospitality Publications.

Market.us (2025) *Global Luxury Food Market Size, Share and Growth Analysis Report*. market.us/report/luxury-food-market (archived at https://perma.cc/VW2J-AXCQ)

McDonald's (2025) *Franchising Overview*. corporate.mcdonalds.com/corpmcd/franchising-overview.html (archived at https://perma.cc/7GYP-3SCS)

NielsenIQ (2022) The changing climate of sustainability: ESG consumer insights. nielseniq.com/wp-content/uploads/sites/4/2022/10/2022-10_ESG_eBook_NIQ_FNL.pdf?utm_source (archived at https://perma.cc/W52N-LLGN)

NielsenIQ (2024) Non-alcohol: A mindful moderator in the US. nielseniq.com/global/en/insights/analysis/2024/non-alcohol-a-mindful-moderator-in-the-us (archived at https://perma.cc/6QQB-LNA7)

Restaurant Dive (2020) Ghost kitchens could be a $1 trillion global opportunity by 2030, says Euromonitor, July 10. restaurantdive.com/news/ghost-kitchens-global-market-euromonitor/581374 (archived at https://perma.cc/VSJ9-V6BX)

Skyquest (2025) *Gourmet Food Market Size, Share, and Growth Analysis*. skyquestt.com/report/gourmet-food-market (archived at https://perma.cc/G27C-2MYG)

Sonoma County Economic Development Board (2023) *Sonoma County Annual Tourism Report 2023*. sonomaedc.org/Microsites/Economic%20Development%20Board/Documents/Reports/2023/2023%20ATR%20FINAL%20ADA.pdf (archived at https://perma.cc/WQ84-4UWQ)

Starbucks (2024) *Financial Releases*. investor.starbucks.com/news/financial-releases/news-details/2024/Starbucks-Reports-Q4-and-Full-Fiscal-Year-2024-Results/default.aspx (archived at https://perma.cc/LN9V-G8L8)

Stone, M., Migacz, S., & Wolf, E. (2021) Learning through culinary tourism and developing a culinary tourism education strategy, *Journal of Tourism and Cultural Change*, 20 (1), 1–19.

Taylor Jr., S., DiPietro, R.B., & So, K.K.F. (2018) Increasing experiential value and relationship quality: An investigation of pop-up dining experiences, *International Journal of Hospitality Management*, 75, 58–68.

Technomic (2024) Global foodservice trends and outlook (blog). technomic.com/blog-global-foodservice-trends-outlook (archived at https://perma.cc/QD4X-QANQ)

The Business Research Company (2024) *Fast Food and Quick Service Restaurant Global Market Report 2025*. thebusinessresearchcompany.com/report/fast-food-and-quick-service-restaurant-global-market-report (archived at https://perma.cc/5PZA-97G7)

TravelAge West (2023) The importance of cuisine in the cruise industry, June 5. travelagewest.com/Thought-Leadership/Importance-of-Cuisine-in-the-Cruise-Industry (archived at https://perma.cc/WWK5-ZSUK)

USDA (2025) *Food Service Industry: Market Segments*. https://www.ers.usda.gov/topics/food-markets-prices/food-service-industry/market-segments (archived at https://perma.cc/E8B4-FGFP)

Van Rooyen, R. (2025) Ghost kitchens in hospitality: The end of the traditional hotel restaurant?, May 5. linkedin.com/pulse/article-8-ghost-kitchens-hotels-end-traditional-hotel-van-rooyen-zpfcf (archived at https://perma.cc/8ZT6-SFUJ)

Verified Market Reports (2024) *Food Delivery Market Size, Market Outlook & Forecast (2021–2027)*. verifiedmarketreports.com/product/food-delivery-market/?utm_source (archived at https://perma.cc/62PK-AP8T)

World Health Organization (2023) Blindness and vision impairment. who.int/news-room/fact-sheets/detail/blindness-and-visual-impairment (archived at https://perma.cc/3UU4-AWT9)

YouGov (2022) Global: Most consumers want to eat local food – but how do climate change beliefs affect appetites? business.yougov.com/content/42811-global-poll-buy-eat-local-food-climate-change (archived at https://perma.cc/5TY4-LY65)

Entertainment and recreation

12

LEARNING OBJECTIVES

- Define the entertainment and recreation industry, highlighting its integral connection to hospitality and tourism.
- Trace historical developments shaping contemporary entertainment and recreation offerings.
- Identify key operational segments, including theme parks, sports venues, live entertainment, cultural institutions, and niche recreation.
- Evaluate emerging trends, including sustainability, technological integration, immersive experiences, and inclusive practices.
- Recognize diverse career paths within entertainment and recreation, including required competencies, advancement opportunities, and their interconnections with broader hospitality and tourism sectors.

Introduction

Imagine turning 21 and eagerly heading to Las Vegas, a city known for vibrant nightlife, glittering casinos, and world-class entertainment. You've heard stories of gaming slots, star-studded shows, and bustling clubs. Upon arrival, you're mesmerized by the diverse and extravagant themes of each hotel. You wander alongside recreated canals of Venice at the Venetian, marvel at dancing fountains outside the Bellagio, and stroll beneath Fremont Street's neon glow. Before you realize it, hours have passed; you've been fully immersed in a world where entertainment meets hospitality in extraordinary ways.

Recall some of your own favorite memories. Perhaps they include the exhilaration of your first roller coaster ride, the mesmerizing energy of a live concert, or the electric atmosphere of cheering on your favorite team. These experiences aren't merely enjoyable—they create lasting impressions and meaningful connections.

The entertainment and recreation industry encompasses a diverse range of experiences and services, including theme parks, gaming resorts, sports venues, live entertainment, museums, zoos, cinemas, and specialized recreational activities, that are designed to engage, entertain, and enrich guests. Closely linked to other hospitality and tourism sectors, this industry enhances visitor experiences, drives economic growth, fosters community engagement, and promotes cultural exchange.

Today's vibrant entertainment landscape reflects a rich historical journey explored in this chapter. Iconic landmarks such as Disneyland, Broadway, and Olympic venues transform cities, energize local economies, and present cultural heritage to global audiences. The industry continually evolves by integrating advanced technology, sustainability, and inclusivity practices. These entertainment and recreation offerings significantly shape tourism patterns, influencing travelers' destination choices and enriching overall visitor experiences worldwide.

This chapter explores entertainment and recreation's dynamic landscape, historical evolution, key segments, emerging trends, and exciting career opportunities.

Historical evolution of entertainment and recreation

Entertainment and recreation have deep historical roots, reflecting humanity's enduring desire for leisure, excitement, and communal experiences. Ancient civilizations laid foundations that continue influencing contemporary forms of entertainment today.

Ancient Greece highly valued leisure, exemplified by the original Olympic Games, which were events combining athletic prowess, community spirit, and religious celebration. Similarly, Roman amphitheaters, such as the iconic Colosseum, hosted spectacles ranging from gladiatorial combats to theatrical performances, serving as focal points for public gatherings based around organized entertainment.

During the Middle Ages and Renaissance, European fairs became significant community hubs. Notably, the Champagne fairs in 12th- and 13th-century France combined trade and entertainment through tournaments, games, music, and theatrical performances. The Renaissance marked a resurgence in performing arts, prominently showcased through Shakespearean drama in England and the improvisational Commedia dell'arte in Italy, delighting audiences with relatable storytelling and humor. This period also saw the rise of organized recreational clubs, including cricket clubs in 18th-century England, laying the groundwork for modern structured leisure.

The 19th century saw the introduction of commercial amusement parks like New York's Coney Island, offering thrilling rides and carnival atmospheres accessible to broader populations. Traveling circuses further captivated audiences worldwide, featuring acrobatics, animal acts, and theatrical performances brought directly to local communities. Crucially, this era also marked the emergence of the leisure class, largely driven by the Industrial Revolution's socioeconomic shifts. Increased urbanization, more transport options, rising incomes, and standardized working hours allowed more people to engage in leisure activities. This trend significantly expanded into the 20th century, enabling broader segments of society to regularly participate in recreational pursuits and entertainment experiences.

The 20th century transformed entertainment globally. Disneyland's debut in California in 1955 revolutionized family entertainment by integrating immersive storytelling and themed environments (see Chapter 9 for more detailed exploration). Subsequent global expansions, such as Tokyo Disneyland and Disneyland Paris, demonstrated cross-cultural appeal. Dubai's landscape similarly evolved rapidly with attractions like Atlantis, The Palm and the Dubai Opera, while technological advances expanded global reach through televised sports, cultural events, and digital entertainment platforms (further detailed in Chapter 10).

These milestones (shown in Figure 12.1) illustrate how entertainment and recreation evolved alongside societal shifts, technology, and cultural trends.

Key segments in entertainment and recreation

Each of the following segments directly contributes to tourism by enhancing destination appeal, drawing visitors globally, and supporting robust economic activities through visitor spending.

Gaming and casino entertainment

Gaming and casino entertainment remains a dynamic and evolving segment within the entertainment and recreation industry, attracting millions of visitors globally and playing a significant role in regional economies. Historically centered on traditional casino gaming, the sector has experienced a significant evolution in recent years, marked by a strategic shift from purely gaming-focused businesses to holistic entertainment experiences. Penn Entertainment (formerly Penn National Gaming), MGM Resorts, and Caesars Entertainment have repositioned themselves as diversified entertainment corporations, combining gaming with live shows, sports, esports, luxury hospitality, culinary excellence, and varied leisure offerings.

This evolution toward integrated entertainment is driven by shifting consumer preferences and technological advances. Modern gaming locations like Bellagio in Las Vegas, Marina Bay Sands in Singapore, and Wynn Macau exemplify comprehensive destination experiences. These venues combine sophisticated gaming floors with live performances, Michelin-star dining, luxury shopping, expansive convention facilities, and upscale accommodations. Such integrated resorts position gaming as one part of a broader experiential package to appeal to families, business travelers, international tourists, and culture-seekers alike (Lucas and Tanford, 2010). This broad

Figure 12.1 Milestones in entertainment and recreation

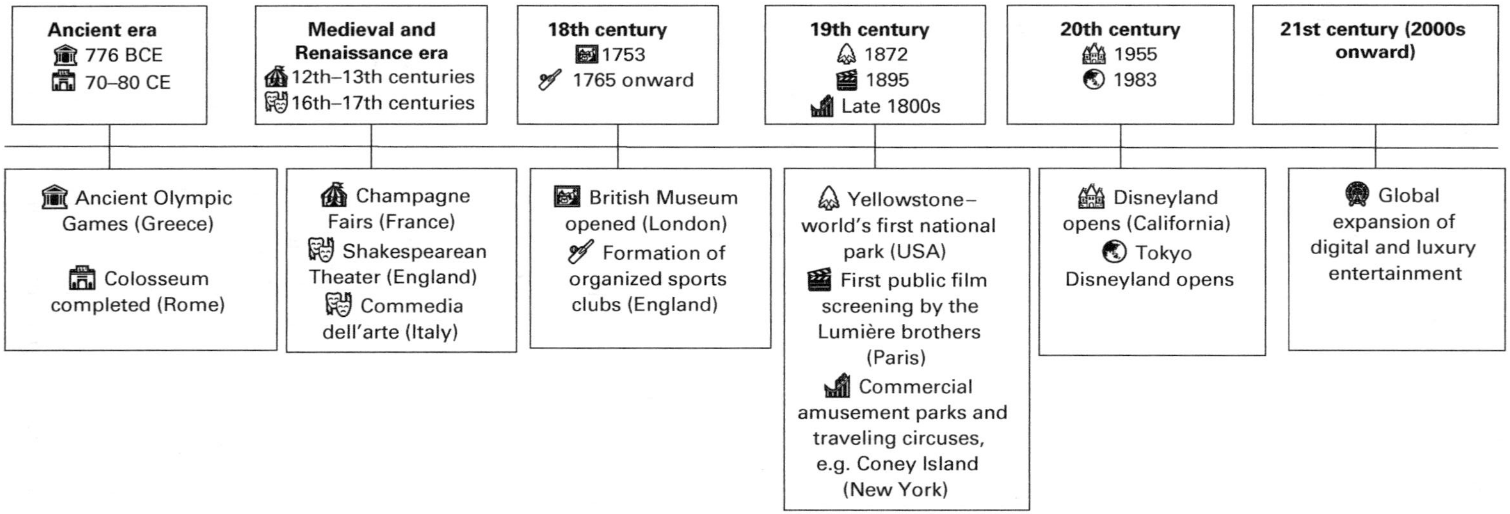

Ancient era	Medieval and Renaissance era	18th century	19th century	20th century	21st century (2000s onward)
776 BCE 70–80 CE	12th–13th centuries 16th–17th centuries	1753 1765 onward	1872 1895 Late 1800s	1955 1983	
Ancient Olympic Games (Greece) Colosseum completed (Rome)	Champagne Fairs (France) Shakespearean Theater (England) Commedia dell'arte (Italy)	British Museum opened (London) Formation of organized sports clubs (England)	Yellowstone – world's first national park (USA) First public film screening by the Lumière brothers (Paris) Commercial amusement parks and traveling circuses, e.g. Coney Island (New York)	Disneyland opens (California) Tokyo Disneyland opens	Global expansion of digital and luxury entertainment

appeal significantly enhances destination competitiveness, bolstering local tourism economies and hospitality sectors:

> Today's gaming industry is much more than casinos and slot machines. At its core, gaming has evolved into a vibrant and dynamic hospitality experience that encompasses entertainment, culinary excellence, e-gaming, live events, and immersive leisure offerings. As our industry grows, we're committed to delivering memorable experiences that cater to diverse audiences, while also embracing our responsibility to support our communities through proactive measures and responsible business practices.
>
> —*Dwayne Adams, vice president of hospitality, Penn Entertainment*

Esports and technological innovations

An exciting and increasingly prominent element within casino entertainment is the rise of esports, reflecting a profound shift in entertainment consumption, particularly among younger demographics. Casinos and integrated resorts worldwide now regularly host esports tournaments, livestream gaming events, and interactive gaming experiences specifically designed to appeal to digitally oriented consumers. For example, the Luxor Resort in Las Vegas features the HyperX Esports Arena, a state-of-the-art gaming facility that attracts global esports competitions, illustrating the industry's proactive approach to engaging emerging demographics.

Economic contributions and career opportunities

Economically, the gaming and casino entertainment sector remains a powerful driver of employment, tourism revenue, and regional stability. In the US, commercial gaming revenue reached a record high of $71.92 billion in 2024, representing a 7.5 percent increase from 2023, supporting approximately 1.8 million jobs, and contributing nearly $329 billion in total economic output (American Gaming Association, 2025). Globally, major gaming hubs show similar robust growth. Macau's gross gaming revenue increased by approximately 24 percent in 2024, totaling around $28.3 billion, despite remaining below pre-pandemic levels (Asgam. com, 2025; Reuters, 2025a). The Macau government also reported collecting roughly $11 billion in gaming taxes, a yearly increase of approximately 35 percent (CDC Gaming Reports, 2025). Singapore's tourism receipts included historical highs in visitor spending on entertainment and gaming, rising by 25 percent year over year to approximately S$22.4 billion from January to September 2024, with projections surpassing S$27.5 billion for the full year (Reuters, 2025b; Singapore Tourism Board, 2025).

From a career perspective, integrated resorts continue to offer diverse professional opportunities, including roles in hospitality management, culinary arts, event planning, entertainment production, and technical specialties such as data analytics, cybersecurity, surveillance, and esports operations. These varied roles underscore the industry's significance as an important global employment hub.

Ethical considerations and responsible gaming initiatives

Despite its significant economic and entertainment value, the gaming and casino sector faces ethical scrutiny regarding gambling addiction and social impact. Critics argue the industry's environment—through gaming-floor layouts, lighting, sound design, and promotional incentives—is intentionally engineered to encourage extended play, disproportionately affecting vulnerable individuals.

In response, major operators have adopted comprehensive responsible gaming measures. Caesars Entertainment's Project 21 campaign, begun in 1989, introduced responsible gambling training for staff, a national problem-gambling hotline, and self-exclusion policies across all its properties. MGM Resorts, through its GameSense program (licensed from the British Columbia Lottery Corporation), expanded training to over 1,000 employees in 2024 and integrates messaging via digital platforms, retail sportsbooks, and NFL stadium sponsorships (MGM Resorts, 2025; PR Newswire, 2025).

Support from nonprofit entities further strengthens these efforts. The Responsible Gambling Council's *2023–24 Annual Impact Report* details its work promoting safer gambling standards, advising businesses, regulators, and communities. Meanwhile, the National Council on Problem Gambling provides industry-wide best-practice guidelines, including its Internet Responsible Gambling Standards and Principles for Sports Gambling Legislation, to help operators prevent harm and support treatment (see ncpgambling.org).

As entertainment options evolve, the sector's future depends on achieving a balance between innovative guest experiences and proactive harm prevention. By deploying consistent, transparent, responsible gaming measures, the industry can demonstrate its commitment to social integrity and long-term sustainability.

> **THINK LIKE A MANAGER**
>
> You're the general manager at a newly launched integrated resort. Guests and media express concerns about responsible gaming. What strategies would you implement to proactively address these concerns and reassure your community?

Theme parks and attractions

Theme parks and attractions represent one of the most impactful segments of the entertainment and recreation industry, captivating millions through immersive, intricately themed experiences. In 2023, major theme parks worldwide drew around 420 million visitors, showing sustained global demand even as the industry recovered from pandemic constraints (AECOM & TEA, 2023). Destinations such as Walt Disney World, Universal Studios Hollywood, Tokyo Disneyland, and Europa-Park continue to exemplify this global appeal.

Effective theme park management hinges on operational rigor, guest services excellence, and strategic revenue management. Disney's celebrated storytelling runs through all its guest touchpoints, from attractions and live entertainment to dining and merchandising. The company employed approximately 233,000 people worldwide in 2024, with a substantial portion dedicated to its parks division (Quartz, 2024). Such major theme parks serve as anchor attractions for tourism, significantly influencing travelers' destination choices and extending regional economic benefits through increased visitation.

Technological innovation enhances the park experience. Attractions such as Universal's Wizarding World of Harry Potter utilize advanced ride mechanics, lifelike animatronics, and intricate set designs to create deeply immersive narratives. Industry-wide, the global theme parks market was valued at $64.6 billion in 2023, with projections estimating a 5.5 percent CAGR through 2032 (Global Market Insights, 2024).

Economic impact extends beyond the gates. Disney's Orlando Magic Kingdom alone hosted approximately 17.7 million visitors in 2023, making it the world's most visited theme park (ABC Action News, 2024). Consumer spending within parks drives regional economies through hotels, restaurants, retail, and transport services, contributing significantly to local development.

Leading operators are also beginning to prioritize inclusion and sustainability. Disney's reimagination of Splash Mountain into Tiana's Bayou Adventure features Disney's first Black princess, indicating a commitment to cultural representation. Similarly, parks like Legoland and Universal Orlando have launched sensory-friendly services to accommodate guests with disabilities or sensory sensitivities. Sustainability efforts are gaining traction. Disneyland Paris, for instance, has shifted 20 percent of its energy sourcing to renewables and ramped up recycling and responsible procurement initiatives (Disneyland Paris, 2024).

Finally, the industry continues to evolve its signature attractions. Expansions such as Star Wars: Galaxy's Edge, Super Nintendo World, and newly opened parks like Universal's Epic Universe in Orlando (May 2025), as well as planned attractions like the Universal Horror Experience in Las Vegas, reflect ongoing investment in integrated IP-driven, immersive environments.

Ultimately, theme parks demonstrate the industry's remarkable ability to blend creativity, operational excellence, innovative technology, guest-centric services, strategic revenue management, and inclusive storytelling to create experiences that resonate deeply.

Cruise entertainment and recreation

Cruise entertainment represents a rapidly evolving segment within global hospitality, blending immersive leisure experiences with sophisticated operations. Modern cruise ships, operated by companies such as Royal Caribbean, Carnival, Norwegian, Disney, and MSC, serve as self-contained resorts at sea, offering diverse entertainment and hospitality experiences comparable to major resorts and theme parks. Guests aboard these floating destinations can enjoy Broadway-style productions, immersive theatrical performances, expansive casinos, luxury spas, specialty dining, comedy clubs, and family-oriented activities.

Cruise tourism significantly impacts global economies. In 2023, approximately 31.7 million passengers cruised globally, making substantial economic contributions through shore excursions, dining, retail, and cultural experiences (CLIA, 2025). Caribbean cruise tourism specifically contributed over $3 billion in 2023–24, supporting over 50,000 local hospitality jobs (Florida-Caribbean Cruise Association, 2024). Cruise tourism thus acts as a vital catalyst for destination economies, supporting extensive tourism-related infrastructure and local business growth.

The industry also offers extensive employment opportunities, with over 1.2 million professionals worldwide in areas such as entertainment management, culinary arts, guest services, maritime operations, revenue management, health and wellness, technology, and environmental management (CLIA, 2025). Leading cruise lines prioritize extensive employee training and career development, fostering global career mobility and professional growth.

Accessibility and inclusivity have become essential, with cruise operators such as Carnival, Norwegian, and Royal Caribbean providing accessible accommodations, sensory-friendly activities, specialized dietary options, and trained staff to assist guests with disabilities. Cruise operators regularly offer themed cruises catering to diverse interests, further enriching the inclusivity of onboard experiences.

Environmental sustainability is increasingly critical, addressing concerns like emissions, waste management, and impacts on marine ecosystems. Leading cruise lines actively invest in cleaner fuel alternatives (such as liquefied natural gas), advanced wastewater systems, and emissions reduction technologies. MSC Cruises, for instance, aims to achieve net-zero carbon emissions by 2050. Technologies such as MSC's OptiCruise itinerary optimization aim to reduce emissions by up to 15 percent by 2026 (Black, 2024). The industry collaborates closely with environmental organizations, port authorities, and communities to adopt stringent international environmental standards, demonstrating commitment to sustainability and community engagement.

Ultimately, cruise entertainment exemplifies hospitality's remarkable ability to innovate, adapt, and responsibly deliver extraordinary guest experiences while promoting environmental stewardship and economic vitality.

REAL-WORLD EXAMPLE:
INDUSTRY SPOTLIGHT   Royal Caribbean's *Wonder of the Seas*

Royal Caribbean's ship *Wonder of the Seas*, launched in 2022, exemplifies innovation and operational excellence in cruise entertainment. As the world's largest cruise ship, it accommodates nearly 7,000 guests and 2,000 crew members, offering unparalleled entertainment such as Broadway-caliber shows, AquaTheater diving performances, ice-skating spectaculars, zip-lining, rock climbing, and surfing simulators (Royal Caribbean, n.d.).

Emphasizing sustainability, the ship integrates advanced environmental technologies to reduce emissions and waste. Accessibility is also prioritized, ensuring inclusive services and accommodations that are tailored to diverse guest needs, demonstrating the company's leadership in both guest experiences and sustainable cruising.

Water parks and aquatic recreation

Water parks uniquely combine excitement, immersive storytelling, and refreshing leisure, capturing the imagination of millions worldwide through larger facilities such as Atlantis Bahamas, Yas Waterworld in Abu Dhabi, and Disney's Typhoon Lagoon as well as smaller local aqua parks.

Modern water park management depends on rigorous safety protocols, guest-service excellence, innovative revenue models, targeted marketing, and efficient logistics. Yas Waterworld leads the way with RFID wristbands for cashless transactions, streamlined queue systems, and interactive attractions, all contributing to guest satisfaction and smooth operations.

Economically, water parks significantly contribute to regional tourism by attracting millions of visitors each year, substantially boosting hotel occupancy, dining, retail, and local services within surrounding communities. This economic impact underscores their importance within the broader entertainment and hospitality industry.

Many water parks also emphasize inclusivity, featuring sensory-friendly zones, accessible facilities, and trained staff catering to guests of all abilities. Sustainability efforts are also increasingly important. Yas Waterworld employs eco-friendly technologies like solar lighting, waste-reduction programs, and water recycling to reduce environmental impact while maintaining guest appeal.

Water parks exemplify how hospitality-driven recreation can integrate operational excellence, curated guest experiences, financial strategy, inclusivity, and environmental responsibility into engaging, sustainable environments.

Sports venues and sporting events

Sports venues uniquely integrate community identity, fan experiences, and significant economic impacts. Iconic stadiums like Wembley in London and Fenway Park in Boston exemplify this. In 2023, Wembley Stadium welcomed approximately 2.2 million spectators, hosting numerous concerts and sports fixtures that solidified London's reputation as a global events destination (Coliseum Online, 2023). Meanwhile, Fenway Park continues to attract large crowds, consistently enhancing Boston's local economy through visitor expenditures on hospitality, dining, and retail associated with events held at the historic venue.

Fan-focused strategies and major investments also shape modern stadium experiences. Tottenham Hotspur Stadium in London, representing a development investment of approximately £1 billion, is recognized as one of Europe's most technologically sophisticated venues, featuring multipurpose design, advanced digital experiences, and sustainable operations (SportsPro, 2019).

Inclusivity and sustainability are increasingly prioritized in venue management. Mercedes-Benz Stadium in Atlanta earned TRUE Platinum certification by successfully diverting over 90 percent of its waste from landfills, demonstrating leadership in environmental sustainability and accessibility practices (Mercedes-Benz Stadium, n.d.). Similarly, Seattle's Climate Pledge Arena operates entirely on renewable energy, recycles over 90 percent of venue waste, and employs innovative features such as rainwater recycling and complimentary public transit options, earning international recognition as a certified net-zero carbon facility (Climate Pledge Arena, 2023).

Collectively, these examples show how contemporary sports venues combine operational excellence, fan engagement, economic contributions, cutting-edge technology, inclusivity, and sustainability and can profoundly enrich communities worldwide. (See Chapter 8 for deeper insights into venue operations and events.)

REAL-WORLD EXAMPLE:
INDUSTRY SPOTLIGHT   Indianapolis Colts' Lucas Oil Stadium

Lucas Oil Stadium, home of the Indianapolis Colts NFL team, anchors the hospitality and events district of downtown Indianapolis. Together with the Indiana Convention Center and adjacent venues, it helps drive a combined annual impact of approximately 29 million visitors, $5.6 billion in local economic activity, and about 83,000 jobs (Visit Indy, n.d.). In addition, Colts games alone have historically contributed roughly $150 million per season to the regional economy (Klacik and Noonan, 2014). Underpinning this significant impact are the stadium's advanced fan amenities, technology systems, and year-round event programming, which contribute to its role in driving community vitality and pride.

Live entertainment and performing arts

Live entertainment and performing arts venues captivate audiences through storytelling, artistry, and cultural expression. Iconic entertainment districts, such as Broadway—a vibrant collection of venues in Manhattan's Theater District—London's West End, and prominent single venues like the Sydney Opera House, attract millions globally. These locations present destination-worthy experiences and significantly contribute to local economies and tourism.

In the 2024–25 season, Broadway collectively welcomed approximately 14.7 million visitors, generating box office revenues of $1.89 billion—a record-setting performance highlighting live theatre's continued global appeal (The Broadway League, 2025).

Staging such high-caliber performances requires extensive collaboration among artistic directors, performers, technical teams, and hospitality staff. Productions like *Hamilton* and *The Lion King* illustrate the meticulous behind-the-scenes planning and coordination necessary for consistently extraordinary performances. Broadway's collective economic contribution surpasses $14.7 billion annually, supporting nearly 97,000 jobs in New York City (Roberts et al., 2024).

Technology plays a significant role in enhancing performances. Advanced projection mapping, surround sound systems, and innovative staging techniques elevate audience enjoyment. Cirque du Soleil's renowned show *O* in Las Vegas, for example, integrates aquatic performances, breathtaking acrobatics, and complex theatrical technology. Cirque du Soleil productions attract millions of visitors annually, showcasing global demand for innovative and extraordinary entertainment.

Performing arts also drive tourism economies. London's West End drew a record 17.1 million theatregoers in 2023, generating an estimated £4.44 billion and supporting more than 230,000 jobs, outpacing even top sports events in visitor appeal (SOLT, 2025). Meanwhile, the Sydney Opera House precinct attracted 10.9 million visitors and contributed about AUD 1.2 billion to the New South Wales economy in 2022–23 (Deloitte, 2023).

Theatre has also become more inclusive. Productions like *Come From Away* and *Six* showcase diverse stories, and approximately 40 percent of Broadway audiences now identify as culturally or ethnically diverse (The Broadway League, 2025).

Looking ahead, live entertainment is exploring immersive and interactive formats. Productions such as *Sleep No More* in New York—an immersive, site-specific interpretation of *Macbeth*—allow audiences to shape their experience. Art collectives like *Meow Wolf* also push boundaries by merging art and environment, offering radically different forms of engagement outside traditional venues.

> **THINK LIKE A MANAGER**
>
> You manage a Broadway theater hosting a popular new show. Demand exceeds available seating, and some guests express dissatisfaction. How would you balance operational efficiency, guest satisfaction, and potential revenue optimization?

Museums and cultural institutions

Picture yourself standing beneath the glass pyramid of the Louvre in Paris, eagerly waiting for your first glimpse of the Mona Lisa, or walking through the Smithsonian National Museum of Natural History in Washington, DC, noticing a child's eyes widen in awe at a towering dinosaur exhibit. Museums and cultural institutions uniquely blend history, art, science, and culture into experiences that are both enjoyable and educational.

World-famous museums and galleries, such as the Smithsonian, the Louvre, and the Guggenheim in Bilbao, attract millions of visitors each year and are major drivers of global tourism. In 2023 alone, the Louvre welcomed over 8.9 million visitors, making it the world's most visited museum (Louvre Press, 2024).

Museum professionals carefully manage extensive collections, using specialized techniques to preserve and display precious artifacts. The Louvre, for example, maintains approximately 35,000 artworks, requiring expert conservation practices to protect masterpieces for future generations (Louvre Press, 2024). For hospitality students, understanding how museums and galleries care for their collections and engage visitors can offer valuable insights into guest experiences and operations management.

Education is another hallmark of museums, setting them apart from other attractions. The Smithsonian National Museum of Natural History educates approximately 6 million visitors annually through interactive exhibits, workshops, and online resources, engaging diverse audiences from around the globe (Smithsonian Institution, 2024).

Museums can significantly impact local economies by encouraging travel, extending hotel stays, and increasing spending at restaurants, transportation services, and shops. In the US, museums contribute about $50 billion annually to local economies, highlighting their critical role within hospitality and tourism (American Alliance of Museums, 2023). Popular museums and galleries like New York City's Metropolitan Museum of Art attract millions of visitors each year, greatly benefiting local businesses and hospitality services.

Digital innovation further expands the reach and accessibility of museums. Amsterdam's Rijksmuseum saw major growth in visitor engagement after launching virtual tours and interactive online experiences, allowing people worldwide to explore its collections (Rijksmuseum, 2023).

Sustainability is also increasingly important. The California Academy of Sciences, known globally for eco-friendly architecture, consumes 40 percent less energy than comparable institutions, setting new standards for museum sustainability (Cal Academy, 2024).

Inclusivity is a key priority too. The British Museum in London provides multilingual resources, accessible programs, and sensory-friendly tours, ensuring everyone in the community can participate fully in museum experiences.

> **Reflect**
>
> Think of a museum or cultural institution you've visited.
>
> - What aspects of your visit enhanced your overall experience?
> - How might these practices inform your approach to guest services in your hospitality career?

Zoos, aquariums, and wildlife parks

Walking through lush pathways at Singapore Zoo, visitors glimpse endangered animals thriving in thoughtfully designed habitats. At Georgia Aquarium in Atlanta, whale sharks glide gracefully through massive tanks, captivating millions of guests each year. Zoos, aquariums, and wildlife parks uniquely blend entertainment, conservation, education, and meaningful interactions with nature, significantly contributing to global tourism.

World-famous institutions such as Georgia Aquarium, Singapore Zoo, and Australia's Taronga Zoo serve as cultural and tourism landmarks. Managing these facilities involves specialized animal care, including rigorous welfare standards, habitat maintenance, veterinary services, and guest experience planning. Educational programs further distinguish these venues. For instance, Georgia Aquarium attracts approximately 2.5 million annual visitors, many engaging directly in interactive conservation-focused activities (Georgia Aquarium, 2023).

The economic contributions of zoos and aquariums are substantial. In the US in 2023, institutions accredited by the Association of Zoos & Aquariums generated around $1.2 billion in revenue and supported more than 35,000 jobs (AZA, 2024).

Sustainability practices are of the highest priority and increasingly shape operations in addition to wildlife consideration and conservation projects. Singapore Zoo, under Mandai Wildlife Group's leadership, has embraced science-based environmental targets, integrating eco-friendly practices throughout its operations. Inclusivity and accessibility initiatives are also central. Taronga Zoo in Sydney offers extensive accessibility features, while its Sydney Zoo counterpart provides sensory-friendly programs and accessible infrastructure, ensuring welcoming experiences for diverse audiences.

Collectively, zoos, aquariums, and wildlife parks integrate conservation, educational engagement, operational excellence, sustainability, inclusivity, and hospitality to offer extraordinary visitor experiences, strengthen global tourism, and promote environmental education.

Cinemas and film festivals

Imagine walking the red carpet at the Cannes Film Festival, with cameras flashing amid the excitement of a film premiere, or settling into a luxury recliner as cinema lights dim, signaling the start of storytelling magic. Cinemas and film festivals combine artistry, culture, community engagement, and tourism into unforgettable experiences.

Iconic events like Cannes, Sundance, and Venice International Film Festival, alongside major cinema chains such as AMC and Cineworld, form a significant element of global tourism and hospitality. The 2023 Cannes Festival regularly hosts around 40,000 guests. Venice draws over 220,000 attendees during its festival period (Comune di Venezia, 2024) and boasts venues like the 1,760-seat Sala Grande that anchor the city's cinematic and cultural significance.

Meanwhile modern cinema chains are enhancing audience experiences through technology. AMC Theatres has launched premium recliner seating, dine-in amenities, and Dolby Cinema, with expected higher occupancy rates than traditional cinemas (Business Wire, 2024).

Managing cinemas and festivals requires meticulous coordination across logistics, programming, technical infrastructure, guest services, and revenue optimization. Sundance, for example, had 72,840 in-person attendees in 2023, along with 361,212 hybrid views, attracting industry professionals and requiring detailed operational planning (Sundance Institute, 2024).

Festivals increasingly embrace inclusivity through multilingual screenings, accessible venues, and cultural diversity. The Toronto International Film Festival attracts over 400,000 attendees annually, celebrating stories from marginalized voices (*Daily Observer*, 2025). Sustainability efforts also grow. The Berlinale cut waste by up to 35 percent in 2024 using renewable energy, recycling, and eco-aware catering (Berlinale, 2024).

Cinemas and film festivals illustrate how entertainment marries storytelling, operational efficiency, innovation, inclusivity, and sustainability, reinforcing their vital roles in culture, tourism, and hospitality.

REAL-WORLD EXAMPLE:
INDUSTRY SPOTLIGHT The Cannes Film Festival

Held annually, the Cannes Film Festival in France is one of the most prestigious and influential events in global cinema. Each year, Cannes hosts approximately 40,000 industry professionals and film enthusiasts, significantly boosting local hospitality sectors by generating around €200 million in economic benefits (*Le Monde*, 2024).

Renowned for premiering groundbreaking films and celebrating the creative, unexpected, and excellent in cinema, the festival meticulously curates international films, welcoming diverse perspectives and inclusive storytelling. Operationally, Cannes exemplifies exceptional event management, combining sophisticated logistics, technical precision, and superior guest services.

Sustainability and inclusivity are integral to the festival's practices, with initiatives such as digital programs, multilingual accessibility, eco-friendly operations, and culturally diverse programming. The festival's global cultural influence, economic impact, and dedication to inclusivity and sustainability underscore its pivotal role in entertainment, tourism, and hospitality.

Family entertainment centers

Imagine a vibrant, laughter-filled space illuminated by arcade games, with casual dining aromas, and buzzing with friendly competition: this captures the essence of family entertainment centers (FECs). Designed to offer accessible, inclusive, and engaging experiences, venues such as Dave & Buster's, Chuck E. Cheese, Topgolf, and Main Event Entertainment combine interactive gaming, dining, sports activities, and events into compact yet dynamic settings.

> **THINK LIKE A MANAGER**
>
> You oversee operations for a growing chain of FECs. You want to expand your customer base to better accommodate guests with special needs. Outline three initiatives you would propose to make your venues more inclusive.

Effective FEC management involves coordinating multiple attractions, including arcade games, bowling alleys, miniature golf, trampoline parks, birthday parties, and interactive dining experiences, across diverse operational disciplines such as guest services, food and beverage, sales, and event management. Dave & Buster's, operating in approximately 150 locations across the US, Canada, and Puerto Rico, skillfully combines casual dining and arcade entertainment, accommodating family events, corporate gatherings, and celebrations.

Technological innovations develop and enhance FEC appeal. Topgolf, known for its advanced ball-tracking technology, interactive screens, and mobile integrations, transforms traditional golf into accessible modern entertainment. Its rapid global expansion highlights the substantial international appeal of technology-driven leisure.

FECs notably benefit local economies by providing affordable, convenient leisure options. According to IAAPA (2024), the broader North American attractions industry, including FECs, generated approximately $188 billion and supported over 1.1 million jobs in 2023.

Inclusivity and accessibility remain core to contemporary FEC operations. Venues such as Main Event Entertainment regularly organize sensory-friendly programs, thoughtfully accommodating guests with diverse needs and fostering inclusive community engagement.

Collectively, FECs uniquely integrate guest services, technological innovation, diverse recreational activities, inclusivity, and community-oriented leisure, underscoring their essential role within the hospitality, tourism, and recreation sectors.

REAL-WORLD EXAMPLE:
INDUSTRY SPOTLIGHT Topgolf Entertainment Group

Topgolf exemplifies innovation within family entertainment centers by redefining traditional golf as interactive, technology-driven experiences. Operating over 100 venues worldwide, Topgolf maintains locations across North America, the UK, Australia, UAE, Mexico, Germany, and Thailand, attracting diverse visitors from families and social groups to corporate events. Using advanced RFID-enabled golf balls and real-time digital scoring, Topgolf delivers engaging, inclusive experiences. Facilities include climate-controlled bays, casual dining, and spaces for private events, maximizing guest comfort and encouraging community engagement.

Topgolf's combination of advanced technology, inclusive design, and broad hospitality illustrates its influential role in modern leisure and recreation.

National and state parks

Picture the scene of hiking beneath Yosemite's towering sequoias, exploring Grand Canyon's dramatic vistas, or marveling at Yellowstone's geothermal wonders.

National and state parks offer profound experiences, connecting visitors with nature's grandeur and sites' cultural heritage. In 2023, US National Park Service sites recorded 325 million recreation visits, with visitors spending an estimated $26.4 billion in gateway communities, supporting local lodging, dining, retail, and transport sectors (NPS, 2024). Iconic parks such as Yellowstone, Yosemite, Banff, and the Great Barrier Reef draw hundreds of millions globally, reinforcing their vital role in international tourism.

Managing parks involves a balance, however, of hospitality operations with wildlife conservation, visitor safety, sustainable infrastructure, and environmental preservation. Multidisciplinary teams, including park rangers, environmental scientists, educators, and hospitality professionals, collaborate to deliver guest experiences while safeguarding fragile ecosystems. Yellowstone, for example, enhances stewardship through ranger-led programs, interactive exhibits, and conservation education designed to deepen visitor awareness and responsibility.

Sustainability efforts are paramount. Banff National Park, for instance, welcomes over 4 million visits annually, and uses comprehensive conservation strategies, such as habitat restoration, energy conservation, and eco-friendly transport, to minimize ecological impact and educate visitors on sustainable practices (Parks Canada, 2023).

Inclusivity is central to park services, with accessible trails, sensory-friendly experiences, and multilingual signage enabling enjoyment for individuals of all abilities and backgrounds. Ultimately, national and state parks illustrate how hospitality effectively integrates outdoor recreation, environmental stewardship, education, sustainability, and accessible guest services to support community vitality and global environmental awareness.

REAL-WORLD EXAMPLE:
INDUSTRY SPOTLIGHT Crystal Cove State Park

Nestled along Southern California's scenic coastline, Crystal Cove State Park presents a harmonious blend of natural beauty, heritage tourism, and hospitality experiences. Spanning three miles of shoreline and hosting approximately 3 million annual visits, the park significantly benefits local lodging, dining, and retail in Orange County (California State Parks, 2023).

The park's Historic District features restored beach cottages from the 1920s and 1930s, offering immersive lodging options that connect guests to California's coastal cultural heritage. Visitors dining at the Beachcomber Café, for example, also engage in this experiential tourism, celebrating local history and cuisine.

Crystal Cove exemplifies sustainable tourism. Park staff implement ecological restoration, wildlife and marine conservation programs, and educational outreach, fostering environmental stewardship and preserving natural habitats. Accessibility and inclusivity are prioritized. The park provides beach wheelchairs, accessible trails, and multilingual interpretive signage, ensuring that everyone can enjoy its scenic and cultural offerings.

Ultimately, Crystal Cove State Park demonstrates how parks can integrate environmental care, cultural preservation, sustainable operations, accessible hospitality, and regional economic benefit into a cohesive and responsible visitor experience.

Specialized and niche recreation segments

Beyond mainstream entertainment and recreation, specialized and niche segments have become compelling drivers of global tourism, enriching destinations and offering transformative traveler experiences. Adventure tourism destinations such as Queenstown in New Zealand, and Interlaken in Switzerland, attract thrill-seekers through activities like skydiving, bungee jumping, and whitewater rafting. Culinary and wine tourism in regions such as Napa Valley in the US and Burgundy in France blends gastronomy, cultural immersion, and hospitality through festivals and authentic dining experiences. Additionally, wellness tourism, including spa retreats in Bali and holistic resorts in Costa Rica, has grown substantially, with a value expected to surpass $1 trillion by 2024 (Global Wellness Institute, 2023). Emerging segments such as ecotourism, wildlife safaris, sustainable retreats, and even space tourism highlight the industry's innovative potential. Inclusive practices within these niches further reinforce hospitality's commitment to welcoming diverse travelers, offering professionals and students innovative pathways for industry engagement and career opportunities.

INTERACTIVE EXERCISE
Exploring specialized recreation

This exercise promotes active learning, reinforcing theoretical knowledge through practical application. You'll also explore how different segments intersect and support other hospitality and tourism sectors (food and beverage, lodging, tourism, events, managed services).

1 **Choose a segment**
    o   Select one specialized recreation segment from this chapter, such as:
        – Adventure and extreme sports tourism
        – Family entertainment centers

- National and state parks
- Museums and cultural institutions
- Zoos, aquariums, and wildlife parks
- Cinemas and film festivals
- Cruise entertainment
- Theme parks and attractions
- Gaming and casino entertainment

2 **Real-world exploration**
   o Research an actual business or attraction representing your chosen segment. Use credible resources such as official websites, industry reports, or news articles to learn more.

3 **Analysis and reflection**
   o Briefly answer these questions about your choice:
   - **Introduction:** What specific business, attraction, event, or destination did you pick? (Name, location, and brief description.)
   - **Why did you choose it?** How does it clearly represent your selected recreation segment?
   - **What's interesting?** Describe one innovative or unique practice, such as technology, sustainability, guest experience, or accessibility, that this business or attraction uses.
   - **Connections:** Name at least one way your choice connects to another area of hospitality or tourism (such as food and beverage, lodging, events, or tourism).
   - **Careers:** Identify one or two possible job roles associated with your choice. How might these roles interact with other hospitality or tourism segments?

4 **Share your findings**
   o **Individual learners:** Summarize your findings in a short reflection, discussion board post, infographic, or brief video.
   o **Groups:** Prepare a short presentation highlighting your choice's unique features, innovative practices, connections with other segments, and related career opportunities. Include visuals or multimedia for engagement.

Key trends in entertainment and recreation

Sustainability and environmental stewardship

Sustainability initiatives are central to many entertainment and recreation operations today, driven by developing consumer expectations and environmental responsibilities. Leading organizations, including Disneyland Paris, Atlantis Bahamas, and MSC Cruises, integrate renewable energy sources, waste reduction, and water conservation in attempts to lower their ecological impact. Disneyland Paris recently completed Europe's largest solar canopy, producing approximately 36 GWh annually—enough for about 17,400 people each year (Urbasolar, 2024). Similarly, MSC Cruises achieved a 6.5 percent reduction in carbon intensity across its fleet in 2023 through measures including ships powered by liquefied natural gas and extensive use of shore-power connections (MSC Group, 2024). Such proactive sustainability efforts not only address global environmental challenges but also enhance operational efficiency, brand reputation, and guest satisfaction, and reinforce the industry's commitment to sustainable tourism and recreation.

Technological innovation

Technological innovation continues to revolutionize entertainment and recreation experiences, with AR, VR, smart ticketing, and AI-driven personalization leading advances. Attractions such as Universal Studios' Super Nintendo World employ AR to immerse guests deeply in interactive storytelling experiences. Digital innovations such as smart wristbands can streamline transactions and queue management, and help to personalize guest interactions, improving visitor convenience and operational efficiency. Technology thus emerges as a critical factor in competitive differentiation, guest satisfaction, and sustained industry growth.

Immersive and interactive experiences

Today's guests increasingly seek immersive experiences that blur spectator and participant roles. As previously mentioned with *Meow Wolf* and *Sleep No More*, attractions such as Tokyo's teamLab Planets, AREA15 in Las Vegas, immersive theater, and escape rooms exemplify this trend. At teamLab Planets, visitors walk barefoot through water and gardens within interactive digital art installations that respond to their presence, creating a deeply sensory, participatory environment. Similarly, AREA15 offers a sprawling arts and entertainment district featuring large-scale immersive exhibits, multisensory performances, and interactive dining, described as "America's #1 immersive art experience" (Area15, 2024). Meanwhile, the escape room trend continues to grow, with the US hosting about 2,000 venues and the global market projected to exceed $21 billion by 2030 (Allied Market Research, 2024). These varied examples illustrate the dynamic appeal of interactive, emotionally resonant experiences across today's entertainment industry.

Inclusive and accessible recreation

Inclusivity and accessibility have become standard expectations within entertainment and recreation, with many venues providing sensory-friendly environments, accessible infrastructure, and multilingual resources to welcome all visitors. (Revisit Chapter 11 for a detailed exploration of inclusive hospitality.)

REAL-WORLD EXAMPLE:
INDUSTRY SPOTLIGHT   Morgan's Inspiration Island

Morgan's Inspiration Island in San Antonio, Texas, is recognized as the world's first ultra-accessible water park, setting a benchmark for inclusive recreation. Designed specifically for guests with physical, cognitive, and sensory disabilities, the park features wheelchair-accessible splash pads, waterproof wheelchairs, temperature-controlled water attractions, and sensory-friendly programming. Staff receive specialized training to ensure all visitors feel welcomed and supported, exemplifying the park's foundational commitment to empathy and inclusivity.

Core business functions in entertainment and recreation

Entertainment and recreation segments integrate all core business functions previously explored across hospitality and tourism. Effective operations require comprehensive guest services, rigorous safety management, strategic revenue optimization, innovative branding and marketing, and diligent risk management practices. Venue operations involve seamless guest experiences, robust safety protocols, crowd management, and meticulous facility maintenance. Strategic revenue management includes dynamic ticket pricing, data-driven decisions, and tailored guest offerings. Branding, digital marketing, and strategic communications foster strong guest relationships and industry competitiveness. Additionally, risk management, regulatory compliance, and ethical practices need to be rigorously maintained to ensure operational sustainability, guest safety, and brand reputation. (For comprehensive details, see Chapters 4 and 5.)

Careers in entertainment and recreation

> My passion for hospitality began as a kid visiting Cedar Point. Working my way from hostess to supervisor strengthened skills like leadership, teamwork, and communication. Now, studying hospitality management, I clearly see how these experiences and skills prepare me for diverse opportunities across entertainment, tourism, and beyond.
>
> —Abigayle Lydy, hospitality management student

The entertainment and recreation industry provides diverse career pathways, characterized by creativity, innovation, and dynamic guest interactions. Careers span operational roles at individual properties to strategic positions at corporate levels, and entrepreneurial opportunities

Property-level careers

Property-level careers are often the most accessible to new hospitality and tourism graduates, with detailed progression paths and hands-on guest interaction. These careers involve daily operational oversight, direct guest engagement, and specialized management roles across various departments, including operations, food and beverage, retail, guest relations, safety, and events (as detailed in Chapters 4 and 5). Each pathway offers structured advancement opportunities, illustrated by the following examples:

- **Theme park manager:** Oversees daily operations, safety compliance, and guest experiences at attractions such as Walt Disney World or Universal Studios. Typical career progression begins with frontline roles (such as attraction operator), advances to supervisory positions (coordinator or supervisor), then to managerial roles overseeing park sections (operations manager), and ultimately senior roles managing comprehensive park operations (senior park manager or general manager).
- **Museum curator:** Manages collections, designs educational programs, and enhances visitor engagement at institutions like the Smithsonian or the Louvre. Career pathways typically start with entry-level roles in local spaces (visitor services associate, collections assistant, or educator), advancing into mid-level positions (assistant curator or exhibit manager), then senior curatorial roles (curator or senior curator), and ultimately leadership positions (chief curator or museum director) that oversee entire museum or gallery operations, strategic initiatives, and stakeholder engagement.
- **Cruise director:** Coordinates onboard entertainment, guest programming, and hospitality services on cruise lines such as Royal Caribbean and Carnival. Career

advancement typically begins in entry-level entertainment positions (entertainment staff or activity host), progresses into supervisory roles (entertainment manager or assistant cruise director), and ultimately leads to senior roles like cruise director, overseeing comprehensive onboard entertainment and guest experiences.

These career paths demonstrate clear advancement opportunities, highlighting versatility, growth potential, and interconnectedness across hospitality and tourism segments.

Corporate and above-property careers

Corporate careers focus on strategic leadership, large-scale operations, and brand management. Examples include:

- **Director of entertainment:** Strategically develops entertainment programming and guest experiences across multiple properties, such as those within MGM Resorts.
- **Vice president of operations:** Manages large-scale operational strategy, infrastructure investments, and innovation implementation for organizations like Disney Parks and Resorts.

Entrepreneurial careers

Entrepreneurial professionals develop innovative concepts, specialized experiences, and niche market ventures:

- **Event entrepreneur:** Launches specialized festivals, immersive entertainment experiences, or pop-up events catering to emerging consumer interests.
- **Niche recreation innovator:** Develops unique recreation offerings such as escape rooms, adventure tourism businesses, or wellness retreats.

Professional development and associations

Career growth within entertainment and recreation benefits from active participation in industry associations and continuous professional development:

- **IAAPA (International Association of Amusement Parks and Attractions):** Offers industry resources, networking events, certification programs, and career development tools.
- **TEA (Themed Entertainment Association):** Provides professional networking, educational events, and industry insights to enhance creative careers in themed entertainment.

- **CLIA (Cruise Lines International Association)**: Supports career growth in the cruise industry through training, certification, and networking opportunities.

Entertainment and recreation careers offer rewarding professional journeys that are impactful, globally connected, and rich with opportunities for advancement and personal fulfillment.

> **Key takeaways**
>
> - **Integral role in hospitality and tourism**: Entertainment and recreation are significant to global hospitality and are involved in experiences across lodging, food and beverage, tourism, managed services, and events. Diverse offerings attract varied demographics, supporting robust economic activity, cultural exchange, and industry innovation.
> - **Historical context and evolution**: From early festivals and ancient arenas to modern theme parks and integrated resorts, entertainment and recreation continually adapt to societal preferences and technological advances, shaping today's dynamic industry landscape.
> - **Segment diversity and operational excellence**: Recognition of distinct segments, such as gaming, theme parks, sports venues, live entertainment, cultural institutions, and specialized niches, enables targeted operational strategies, effective guest engagement, and sustained competitive advantage.
> - **Emerging trends and innovations**: Entertainment and recreation professionals must remain responsive to trends such as sustainability initiatives, immersive and interactive experiences, technological innovations like AR/VR and AI personalization, and inclusive practices. Proactively embracing these trends elevates visitor satisfaction and operational effectiveness.
> - **Core business functions across segments**: Successful operations within entertainment and recreation integrate core hospitality functions, including guest services, revenue management, marketing, brand strategy, and risk management, demonstrating the industry's interconnectedness and complexity.
> - **Diverse career pathways and skill sets**: Career opportunities within entertainment and recreation are diverse, spanning property-level management, corporate leadership, entrepreneurship, and specialized niches. Key competencies include operational excellence, creative innovation, strategic thinking, and interdisciplinary collaboration, positioning professionals for ongoing growth and advancement.
> - **Tourism linkages**: Entertainment and recreation strongly influence tourism by enhancing destination attractiveness, motivating visitation, and driving significant economic impacts through visitor spending.

Looking ahead

In Chapter 13, on wellness, the health industry, and healthcare, you'll explore how hospitality uniquely intersects with health and wellness, highlighting the growth and innovation opportunities in wellness tourism, senior living provision, healthcare hospitality, and specialized wellness-focused experiences. You'll learn how hospitality skills transfer effectively across industries, enhancing quality of life, care experiences, and guest satisfaction through thoughtful, empathetic service.

References

ABC Action News (2024) Magic Kingdom was the most visited theme park in the world in 2023, report says, August 15. abcactionnews.com/news/state/magic-kingdom-was-the-most-visited-theme-park-in-the-world-in-2023-report-says (archived at https://perma.cc/JF5H-FBQ7)

AECOM & TEA (2023) *Theme Index Museum Index: Global Attractions Attendance Report*. aecom.com/wp-content/uploads/documents/reports/AECOM-Theme-Index-2023.pdf (archived at https://perma.cc/2FFW-GWFM)

Allied Market Research (2024) *Escape Room Market Forecast 2030*. alliedmarketresearch.com/escape-room-market-A85137 (archived at https://perma.cc/C9YD-45YZ)

American Alliance of Museums (2023) Economic impact of museums: US data. aam-us.org/programs/about-museums/museum-facts-data (archived at https://perma.cc/3AWZ-BKGK)

American Gaming Association (2025) 2024 commercial gaming revenue reaches $71.9 billion, marking fourth straight year of record revenue (press release), February 19. americangaming.org/resources/commercial-gaming-revenue-tracker (archived at https://perma.cc/5WUD-STT7)

Area15 (2024) *Explore AREA15 – Immersive Entertainment in Las Vegas*. area15.com (archived at https://perma.cc/Z4VZ-86UB)

Asgam.com (2025) Macau's gross gaming revenues come in at MOP 226.8 billion in 2024, up 24% YoY, January 1. asgam.com/2025/01/01/macaus-gross-gaming-revenues-come-in-at-mop226-8-billion-in-2024-up-24-year-on-year-zh (archived at https://perma.cc/8LUR-6X3N)

AZA (Association of Zoos & Aquariums) (2024) *2024 AZA Annual Report*. assets.speakcdn.com/assets/2332/aza_annual_report_2024_final.pdf (archived at https://perma.cc/DG6H-2243)

Berlinale (2024) Sustainability initiatives at the Berlin International Film Festival. berlinale.de/en/festival/sustainability.html (archived at https://perma.cc/Q7M4-3BLL)

Black, A. (2024) Game-changing technology helping cruise lines reduce emissions, *Escape*, August 22. escape.com.au/experiences/cruises/gamechanging-technology-helping-cruise-lines-reduce-emissions/news-story/5ebd1678809a30d7e95afdf30c404843 (archived at https://perma.cc/E967-4EHA)

Business Wire (2024) AMC Theatres announces AMC's Go Plan, November 7. businesswire. com/news/home/20241107098160/en/AMC-Theatres-Announces-AMCs-Go-Plan-a-Multi-Year-Plan-to-Invest-up-to-1.5-Billion-Over-Four-to-Seven-Years-Greatly-Improving-the-Movie-Going-Experience-at-AMC (archived at https://perma.cc/JV5B-UDE2)

Cal Academy (2024) Sustainability in action: Green building & operations. calacademy.org/about-us/sustainability-in-action/green-building-operations (archived at https://perma.cc/L4Z4-XTX7)

California State Parks (2023) *Crystal Cove State Park Historic District, Sustainability & Visitor Stats.* https://crystalcove.org/annual-report-2023/ (archived at https://perma.cc/N69M-KCK5)

CDC Gaming Reports (2025) Macau's government collected US$11 billion in gaming tax in 2024, April 3. cdcgaming.com/brief/macaus-government-collected-us11-billion-in-gaming-tax-in-2024 (archived at https://perma.cc/SU4Z-EXSJ)

CLIA (2025) *2024 State of the Cruise Industry Report.* cruising.org/-/media/clia-research/state-of-the-industry-report-2024.pdf (archived at https://perma.cc/ML56-4WGG)

Climate Pledge Arena (2023) Climate Pledge Arena is proud to be the first zero-carbon certified arena in the world, October 20. theclimatepledge.com/content/amazonclimatepledge/us/en/Stories/climate-pledge-arena-first-zero-carbon-certified-arena.html#main-navigation (archived at https://perma.cc/XE8X-PEY9)

Coliseum Online (2023) The O2 and Wembley enjoy bumper 2023, March 1. coliseum-online.com/the-o2-and-wembley-enjoy-bumper-2023 (archived at https://perma.cc/3FJC-E6W3)

Comune di Venezia (2024) *2023 Venice Tourism Data.* comune.venezia.it/sites/comune.venezia.it/files/documenti/Turismo/Yearbook_of_tourism_data_2023.pdf (archived at https://perma.cc/4G5H-9WK9)

Daily Observer (2025) Toronto film festival celebrates 50th edition with star-studded premieres and global flair, September 2. observerbd.com/news/542255 (archived at https://perma.cc/CJ6U-4548)

Deloitte (2023) *Valuing 50 Years of Australia's Icon.* deloitte.com/au/en/services/economics/analysis/valuing-50-years-australias-icon.html (archived at https://perma.cc/8TDG-89DA)

Disneyland Paris (2024) *Environmental responsibility at Disneyland Paris.* disneylandparis.com/en-usd/environmental-responsibility-at-disneyland-paris (archived at https://perma.cc/47EG-ZK2R)

Florida-Caribbean Cruise Association (2024) *Economic Contribution of Cruise Tourism to the Caribbean: 2023–24 Report.* f-cca.com/downloads/2024-Caribbean-Cruise-Analysis-Vol-I.pdf (archived at https://perma.cc/GUQ6-UTFN)

Georgia Aquarium (2023) *2023 Annual Report.* georgiaaquarium.org/wp-content/uploads/2024/11/2023-Annual-Report-Web_final.pdf (archived at https://perma.cc/ZLV7-6PU4)

Global Market Insights (2024) *Theme Parks Market Size & Share, Growth Trends 2024–2032.* gminsights.com/industry-analysis/theme-parks-market (archived at https://perma.cc/NEG4-TEUJ)

Global Wellness Institute (2023) Wellness tourism will cross the $1 trillion mark in 2024. globalwellnessinstitute.org/global-wellness-institute-blog/2023/11/28/wellness-tourism-will-cross-the-1-trillion-mark-in-2024 (archived at https://perma.cc/D6KS-BCVT)

IAAPA (2024) How innovative technology can revolutionize the attractions industry, April 25. iaapa.org/how-innovative-technology-can-revolutionize-attractions-industry (archived at https://perma.cc/N9HM-Z5NV)

Klacik, D. & Noonan, D. (2014) *An Initial Look at the Economic Capital of Sports in Indianapolis*. Indiana University.

Le Monde (2024) Festival de Cannes: Economic returns exceed €200 million. lemonde.fr/economie/article/2024/05/20/festival-de-cannes-la-ville-table-sur-des-retombees-de-plus-de-200-millions-d-euros_6234464_3234.html (archived at https://perma.cc/EM3A-6NZ4)

Louvre Press (2024) 8.9 million visitors to the Musée du Louvre in 2023. presse.louvre.fr/?p=1063000215090 (archived at https://perma.cc/L3L6-6R8E)

Lucas, A.F. & Tanford, S. (2010) Evaluating the impact of a new resort amenity on gaming business volumes, *UNLV Gaming Research & Review Journal*, 14 (2).

Mercedes-Benz Stadium (n.d.) *Accessibility and sustainability*. mercedesbenzstadium.com/accessibility (archived at https://perma.cc/3RSM-SHD7)

MGM Resorts (2025) MGM Resorts, BetMGM expand commitment to responsible gaming messaging (press release), February 28. https://sbcamericas.com/2025/02/28/mgm-resorts-betmgm-responsible-gambling/

MSC Group (2024) *Sustainability Report 2023*. issuu.com/msc-cruises/docs/msc-cruises-cor-sustainability-report-2023?fr=xKAE9_zU1NQ (archived at https://perma.cc/NT2P-CGUV)

NPS (National Park Service) (2024) *2023 National Recreation Visits Report – 325 Million Visits*. nps.gov/nature/customcf/NPS_Data_Visualization/docs/NPS_2023_Visitor_Spending_Effects.pdf (archived at https://perma.cc/RKX3-JC9E); *2023 Visitor Spending Effects – Economic Contributions of National Park Visits*. nps.gov/subjects/socialscience/vse.htm (archived at https://perma.cc/SQ3G-YFUQ)

Parks Canada (2023) *Learn About Banff: Visitor Statistics*. banff.ca/252/Learn-About-Banff (archived at https://perma.cc/7URE-63MV)

PR Newswire (2025) MGM Resorts and BetMGM expand commitment to problem gambling research (press release), February 28. prnewswire.com/news-releases/mgm-resorts--betmgm-expand-commitment-to-problem-gambling-research-treatment--public-awareness-302388180.html (archived at https://perma.cc/9STC-Z3DE)

Quartz (2024) Disney to lay off hundreds of employees as part of restructuring, September 11. qz.com/disney-layoffs-bob-iger-entertainment-disney-1851783390?utm_source (archived at WSKV)

Responsible Gambling Council (2024) *2023–24 Annual Impact Report*. responsiblegambling.org/about-rgc/annual-report (archived at https://perma.cc/GUP3-UG86).

Reuters (2025a) Macau 2024 casino revenues top official estimate but below pre-pandemic levels, January 1. reuters.com/business/macau-2024-casino-revenues-top-official-estimate-below-pre-pandemic-levels-2025-01-01 (archived at https://perma.cc/N3GA-EGZU)

Reuters (2025b) Singapore says visitor arrivals rise 21% in 2024, February 5. reuters.com/world/asia-pacific/singapore-says-visitor-arrivals-rise-21-2024-2025-02-05 (archived at https://perma.cc/3WAL-BJAW)

Rijksmuseum (2023) Rijksmuseum rounds off historic year (press release) December 14. rijksmuseum.nl/en/press/press-releases/rijksmuseum-rounds-off-historic-year (archived at https://perma.cc/4DYW-JXAK)

Roberts, L.M., Hewlin, P.F., & Simon, L. (2024) The show must go on! SHRM Business, February 22, shrm.org/executive-network/insights/people-strategy/show-must-go-on (archived at https://perma.cc/2NH5-JWHR)

Royal Caribbean (n.d.) *Wonder of the Seas Overview*. royalcaribbean.com/cruise-ships/wonder-of-the-seas (archived at https://perma.cc/4WEM-UFU3)

Singapore Tourism Board (2025) Singapore achieves historical high in tourism receipts in 2024, February 4. stb.gov.sg/about-stb/media-publications/media-centre/singapore-achieves-historical-high-in-tourism-receipts-in-2024 (archived at https://perma.cc/WE4D-H92T)

Smithsonian Institution (2024) *National Museum of Natural History – visitor and education stats*.naturalhistory.si.edu (archived at https://perma.cc/7W87-3YGK).

SOLT (Society of London Theatre) (2025) London's West End: A cultural and economic powerhouse, April 3. solt.co.uk/londons-west-end-a-cultural-and-economic-powerhouse (archived at https://perma.cc/7748-D5FE)

SportsPro (2019) Tottenham Hotspur's new £1bn stadium analysis. sportspro.com/insights/analysis/tottenham-new-stadium-all-you-need-to-know-design-tech-nfl (archived at https://perma.cc/63DC-D3GC)

Sundance Institute (2024) *2024 Sundance Film Festival Attendance Recap*. sundance.org/wp-content/uploads/2024/10/2024-Sundance-Film-Festival-Attendance-Recap-and-Economic-Impact-Report-1.pdf (archived at https://perma.cc/G33R-J79P)

The Broadway League (2025) Broadway's 2023–2025 season wraps with 14.7 million attendees and grosses of $1.89 billion (press release), May 28. broadwayleague.com/press/press-releases/broadways-2024-2025-season-wraps-with-147-million-attendances-and-grosses-of-189-billion (archived at https://perma.cc/3ULH-P9A9)

Urbasolar (2024) Disneyland Paris and Urbasolar commission Europe's largest photovoltaic solar canopy. urbasolar.com/disneyland-paris-and-urbasolar-commission-europes-largest-photovoltaic-shadow-power-plant (archived at https://perma.cc/CM46-2KAA)

Visit Indy (n.d.) *Visit Indy 2025 Community Report*. cloud.3dissue.com/1527/1988/3911/2025VisitIndyCommunityReport/index.html?r=20 (archived at https://perma.cc/A4FT-QRJC)

Intersection of the wellness and health industry with healthcare

13

> **LEARNING OBJECTIVES**
>
> - Define the wellness and health sectors within the hospitality industry and healthcare, identifying their growth trends and intersections.
> - Trace historical developments shaping contemporary wellness hospitality practices.
> - Identify and differentiate key operational segments: spas, wellness retreats, fitness facilities, senior living communities, hospitals, and clinics.
> - Evaluate emerging wellness hospitality trends, including technology-driven solutions, personalized wellness experiences, and inclusive wellness practices.
> - Recognize diverse career pathways within wellness hospitality, senior living, and healthcare, highlighting required competencies and advancement opportunities.

Introduction

Imagine you've just accepted a post as an engagement coordinator at an upscale independent living and memory care community. On your first day, you walk through lush landscaped gardens bursting with vibrant flowers and along tranquil shaded pathways dotted with inviting benches—spaces intentionally crafted for leisurely strolls and friendly conversations.

As you step inside, the beautifully designed interiors catch your attention. Spacious, sunlight-filled common areas are thoughtfully arranged to encourage residents to socialize and engage in activities. Elegantly appointed residences reflect not only luxury but also dignity and independence, embodying the core principles of exceptional hospitality.

During orientation, you dive into the community's culture and wellness offerings, which range from music therapy and memory-enhancement workshops to tailored fitness programs and culinary demonstrations. Amid this training, you learn that the roots of this community trace back to Marriott's pioneering Marriott Senior Living Services. Although Marriott strategically exited the senior living business in 2003 (selling its properties to Sunrise Senior Living), the original vision of Marriott's hospitality excellence continues to shape the senior living industry.

This revelation vividly illustrates Pine and Gilmore's (1999) experience economy model, showing how experiences designed with intention can transform guest and resident interactions beyond basic services. This intersection between hospitality and healthcare is just the beginning, but shows how deeply hospitality principles can improve lives, foster meaningful connections, and support well-being in healthcare and senior living environments.

The intersection of the hospitality and tourism industry with wellness, health sectors, and healthcare continues to expand globally, driven by consumer demand for experiences that support personal well-being and quality of life. In this chapter, we explore these intersections in depth, examining historical contexts, clearly defining operational segments, identifying emerging trends, and spotlighting career opportunities that await hospitality professionals in wellness and healthcare settings.

Historical evolution of health and wellness hospitality and tourism

The integration of wellness practices into hospitality has deep historical roots. Wellness tourism and hospitality have existed in various forms for thousands of years, reflecting humanity's enduring pursuit of health, rejuvenation, and relaxation.

Ancient civilizations laid the foundational traditions that profoundly shaped today's wellness hospitality and tourism. For example, ancient Roman baths offered sophisticated wellness experiences with facilities for hydrotherapy, massages, and exercise, functioning as both social and therapeutic hubs (Britannica, n.d.). Similarly, traditional Ayurvedic practices from ancient India emphasized holistic wellness, integrating personalized herbal treatments, yoga, and dietary guidelines that continue to influence contemporary wellness retreats worldwide (Johns Hopkins Medicine, 2023).

In Europe, the rise of spa towns like Bath in England, Baden-Baden in Germany, and Karlovy Vary in Czechia during the 18th and 19th centuries marked the formal emergence of structured wellness tourism. Visitors flocked to these towns seeking therapeutic benefits from mineral-rich thermal waters and social connections through shared wellness experiences, laying the groundwork for modern spa resorts (Nahrstedt, 2004).

The modern wellness hospitality movement accelerated significantly from the late 20th century onwards, expanding beyond traditional spa offerings to embrace holistic health principles that encompassed physical, mental, emotional, and spiritual well-being. This shift gave rise to integrative wellness resorts and specialized retreats designed to cater to an increasingly health-conscious global market. Brands like Canyon Ranch and Miraval emerged, offering comprehensive wellness experiences that combined luxury accommodations, health education, fitness, and mindfulness practices.

Ancient wellness traditions, such as the Roman hydrotherapy baths and Indian Ayurvedic practices, have directly inspired contemporary treatments in integrative wellness resorts. They inform modern spa therapies, nutritional counseling, yoga retreats, and holistic wellness programs offered by global hospitality leaders such as Canyon Ranch and Ananda Spa.

Today's wellness hospitality is a thriving global industry, reflecting the evolving consumer demand for experiences that meaningfully enhance quality of life. From ancient roots to contemporary innovation, the wellness hospitality industry continues to develop, shaped by cultural traditions, technological advances, and changing consumer preferences.

> **THINK LIKE A MANAGER**
>
> Imagine managing a wellness retreat inspired by ancient Roman bathhouses. What contemporary wellness services would you integrate, and how would you authentically blend historical traditions with modern expectations?

Segment overview: Spas, health clubs, and wellness retreats

Spas

Spas have become integral to hospitality and tourism, significantly influencing travel destination choices, lengthening stays, and enhancing overall guest experiences. Wellness-focused hospitality, exemplified by diverse spa offerings, not only enriches individual well-being; it also positively impacts local tourism economies.

Destination spas

Canyon Ranch and Miraval Resorts, for example, offer immersive wellness experiences, combining spa treatments, fitness classes, nutritional counseling, and mindfulness practices. Guests typically engage deeply over extended stays, prioritizing holistic wellness and rejuvenation. Canyon Ranch, founded in 1979 in Tucson, Arizona, initially focused on a holistic approach combining health, fitness, and nutrition in an all-inclusive luxury setting. Over time, it evolved to include personalized wellness assessments, educational programs, integrative medical treatments, and mindfulness-based therapies, establishing itself as a leader in comprehensive wellness tourism.

The global spa services market was valued at approximately $96.5 billion in 2024 and is projected to grow to about $147 billion by 2030 and even $201 billion by 2034, driven by rising global interest in structured wellness programs (Grand View Research, 2024b; Precedence Research, 2025). Brands like Canyon Ranch exemplify success in this segment, consistently achieving strong guest loyalty and repeat visitation rates by effectively integrating wellness and hospitality practices.

Day spas

Day spas, often conveniently located in urban and suburban settings, offer shorter, accessible wellness experiences. These establishments cater primarily to local clientele and tourists who seek brief yet revitalizing breaks from daily stressors, or require a particular treatment. Treatments range widely, from massages and facials to specialized services such as hydrotherapy and aromatherapy. Day spas are often available in metropolitan hotels, drawing travelers and local residents who frequently combine spa visits with dining or shopping, generating additional economic benefits for surrounding communities.

Medical spas

Medical spas represent a specialized segment of the spa industry, uniquely blending traditional spa services with advanced medical treatments overseen by licensed medical professionals. These facilities address specific health-related concerns and include skin treatments and rejuvenation therapies, weight management programs, and other wellness-based medical services. According to Grand View Research (2024a), the global medical spa market reached $18.6 billion in 2023 and is projected to reach $49.4 billion by 2030, growing at an annual rate of approximately 15 percent. Leading examples such as SkinSpirit and Ideal Image have expanded rapidly across North America, highlighting the profitable intersection of healthcare and hospitality services.

Reflect

- Among day spas, destination spas, and medical spas, which segment do you believe offers the greatest growth potential over the next decade? Why?
- How might hospitality leaders strategically adapt their services to capitalize on these evolving wellness expectations?

Health clubs and fitness centers

Health clubs and fitness centers have emerged as integral components of hospitality and tourism, both as amenities within lodging establishments and as standalone facilities offering hospitality-rich experiences. They provide extensive wellness amenities that can enhance guest satisfaction, influencing customer loyalty, length of stay, and destination choice.

Within lodging environments, brands like Marriott, Hilton, and Hyatt prominently feature comprehensive health suites as essential parts of their guest experience strategy. Hilton's innovative Five Feet to Fitness initiative, for example, incorporates specialized in-room exercise equipment and tailored wellness amenities in guest accommodations, which indicates the strategic value placed on guest health and convenience.

Beyond hotel settings, independent fitness centers and health clubs also exemplify hospitality principles through exceptional service quality, personalized interactions, and curated wellness experiences. Premium brands such as Equinox and Lifetime Fitness emphasize hospitality-driven elements, including luxurious locker rooms, concierge-level guest services, member-focused events, wellness workshops, and sophisticated design aesthetics. These elements attract members who seek not just fitness facilities but also holistic wellness and social experiences akin to high-end hospitality and tourism settings.

Additionally, health clubs contribute substantially to local tourism economies. Travelers often select destinations based on proximity to high-quality fitness facilities, particularly when traveling for extended periods or engaging in wellness tourism. Cruise lines, such as Norwegian and Royal Caribbean, further illustrate this trend by offering expansive fitness facilities and personalized wellness programming onboard, directly boosting customer retention and cruise satisfaction scores (CLIA, 2024).

Economic impacts from fitness-oriented travelers extend to ancillary spending on nearby hotels, restaurants, spas, and retail outlets, underscoring health clubs' roles as important drivers of local tourism. According to Fortune Business Insights (2025), the global health and fitness club market surpassed $104 billion in 2022 and is projected to grow annually by almost 9 percent, driven significantly by the intersection of wellness tourism and local hospitality offerings. Thus, whether affiliated with lodging brands or operating independently, health clubs and fitness centers significantly enrich hospitality and tourism by elevating guest experiences, driving economic growth, and reinforcing the holistic integration of wellness into travel and lifestyle.

> **Reflect**
>
> How do hospitality principles, such as personalized services and luxurious amenities, enhance guest experiences in fitness centers, both within hotels and standalone facilities?

Wellness retreats

Wellness retreats offer specialized and immersive experiences that cater to individuals seeking focused and comprehensive approaches to personal health and well-being. Unlike traditional vacation destinations, wellness retreats combine accommodations, nutrition, physical activities, mindfulness practices, and educational workshops, creating transformative experiences that can significantly impact guest lifestyles and health behaviors long after their stay.

> **THINK LIKE A MANAGER**
>
> Leading a wellness retreat focused on emotional and mental wellness, how would you curate programs to effectively cater to diverse international guests?

According to the Global Wellness Institute (Mcgroarty, 2022), wellness tourism, including retreats, reached a market size of approximately $817 billion in 2022, and was expected to surpass $1.3 trillion by 2025. This growth reflects a powerful consumer shift toward vacations prioritizing health, self-improvement, and sustainable living.

Yoga and meditation retreats have seen particularly robust growth. Destinations such as Ananda in the Himalayas and the Omega Institute in New York offer structured retreats emphasizing mindfulness, stress reduction, and emotional balance. Yoga tourism has grown significantly, driven by Western travelers embracing Eastern mindfulness practices, and is expected to continue expanding as a major segment of global wellness tourism (Bowers and Cheer, 2022). These retreats attract global visitors and contribute to local hospitality and tourism economies by drawing travelers specifically interested in these unique wellness experiences.

Detox and nutritional wellness retreats, such as SHA Wellness Clinic in Spain and Kamalaya Wellness Sanctuary in Thailand, provide specialized programs aimed at cleansing the body and resetting dietary habits. These retreats frequently integrate medical expertise with holistic wellness practices, appealing to diverse international clientele seeking medically informed wellness solutions.

Additionally, mental and emotional wellness retreats have surged in popularity, particularly in response to heightened awareness of mental health issues exacerbated by the Covid pandemic. Retreat centers like Esalen Institute in California and The Ranch Malibu offer therapeutic programs featuring professional psychological counseling, emotional resilience training, and personalized wellness coaching. This segment is expected to continue to grow strongly, developing its role in wellness hospitality.

REAL-WORLD EXAMPLE:
INDUSTRY SPOTLIGHT   Six Senses Bhutan: A journey of transformation

Six Senses Bhutan exemplifies transformative hospitality by blending wellness, culture, and sustainability into unique guest journeys across several locations. Six Senses Bhutan provides an exemplary model of how wellness retreats can offer transformative hospitality experiences that benefit both guests and local communities. Set in the majestic Himalayan kingdom of Bhutan, this innovative retreat concept comprises five distinct lodges spread across diverse sites, each uniquely designed to reflect local culture, environment, and spiritual heritage. Guests journey between these lodges, experiencing holistic wellness programs deeply rooted in Bhutan's philosophy of Gross National Happiness, which prioritizes emotional balance, mindfulness, and sustainable living.

At the resort, wellness transcends typical spa services to encompass personalized meditation sessions, yoga, traditional Bhutanese healing rituals, nutrition-based culinary programs, and guided immersive experiences that connect visitors intimately with nature and culture. Guests often report transformative and lasting changes to their lifestyle and health habits.

Retreats like these contribute significantly to their local economies, as wellness tourists at destinations like Six Senses Bhutan typically spend 53 percent more than the average traveler, stimulating economic activity across hospitality, tourism, retail, culinary, and transportation sectors (Global Wellness Institute, 2023).

By harmoniously integrating authentic wellness practices, luxury hospitality, and sustainable community engagement, Six Senses Bhutan showcases the powerful role wellness retreats play in improving individual lives and bolstering regional economies.

Wellness retreats not only contribute significantly to individual health outcomes, they improve economic sustainability and vitality in regions strategically aligned with wellness tourism, thus highlighting their critical role in contemporary hospitality and tourism industries.

> **Reflect**
>
> Consider how wellness retreats differ from typical vacations. How do hospitality principles such as personalized service, curated experiences, and attentive guest care influence guest satisfaction and loyalty in wellness retreats?

Hospitality in senior living communities

Hospitality has become an essential component of modern senior living, transforming traditional elder care into vibrant communities reminiscent of upscale resorts. Driven by demographic shifts and rising expectations, senior living communities increasingly emphasize personalized services, gourmet dining, extensive wellness programs, and thoughtfully designed environments that foster social interaction, dignity, and independent living. This hospitality-inspired approach is fueling significant industry growth, with the global senior living market projected to reach approximately $480 billion by 2027 (McCracken, 2025).

Professionals with hospitality expertise often find a natural and impactful transition into senior living roles. Hospitality skills such as personalized guest service, operational management, event coordination, and culinary excellence directly transfer into senior living contexts, supporting resident satisfaction, operational efficiency, and overall community success.

The success of hospitality-driven senior living communities hinges on several key components that elevate resident experiences, strengthen community reputation, and promote operational excellence. Exceptional dining, active resident engagement, strategically designed residences, sophisticated sales and marketing, proficient administration, effective human resources management, and memorable special events collectively differentiate these communities, positioning them as leaders in both senior care and the broader hospitality industry.

Dining excellence

Exceptional dining experiences are a cornerstone of good hospitality in senior living communities. Meals might be curated by professional chefs and emphasize nutrition, taste, and visual presentation in restaurant-quality settings. Dining venues often offer varied menus, locally sourced ingredients, seasonal specialties, and customizable options that cater to dietary needs and preferences. According to Argentum (Gresham, 2025), sophisticated dining services are critical to resident satisfaction, social engagement, and community appeal. *FoodService Director* (2013) reports that enhanced dining programs have measurable positive impacts on resident well-being and community atmosphere.

REAL-WORLD EXAMPLE:
INDUSTRY SPOTLIGHT Atria Senior Living: Redefining hospitality in senior care

Atria Senior Living exemplifies the intersection of hospitality and senior care, operating in over 350 communities across North America with a resident-centric philosophy. Atria integrates luxury hospitality standards—professional chefs, diverse wellness programming (yoga, gardening, cultural outings, lifelong learning), and thoughtfully designed residences—into its offerings. According to *Senior Living News* (Nelson, 2024), Atria's hospitality-inspired approach has yielded consistently high resident satisfaction and occupancy rates, setting a benchmark in the senior living industry.

Resident engagement

Another critical hospitality component in senior living is active resident engagement. Communities often employ dedicated resident engagement managers who organize and facilitate diverse activities, events, and programs tailored to residents' interests, abilities, and well-being needs. These might include educational seminars, creative arts workshops, fitness classes, cultural outings, and social gatherings, fostering vibrant communities where residents form meaningful relationships and remain socially and physically active. Engaged residents report higher levels of happiness and overall wellness, which emphasizes the importance of intentional, thoughtfully designed engagement programs.

THINK LIKE A MANAGER

As the resident engagement manager at a luxury senior living community, how would you ensure your events are not only enjoyable but also contribute to residents' emotional, physical, and social wellness?

Thoughtfully designed residences

Residential spaces within hospitality-driven senior living communities are carefully planned to maximize comfort, accessibility, and independence. Quality residences feature elegant designs, high-quality finishes, accessible layouts, and personalized amenities that support both functional needs and aesthetic preferences. Common areas, such as lounges, libraries, gardens, and fitness centers, are intentionally designed to encourage social interaction and active living, enhancing residents' sense of community and belonging.

Sales and marketing excellence

Effective sales and marketing strategies are essential in hospitality-oriented senior living communities. Sales teams often draw directly from hospitality industry practices by employing relationship-based selling techniques, emphasizing personalized guest experiences and proactive communication. For example, skilled hospitality professionals leverage guest service experience to create warm, personalized tours for prospective residents and their families, highlighting not just amenities, but the emotional and lifestyle benefits of joining the community.

Additionally, sophisticated digital marketing campaigns, similar to those used by upscale hotels, incorporate storytelling and resident testimonials, showcasing real-life experiences to build authenticity and emotional connections. By applying hospitality-driven CRM tools and guest satisfaction metrics, sales and marketing can increase occupancy levels, strengthen market differentiation, and foster lasting relationships with residents and families.

Administration and operational oversight

Efficient administration and operational management ensure seamless delivery of hospitality services in senior living communities. Administrators frequently transfer core hospitality management skills, such as meticulous attention to detail, quality assurance, and service excellence, into the senior living context. This involves not only overseeing critical operations such as budgeting, compliance, staffing, and maintenance but also maintaining a hospitality-centric environment that prioritizes resident satisfaction at every level. For instance, operational oversight often includes routine quality audits and guest satisfaction surveys, similar to those implemented in luxury hotels, ensuring that services consistently meet or exceed resident expectations. Strong administrative leadership, drawing from hospitality best practices, creates a culture of proactive service, continuous improvement, and operational excellence, which can contribute directly to enhanced resident well-being and community reputation.

Special events and celebrations

Hosting special events and celebrations is integral to senior living hospitality, creating memorable experiences and fostering community connections. Hospitality-trained event coordinators often plan sophisticated events that follow luxury hospitality standards, from meticulously themed holiday parties and elegant milestone celebrations to enriching guest speaker series and cultural performances. These thoughtfully executed events foster a vibrant social atmosphere and enhance resident engagement and community appeal. According to McKnight's Senior Living (2024), senior living communities that emphasize purposeful engagement and meaningful programming are increasingly recognized for enhancing resident satisfaction, strengthening family connections, and fostering a strong sense of community—underscoring the vital role of hospitality practices in senior living.

Hospitality in hospitals and clinics

When hospitality principles extend into hospitals and clinics, they can enhance patient experience through personalized attention, comfort, responsiveness, and empathy. According to Deloitte (2023), hospitality-driven, patient-centered care significantly improves patient satisfaction, clinical outcomes, and provider reputation. Institutions such as Bumrungrad International Hospital in Thailand and Albert Einstein Hospital in Brazil exemplify this integration.

REAL-WORLD EXAMPLE:
INDUSTRY SPOTLIGHT Bumrungrad International Hospital: A leader in healthcare hospitality

Bumrungrad International Hospital demonstrates global leadership in healthcare hospitality by consistently delivering exceptional, hotel-level patient care and services. Located in Bangkok, Bumrungrad International combines clinical excellence with luxury-hotel-level service, which makes it a globally renowned destination for medical tourism. The hospital provides highly personalized care, including luxurious patient accommodations, multilingual concierge support, and attentive, responsive service that rivals top-tier hospitality providers. Its distinctive integration of hospitality principles into patient care has consistently earned the hospital international recognition and high patient satisfaction ratings (Veerasoontorn et al., 2011).

Transferability of hospitality skills between hotels and hospitals

Hospitality skills seamlessly transfer between hotels and hospitals, as both sectors share essential priorities: exceptional guest care, comfort, and attention to detail. Hospitality professionals effectively contribute competencies like empathetic communication, proactive problem-solving, and operational excellence in healthcare roles such as guest services managers, dietary directors, environmental services teams, and facilities management leaders. It has been seen that these transferable skills enhance patient satisfaction and improve operational outcomes, demonstrating the value of hospitality experience in healthcare settings.

REAL-WORLD EXAMPLE:
INDUSTRY SPOTLIGHT Cleveland Clinic: Redefining healthcare through hospitality excellence

Cleveland Clinic consistently ranks among the world's best hospitals, blending top-tier medical care with hospitality-inspired patient experiences. Its US main campus and Cleveland Clinic, Abu Dhabi, prioritize comfort, warmth, and personalized service—experiences you would expect from a luxury hotel rather than a typical hospital.

At the Abu Dhabi clinic, hospitality extends beyond healthcare: patients experience culturally tailored amenities, multilingual support teams, chef-prepared meals, and thoughtfully designed private rooms. This intentional approach has earned Cleveland Clinic second place in the global rankings by Newsweek (2024) for patient experience and medical excellence.

Through genuine hospitality, Cleveland Clinic is redefining expectations in healthcare—creating spaces of healing and comfort.

Patient satisfaction

Patient satisfaction is central to healthcare hospitality, reflecting the overall quality and effectiveness of care provided. Hospitals emphasizing patient satisfaction invest in training healthcare professionals to deliver empathetic, clear, and responsive communication. Patient satisfaction surveys guide continuous improvement initiatives, aligning services with patient expectations. High patient satisfaction correlates strongly with increased loyalty, positive referrals, and strengthened provider reputations. According to Press Ganey (Daniels, 2024), hospitals ranking highly in patient satisfaction achieve significantly higher patient loyalty, resulting in increased referrals, greater utilization of additional healthcare services, and enhanced institutional reputations compared to lower-performing peers.

> **CAREER SPOTLIGHT**
> Jason Mack, director of patient experience, OSU Comprehensive Cancer Center
>
> Jason Mack, currently director of patient experience at The Ohio State University's Comprehensive Cancer Center, transitioned into healthcare after an extensive career managing strongly branded, reputable hotel properties such as Le Meridien and AC Hotel by Marriott. His hospitality-centric leadership directly translates into patient experience management, prioritizing personalized care and positive interactions that significantly improve patient satisfaction.
> Reflecting on the valuable intersection of hospitality and healthcare, Mack shares:
>
> Decades of experience in hospitality have proven invaluable in a healthcare setting. At a time of unparalleled access to knowledge and many choices in where to seek care, it becomes even more critical that we are hyper-focused on curating memorable experiences through a human-centered lens. Experience in hospitality has taught me to anticipate the needs of the guest, recognizing that emotional needs are equally important to physical needs. At the end of the day, The James is just a big hotel that no one really wants to check-in to *and* they cannot wait to leave… Our ability to connect at a human level is absolute in driving top-decile patient satisfaction.
>
> This perspective underscores how hospitality expertise, particularly in personalized guest service and meaningful human interactions, can significantly elevate patient experiences and overall satisfaction in healthcare settings.

Guest services

Guest services in hospitals and clinics worldwide provide personalized assistance that is comparable to luxury hotel environments. Services include personalized patient admissions, concierge support, appointment assistance, wayfinding, and family support. Singapore's Mount Elizabeth Hospital, for example, employs guest service teams trained in hospitality, significantly enhancing patient comfort and satisfaction and creating seamless healthcare experiences. Healthcare providers adopting these concierge-style practices increasingly view them as central to patient satisfaction and differentiation in a competitive marketplace.

> **THINK LIKE A MANAGER**
>
> As director of patient experience, how would you implement hospitality practices to humanize and improve patient journeys, from admission through discharge?

Dietary services

Exceptional dietary services significantly contribute to patient satisfaction and recovery. Many healthcare dietary departments increasingly emphasize providing nutritious, visually appealing, and customized meals tailored to specific patient dietary requirements, aligning closely with culinary practices seen in quality restaurants and hospitality settings. High-quality dietary services play a critical role in healthcare by supporting patient recovery, comfort, and overall satisfaction. Many hospitals now view food not only as nourishment but also as an extension of care, integrating culinary excellence, nutrition science, and hospitality principles into their operations. Thoughtful meal planning, sustainable sourcing, and personalized menus help improve patients' well-being, reduce stress, and create a more positive healthcare experience. By treating food as part of the healing process, healthcare organizations can enhance outcomes while elevating the patient experience.

Facilities management

Effective facilities management maintains safe, comfortable, and aesthetically pleasing healthcare environments. Directors oversee housekeeping, sanitation, maintenance, and infrastructure, applying hospitality standards. Effective facilities management is essential for maintaining safe, comfortable, and welcoming healthcare environments. Directors oversee areas such as housekeeping, sanitation, maintenance, and infrastructure, often applying hospitality standards to ensure spaces are both functional and patient-centered. A well-maintained environment not only supports safety and efficiency but also shapes how patients and families perceive the overall quality of care. When healthcare settings are clean, orderly, and thoughtfully designed, they reinforce trust and contribute to a more positive healing experience.

Environmental services

Environmental services (EVS) teams ensure hygienic, safe, and visually appealing healthcare environments. Hospitality-trained EVS professionals might manage cleaning protocols, infection prevention, linen services, and waste management.

Internationally recognized hospitals, such as Sheba Medical Center in Israel, demonstrate the crucial role of EVS in patient satisfaction through meticulous environmental standards and empathetic interactions. Various studies have shown that enhanced EVS practices lead to a significant reduction in hospital-acquired infections.

Robust infection prevention practices, however, extend beyond hospitals. Public spaces—including hotels, restaurants, event venues, airports, cruise ships, and educational institutions—also rely heavily on rigorous EVS protocols to ensure customer safety and satisfaction. Recognizing this need, resources such as *Infection Prevention 101*, a free online course accessible globally (see cloroxpro.com), offer critical foundational training in infection prevention and control. Widely used by professionals across various hospitality segments as well as healthcare settings, this resource emphasizes the universal importance of EVS principles in maintaining safe, welcoming environments.

CAREER SPOTLIGHT
Kamila Sledzinska, senior general manager of environmental services, Mount Carmel Health System (Trinity Health)

Kamila Sledzinska began her career in hospitality management with renowned hotel brands, including Hilton and Marriott. In these roles, she excelled in delivering exceptional guest experiences through meticulous attention to detail, cleanliness, and operational excellence—qualities fundamental to luxury hospitality.

Recognizing the transferability of these skills beyond traditional hospitality settings, Sledzinska transitioned into healthcare, initially as environmental services operations manager at The Ohio State University East Hospital.

After about five years' healthcare operations experience at major medical centers of The Ohio State University's hospitals, Sledzinska advanced to director of environmental services at Mount Carmel St. Ann's, overseeing the entire department. Recently promoted again, she now leads the environmental services and linen departments across all Mount Carmel hospitals in Central Ohio.

Reflecting on her career transition, she says:

> My goal is always to provide the best experience to customers, whether it be in hotel or hospital settings. Positive feedback from patients can determine where future patients seek care. My mindset about a clean environment is that cleanliness promotes healing. I always think about myself as the patient, what would I want? A clean, safe, and welcoming hospital away from the comfort of my home. In addition to serving patients and external customers, we also provide a clean environment to our Clinical Care Teams so they're able to care effectively for patients.

Security and safety

Integrating hospitality principles into security and safety operations creates secure yet welcoming environments that emphasize patient-centered care during critical situations. Hospitality-trained security personnel proactively engage patients and visitors, offer clear and comforting communication, and deliver empathetic emergency responses. This transforms security roles into compassionate, reassuring interactions, significantly enhancing patient confidence and overall satisfaction.

Patient transport services

Patient transport teams deliver personalized, compassionate mobility services, transforming routine transfers into comforting interactions. Hospitality-oriented training equips transport staff with advanced communication skills, empathy, and attentive care practices that can reduce patient anxiety and stress. A supportive approach to this aspect of the healthcare environment significantly contributes to positive patient experiences.

Technology integration

Advanced hospitality-driven technologies enable greater patient comfort, convenience, and engagement. Where available, interactive entertainment systems provide tailored content, telehealth services offer efficient care access, and smart-room technologies empower patients to control their particular environments. These innovations foster patient autonomy and satisfaction and can improve overall well-being and institutional effectiveness, aligning with insights detailed in Chapter 5.

Integration of Pine and Gilmore's experience economy model

Pine and Gilmore's experience economy model (introduced at the beginning of the chapter) focuses on meaningful patient experiences rather than just basic provision of services. The approach prioritizes emotional and psychological care aspects, which enhance patient satisfaction, institutional reputation, and health outcomes. This aligns with hospitality's broader objectives of providing memorable and impactful experiences for guests and patients alike.

Reflect

- Considering Pine and Gilmore's experience economy model, what specific hospitality skills do you believe are most essential to enhancing patient satisfaction in hospitals?
- Provide concrete examples that illustrate how these skills could positively impact patient experiences.

Integrating wellness across hospitality and tourism

Integrating wellness initiatives across hospitality and tourism segments has become increasingly important, driven by evolving guest expectations for holistic health and well-being. Hospitality businesses, including in food and beverage, events, and technology, actively incorporate wellness strategies to differentiate their offerings, enhance guest satisfaction, and foster customer loyalty.

Wellness initiatives in food and beverage operations

Wellness-centric dining has emerged as a key trend within hospitality food and beverage operations. Restaurants and hotels now prioritize nutritious, balanced menus that show dietary information, ingredient sourcing, and health benefits. According to the National Restaurant Association (2024), over 70 percent of customers actively seek healthier menu options when dining out, prompting hotels and restaurants to offer diverse, appealing, and nutritional meals.

Hospitality establishments like Westin Hotels & Resorts emphasize wellness dining through initiatives such as their Eat Well Menu, which features nutrient-rich, balanced dishes designed to nurture guests' energy and well-being. It includes flexible portion sizes, clean sourcing, and dishes such as organic salmon with roasted vegetables, crafted to support guests' wellness.

Additionally, farm-to-table concepts have gained traction, reflecting consumer demand for locally sourced, organic, and sustainably produced ingredients. The Global Wellness Institute (2024a) forecasts that wellness-focused dining will grow at approximately 8 percent annually, as increasing global awareness underscores nutrition's central role in overall wellness.

Wellness-centric events, meetings, and programs

The hospitality events industry continues to evolve by integrating meaningful wellness features, such as quiet zones, mindfulness breaks, nutritious catering, and thoughtful pre-event communication, to enhance attendee well-being. For example, Hilton's *2025 Meetings & Events Trends Report* highlights growing attendee preferences for wellness-enhanced events, including the desire for quiet spaces and mindful pauses. Industry-wide, events that integrate wellness components see approximately 15 percent higher participant satisfaction and repeat attendance rates compared to traditional formats (Eventbrite, 2024). By incorporating wellness practices, hospitality providers increase attendee productivity and satisfaction while positioning themselves as responsive, forward-thinking leaders in an increasingly wellness-conscious marketplace.

Digital wellness innovations, telehealth applications, and personalized wellness apps

Technology can significantly affect wellness experiences within hospitality and tourism, enabling personalized, convenient, and engaging services. Digital wellness innovations range from personalized wellness apps and wearable health technology to telehealth applications that facilitate seamless healthcare access.

Hospitality providers are increasingly incorporating personalized wellness apps, allowing guests to tailor their wellness experiences to individual preferences, fitness goals, and dietary needs. Leading brands such as Four Seasons and Hilton offer customized wellness platforms featuring fitness routines, nutrition advice, mindfulness practices, and sleep improvement techniques. Personalized technology enhances guest satisfaction by making experiences feel more individual. Deloitte (2024) reports that personalization can boost guest satisfaction by as much as 15 percent, emphasizing the high-impact potential of these innovations.

Telehealth applications within hospitality enable guests to access healthcare services remotely, greatly improving convenience and peace of mind. Platforms like Amwell and Teladoc can be integrated into hospitality settings, offering prompt virtual medical consultations. For instance, Amwell's Converge platform supports telehealth access through hotel systems and devices, bringing care directly into guest rooms and building trust through integrated, on-demand healthcare solutions. Additionally, a recent report (TechTarget, 2024) notes that major providers including Amwell and Teladoc Health supply telehealth systems for over 240 hospital settings, indicating their reliability and widespread adoption.

INTERACTIVE EXERCISE
Wellness during conference provision

Imagine you are the general manager at an upscale urban hotel known for hosting high-profile business conferences and events. Your property recently received feedback indicating that guests increasingly value wellness-focused experiences during their stay. You therefore aim to integrate wellness initiatives throughout your operations.

1. Identify three wellness initiatives you would incorporate into your hotel's food and beverage offerings.
2. Design a wellness-focused event or program you would introduce to enhance guest experiences and satisfaction during conferences.
3. Select one technology-driven wellness innovation you believe would significantly benefit your guests. Explain why you chose this innovation and how you would implement it practically within your hotel operations.
4. Discuss how you would measure the effectiveness and guest satisfaction of these wellness initiatives.
5. Summarize your ideas in a brief management report. Clearly outline your steps and how you can measure their effectiveness.

Emerging trends and future directions

As wellness continues to evolve within hospitality and tourism, several emerging trends suggest new directions and opportunities, driven by technological advances, heightened awareness of mental and emotional health, and the rise of micro-wellness in urban environments. Additionally, international innovations are shaping global wellness trends, creating individual and impactful experiences.

REAL-WORLD EXAMPLE:
INDUSTRY SPOTLIGHT Zulal Wellness Resort by Chiva-Som: Pioneering wellness in the Middle East

Zulal Wellness Resort managed by global wellness leader Chiva-Som illustrates groundbreaking wellness innovation by uniquely blending Middle Eastern cultural traditions with advanced technological and personalized solutions. It is redefining the future of wellness hospitality through its innovative, culturally rooted approach in Qatar. As the region's first full-immersion wellness retreat, Zulal uniquely blends traditional Arabic and Islamic medicine with contemporary wellness practices, cutting-edge technology, and sustainable luxury.

Zulal aims to elevate its guests' wellness journeys with AI-driven assessments, custom wellness apps, and techno-enhanced mindfulness and fitness programs. The resort's adoption of genomic testing demonstrates its commitment to bespoke, data-informed wellness.

Emphasizing mental and emotional wellness, Zulal offers extensive programs in mindfulness, meditation, resilience coaching, and stress-management therapies that combine Middle Eastern healing traditions and modern techniques.

The resort also promotes micro-wellness with short rituals, such as mini-meditation sessions and express wellness cleanses, designed for busy professionals and global travelers seeking instant rejuvenation.

According to *Forbes* (Hill, 2024), Zulal stands out as "the first wellbeing retreat of its kind in the Middle East," and offers culturally enriching, full-immersion retreats. Building on its leadership in the region, Zulal was named the Middle East's Leading Retreat at the World Travel Awards in 2024. The resort's prominence at the Arabian Travel Market conference in 2024 demonstrates its leadership in the growing wellness sector in the region.

Reflect

Which emerging wellness trend do you think will have the greatest impact on hospitality careers in the next five years? Why?

Personalized wellness technologies

Personalized wellness technologies, particularly AI-driven platforms and digital solutions, are transforming hospitality and tourism experiences. AI technologies provide tailored recommendations and can enhance guest wellness journeys by adapting in real-time to personal preferences, health goals, and behavior patterns. Personalized wellness technologies, particularly AI-driven platforms and digital solutions, are transforming hospitality and tourism experiences. These tools deliver tailored recommendations that adapt in real time to individual preferences, health goals, and behavior patterns, enhancing each guest's wellness journey.

Hotels such as Hyatt's Miraval and Mandarin Oriental utilize AI-driven wellness applications to help deliver personalized spa treatments, fitness routines, nutritional guidance, and mindfulness activities. Such customized approaches enable personalized and memorable wellness experiences that improve guest engagement and satisfaction.

Emphasis on mental and emotional wellness

The hospitality and tourism industry increasingly recognizes the importance of mental and emotional wellness, prompted by a global rise in mental health awareness. Many hospitality providers are incorporating wellness offerings that address stress management, emotional resilience, and overall mental well-being. Establishments such as Canyon Ranch and Aman Resorts offer comprehensive mental wellness programs, including mindfulness meditation, counseling services, emotional resilience workshops, and stress-relief therapies. According to the Global Wellness Institute (2024b), mental wellness experiences within hospitality are growing at an annual rate of nearly 10 percent, which reflects the strong global demand for emotional and mental well-being initiatives. By addressing mental health needs, hospitality operators understand guest preferences and can position themselves as leaders in holistic wellness.

Micro-wellness and urban hospitality trends

Micro-wellness, characterized by accessible, short wellness experiences, is increasingly popular in urban hospitality settings, catering to busy working people and travelers seeking brief yet impactful wellness rituals. These micro-practices include compact meditation pods, express spa treatments, quick wellness-focused dining options, and short, effective fitness sessions.

Urban hospitality brands like EVEN Hotels and citizenM have successfully introduced micro-wellness amenities into urban guest experiences. Hotels adopting micro-wellness strategies report approximately 15 percent higher guest retention rates, demonstrating the strategy's impact on loyalty and satisfaction (Hospitality Net, 2024). This trend indicates the value of delivering bite-sized wellness experiences in effectively enhancing urban hospitality offerings.

International innovations: Wellness examples from Europe, Asia, and the Middle East

Hospitality providers globally are pioneering wellness innovations often combining cultural authenticity with advanced programming. Lanserhof Tegernsee in Germany merges medical expertise with luxury hospitality under its Medicine 3.0 concept, earning recognition as the World's Best Medical Spa at the World Spa Awards 2024.

Hoshinoya Resorts in Japan features wellness offerings like forest bathing (Shinrin-yoku) and hot spring therapies, drawing on Japanese nature-centric traditions. Ananda in the Indian Himalayas integrates Ayurveda, yoga, and meditation into its luxury retreat experiences, earning global acclaim.

As previously mentioned, the Middle East's wellness hospitality sector includes leaders like Zulal Wellness Resort in Qatar, the region's first "full-immersion wellness destination," recognized as the Middle East's Leading Retreat at the 2024 World Travel Awards. The Middle East is another growth region for wellness tourism.

These global developments point to hospitality's evolving role in blending tradition, personalization, and cultural respect to set new standards in experiential wellness.

Nuanced considerations in wellness and healthcare hospitality

Authenticity in wellness messaging has become critical in hospitality, as customers grow increasingly discerning about wellness claims and initiatives. Clearly and transparently communicating wellness offerings and benefits, coupled with genuinely researched and integrated practices, has never been more essential. The 2024 *Edelman Trust Barometer* underscores this, revealing that 82 percent of global consumers regard trust in a brand's parent company as a decisive factor influencing their purchasing decisions (Edelman, 2024).

Data privacy is another significant consideration, particularly as personalized wellness services increasingly depend on guest data. McKinsey (2023) notes that approximately 85 percent of consumers stress the importance of understanding a company's data privacy policies before they engage with personalized services. Hospitality businesses must therefore prioritize robust data protection measures, transparent privacy policies, and clear communication about data handling practices to maintain guest confidence and regulatory compliance.

Ensuring *culturally responsive* wellness practices is equally essential, as detailed in Chapter 3. Wellness initiatives must support diverse cultural understandings, preferences, and practices. Hospitality providers should collaborate with local cultural experts, adapt wellness programs to align with regional traditions and sensitivities, and foster inclusive environments that honor different cultural perspectives. Incorporating culturally varied wellness practices, such as Ayurveda from India or Hammam rituals from the Middle East, allows hospitality businesses to resonate with global audiences, promote cultural appreciation and enhance guest satisfaction. Culturally responsive wellness programs not only elevate guest experiences; they also offer a competitive advantage in attracting diverse international travelers.

These nuanced considerations—authenticity in wellness messaging, robust data privacy measures, and culturally responsive wellness programs—are essential for hospitality leaders seeking sustainable global success and competitive differentiation. Leaders must proactively integrate these considerations into strategic planning, operations, and guest interactions to build trust, credibility, and loyalty in increasingly diverse global markets.

Core business functions in wellness hospitality

Operations management in wellness hospitality involves coordinating multiple dimensions, including facility upkeep, staff training, guest service delivery, and maintaining wellness-specific standards. Effective operational management ensures seamless guest experiences, supports consistent service quality, and enables scalability of wellness programs, referencing insights discussed in Chapter 4.

Financial strategies and revenue management in wellness hospitality require targeted approaches that account for specialized wellness offerings, seasonal demand fluctuations, and premium pricing strategies. Dynamic pricing, wellness package bundling, and strategic promotional efforts aim to enhance profitability while ensuring value perception among guests.

Within wellness hospitality, maintaining exceptional service quality and robust risk management requires a specialized focus on guest health, safety, and well-being. Critical considerations include ensuring wellness staff hold appropriate professional certifications, effectively managing liability risks in medical spa environments, and upholding meticulous hygiene and sanitation standards to protect guest health. Compliance with relevant regulatory guidelines and proactive risk management practices ensures guest safety, reinforces brand integrity, and supports sustained operational excellence. This specialized focus complements and expands upon the broader risk management and service quality principles detailed in Chapter 5.

Career pathways and industry associations

Wellness hospitality offers diverse and rewarding career opportunities across various segments, including spas, wellness resorts, healthcare hospitality, senior living communities, and corporate wellness programs. Career pathways include roles such as spa director, wellness program manager, patient experience director, dietary services director, and facilities management leader. Each position demands specialized skills in wellness practices, operational excellence, guest service, and business management.

Recommended professional resources and industry associations supporting career development and expertise in wellness hospitality include:

- **International Spa Association (ISPA)**: Provides comprehensive resources, education, and networking opportunities focused on spa and wellness industry professionals.
- **American College of Healthcare Executives (ACHE)**: Offers professional development, certification, and resources tailored to healthcare hospitality leaders.
- **LeadingAge (Senior Living Professionals Association)**: Specializes in advocacy, education, and networking specifically for senior living and wellness professionals.
- **Global Wellness Institute (GWI)**: A leading research organization providing insights, resources, and networking opportunities for professionals across all wellness sectors, emphasizing culturally responsive wellness practices globally.

> **Key takeaways**
>
> - **Historical significance, contemporary growth, and tourism impact**: Wellness hospitality, rooted historically, has evolved significantly, enhancing contemporary hospitality experiences and driving wellness tourism globally.
> - **Segmentation across wellness hospitality**: Wellness segments, such as spas, senior living communities, and healthcare, uniquely integrate wellness principles to enhance guest satisfaction.
> - **Transferable hospitality skills and career opportunities**: Hospitality skills such as exceptional guest service and operational excellence are directly transferable, offering diverse career paths.
> - **Authenticity, technology, privacy, and cultural responsiveness**: Authentic messaging, innovative technology integration, robust privacy measures, and culturally responsive practices are essential for global guest trust and engagement.
> - **Emerging trends and professional development**: Continuous innovation in personalized wellness and mental health, supported by professional industry associations, sustains growth.

Looking ahead

In Chapter 14, "Resilience in the hospitality and tourism industry," you'll explore strategies that strengthen the capacity of hospitality businesses to adapt, respond, and thrive amid challenges, focusing on long-term sustainability and growth through resilient business practices.

References

Bowers, H. & Cheer, J.M. (2022) Yoga tourism: Commodification and Western embracement of Eastern spiritual practice, *Tourism Management Perspectives*, 42.

Britannica (n.d.) Thermae. britannica.com/technology/thermae (archived at https://perma.cc/F5A4-LZ48)

CLIA (Cruise Lines International Association) (2024) *State of the Cruise Industry Report May 2024*. cruising.org/sites/default/files/2025-03/2024%20State%20of%20the%20Cruise%20Industry%20Report_updated%20050824_Web.pdf (archived at https://perma.cc/GZD5-3MY7)

Daniels, C. (2024) Patient experience in 2024: Bridging the gap in the patient care journey, Press Ganey, August 20. info.pressganey.com/press-ganey-blog-healthcare-experience-insights/patient-experience-in-2024-bridging-the-gap (archived at https://perma.cc/9RAU-SKGD)

Deloitte (2023) The value of patient experience: Hospitals with better patient experiences perform better financially. deloitte.com/us/en/Industries/life-sciences-health-care/articles/hospitals-patient-experience.html (archived at https://perma.cc/E5QS-8K3B)

Deloitte (2024) Humanising hospitality through technology. https://www.deloitte.com/uk/en/Industries/consumer/blogs/humanising-hospitality-through-technology.html (archived at https://perma.cc/3RZ7-2Q2R)

Edelman (2024) *2024 Edelman Trust Barometer: Innovation in Peril*. edelman.com/trust/2024/trust-barometer (archived at https://perma.cc/Y25Q-GK3H)

Eventbrite (2024) *2024 Event Trends Report: Wellness Events*. eventbrite.com/blog/event-statistics-ds00 (archived at https://perma.cc/9PSD-36W6)

FoodService Director (2013) Senior living dining programs impact residents' satisfaction, September 30. foodservicedirector.com/senior-dining-meals/senior-living-dining-programs-impact-residents-satisfaction (archived at https://perma.cc/XCR4-L69P)

Fortune Business Insights (2025) *Health and Fitness Club Market Size & Share*. fortunebusinessinsights.com/health-and-fitness-club-market-102849 (archived at https://perma.cc/4KMS-VUXZ)

Global Wellness Institute (2023) *Global Wellness Economy Monitor 2023*. globalwellnessinstitute.org/industry-research/2023-global-wellness-economy-monitor (archived at https://perma.cc/9HZ6-YELU)

Global Wellness Institute (2024a) *2024 Global Wellness Economy Monitor*. globalwellnessinstitute.org/industry-research/2024-global-wellness-economy-monitor (archived at https://perma.cc/S8RG-PWC3)

Global Wellness Institute (2024b) Mental wellness initiative trends for 2024. globalwellnessinstitute.org/global-wellness-institute-blog/2024/04/30/mental-wellness-initiative (archived at https://perma.cc/U274-G6EU)

Grand View Research (2024a). *Medical Spa Market Size, Share & Trends Analysis Report*. grandviewresearch.com/industry-analysis/medical-spa-market (archived at https://perma.cc/23ZX-QBH2)

Grand View Research (2024b). *Spa Services Market Size, Share & Trends Analysis Report*. grandviewresearch.com/industry-analysis/spa-market (archived at https://perma.cc/6XXE-77F3)

Gresham, T. (2025) Why dining matters in senior living—and what's changing, Argentum, April 16. argentum.org/why-dining-matters-in-senior-living-and-whats-changing (archived at https://perma.cc/U3TV-6WLV)

Hill, L.J. (2024) Inside Qatar's most serene retreat, Zulal Wellness Resort by Chiva-Som, *Forbes*, April 29. forbes.com/sites/laurenjadehill/2024/04/29/inside-qatars-most-serene-retreat-zulal-wellness-resort-by-chiva-som (archived at https://perma.cc/22J9-D9W7)

Hilton (2025) *2025 Meetings & Events Trends Report*. stories.hilton.com/releases/hilton-announces-meetings-and-event-trends-report (archived at https://perma.cc/84WQ-MWU2)

Hospitality Net (2024) What wellness features provide the best returns? hospitalitynet.org/opinion/4124696.html (archived at https://perma.cc/HH9R-SGVX)

Johns Hopkins Medicine (2023) Ayurveda. hopkinsmedicine.org/health/wellness-and-prevention/ayurveda (archived at https://perma.cc/9KL8-XJ33)

McCracken, L. (2025) 2025 growth outlook for senior housing & care, National Investment Center for Seniors Housing & Care, January 9. nic.org/blog/2025-growth-outlook-for-senior-housing-care (archived at https://perma.cc/PL9U-UQ7P)

Mcgroarty, B. (2022) New data on wellness tourism: Projected to hit $817 billion this year, $1.3 trillion in 2025, Global Wellness Institute, January 11. globalwellnessinstitute.org/global-wellness-institute-blog/2022/01/11/industry-research-new-data-on-wellness-tourism-projected-to-hit-817-billion-this-year-1-3-trillion-in-2025 (archived at https://perma.cc/8WGG-MA7T)

McKinsey & Company (2023) What is personalization? https://www.mckinsey.com/featured-insights/mckinsey-explainers/what-is-personalization (archived at https://perma.cc/49JM-MKYW)

McKnight's Senior Living (2024) *Resident Engagement in 2024: Opportunities Abound*. www.mcknights.com/marketplace/marketplace-experts/resident-engagement-in-2024-opportunities-abound/ (archived at https://perma.cc/B7CP-A49S)

Nahrstedt, W. (2004) Wellness: A new perspective for leisure centers, health tourism, and spas in Europe. In K. Weiermair & C. Mathies (eds.), *The Tourism and Leisure Industry: Shaping the Future*. New York: Haworth Hospitality Press (pp. 181–198).

National Restaurant Association (2024) *Food and Beverage Trends: 2024 Culinary Forecast*. restaurant.org/education-and-resources/learning-center/food-nutrition/food-and-beverage-trends (archived at https://perma.cc/2BVG-AFXW)

Nelson, J. (2024) NIC MAP vision report projects massive investment shortage in senior housing, *Senior Living News*, June 27. seniorlivingnews.com/nic-map-vision-report-projects-massive-investment-shortage-in-senior-housing (archived at https://perma.cc/H9VC-VSFR)

Newsweek (2024) *World's Best Hospitals 2024*. newsweek.com/rankings/worlds-best-hospitals-2024 (archived at https://perma.cc/4659-BCN3)

Pine, B.J. & Gilmore, J.H. (1999) *The Experience Economy: Work is Theatre & Every Business a Stage*. Boston, MA: Harvard Business School Press.

Precedence Research (2025) *Spa Services Market Size Share and Trends 2025 to 2034*. precedenceresearch.com/spa-services-market (archived at https://perma.cc/Q6EQ-KD2K)

TechTarget (2024) Healthcare organizations plan to expand telespecialty, virtual sitting. techtarget.com/virtualhealthcare/news/366596648/Healthcare-organizations-plan-to-expand-telespecialty-virtual-sitting (archived at https://perma.cc/789U-CLB2)

Veerasoontorn, R., Beise-Zee, R., & Sivayathorn, A. (2011) Service quality as a key driver of medical tourism: the case of Bumrungrad International Hospital in Thailand, *International Journal of Leisure and Tourism Marketing*, 2 (2), 140–158. https://doi.org/10.1504/IJLTM.2011.038886 (archived at https://perma.cc/D2X8-D3CV)

Resilience in hospitality and tourism

14

LEARNING OBJECTIVES

- Define resilience within hospitality and tourism contexts.
- Analyze historical economic challenges and identify resulting opportunities.
- Explain essential principles of effective crisis management.
- Recognize hospitality skills as transferable across industries.
- Identify inclusive, adaptive strategies businesses use to develop resilience.

Introduction

Envision hospitality and tourism as resilient companions who, despite facing numerous challenges, always finds a way to bounce back stronger, wiser, and ready to embrace new opportunities. Whether it's navigating through economic downturns, responding promptly to global health crises, or adapting creatively to unexpected environmental events, resilience is at the heart of this vibrant, ever-evolving industry.

In this final chapter, we'll dive into the fascinating ways resilience shapes hospitality and tourism. You'll journey through historical moments when economic challenges sparked groundbreaking innovation and discover how each setback laid the groundwork for remarkable growth and transformation. You'll gain practical insights into managing crises with confidence and learn proven strategies that businesses use to adapt successfully.

We'll also explore how the skills you've built throughout this book can help you navigate new opportunities and industries. You'll see how these transferable skills empower you to navigate your professional journey with confidence.

Additionally, we'll uncover how hospitality organizations can support and strengthen their teams during challenging times, ensuring everyone moves forward together. You'll explore emerging trends designed to "future-proof" the industry and discover exciting career pathways focused specifically on resilience and crisis management.

As you read through this closing chapter, I encourage you to consider your own growth and experiences and how resilience can support you both personally and professionally. Remember that your ability to anticipate change, adapt proactively, and respond with confidence will position you not just to succeed, but to flourish in your hospitality career—and beyond.

Historical timeline of economic challenges and industry responses

Over the past several decades, the hospitality and tourism industry has faced significant global disruptions, from economic crises to pandemics. But, if there's one thing this industry does well, it's bouncing back. Every challenge has sparked new innovations and creative pivots and provided clear evidence that hospitality is built on resilience.

1970s oil crisis

When fuel prices skyrocketed during the oil crises of the 1970s, travel costs surged sharply, posing significant challenges for the hospitality and tourism industries. Airlines responded with innovation, adopting more fuel-efficient aircraft and implementing aerodynamic improvements, such as winglets and high-bypass-ratio engines, which collectively reduced fuel consumption by approximately 30–50 percent per passenger-kilometer compared to earlier models (ICCT, 2015; Lee et al., 2001). Meanwhile, hospitality providers and tour operators developed budget-friendly travel packages by bundling transportation, lodging, and dining services, helping maintain travel affordability despite economic turmoil.

September 11 attacks (2001)

In the aftermath of 9/11, global travel faced immediate challenges, with air passenger numbers dropping by nearly 30 percent almost overnight (IATA, 2021). Working with federal agencies, US airports implemented extensive investments in advanced security screening technologies, rigorous passenger checks, and expanded security staffing to reassure travelers and support a recovery in travel demand (FAA, 2002). Concurrently, domestic tourism surged as travelers explored destinations closer to home. In Europe, similarly tightened airport security measures initially caused a downturn in air travel but ultimately contributed to renewed traveler confidence and increased intra-European tourism.

Global financial crisis (2007–2009)

When the global economy faced a severe downturn during the 2007–2009 financial crisis, hospitality companies had to adapt rapidly. Technology emerged as a crucial support, with online travel agencies (OTAs) such as Expedia and Booking.com experiencing substantial growth. Expedia, for instance, saw its gross bookings rise by 7 percent in 2009 despite restrained consumer spending (Expedia, 2010). OTAs thrived primarily because they provided cost-effective solutions by streamlining the booking process, eliminating traditional intermediaries, and allowing travelers direct access to discounted rates and last-minute deals. Consumers, increasingly price-conscious due to economic uncertainties, were drawn to the transparency, convenience, and affordability of OTAs.

At the same time, Airbnb's growth was dramatic, climbing from 21,000 bookings in 2009 to over 5 million by 2011 (Airbnb, 2011). The company's appeal, particularly to millennials, was rooted in its financial and experiential advantages. Airbnb rentals presented good-value alternatives to traditional hotels, with spacious villas or apartments suitable for family and group travel, often significantly reducing per-person costs. Additionally, these accommodations provided cooking facilities, thereby enabling travelers to minimize costly dining out. This combination of affordability, flexibility, and unique accommodation options resonated strongly with younger, cost-conscious travelers during and beyond the financial crisis.

Hotels responded by enhancing loyalty programs, launching special offers, and creating bundled packages. These initiatives aimed to retain customer loyalty, provide attractive value propositions, and maintain competitiveness in a cautious spending environment.

Covid-19 pandemic (2020–22)

No recent event impacted hospitality like the Covid-19 pandemic. In 2020 alone, global tourism faced an estimated $1.3 trillion loss in export revenue (UN Tourism, 2025), marking the sector's most severe downturn. In response, touchless technologies rapidly became standard: mobile check-in, digital menus, and contactless payment systems ensured safety and maintained guest confidence.

Hotels introduced "work-from-hotel" and extended-stay packages to serve remote workers, while restaurants pivoted swiftly to takeout and delivery services. The global online food delivery market surged from $115 billion in 2020 to $127 billion in 2021, a growth of roughly 10 percent (Business Wire, 2021).

Innovation and flexibility proved essential. In Southeast Asia, for example, hospitality providers partnered with governments to convert hotels into quarantine accommodations, generating some revenue while supporting critical public health efforts during lockdowns.

> Creativity and innovation are the heartbeat of the restaurant industry. When tastes change, we create new dishes; when the economy softens, we roll out value menus; and when dining rooms closed, we launched curb-side pick-up. Our industry's resilience stems from entrepreneurs and out-of-the-box thinkers who continually devise new solutions to every challenge.
>
> —Rick Postle, *restaurant entrepreneur*

Trade wars and political shifts (2018 onward)

Recent geopolitical tensions, including the US–China trade war and Brexit, disrupted global supply chains and introduced uncertainty into international travel. By late 2019, tariffs had impacted approximately $550 billion in Chinese goods, prompting reciprocal tariffs from China on US products (Congressional Research Service, 2019; Reuters, 2019). In response, hospitality and tourism businesses adapted by diversifying supply chains, increasing local sourcing, and placing greater emphasis on domestic travel options. These shifts developed the industry's commitment to sustainability, operational agility, and resilience, helping businesses effectively navigate ongoing geopolitical uncertainties while meeting evolving traveler preferences.

Recent trends and ongoing economic uncertainty

As the hospitality and tourism industry recovers, challenges such as inflation, labor shortages, and supply chain disruptions continue to reshape operations globally. In response, businesses across the sector are rethinking their models by significantly investing in employee training, prioritizing retention, and embedding sustainability into their core strategies.

Sustainability-focused travel has experienced substantial growth, with strong consumer demand underscoring a clear preference for responsible, ethical, and values-driven hospitality experiences. Booking.com's 2023 *Sustainable Travel Report* (GSTC, 2023) found that 76 percent of travelers say they intend to travel more sustainably in the coming year, reflecting the growing mainstream appeal of sustainable tourism, and many global travelers are willing to pay a premium for environmentally friendly accommodations, underscoring the commercial viability of sustainable practices. Younger travelers, in particular, are driving this shift, with Gen Z and millennials frequently identified as the most likely to prioritize eco-friendly accommodations and experiences, emphasizing sustainability's critical role in shaping the future of hospitality and tourism.

Labor challenges have proven particularly persistent across both hospitality and tourism sectors worldwide. According to the World Travel & Tourism Council (WTTC, 2024), global labor shortages in travel and tourism remained at 10 percent below pre-pandemic levels in early 2024, with key shortages noted in positions such as tour guides, airline crew, and hotel operations staff. To address this, businesses raised wages (the American Hotel & Lodging Association (AHLA, 2023) noted an average 12 percent wage increase), extended employee benefits, provided flexible scheduling, and introduced comprehensive professional development initiatives. Industry-wide, there has been a notable rise in partnerships with educational institutions and government training programs aimed at cultivating a more robust, skilled workforce prepared to meet evolving customer expectations and industry demands.

REAL-WORLD EXAMPLE:
INDUSTRY SPOTLIGHT Hilton's commitment to workforce excellence

Hilton Worldwide, consistently ranked among the top global workplaces, stands as a leading example of strategic workforce management and employee development. Recognized as the World's Best Workplace in 2024 by Great Place to Work, Hilton emphasizes comprehensive employee training, inclusive workplace culture, and meaningful career growth opportunities. A cornerstone of Hilton's workforce strategy is its robust tuition reimbursement program, which provides employees with substantial financial support toward degrees from traditional colleges and universities. Complemented by additional offerings through partnerships such as with Guild Education, Hilton covers a significant portion of tuition costs, books, and fees, encouraging employees to pursue higher education and professional certifications. The company also proactively addresses labor shortages through competitive compensation, enhanced benefit packages, and flexible scheduling, making Hilton a model of how investing in education and employee well-being can drive sustained success and loyalty.

Reflect

Which historical challenge or industry response resonates most strongly with you, and why?

- Reflect on how specific examples of innovation, adaptability, or leadership shaped the industry's recovery during that time.
- How might these lessons influence your approach and mindset as you prepare for your career in hospitality and tourism?

Crisis management and recovery

Navigating crises successfully is vital for hospitality businesses, and the industry offers many inspiring examples of how leaders have responded with empathy, agility, and innovation. Imagine managing a hotel during a hurricane or leading a restaurant through sudden supply chain disruptions. What strategies might you use to ensure safety, continuity, and guest trust?

When Hurricane Irma struck the US Virgin Islands in September 2017, Marriott famously chartered a private ferry to evacuate about 600 stranded guests from its St. Thomas properties to Puerto Rico, demonstrating a commitment to guest safety during a crisis (Solomon, 2017). Staff worked under intense pressure to coordinate this evacuation, and Marriott's leadership communicated openly with guests throughout the process, maintaining transparency and prioritizing safety.

In the restaurant sector, Chipotle introduced Chipotlanes—dedicated drive-through lanes for mobile orders—boosting digital sales to over 46 percent of total food and beverage revenue by the end of 2020, significantly higher than the previous year's 10.9 percent (Chipotle, 2021). This innovation improved convenience and safety for customers and helped the brand stay competitive and resilient during a major public health crisis. That same spirit of experimentation was summed up beautifully by restaurateur Rick Postle, quoted earlier.

Businesses worldwide demonstrated similar creativity. Singapore Airlines launched several innovative customer engagement strategies while flights were grounded. One of its most notable initiatives was Restaurant A380 @ Changi, which transformed a grounded Airbus A380 into a pop-up dining experience. The concept resonated widely, with over 900 seats selling out in just 30 minutes (Gene, 2020). The airline also introduced Discover Your Singapore Airlines, a behind-the-scenes experience offering public access to flight simulators, cabin-crew training sessions, and more, fostering brand loyalty and aiming to keep the company top-of-mind during a prolonged crisis.

> **THINK LIKE A MANAGER**
>
> A winter storm has caused power outages and flight cancellations. Guests are stranded, staff are limited, and locals are seeking shelter at your hotel. Identify your top three priorities to ensure guest safety and business continuity during the first 24 hours of the crisis.

Theoretical foundation: Faulkner's tourism disaster management framework

Hospitality professionals are likely to encounter unexpected challenges at some point, from economic downturns to natural disasters or global disruptions. To confidently navigate disruptions, it's beneficial to have a structured approach. Faulkner's (2001) tourism disaster management framework provides a practical guide for hospitality and tourism businesses to respond effectively and emerge stronger.

The framework includes six critical stages, guiding organizations systematically through a crisis. Let's explore each stage with real-world examples.

1. Preparation

Preparation involves proactively assessing risks, establishing contingency plans, and regularly training your team to respond swiftly and confidently in a crisis. By investing in preparation, businesses significantly reduce response times and protect guests and staff. For example, Hyatt regularly conducts crisis management simulations and emergency preparedness training across its properties, enabling immediate and effective responses during real crises.

2. Early warning

Early warning means recognizing initial indicators of potential disruptions and swiftly activating predetermined responses. This proactive vigilance helps organizations mitigate the severity of potential crises and maintain stakeholder confidence. At the onset of Covid-19, Hilton swiftly introduced robust safety protocols and used its Hilton Honors app for clear, real-time communication. This helped maintain guest trust and facilitated recovery ahead of competitors.

3. Immediate response

Immediate response requires rapid, coordinated actions to manage the initial impacts of a crisis and ensure stakeholder safety and operational continuity. Effective, immediate responses help stabilize situations and minimize long-term damage.

Following the terrible events of September 11, global air travel immediately halted, leaving thousands stranded. Marriott hotels in affected areas promptly provided shelter, resources, and compassionate assistance to travelers. The Marriott Marquis in Times Square, for example, accommodated hundreds of stranded guests, demonstrating timely responsiveness during profound uncertainty.

4. Recovery efforts

Recovery efforts focus on implementing short-term solutions to quickly restore critical operations and regain guest confidence. Businesses that can rapidly adapt and clearly communicate their recovery strategies generally experience shorter disruptions and stronger customer loyalty. In response to the dramatic decline in air travel after 9/11 (approximately a 30 percent drop in air passenger traffic globally (IATA, 2021))—airlines swiftly strengthened security protocols, including toughened cockpit doors, extensive passenger screenings, and detailed security audits in attempts to restore passenger confidence. Southwest Airlines, in particular, was recognized for quickly implementing and clearly communicating enhanced safety measures, which helped regain traveler trust and enabled the airline to retain higher passenger volumes compared to industry averages.

5. Long-term recovery

Long-term recovery involves strategically adapting to new market conditions after a crisis. Successful organizations reassess their business models, operational strategies, and customer preferences to position themselves for sustained growth. For example, during the Covid pandemic, Airbnb shifted from primarily short-term rental accommodations to longer stays, particularly catering to remote workers. By mid-2020, stays of 28 days or more became their fastest-growing category, more than doubling since 2019, and making up nearly 50 percent of weekly bookings in early 2021 (Airbnb, 2020; Reinhold and Dolnicar, 2021). This pivot enabled Airbnb to tap into the remote-work trend and provided a new revenue stream during uncertain times.

6. Learning and improvement

Learning and improvement involve reviewing crisis responses, identifying key lessons, and strengthening future preparedness. Organizations that institutionalize these lessons tend to emerge more resilient. For example, Starbucks significantly enhanced its employee support programs following Covid-19. In 2020, the company introduced up to 20 free therapy sessions per year for US employees and their eligible family members, and trained managers to better recognize and support employee mental-health needs. These initiatives underscore the growing recognition of well-being investments in supporting staff retention (Fast Company, 2020).

> **THINK LIKE A MANAGER**
>
> Your hotel is experiencing flooding. Using Faulkner's crisis management model, briefly identify:
>
> - One preparedness action
> - An early warning indicator
> - Your immediate priority
> - A step toward recovery
> - A long-term adaptation strategy
> - One improvement for future crises
>
> Which stage presents the greatest challenge, and how might you address it?

Applying crisis management principles to your career

Think of your career as an exciting journey; one that, like hospitality itself, may encounter occasional unexpected twists and turns. Just as industry leaders adapt to disruption, you can apply structured crisis management tools to your own career path. Doing so ensures that, rather than being caught off guard, you're prepared, resilient, and able to thrive through any circumstance.

Preparation: Invest in yourself

Proactively invest in your own growth. Attend industry workshops, seek additional certifications, or expand your skills through internships or volunteering. Think of these activities as "career insurance" that helps you stay valuable, relevant, and ready for new opportunities, even if the industry faces temporary setbacks.

Early warning: Stay alert to change

Keep your eyes and ears open for subtle shifts within your workplace, industry, or personal interests. Rather than worrying at the first sign of change, treat it as an opportunity. For example, if you notice growing trends toward sustainability, proactively explore related courses or projects. Staying aware helps you stay ahead.

Immediate adaptation: Demonstrate adaptability

When unexpected disruptions occur, such as during Covid, your ability to adapt swiftly makes you invaluable. Consider how you can demonstrate adaptability within your current role or organization. For example, if you work in guest services and travel declines, proactively suggest creative ways to enhance guest experiences locally or virtually. If your restaurant faces reduced dining capacity, recommend innovative ideas like expanded takeout services, outdoor dining solutions, or meal kits. Event planners could swiftly pivot by organizing virtual or hybrid events, maintaining engagement without compromising health and safety. By actively proposing solutions, staying flexible, and identifying new opportunities right where you are, you demonstrate value and resilience, positioning yourself for continued growth and leadership within hospitality and tourism.

Short-term recovery: Step up and add value

Short-term recovery focuses on quickly responding to immediate challenges by proactively adapting within your current role or organization. When disruptions occur, step up by proposing solutions, taking initiative, or offering your skills in new ways. For example, if travel demand decreases unexpectedly, suggest creative local experiences or virtual engagements for guests. If dining capacities reduce, consider innovative takeout or outdoor dining options. By demonstrating immediate adaptability, you showcase value, resilience, and leadership, enhancing your professional visibility and opportunities.

Strategic career planning: Plan with purpose

Strategic career planning involves thoughtfully aligning your long-term career direction with evolving industry dynamics. Regularly reassess your professional objectives and remain open to integrating new interests or skills developed during disruptions. For instance, if recent trends or challenges have sparked your interest in wellness tourism, sustainable hospitality practices, or technology-driven services, proactively seek relevant training, certifications, or mentorships. Collaborate on innovative projects, participate in industry workshops, or engage with professional networks to steer your career purposefully toward emerging growth areas. This intentional approach positions you strategically, supporting your sustained adaptability and professional success in hospitality and tourism.

Learning and improvement: Tell your story

Regularly reflect on your professional experiences, especially challenging situations, and clearly identify what you've learned. Rather than simply listing tasks on your résumé, LinkedIn profile, or in job interviews, thoughtfully articulate the impact of your actions, explaining how you overcame obstacles, adapted creatively, or contributed to positive outcomes. Sharing these stories demonstrates resilience and positions you as a proactive, growth-oriented professional.

Additionally, cultivate your resilience by consistently investing in professional relationships and ongoing learning opportunities. Engage actively in industry networks, seek out mentorship, and participate in professional communities or workshops. These intentional actions help you anticipate and navigate change and build a robust, adaptable career that can thrive amid disruption.

Building your own resilient career network

In hospitality, professional relationships play a critical role in both your immediate success and long-term career resilience. Whether you're navigating a new opportunity or responding to a challenge, the strength and diversity of your network can influence how quickly and effectively you move forward. Career resilience is not just about reacting well to disruption—it's about proactively cultivating a professional support system. These relationships typically fall into three categories: operational, personal, and strategic. Understanding the role each plays can help you build a network that supports your goals, growth, and adaptability:

> The evolving relationship between employers and employees offers new opportunities. Rather than relying on a single organization, employees today shape their own careers by building and nurturing strong professional networks. Those who actively engage in cultivating these connections will find greater career flexibility, rewarding opportunities, and long-term growth.
>
> —*Dr. Erik Porfeli, professor and department chair, human sciences*

Operational relationships: Your immediate support system

Operational relationships include the colleagues, supervisors, vendors, and suppliers who support your daily responsibilities. These connections are often your go-to contacts for service delivery, scheduling, logistics, and immediate problem-solving. For example, if you're managing a catering event and suddenly face an equipment shortage, having a well-established relationship with a local vendor or partner venue can help you resolve the issue quickly and keep the event on track.

These relationships contribute to smoother operations, minimize disruptions, and serve as a first line of defense during unexpected challenges. Developing operational relationships requires professionalism, clear communication, and mutual trust—qualities that are cultivated by showing appreciation, being dependable, and following through on commitments.

Personal relationships: Your trusted mentors and advisors

Personal relationships play an important role in long-term career resilience by offering emotional support, career guidance, and perspective during times of transition or uncertainty. These connections might include professors, internship supervisors, managers, or colleagues who have taken an interest in your growth. For instance, if you're considering a move from hotel operations to event management, a trusted mentor can help you evaluate your strengths, explore new roles, and connect with relevant industry contacts.

These relationships are built on mutual respect and care, and they thrive with ongoing communication. Keeping mentors updated on your progress, seeking their advice, and expressing gratitude not only strengthens your support network, it also reinforces your confidence during career pivots.

Strategic relationships: Your window to the future

Strategic relationships expand your awareness of emerging trends, new opportunities, and future-focused career pathways. These include connections made through alumni networks, industry associations, guest speakers, or leaders in fields you're exploring. Unlike operational or personal contacts, strategic relationships may not be involved in your day-to-day work, but they can open doors to new roles, industries, or innovations. For example, attending a conference and engaging in a conversation with a sustainability leader might inspire you to pursue certification in green operations, aligning your career with one of the industry's most in-demand growth areas.

Building strategic relationships requires initiative, curiosity, and thoughtful follow-up. Staying engaged with these contacts helps you remain adaptable, informed, and well-positioned to lead through change.

> **Reflect**
>
> Think about someone in your life who fits into each of the three relationship categories: operational, personal, and strategic.
>
> - How has each relationship supported your growth so far?
> - Are there areas where you could expand or strengthen your network to better support your career goals?

> **INTERACTIVE EXERCISE**
> Building your career crisis management plan
>
> Hospitality leaders plan for disruption—you can too. Drawing up a personal crisis management plan empowers you to stay adaptable and confident through career challenges.
>
> 1 **Identify potential career "crises"**
>   o Think of two realistic scenarios that could disrupt or redirect your planned career path. Examples might include:

- An economic downturn affecting job opportunities
- A personal change requiring relocation or career adjustment
- Technological advances transforming your chosen industry segment

2 **Your immediate response**
   o For each scenario, outline a brief action plan using the following prompts:
   - *Preparation*: What steps can you take now (certifications, networking, upskilling, and so on) to increase your resilience?
   - *Communication*: Who in your personal or professional network would you reach out to first? Why?
   - *Short-term adaptation*: What immediate changes might you make to your strategy to remain relevant and forward-moving?

3 **Long-term recovery and growth**
   o Identify one strategic move you could take after overcoming the disruption. Would you:
   - Pursue a new credential?
   - Explore a different industry segment?
   - Seek mentorship?

4 **Personal insights**
   o Consider the following:
   - What surprised or challenged you as you worked through this exercise?
   - How has this process shaped your understanding of career resilience?

Sustainable tourism and resilience

As explored in Chapter 9, sustainable tourism isn't just ethical—it's a strategic business tool that enhances resilience in the face of economic, environmental, and social disruptions. Organizations that integrate sustainability, through energy efficiency, resource management, waste reduction, and community engagement, are better equipped to navigate challenges like resource shortages or shifting market demands.

A compelling example is Delta Air Lines. In February 2020, Delta announced a $1 billion investment over 10 years to achieve carbon neutrality, emphasizing fleet modernization, improved operational efficiency, and carbon offset initiatives (Delta Air Lines, 2020). By 2023, it had progressed by transitioning to more fuel-efficient aircraft, reducing onboard single-use plastics, and collaborating with environmental partners—actions detailed in its 2024 *Delta Difference* report. Additionally, global consumer research indicates that over 50 percent of travelers now consistently seek out sustainable options when booking travel, and around 75 percent indicate willingness to pay a premium for sustainable travel choices (Trip.com, 2024).

During the Covid pandemic, Delta's existing focus on efficiency and brand trust allowed it to manage costs effectively and maintain customer loyalty, which demonstrates how sustainability strategies can directly support recovery and strengthen brand positioning during crises. For students and early-career professionals, this example underlines how adopting sustainable practices, such as minimizing waste, enhancing energy efficiency, and engaging with local communities, can reinforce their operational value and preparedness in any hospitality or tourism role.

Building resilient businesses

Resilient organizations don't just react to crisis—they prepare for it, adapt quickly, and emerge stronger. This kind of resilience is built through strategic leadership, workforce investment, diversified operations, technological agility, and strong community partnerships. Let's take a closer look at how these elements work together.

Cultivating adaptive and inclusive leadership

Effective hospitality leaders demonstrate flexibility, empathy, and cultural intelligence—key qualities that enable teams to respond adeptly to evolving challenges and guest expectations. Hyatt Hotels exemplifies this leadership approach through structured global training programs under its World of Care initiative. These programs incorporate inclusive leadership workshops, modules on emotional and cultural intelligence, and crisis preparedness simulations, designed to empower employees at all levels to make decisions, solve problems, and lead with empathy across diverse environments. This investment in leadership development lays the groundwork for agile, responsive operations in times of both challenge and opportunity.

Strategic workforce development and retention

A strong workforce is a vital asset during crises. Investing in employee development not only builds skills; it fosters loyalty and long-term capacity. The Emirates Group exemplifies this through its dedicated training arm, Emirates Aviation University (EAU), which offers high-quality education even amid uncertainty. In January 2024, EAU celebrated a graduating cohort of 302 aviation leaders, highlighting its commitment to preparing employees with relevant industry skills. The university graduates maintain impressive employability, with approximately 84 percent employed within six months, demonstrating the effectiveness of its structured internships, diploma programs, and academic degrees that directly connect with Emirates operations (EAU, 2023).

According to Emirates' *Annual Report 2022–2023*, the group continued to invest heavily in learning and development across both Emirates and dnata, supporting workforce resilience and maintaining operational momentum during economic fluctuations (Emirates, 2023). By cultivating internal talent pipelines, organizations like Emirates ensure they can respond to disruptions without losing critical skills or momentum.

Diversification and revenue stability

Diversified operations can be a safety net when one segment of the business is impacted. TUI Group operates across multiple segments, including tours, airlines, cruises, and hotels, enabling it to stabilize revenue by shifting focus when specific markets fluctuate.

Digital transformation and technological agility

These technologies can prove invaluable for safety and operational efficiency during global disruptions. Royal Caribbean Cruises, for example, accelerated its digital transformation by introducing RFID-enabled wearables (WOW Bands) and enhancing its mobile app to streamline key operations including contactless check-in, mobile room access, onboard purchases, and health-related features.

Proactive risk management and contingency planning

Anticipating potential risks, and developing strategies to address them, can mean the difference between survival and success. Qantas Airways exemplifies proactive risk management through strategic scenario planning and operational agility. When international travel halted during Covid, the airline swiftly rerouted resources to domestic flights and cargo operations, maintaining some revenues and demonstrating operational resilience.

Creating a culture of continuous innovation

Organizations that can view disruption as an opportunity often emerge stronger. Disney Parks, for example, continuously invest in immersive experiences, digital enhancements like interactive attractions, and sustainability initiatives such as waste reduction and energy efficiency. These proactive innovations delight guests, match evolving consumer values, and create operational agility. In dynamic environments, innovation isn't just a competitive advantage—it's a core strategy for resilience.

Strengthening community and stakeholder relationships

Community relationships provide critical support during times of uncertainty. G Adventures, a global adventure travel company known for immersive, small-group tours emphasizing responsible tourism, actively partners with local communities to invest in sustainable travel and regional development. Through community-centered initiatives, such as locally-owned accommodations, authentic cultural experiences, and community-led tourism projects, G Adventures builds lasting relationships, mutual trust, and operational resilience. This approach helps the company effectively navigate disruptions by strengthening community ties and maintaining traveler loyalty and trust.

Reflect

- Which of the resilience-building strategies highlighted in this section—adaptive leadership, workforce development, diversification, technology, innovation, risk management, or community partnerships—resonates most with your career goals?
- What is one action you could take now or in the near future to begin strengthening that area in your own career journey?

Career mobility: The hospitality and tourism subway map

Having explored how resilience shapes the hospitality and tourism industry and your career, let's visualize how your skills and experiences lay out versatile career pathways within and beyond hospitality and tourism.

Imagine your hospitality and tourism career as an intricate subway map—colorful, interconnected, and filled with exciting stops and transfers. Throughout your educational journey, you've gained essential skills, specialized knowledge, and practical experiences. Like navigating a subway system, your hospitality and tourism career offers numerous opportunities for smooth transitions from one professional path to another. Your hospitality and tourism skills act as your "unlimited pass," granting access to diverse career routes, ensuring adaptability and resilience throughout your professional life.

Central station: The core of your hospitality skills

At the heart of your hospitality and tourism subway map lies your central station, which houses the essential skills and attributes explored in Chapter 2:

- **Empathy and exceptional guest service:** Understanding guests' needs to deliver personalized, memorable experiences.
- **Effective communication:** Clearly conveying ideas for diverse groups and individuals.
- **Adaptability:** Quickly adjusting to new scenarios, guest expectations, and challenges.
- **Operational excellence:** Mastering your role and responsibilities, delivering efficiently on the basics, and brilliantly managing teams, resources, and processes.
- **Cultural intelligence:** Skillfully navigating cultural diversity (Chapter 3).

These foundational competencies enable smooth career transitions across sectors.

Navigating hospitality and tourism subway lines: Practical career pathways

Each chapter in this book has explored a different segment of the hospitality and tourism industry, each with unique skills that connect across roles and sectors like subway lines. This section explores just a few of the many directions in which hospitality can lead you.

One possible route starts in food and beverage and leads into healthcare. A hotel food-and-beverage manager, for example, might transition into a senior living community or healthcare hospitality setting, using their operational expertise and guest service background to enhance patient satisfaction. Such roles, like patient experience coordinator or dining operations manager, rely on the same attention to detail, empathy, and logistics you've developed in hospitality and tourism.

CAREER SPOTLIGHT

Kamila Sledzinska, senior general manager of environmental services, Trinity Health

As we saw in Chapter 13, Kamila Sledzinska began her career in hospitality operations at Hilton and Marriott, where she built expertise in service excellence and team leadership. Today, she applies those same skills in healthcare, leading environmental services for Trinity Health; an essential function that shapes patient well-being and experience. She notes:

> Hospitality taught me that service is about care, not context... My hospitality foundation didn't just transfer—it elevated my ability to lead in healthcare.

Sledzinska's journey is a powerful reminder that your career can take many turns, and the skills you gain in hospitality will continue to serve you in settings far beyond traditional hotels or restaurants.

Another route might take you from the events industry into corporate event management. Event planning skills such as vendor negotiation, cross-cultural communication, and logistics management transfer well into roles with professional associations, large-scale meetings, or internal corporate events. The ability to create memorable experiences is valued far beyond the hospitality sector.

Tourism is another stop along the way, with potential to cross into destination marketing and brand strategy. Graduates with a strong foundation in cultural intelligence and tourism trends often find themselves leading campaigns that promote regional travel, cultural experiences, or sustainability-focused tourism initiatives.

The lodging industry can also take you into luxury customer service and private client experiences. Managers skilled in guest satisfaction and relationship-building might move into managing high-end private clubs or residential communities, where personalized service is everything.

Or you might shift from food and beverage into supply chain roles, such as procurement or inventory management, especially if you've developed expertise in vendor relationships and operational efficiency. These roles are critical to maintaining consistency, quality, and cost control across brands and regions.

Finally, entertainment and recreation roles can lead naturally into experiential marketing. An entertainment manager who designs engaging, culturally relevant programs for guests can transfer those talents to creating branded experiences, festivals, or promotional events across industries.

CAREER TIP
Your skills travel well

Don't limit yourself to one "track." The hospitality industry thrives on versatility. Your skills are valuable in places you may not have considered yet. Many professionals move between lodging, events, tourism, and even into fields like wellness, healthcare, or corporate services. Your career map is yours to build, and you have an unlimited pass.

Your universal transfer ticket: Empathy and exceptional guest service

Two particular competencies consistently emerge—empathy and exceptional guest service. These skills serve as your universal "transfer ticket," helping you navigate transitions between industries and career phases. By proactively delivering personalized experiences and prioritizing genuine connections, you increase your ability to adapt, build trust, and succeed in new professional settings.

Reflect

- Where have empathy or guest service made a difference in your work, class, or internship experience?
- How might those same skills serve you in a new setting?

Reinforcing your hospitality career mobility

Reflecting on your hospitality journey reveals endless opportunities extending beyond traditional boundaries. Each chapter of this book has discussed insights and skills, including empathy, guest service, adaptability, and cultural intelligence, that empower your long-term professional resilience. In hospitality, career possibilities are dynamic and continuously expanding, ensuring you remain adaptable and successful throughout your professional journey.

INTERACTIVE EXERCISE
Creating your personal hospitality subway map

Use this activity to map out how your skills, interests, and goals intersect across the hospitality industry, and how you can navigate your next steps with purpose and flexibility.

1 **Central station—your core skills**: List your top three transferable skills developed through your hospitality experience so far. These might include communication, adaptability, cultural intelligence, or service excellence.

2 **Career lines—exploring new directions**: Choose two career paths outside your original plan that align with your core skills and spark your interest. These might come from chapters you hadn't considered before, such as managed services, wellness hospitality, or experiential marketing.

> 3. **Career transfers—charting your route**: Outline a few realistic steps to help you transition toward these new opportunities. Think about what training, certifications, internships, or networking connections could support your journey.
> 4. **Making the connection**: How do these new directions relate to what you've learned in this course or read in earlier chapters? Identify key moments, skills, or stories that inspired you to broaden your career map.

Inclusive strategies for workplace resilience

As we've explored throughout this chapter, building a resilient hospitality business requires intentional planning and adaptability. Just as critical, however, is ensuring that resilience strategies include everyone. Inclusive practices help organizations respond more effectively to disruptions, foster stronger team cohesion, and thus promote long-term sustainability.

Inclusive resilience means more than policy—it involves culturally responsive communication, equitable access to support and training, flexible operations, and a commitment to listening and learning from diverse perspectives. The following strategies draw on global examples designed to support a wide range of employees and communities; not just during crises, but as part of everyday organizational success.

Clear, multilingual communication

Effective multilingual communication, including translated signage, training materials, and operations briefings, is essential in culturally diverse hospitality and tourism environments. Research indicates that staff proficiency in foreign languages significantly enhances service quality and reduces cultural misunderstandings, leading to better guest satisfaction (Tziora et al., 2016). Additionally, industry analysis highlights that fluency in multiple languages (particularly Spanish, German, French, Mandarin, or Arabic) adds considerable value to hospitality professionals, improving employability and providing a competitive edge in global operations (Lobertréau, 2023).

Equitable access to training, development, and advancement

Ensuring fair access to professional development ensures diverse talent can thrive, supporting both individual growth and organizational resilience. Scandinavian Airlines, for example, actively empowers women through targeted Employee Inclusion Groups, comprehensive leadership training, and visible representation in operational roles, such as all-female flight crews. Marriott strengthens equitable access by creating defined pathways to advancement through structured mentorships, scholarships, and internships at the Marriott Sorenson Center for Hospitality Leadership, developed in partnership with Howard University. These initiatives support students from underrepresented backgrounds, directly preparing them for future leadership within hospitality.

These approaches demonstrate how deliberate investments in equitable training, development, and clear pathways for career progression can foster inclusive, resilient workplaces.

Inclusive well-being support

Supporting employee well-being across diverse cultural and personal needs strengthens morale and performance. Disney offers wellness initiatives such as health coaching, fitness discounts, mental-health resources, and educational wellness materials for its employees. These programs are available through the company's global well-being platform, which emphasizes access to counseling, wellness tools, and stress-management support. By providing these accessible resources, Disney enhances overall employee health and creates a workplace culture that values well-being and inclusivity.

Flexible operational policies

Flexibility in work schedules, remote access, and leave policies recognizes that employees' lives and responsibilities vary widely. Research indicates that offering flexible work practices improves perceptions of workplace support, particularly for employees with caregiving responsibilities.

Feedback-driven leadership

Inclusive leadership requires consistent feedback and follow-through. Grupo Xcaret, a family-owned hospitality and leisure group based in Mexico, operates integrated parks, hotels, and tours built around Mexican culture and ecological preservation. Through its comprehensive Xustainability model, the company embeds feedback-driven leadership in its core operations, continuously evaluating and improving its sustainability efforts to align with both community and employee needs.

The *2021 Xustainability Report* highlights that Grupo Xcaret instituted an evaluation and continuous improvement system allowing coworkers, community partners, and guests to offer feedback on environmental, cultural, and social practices. This feedback loop fuels changes such as enhanced biodiversity programs, improved cultural workshops, and strengthened safety protocols, all overseen by cross-functional leadership teams. By maintaining these feedback mechanisms, Xcaret ensures its management approaches are responsive, inclusive, and aligned with internal and external stakeholder expectations; modeling effective, feedback-driven leadership.

Community partnerships

Resilience extends beyond operations. Organizations that invest in communities build social capital and long-term trust. The Hilton Global Foundation, for instance, has funded local initiatives globally since 2019, supporting over 211,000 learning and career opportunities, distributing 11.6 million meals, and providing access to clean water for 241,000 people (Hilton Global Foundation, 2024). Its Unlocking Doors program, in partnership with NGOs including DC Central Kitchen, has trained over 2,300 individuals facing homelessness or incarceration, enabling careers in hospitality and showing how long-term community engagement enhances resilience and builds local workforce capacity.

INTERACTIVE EXERCISE

Developing inclusive resilience during disruption

You're the HR manager at a regional hospitality group with properties in multiple countries. A recent global disruption (a public health emergency or political instability) has affected operations in several locations. Your leadership team wants to support staff equitably but needs help identifying strategies that reflect cultural differences, language needs, and varied access to resources.

1. Select three inclusive strategies (from the earlier list) that you would prioritize across the company.
2. Tailor your plan to meet the diverse needs of teams in different regions (such as urban vs. rural, multilingual vs. single-language, high digital access vs. limited).
3. Communicate your approach to senior leadership. How would these strategies contribute to both short-term support and long-term organizational resilience?

Reinforcing inclusive workplace resilience

Inclusive resilience isn't simply a set of strategies—it's a mindset prioritizing equity, empathy, and adaptability. By genuinely integrating inclusivity into workplace practices, hospitality organizations effectively navigate disruptions and build cohesive, engaged, and highly resilient teams, which should ensure sustained success in a rapidly changing world.

Emerging trends in hospitality and tourism: Personalization, values, and flexibility

As hospitality and tourism continue to evolve amid rapid global changes, several key trends are emerging, each emphasizing personalization, purpose, and flexibility in service design and delivery. Understanding these evolving areas equips you, as a future hospitality professional, to anticipate shifts, innovate creatively, and stay agile in an increasingly complex environment.

Trend 1: Hyper-personalized guest experiences through AI and technology

AI and advanced technologies are transforming how hospitality providers anticipate and meet guest needs. Tools such as predictive analytics, chatbots, and digital concierge platforms enable efficient, tailored service that can enhance convenience and drive engagement. A striking example is Japan's Henn-na Hotel, the world's first robot-staffed hotel, where AI-powered robots handle check-ins, concierge tasks, and room personalization (Söderberg Granström et al., 2023).

Beyond physical automation, generative AI tools like ChatGPT are reshaping digital guest interactions. A recent study reveals that integrating ChatGPT into service workflows improves staff efficiency, bridges language barriers, and enhances overall guest satisfaction, with employees reporting better productivity and service delivery (Limna and Kraiwanit, 2023). This illustrates how AI can support real-time responses and personalized recommendations.

Another recent analysis further outlines how AI-driven digital concierges—leveraging natural language processing and behavioral insights—can anticipate guest needs and suggest tailored experiences, while still preserving authentic human engagement (Liu et al., 2024).

Together, these real-world and academic examples show how AI and ChatGPT tools are enhancing guest experiences, without losing sight of the personal, human-focused service central to hospitality (as discussed in Chapter 2).

Global snapshot: Approaches to AI in hospitality vary by region

The use of AI in hospitality varies widely. In Japan, robots have taken center stage in guest service. In contrast, hotels in the UK often focus on behind-the-scenes automation, such as AI-driven CRM systems and mobile check-in, while preserving high-touch guest experiences. Meanwhile, in the US, the trend leans toward mobile-first personalization and self-service convenience over robotic staffing. These regional differences reflect local labor markets, service expectations, and brand positioning strategies.

Trend 2: Expanding sustainability: Social, economic, and cultural dimensions

Sustainability is no longer limited to environmental practices—it now encompasses broader commitments to social equity, economic fairness, and cultural inclusion. Travelers increasingly seek purpose-driven experiences that align with their values, prompting hospitality businesses to adopt more holistic sustainability strategies. A global leader in this space, Intrepid Travel has built its business model around culturally responsible tourism, supporting indigenous communities and promoting economic equity. Its work directly illustrates the connection between sustainability and cultural intelligence, themes explored in Chapter 3.

Trend 3: Rise of flexible, remote-work friendly hospitality models

The rise of remote and hybrid work has transformed how, why, and where people travel. Bleisure travel—blending business with leisure—has driven demand for long-term stays and flexible hospitality experiences. Companies such as Selina, which operates across Latin America and Europe, have responded by integrating coworking spaces, wellness offerings, and cultural immersion into their lodging models. This evolution is changing the role of hotels from temporary stops to dynamic lifestyle hubs, as explored in Chapter 10.

Emerging trends in wellness, immersive experiences, and resilience

Let's now turn our attention to how the industry is responding to global health shifts, rising demand for immersive guest experiences, and the increasing need to build resilience across operations. These trends represent some challenges, but also exciting opportunities for forward-thinking professionals.

Trend 4: Wellness integration across hospitality sectors

Wellness has become a core expectation across hospitality; not just in spas, but in hotels, restaurants, airlines, and event experiences. Singapore Airlines, for instance, introduced healthier in-flight meals, wellness content, and improved air quality systems as part of a broader commitment to traveler well-being. This cross-sector integration of wellness echoes themes in Chapter 13.

Trend 5: Experiential and immersive hospitality

Many of today's travelers increasingly seek experiences that are meaningful, immersive, and culturally enriching. Rather than focusing solely on amenities, they value engagement, local connection, and opportunities for learning. Fogo Island Inn in Canada aims to meet this shift, offering guest experiences rooted in community, storytelling, and regional tradition. Visitors participate in traditional crafts and engage with local artisans, reinforcing the principles of cultural intelligence and meaningful interaction discussed in Chapters 3 and 12.

Trend 6: Crisis-proofing through operational diversification

One of the clearest lessons from recent disruptions is the need for operational agility. Businesses that diversify not just revenue streams but delivery models are better equipped to adapt in uncertain environments. Asia-based events company Pico Group did just that—pivoting to hybrid events and digital experiences that kept clients engaged despite travel restrictions. Its approach aligns with the crisis response principles explored earlier in this chapter.

> **INTERACTIVE EXERCISE**
> Forecasting the future of hospitality
>
> To actively engage with these trends, complete the following reflective exercise:
>
> 1 **Choose a key trend**: Select one of the previously listed trends that excites or interests you the most.
> 2 **Predict industry impact**: Briefly describe how this trend might shape the hospitality industry over the next five years. Consider guest expectations, competition, and operations.
> 3 **Plan your preparation**: List three realistic steps you could take now (courses, certifications, experiences) to prepare for roles aligned with this trend.
> 4 **Share and compare**: Discuss your forecast with classmates or peers. What trends or actions overlap? Where do your ideas diverge?

Reinforcing your hospitality resilience mindset

As you reflect on emerging trends, consider how each connects to core skills, industry insights, and concepts explored in earlier chapters. Hospitality and tourism remain dynamic, ever-evolving fields requiring continuous learning, change, empathy-driven service, cultural intelligence, and innovation—all qualities you've been developing throughout your studies.

By seeking to understand and anticipate industry trends, you position yourself to confidently navigate future challenges, seize new opportunities, and become an adaptable, resilient hospitality leader in a rapidly developing global environment.

> **Key takeaways**
>
> - **Resilience as an industry cornerstone**: Resilience enables hospitality and tourism businesses to effectively navigate disruptions such as economic downturns, health crises, and environmental challenges. Adaptable business models, strategic innovation, and proactive planning help organizations emerge stronger from each challenge.
>
> - **Historical context of industry adaptability**: Significant historical events, including the 1970s oil crisis, the aftermath of 9/11, the global financial crisis, and the Covid pandemic, demonstrate the industry's persistent ability to evolve and capacity for innovation during challenging periods.
>
> - **Effective crisis management strategies**: Utilizing theoretical frameworks like Faulkner's tourism disaster management framework, hospitality businesses can systematically respond to crises through preparation, clear communication, operational flexibility, and strategic learning, ensuring rapid recovery and enhanced resilience.
>
> - **Inclusive workplace practices and resilience**: Inclusivity strengthens organizational resilience by fostering clear multilingual communication, equitable employee support, flexible operational policies, responsive leadership, and community-focused initiatives. Inclusive workplaces sustain morale, loyalty, and operational effectiveness during challenges.
>
> - **Strategic career networking and agility**: Building and nurturing operational, personal, and strategic professional relationships enhances personal career resilience. Effective networking through consistent, authentic engagement positions hospitality professionals to confidently navigate industry shifts and career transitions.
>
> - **Career mobility and transferable skills**: Hospitality careers offer remarkable elasticity through diverse pathways. Transferable skills, such as flexibility, empathy-driven service, cultural intelligence, and operational excellence, provide powerful career mobility and professional resilience across hospitality segments and intersecting industries.

References

AHLA (American Hotel & Lodging Association) (2023) *State of the Hotel Industry Report*. ahla.com/sites/default/files/AHLA.SOTI_.Report.2023.final_.002.pdf (archived at https://perma.cc/EHY3-C2XQ)

Airbnb (2011) Airbnb growth statistics (press release), December. assets.airbnb.com/press/press-releases/Airbnb_1M_Nights_Booked_Print.pdf (archived at https://perma.cc/TJ2B-SSV2)

Airbnb (2020) New insights into how guests are using Airbnb for longer-term stays, April 15. news.airbnb.com/new-insights-into-how-guests-are-using-airbnb-for-longer-term-stays (archived at https://perma.cc/SP2E-QBEE)

Business Wire (2021) Global online food delivery services market report 2021, April 29. businesswire.com/news/home/20210429005768/en/Global-Online-Food-Delivery-Services-Market-Report-2021-COVID-19-Growth-Impacts-and-Change-to-2030---ResearchAndMarkets.com (archived at https://perma.cc/P6CQ-XBSH)

Chipotle (2021) *Form 10-K Annual Report 2020*. annualreports.com/HostedData/AnnualReportArchive/c/NYSE_CMG_2020.pdf (archived at https://perma.cc/MS5K-YA5E)

Congressional Research Service (2019) China's Retaliatory Tariffs on U.S. Agriculture, September 24. sgp.fas.org/crs/row/R45929.pdf (archived at https://perma.cc/BL8Y-DSDC)

Delta Air Lines (2020) Delta commits $1 billion to become first carbon neutral airline globally (press release), March 1. pro.delta.com/content/agency/us/en/news/news-archive/2020/february-2020/delta-commits--1-billion-to-become-first-carbon-neutral-airline-.html (archived at https://perma.cc/MAF5-JBNK)

EAU (Emirates Aviation University) (2023) Graduation addresses industry's skill shortages, EAU News, January 12. eau.presspage.com/emirates-aviation-universitys-graduation-addresses-industrys-skill-shortages (archived at https://perma.cc/T4HQ-42EW)

Emirates (2023) *Annual Report 2022–2023*. c.ekstatic.net/ecl/documents/annual-report/2022-2023.pdf (archived at https://perma.cc/J983-WZ7V)

Expedia (2010) *Expedia Annual Report 2009*. s202.q4cdn.com/757635260/files/doc_financials/2009/ar/ar09.pdf (archived at https://perma.cc/X95K-76T9)

FAA (Federal Aviation Administration) (2002) Aviation Security Technology and Passenger Screening: Post-9/11 Initiatives, faa.gov/media/76196 (archived at https://perma.cc/S9BB-4DPM)

Fast Company (2020) U.S. Starbucks employees can now get up to 20 free therapy sessions. Stephanie Mehta (March 16) fastcompany.com/90476917/starbucks-employees-in-the-u-s-can-get-up-to-20-therapy-sessions (archived at https://perma.cc/7CJV-2CP3)

Faulkner, B. (2001) Towards a framework for tourism disaster management, *Tourism Management*, 22 (2), 135–147.

Gene, N.K. (2020) More than 900 SIA A-380 lunches sold out in half an hour, *The Straits Times*, October 12. straitstimes.com/singapore/more-than-900-sia-a-380-lunches-sold-out-in-half-an-hour (archived at https://perma.cc/Y2YW-FLT9)

Grupo Xcaret (2021) *Xustainability Report 2021*. grupoxcaret.com/en/wp-content/uploads/2022/09/Sustainability-Report-Grupo-Xcaret-2021_b.pdf (archived at https://perma.cc/Z4GG-38US)

GSTC (2023) Booking.com releases 2023 Sustainable Travel Report. gstc.org/booking-com-2023-sustainable-travel-report (archived at https://perma.cc/RT8A-AT6T)

Hilton Global Foundation (2024) Hilton Global Foundation unveils record $5.3 million commitment, stories.hilton.com/releases/hilton-global-foundation-unveils-record-5-3-million-commitment-towards-organizations-championing-people-and-planet (archived at https://perma.cc/EGY3-X4LB); *Our impact*, hiltonglobalfoundation.hilton.com/impact (archived at https://perma.cc/VET9-4XW9)

IATA (International Air Transport Association) (2021) *9/11 Fact Sheet: Impact on Aviation*. iata.org/contentassets/49a331cdfb85447cac12894e01aabb5c/fact-sheet-iata-9-11.pdf (archived at https://perma.cc/66F4-2BR2)

ICCT (International Council on Clean Transportation) (2015) *Fuel Efficiency Trends for New Commercial Jet Aircraft: 1960 to 2014*. theicct.org/wp-content/uploads/2021/06/ICCT_Aircraft-FE-Trends_20150902.pdf (archived at https://perma.cc/6UE6-693S)

Lee, J.J., Lukachko, S.P., Waitz, I.A., & Schafer, A. (2001) Historical and future trends in aircraft performance, cost, and emissions, *Annual Review of Energy and the Environment*, 26, 167–200.

Limna, P. & Kraiwanit, T. (2023) The role of ChatGPT on customer service in the hospitality industry: An exploratory study of hospitality workers' experiences and perceptions, *Tourism and Hospitality Management*, 29 (4), 583–592.

Liu, S.Q., Vakeel, K.A., Smith, N.A., Sadat Alavipour, R., Wei, C.(V.), & Wirtz, J. (2024) AI concierge in the customer journey: What is it and how can it add value to the customer?, *Journal of Service Management*, 35 (6), 136–158. https://doi.org/10.1108/JOSM-12-2023-0523?urlappend=%3Futm_source%3Dresearchgate (archived at https://perma.cc/LRG9-XQK4)

Lobertréau, B. (2023) The best languages to learn for business and the hospitality industry, *Hospitality Insights*, April 25. hospitalityinsights.ehl.edu/languages-to-learn-for-business (archived at https://perma.cc/VCK3-FHHL)

Reinhold, S. & Dolnicar, S. (2021) The evolution of Airbnb's business model, in S. Dolnicar (ed.), *Airbnb Before, During and After Covid-19*. University of Queensland.

Reuters (2019) Trump raises tariffs on $550 billion of Chinese goods, May 5. reuters.com/article/world/trump-heaps-another-5-tariff-on-chinese-goods-in-latest-tit-for-tat-escalation-idUSKCN1VD21E (archived at https://perma.cc/53U8-ZCC5)

Söderberg Granström, D., Pronk, A., & Criscione-Naylor, N. (2023) Robotic services in the hotel industry: An examination of Henn-Na Hotels, *International Journal of Gaming Hospitality and Tourism*, 3 (1). stockton.edu/light/documents/ijght_vol.3no.1/robotic_services_henn_na_hotels-6.7.23.pdf (archived at https://perma.cc/J2FQ-7VGH)

Solomon, M. (2017) The inside story of Marriott's highseas rescue after Irma stranded 620 hotel guests in St. Thomas, *Forbes*, September 12. forbes.com/sites/micahsolomon/2017/09/12/the-inside-story-of-marriotts-high-seas-rescue-of-620-hotel-guests-stranded-by-irma-on-st-thomas (archived at https://perma.cc/6YGR-8RLK)

Trip.com (2024) *Trip.com Group Sustainable Travel Consumer Report 2024*. images3.c-ctrip.com/marketing/grouptrip/Trip.com%20Group%20Sustainable%20Travel%20Consumer%20Report%202024-ENG.pdf (archived at https://perma.cc/6SG9-PZ66)

Tziora, N., Giovanis, N., & Papacharalabous, C. (2016) The role of foreign languages in hospitality management, *International Journal of Language, Translation and Intercultural Communication*, 4 (1), 89–97.

UN Tourism (2025) 2020: Worst year in tourism history with 1 billion fewer international arrivals. untourism.int/news/2020-worst-year-in-tourism-history-with-1-billion-fewer-international-arrivals (archived at https://perma.cc/4WZD-BCHT)

WTTC (2024) Travel & tourism economic impact research, WTTC Research Hub. wttc.org/research/economic-impact (archived at https://perma.cc/3HR8-N84A)

INDEX

Note: Page numbers in *italics* refer to figures or tables.

ADR (average daily rate) 118, *119*, 120, 292
Airbnb 6, 16, 273, 276, 286, 393, 398
AMC Theaters 326, 350
American Hotel & Lodging Association (AHLA) 105–06, 299
American Hotel & Lodging Educational Institute (AHLEI) 299
Aramark 150, 174–75, 182, 309, 320
artificial intelligence (AI) 6, 8, 50, 175, 187
   building resilient businesses 404–06
   career mobility 406–10
   hospitality and tourism, emerging trends in 413–14
   inclusive strategies for 410–12
   smart tech and personalization 222
   sustainable tourism and resilience 403–04
   wellness, immersive experiences, and resilience, emerging trends in 414–16
augmented reality (AR) 8, 51, 52, 221, 248–49, 356
Australia 188, 231, 243, 253, 255, 349, 352

Bed and breakfast providers (B&Bs) 277
Bellagio 277, 337, 339
Booking.com 251, 276, 393
business trips 2, 257

Cannes Film Festival 350–51
Canyon Ranch 89, 287, 367, 368, 385
career fairs 165, 168
Chatbots 50, 222, 285, 413
Chick-fil-A 36–37
Chipotle 305, 396
Cleveland Clinic 47, 176, 186, 187, 376
Coachella 89, 202, 203, 235
Colosseum 244, 257, 338
communication styles 62, 63, 78, 104
Compass Group 21, 126–27, 132–33, 136, 150, 175, 184, 185, 228, 229, 309, 320
compound annual growth (CAGR) 191, 311, 312
Consumer Electronics Show (CES) 203, 207
core values 46, 73, 212
Costa Coffee 308, 318
Covid-19 pandemic 6–7, 187–88, 203, 237, 239, 249, 259, 371, 393–94, 397, 398–99, 404
cultural awareness 29, 30, 65, 77–78
cultural competence 143, 294
   application process 81–82
   components in hospitality 77–81
   definition and importance 57–59
   significances of 82–83
cultural diversity
   belongingness theory 59
   definition and importance 57–59
   Maslow's hierarchy of needs 60–62, *61*
   social identity theory 62–64
cultural exchange 2, 11, 13, 59
   global connections and 16–17
   hospitality professionals role in 141, 157–58

Delta Airlines 73, 404, 405
dietary restrictions 60, 81, 176, 184–85, 326
digital age 6, 101
digital menus 6–7, 186, 321, 393
Disney 5–6, 28, 343, 345, 411
   five keys to guest experience 45, 46
   internships 161
   parks 92, 97–98, 405
Disneyland 206–07, 237, 338, 339
Disneyland Paris 31, 153, 339, 343, 355
diversity, equity, inclusion, belonging, and accessibility (DEIBA) 241, 287, 300
dynamic pricing 118, 120, 273, 296, 387

economic contributions 13–15, 190, 272, 341, 343–44, 346
Edinburgh Fringe Festival 208
emails 89, 99, 216
emergency protocols 121
Emirates
   Airline 33–34
   Aviation University (EAU) 404–05
   Group 404–05
emotional connections 49, 88, 91–92, 101, 247, 293
emotional health 35, 383
emotional intelligence 25, 28, 36–37, 39, 141, 149
employee
   engagement 57, 103, 106–07, 108, 290
   experience 60, 93, 105, 107
   satisfaction 87, 93, 106, 123, 180, 325
   training 87, 106, 121, 344, 394
   turnover 102, 105–06
   trends 190, 272
energy efficiency 115, 129, 130–31, 136, 403, 404, 405

Index

entertainment and recreation
　careers in 357–60
　historical evolution of 338–39
　key segments in 339–53, *340*
　key trends in 355–57
　specialized and niche recreation segments 354–55
event(s)
　across key sectors 204–12
　career exploration 229–31
　career pathways within 225–29, *225–26, 226–27, 228*
　coordinators 15, 375
　emerging trends in 220–24
　management structures 224–25
　overview and evolution of 202–04
　safety 122
Expedia 6, 99, 252, 259, 393

FIFA World Cup 203, 209, 249
"first in, first out" (FIFO) 115, 127
food and beverage industry
　career development and professional associations 331–33
　careers and professional development 328–31
　core business functions in 323–25
　Historical evolution 305–07
　inclusive practices in 325–28
　key beverage segments 314–18, *314–15*
　key food and beverage segments 307–14
　key trends in 321–23
　ownership, management, and branding in food and beverages 319–21
　universal language of 303–05

Gen Z 247, 252, 259, 277, 395
General Data Protection Regulation (GDPR) 285, 294
global economy 11, 13–14
Google 98, 101, 180
Great Barrier Reef 243, 254, 255, 258, 352
guest engagement 7, 30, 148, 205, 327, 385
　CARES and REACT models 42–45, 47–49

Hazard Analysis and Critical Control Points (HACCP) 123, 325
healthcare facilities 21, 134, 173, 176, 191
Hilton 5, 28, 273, 274, 275, 276, 281, 288, 292, 294, 327
　economic challenges and industry responses, historical timeline of 392–96
　health clubs and fitness centers 369–70
　HEART 39, 41–42
　hospitals and clinics, hospitality in 375–81
hospitality
　application of industry service models 39–49, *46*
　building resilient businesses 404–06
　career mobility 406–10

　crisis management and recovery 396–403
　economic challenges and industry responses, historical timeline of 392–96
　emerging trends in 413–14
　facilities and asset management 134–37, *137*
　financial management 113–16, *114*
　global interconnectedness 19–23
　guest experience management 88–93
　human resources management 102–07
　importance of industry experience 17–19
　inclusive strategies for 410–12
　reputation management 101–02
　revenue and yield management 117–21, *119*
　risk management and compliance 121–24
　role of operations management 93–96
　sales and marketing goals 96–101
　social identity wheel 65–69, *66*
　supply chain and procurement management 124–29, *128*
　sustainability and environmental management 129–33, *133*
　housekeeping supervisors 15, 296
Hyatt 57, 73, 80–81, 280, 288, 289, 286, 294, 298, 384–85, 397, 404
health clubs and fitness centers 369–70

IHG 274, 276, 280, 288, 289
inclusive event planning framework 212–20, *213, 217*
Industrial Revolution 3–4, 203, 337–38
Instagram 203, 324
international conferences 152, 165
Internet of Things (IoT) 8, 50, 51, 52, 128, 188

Japan 3, 188, 222, 244, 308, 320, 386, 413
job satisfaction 35, 102, 105

key performance indicators (KPIs) 124, 133, *133*, 137, *137*
kosher 8, 81, 192

leadership skills 17, 70, 167, 295
LEED (Leadership in Energy and Environmental Design) 7, 132, 222
LinkedIn 164, 168, 203
lodging
　career pathways in 295–98
　core business and operational functions 290–95, *291*
　emerging trends and innovations in 284–89
　executive leadership and operations, Understanding 289–90
　historical evolution of 272–74
　lodging segments 274–79
　structures, understanding the 279–83, *282*
London 179, 203, 243, 271, 273, 317, 321, 326, 345, 346, 347, 348
loyalty programs 8, 99, 100–01, 116

Index

managed services
    business and industry sector 180–82
    core business functions application 183
    global impact and scope 190–93
    historical evolution 174–75
    impacts on education sector 177–78
    leisure, sports, and entertainment 179–80
    military and government 182–83
    operational considerations: conversational approach 184–86
    property, above-property, and corporate levels 194–96
    role in healthcare 175–76
    technology and innovation 186–90
Marriott 5, 89, 101, 116, 126, 228, 273, 274, 276, 280, 281, 285, 286, 292, 293, 325, 327, 366
    Bonvoy 293
    health clubs and fitness centers 369–70
    hospitals and clinics, hospitality in 375–81
    International 284, 297
    Management Services 228
    Marquis 274, 275, 276, 398
    Senior Living 366
    Serve 360 initiative 7
McDonald 305, 307, 319, 328
millennials 252, 259, 395
Mobile check-ins 6–7, 50, 88

Ohio State University (The) 177, 178, 377
Olympic Games 202, 249, 337
operational excellence 20, 58, 134, 152, 184
operational realities 46
organizational goals 46, 174, 195

personal growth 2, 15, 141, 247
positive reviews 93, 101
post-visit surveys 89
professional confidence 167

Quick-service restaurants (QSRs) 307–08, 309, 310

recycling programs 131, 180
resource allocation 195
revenue per available room (RevPAR) 116, 118, 275, 292
RFID 90, 222, 345, 405
Ritz-Carlton 28, 30, 35, 275
    gold standards of service 39–41, 47–49, 93
robotics 51, 186, 321
Royal Caribbean 73, 278, 343, 344–45, 358, 369, 405

sales strategies 95, 99–100
self-awareness 28, 29, 36, 62, 69, 83
sensory sensitivities 62, 91, 326, 343

September 11 attacks (2001) 392–93, 398
service excellence 20, 22, 25
    empathy and emotional intelligence 32–39
service skills 102, 103
small to medium-sized enterprises (SMEs) 17, 225–29
social skills 29, 36
Sodexo 7, 20, 57, 175, 228, 309
    cloud-based inventory systems 127
    culinary excellence 21–22
    food and beverage operations 320
    menu designing 191–92
    Spirit of Inclusion program 82
    WasteWatch powered by Leanpath program 188
solar panels 130, 131, 136
South by Southwest (SXSW) festival 203, 223
Starbucks 88, 306, 308, 318, 319–20, 325, 330, 398
Sundance Film Festival 222, 350

TikTok 98, 203, 248, 259, 324
Tokyo
    2020 Olympics 179, 239
    Disneyland 153, 179, 339, 343
    DisneySea 153
tourism industry
    application of industry service models 39–49
    building resilient businesses 404–06
    career mobility 406–10
    crisis management and recovery 396–403
    customer behaviour and traveller influences 247–50
    economic, community, and global impact 237–42, *238*, *240*
    emerging trends in 413–14
    global significance 13–17, 235–36
    guest experience management 88–93
    inclusive strategies for 410–12
    pathways and opportunities 261–67, *265*
    service and exploration 10–12
    sustainability and environmental management 129–33, 250–53, 403–04
    UNESCO World Heritage and tourism 253–57
    see also managed services; service excellence
transferable skills
    club management 155–56, *155–56*
    cross-sector opportunities and 142–47
    cruising 156–57, *157*
    internships, employment, and practical learning 159–63, *160*
    key industry segments 147–59, *148*, *150–51*, *154*
    mentorship impacts on career growth 167–68
    networking and industry engagement 163–66, *164*

supply chain and vendor management 158–59, *158, 159*
travel and tourism 157–58

UNESCO World Heritage sites 253–57, 244
United Nations Sustainable Development Goals (UN SDGs) 129, 132–33
Universal Studios 179, 206–07, 343, 356, 358

value propositions 96, 393
vegan 81, 322, 326
vendor shortages 126
virtual reality (VR) 8, 51, 221, 248–49, 254, 356
Vrbo 6, 273, 276

waste reduction 129, 130, 136, 178, 185
wellness and health industry

career pathways and industry associations 387–88
emerging trends and future directions 383–86
health clubs and fitness centers 369–70
hospitals and clinics, hospitality in 375–81
integrating wellness 381–83
nuanced considerations in 386–87
senior living communities, hospitality in 372–75
spas 367–69
wellness retreats 370–72

Yellowstone 255, 352–53
Yelp 101, 324

Zoom 203
Zulal Wellness Resort 383–84, 386

Looking for another book?

Explore our award-winning books from global business experts in Tourism, Leisure and Hospitality

Scan the code to browse

www.koganpage.com/tlh

supply chain and vendor management 158–59, *158*, *159*
travel and tourism 157–58

UNESCO World Heritage sites 253–57, 244
United Nations Sustainable Development Goals (UN SDGs) 129, 132–33
Universal Studios 179, 206–07, 343, 356, 358

value propositions 96, 393
vegan 81, 322, 326
vendor shortages 126
virtual reality (VR) 8, 51, 221, 248–49, 254, 356
Vrbo 6, 273, 276

waste reduction 129, 130, 136, 178, 185
wellness and health industry
    career pathways and industry associations 387–88
    emerging trends and future directions 383–86
    health clubs and fitness centers 369–70
    hospitals and clinics, hospitality in 375–81
    integrating wellness 381–83
    nuanced considerations in 386–87
    senior living communities, hospitality in 372–75
    spas 367–69
    wellness retreats 370–72

Yellowstone 255, 352–53
Yelp 101, 324

Zoom 203
Zulal Wellness Resort 383–84, 386

Looking for another book?

Explore our award-winning books from global business experts in Tourism, Leisure and Hospitality

Scan the code to browse

www.koganpage.com/tlh

From 4 December 2025 the EU Responsible Person (GPSR) is:
eucomply oÜ, Pärnu mnt. 139b – 14, 11317 Tallinn, Estonia
www.eucompliancepartner.com

www.ingramcontent.com/pod-product-compliance
Lightning Source LLC
Chambersburg PA
CBHW060456010526

44118CB00018B/2439